Power, Prayers, and Protection

A Cultural History of the Utah San Juan River Navajos

ROBERT S. MCPHERSON

Robert S. McPherson is a professor of history emeritus at Utah State University–Blanding and is the author of numerous books about the history and cultures of the Four Corners region.

Other books of related interest by the author:

Scouting for the Bluecoats: Navajos, Apaches, and the U.S. Military, 1873–1911 (distributed by University Press of Colorado)

Stories from the Land: A Navajo Reader about Monument Valley (distributed by University Press of Colorado)

Navajo Women of Monument Valley: Preservers of the Past (distributed by University Press of Colorado)

Traditional Navajo Teachings: A Trilogy (distributed by University Press of Colorado)
        Volume I: *Sacred Narratives and Ceremonies*
        Volume II: *The Natural World*
        Volume III: *The Earth Surface People*

Traders, Agents, and Weavers: Developing the Northern Navajo Region (University of Oklahoma Press)

Both Sides of the Bullpen: Navajo Trade and Posts of the Upper Four Corners (University of Oklahoma Press)

Viewing the Ancestors: Perceptions of the Anaasází, Mokwič, and Hisatsinom (University of Oklahoma Press)

Under the Eagle: Samuel Holiday, Navajo Code Talker (University of Oklahoma Press)

Dinéjí Na'nitin: Navajo Traditional Teachings and History (University Press of Colorado)

Navajo Tradition, Mormon Life: The Autobiography and Teachings of Jim Dandy (University of Utah Press)

Along Navajo Trails: Recollections of a Trader, 1898–1948 (Utah State University Press)

A Navajo Legacy: The Life and Teachings of John Holiday (University of Oklahoma Press)

Navajo Land, Navajo Culture: The Utah Experience in the Twentieth Century (University of Oklahoma Press)

The Journey of Navajo Oshley: An Autobiography and Life History (Utah State University Press)

Sacred Land, Sacred View: Navajo Perceptions of the Four Corners Region (University Press of Colorado)

The Northern Navajo Frontier, 1860–1900: Expansion through Adversity (University of New Mexico Press)

Editing, indexing, and design by Kerin Tate, Three Trails Publishing Services.

CONTENTS

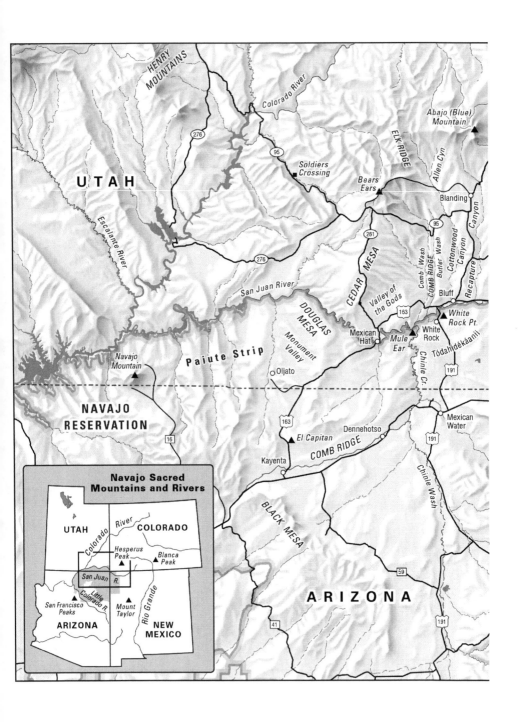

HENRY MOUNTAINS

Colorado River

Abajo (Blue) Mountain

276

95

ELK RIDGE

Soldiers Crossing

Allen Cyn

UTAH

Bears Ears

Blanding

Escalante River

261

95

Cottonwood Canyon

276

Comb Wash

Butler Wash

COMB RIDGE

Recapture Canyon

San Juan River

CEDAR MESA

Valley of the Gods

Bluff

DOUGLAS MESA

163

White Rock Pt.

Navajo Mountain

Paiute Strip

Monument Valley

Mexican Hat

Mule Ear

White Rock

Tódahidéékáanii

Oljato

Chinle Cr.

191

NAVAJO RESERVATION

Mexican Water

16

163

Dennehotso

191

El Capitan

COMB RIDGE

Kayenta

Chinle Wash

Navajo Sacred Mountains and Rivers

UTAH

Colorado River

COLORADO

BLACK MESA

Hesperus Peak

Blanca Peak

San Juan R.

Little Colorado R.

59

San Francisco Peaks

Mount Taylor

Rio Grande

ARIZONA

ARIZONA

NEW MEXICO

41

191

vi

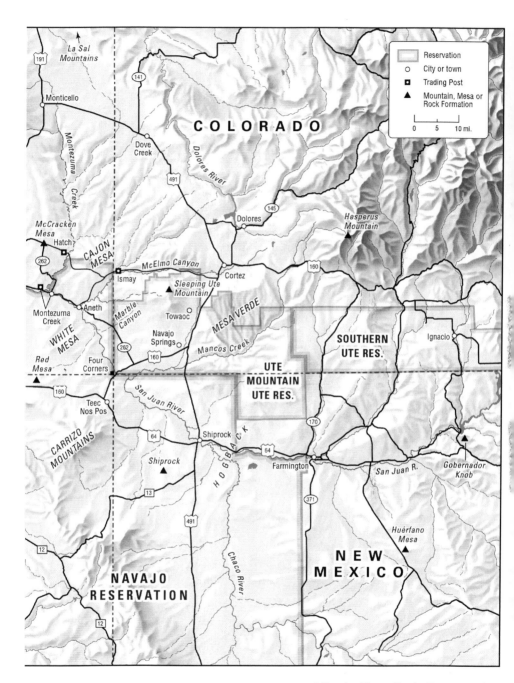

Map by Erin Greb Cartography

INTRODUCTION

A Glimpse of the Water People

B eginning in the 1960s, then gaining full steam in the 1970s, the New Social History, manifested through New England Town Studies, became a popular means to examine the daily life of "everyman" living in colonial America. Authors such as John Demos (*A Little Commonwealth*), Kenneth Lockridge (*A New England Town*), and Michael Zuckerman (*Peaceable Kingdom*) diminished the role of many traditional elements found in previously written history such as politics, economy, humanities, and diplomacy, as well as quantitative and religious history, in favor of a more journalistic rendering. Certain aspects of these genres still found their way into the New Social History, but the main emphasis now was the life and thought of the common man in both a cultural and social context. A single or small group of New England towns became the laboratory explored through journals, diaries, written statements, and recollections to better understand what the colonial experience was like for people now silent. Their voices resurrected a past, much of which had been lost through other types of writing.

Native Americans, on the other hand, have had their story told through anthropology, with the assistance of disciplines such as ethnohistory, military reports, biography, and autobiography—all of which have their strengths and weaknesses as well as their format for presentation. Anthropologists examined the mechanics of language, kinship, and other cultural dynamics; those involved in war studied the elements that led to victory or defeat on the battlefield, while biography and

1

autobiography focused on an individual's life and influences that affected it. Often, however, it was a matter of professional outsiders looking in rather than insiders looking out. Here, the reader will encounter more of the New Social History approach of the New England Town Studies as Navajo people, born and raised in the first third of the twentieth century, discuss what their life was like living along the San Juan River—more particularly the Four Corners area, ranging from Aneth and Montezuma Creek to Bluff, Utah, to just below Mexican Water, Arizona. This fifty-seven-mile stretch of water, whose upper end flows through Shiprock, New Mexico, has historically had a group of Navajos living along its banks primarily for agricultural purposes.

When I asked medicine man and traditionalist Perry Robinson how Navajos categorize or think about different communities on the reservation, he noted that a number of areas had their own reputation based on geographical features and the qualities of the people living there. For instance, in his view, the "Black Mesa/Mountain Navajos" living in that region were the most traditional on the reservation, inhabiting a place where many of the stories found in Navajo religion had their genesis. Those residing in the Navajo Mountain area were also very traditional and were referred to in the past as "The Ones Who Had Long Hair Buns," a symbol of their deep-seated customs and beliefs. Those inhabiting the Many Farms–Rock Point–Rough Rock region were the "Valley People"; others in the Lukachukai-Chuska area were "Whities" because of the white reeds growing there; and those residing on the desert land that extends south to Gallup and from Albuquerque, New Mexico, to Window Rock, Arizona, were known as the "Middle Line" or "Railroad People" because of the tracks passing through their land. Those inhabiting the Farmington, Shiprock, and region north adjacent to the San Juan River were called "Along the River" or "Water People."[1] The latter are the focus of this book, with a primary emphasis on their telling about the everyday life and beliefs of the residents of this part of southeastern Utah.

Their story has been partially told at other times in other ways. For instance, anthropologist Walter Dyk in 1947 published *A Navaho Autobiography* concerning Old Mexican (1865–1933), a resident of the Aneth–Montezuma Creek–Wooded Hill Point (ten miles south of Aneth) area.[2] From his life story, three major themes emerge: acculturation, the difficulties of farming, and troubles in married life. Very little of his intellectual thought and beliefs were covered, just the day-to-day grind of eking out an existence on a difficult landscape. On the other hand, anthropologist David M. Brugge in 1966 completed an unpublished manuscript entitled "Navajo Use and Occupation of Lands North of the San Juan River in Present-Day Utah to 1935" based on historic documents found in the National Archives in Washington, D.C.[3] It is a treasure trove of information, most of which is from the Anglo perspective, that provides a chronology of events affecting the Navajos living along the river. There have also been more specialized studies, ranging from a singular topic to poetic musings. For instance, Margaret K. Brady wrote *"Some Kind of Power": Navajo Children's Skinwalker Narratives* examining Montezuma Creek elementary and middle school children's beliefs concerning witchcraft; *Pieces of White Shell: A Journey to Navajoland*, by Terry Tempest Williams, offers a contemplative interpretation of her experiences with Navajo culture; and J. Lee Correll's *Bai-a-lil-le: Medicine Man or Witch?* is a short monograph about a powerful figure in the Aneth community near the turn of the century.[4] Other than that, this area has not had much written specifically about it, with the exception of the work I have done.

The Aneth–Montezuma Creek–Bluff region has an interesting, and at times, turbulent history. Perhaps more than any other place on the reservation, there has been a mix of Navajos, Utes, Paiutes, Mormons, cowboys, miners, evangelists, agents, government farmers, military personnel, educators, and entrepreneurs of all kinds who have played their part in these Navajos' history. Many have left some type of record—whether written on paper or upon the land—allowing others to later encounter their presence. Over the past thirty-plus years, I have been able to document these activities in some wide-ranging histories of the region, presented in a traditional approach, yet liberally sprinkled with oral history.[5] These works, however, did not emphasize an "everyman" approach held by its occupants. Instead, they examined historic events from a more traditional perspective.

This book intends to be different. During the late 1980s and 1990s, I had the opportunity to conduct interviews with many of the Navajo people living in southeastern Utah. My efforts in writing an inclusive history of San Juan County for the Utah Centennial, providing public programming on and off the reservation for the Utah Humanities Council, teaching college classes in both the Montezuma Creek and

Monument Valley areas, and working with Navajo people in different civic capacities led to interaction that allowed me to meet many elders who were raised in the 1920s and 1930s during the livestock era, when much of the traditional culture was still intact.[6] I recorded many aspects of their life histories and events with their permission and understanding that what they shared would be given back to their children and grandchildren. They expressed a strong desire for the young people to learn what life had been like in the old days and how the traditional teachings had framed their world. I agreed to facilitate this. While their views and testimonies have been part of everything I have written to this point, much of it is structured in a more traditional, chronological, western style of writing instead of a manner that highlights Navajo thought and teachings.

I considered taking all that I have written thus far and combining it into a single book that followed a more cultural approach to Navajo traditions and history. To do so, however, would create a large compilation of works that would be unwieldy in length and that was already available to the public. A long rehash seemed undesirable. At the same time, for those who want a more detailed history of the area accompanied by names, dates, and movements, there needed to be an inclusive approach that referenced where this material could be found. For instance, the early years of the Montezuma Creek–Aneth area were dominated by contention and change. In the book *The Northern Navajo Frontier, 1860–1900*, there are chapters on Ute, Paiute, and Navajo interaction; Mormon and non-Mormon friction; competition with non-Navajo livestock owners; the role of trading posts; and boundary shifts fostering reservation expansion that changed lives and either diminished or increased natural resources.[7] Rather than duplicate this information, I have decided to reference it in this introduction, while providing a minimal context for the reader of these chapters so that the elders could tell their own story. In my previous work, government documents, military reports, settlers' perspectives, diaries, and journals tell the story in a more traditional approach, while here, oral history and cultural teachings dominate the page.

A second factor that has influenced the writing of this book is that of another entitled *Stories from the Land: A Navajo Reader about Monument Valley*.[8] Actually, it is a companion piece in that the entire text is based in oral history of the people living in that area. There are, of course, many elements that this community shares with those of the people in the Aneth–Montezuma Creek area, but there is also additional information that is unique or not stressed in interviews conducted in the other community. For instance, the role of the river, the large number of trading posts as opposed to the two in Monument Valley, the school experience in Shiprock, and the oil industry compared to that of tourism in Monument Valley are just some of the teachings that the elders shared that were different. On the other hand, major events or concerns such as the Long Walk, witchcraft, and livestock reduction shared similarities but also offered unique perspectives. I have tried to incorporate as much different material, in either case, to give the reader a more complete picture of the life of the Navajos in southeastern Utah. In summary, these are companion volumes that expand and illuminate rather than repeat what the other has said.

A few caveats. Those elders recorded represent a wide variety of both men and women aged sixty-five or older at the time of meeting. The ability to speak English ranged from little to nonexistent, and so all information that they shared was in Navajo with the help of a transla-tor, in most instances Baxter Benally, who lived in Bluff and has since passed away. He did an excellent job being well versed in the topics set for discussion, but once the elder began to answer, the information just flowed without clarifying questions from me. We both understood that the less interruption on our part, the more complete the response of the individual being interviewed. In general, this worked well, but there was one area that should have been clarified at the time but was not—that of specific geographical references with Navajo names. While most could be determined through internal information from the interview or by other people referring to the same location, then adding some type of identifying feature, there were some places that were hard to identify. In these instances, the reader can determine the general vicinity of those spots based on the area where the interviewee lived. All of the individ-uals interviewed have died, and unless this information has been passed on to children or grandchildren, it is lost in time.

The spelling of the names of people, places, and things follows the standards used by the Navajo Nation today. Two Navajo linguists, Clayton Long and Charlotta Nez Lacy, have helped to ensure correct spelling whenever possible. There were some terms and names used by the elders that could not be deciphered, and so those have been left as found in the initial manuscript translation performed by another Navajo speaker unfamiliar with the rules of standardization. Diacritical marks may also vary with how a word is pronounced within a region, which is more the concern of specialists. In the same vein, chapters 5 and 6 contain the life experiences and teachings of a medicine man named David Kindle, recorded in the 1970s by Robert W. Putsch, a clinical psychologist. Kindle shared important information about origin stories of various ceremonies as well as how and why they are performed. The first of these chapters was of a personal nature, straightforward in its approach and in the vocabulary used. The second chapter was more difficult to translate because of the complexity of the sacred narratives and specialized ceremonial terms. Again, every effort has been made to ensure accuracy, but there were some places that required interpolation and interpretation.

The Navajo oral tradition is rich in stories and themes that form the basis for ceremonial performance. Everything that is physical, emotional, or spiritual has been placed in this world by the holy people at the time of creation, a process specified in these stories and teachings. Each chapter in this book references these sacred narratives that provide power through prayers that bring protection and a path for believers to follow. These are the elders' stories and views, and so their thoughts are center stage, providing their way of looking at their experience. Yet beyond oral history, there are views and interpretations that depend on the written record and other sources. For those who would like additional information and a different perspective, I suggest sources that I have written, which are identified by endnotes in each of the chapters outlined below. The intent is that this will provide a ready reference for those wishing to pursue further research.

Going back to the earliest documentary history of Navajos living in this area along the San Juan River and buttressing that information with the People's recollections, chapter 1 examines what their life was like from 1850 to 1890, as they interacted with their Indian neighbors the Utes and Paiutes, and the new move-ins—Anglos—who were, for the most part, members of the Church of Jesus Christ of Latter-day Saints (Mormons). These turbulent times embraced three Navajo-Ute wars including the devastating events of the Fearing Time and Long Walk era, the entrance of farmers and ranchers from Colorado, and the establishment of pioneer homes in Bluff, Montezuma Creek, and Aneth.

Inroads by the dominant culture had started.[9] Chapter 2 discusses the Navajos' ties to this land through sacred geography and how the chantways, the basis of Navajo religion, identify specific land formations in which power and protection reside. Established by the holy people, this relationship between man and his surroundings is the basis of much traditional teaching.[10] In the high desert environment of the Colorado Plateau, quality of life is determined by the water that is available, and so it is not surprising that this resource weighs heavily in Navajo thought and is the topic of the third chapter. Water was a blessing that brought Navajos to the San Juan River for farming, that focused prayers on rain and snow, and that encouraged government farmers to assist the people. It was also a curse as floodwaters inundated the land and eroded the soil.[11]

The next three chapters are devoted to the teachings and experiences of the medicine people. In chapter 4 herbalists, primarily women like Gladys Yellowman and Mary Blueyes, share their encyclopedic knowledge of plants and their uses as ordained by the holy people. Everything from food and fuel to changing the sex of a baby is found in their teachings, but it is the relationship an individual has with a plant that determines how effective their interaction will be. David Kindle, a medicine man of long standing, spoke of his experiences as a hand trembler, raconteur of origin stories, and chanter of the Windway ceremony. He was also a preservationist who wanted to see this information recorded for future generations. His experiences with divination, witchcraft, and healing through both Navajo and Anglo mediums are instructive.[12] Chapter 7 is a potpourri of daily life events when life along the river was still heavily dependent on livestock and traditional practices in use since the Navajos returned from the Long Walk and Fort Sumner. Starting with childhood memories of being raised in a strict, sometimes harsh, manner prepared both boys and girls for difficulties in the future. Puberty ceremonies set youth on the road to adulthood, as life became more complicated and difficult. Raising children, obtaining a livelihood, participating in the community, and eventually embracing death were all part of Navajo life. The San Juan River was at the center of much of what transpired for those living along its banks.[13]

The last five chapters look at the ever-increasing influence of the dominant culture as it worked its way into traditional practices. In some instances, it proved highly desirable, such as the trading posts that proliferated along the San Juan. Chapter 8 discusses the unique situation of having boats as part of the trading experience, why and where posts were established, the names of and relationships with traders, and what took place in this culturally laden activity. Extensive research is available on the posts located in the Aneth–Montezuma Creek–Bluff area.[14] Zealous advocates of providing Anglo education to the Navajos received a boost when the Shiprock Boarding School came into existence. Chapter 9 shows how Navajos living along the river were strenuously urged to send their children to this school. Some complied; others did not. For those who did, the experience appeared to be beneficial but strictly controlled. For those who did not, running away became an option fraught with danger. Starting with the children, a more frontal approach to making inroads into the culture began.[15]

By the mid-1920s, the reservation was changing dramatically. Navajos understood that as new technology wended its way into their culture, many of their values and much of their lifestyle started to shift. Like the Anasazi of the prehistoric past, this meant loss of traditional practices and moving away from the holy people—even though some of the change was highly desirable. Cars, improved roads, airplanes, and the Civilian Conservation Corps all brought good things to the People, while the influenza epidemic of 1918 was a disaster, with off-reservation employment receiving mixed reviews. This was also a time when change, for better or worse, became inescapable.[16] If there was a single event that shifted the Navajo economy that had been in place for the past hundred years, it was livestock reduction, culminating in the mid to late 1930s. Loss of half of the animals—sheep, goats, horses, and cows—which they depended on, impoverished many. The trauma was palpable, but as chapter 11 points out, there was no turning back. Off-reservation employment for many was the only answer.[17] The final chapter looks at more contemporary concerns bothering the elders, most importantly the desecration of the land by oil companies operating in the Aneth Oil Field. The eventual outcome—the Aneth takeover—solved some of the problems but left many issues still dangling. When added to concerns about education, alcohol, and major cultural loss, there is little surprise that the elders wondered and feared for the younger generations. Ending on a somber note, they share their thoughts about what the future holds for their loved ones.[18]

Perhaps the best way to close this introduction is to open the way for what follows by listening to eighty-eight-year-old Cyrus Begay, one of those asked to share his life's experience. His response was similar to what many other elders queried:

> What will become of this interview? What is going to be done with it? It can be useful in many ways. Either something good will come out of it or something bad. If it is to be documented for our people's history, then it is good. Someday our children will discover and research our heritage and grow to appreciate the significance of our people and their past. I think it is good that you are doing this. I'm sure there are many elderly people around here who could tell you some more interesting stories. Some are medicine men, others are counselors and leaders. They love their people, want to help, and are very knowledge-able. I am not a medicine man, but I do offer prayers and believe there is a God who created us. My voice is but a cry in the dark, but I want to be heard. I hope what I and others say now will bring good results. Words are words. I have been talking as a leader to my people for many years, stressing the importance of caring for themselves and their children, to teach them the good ways of life and to live in harmony, with beauty before them, behind them, below them, beside them, and all around them, and to have beauty in their voices when they speak. This should be our prayer and teachings—our way of life. I also thank you, Baxter, my brother, for you are my uncle's son. Thank you also, Mr. McPherson, my brother, for coming to see me. May you take my stories and voice to make good their purpose, to benefit our children and future generations. Let these teachings live on through them and forever after.[19]

That is the theme of this book.

CHAPTER ONE

Early Days along the San Juan, 1850–1890

Food, Friends, and Foe

Exactly when the Navajo (Diné) people arrived in the Southwest is a topic with wide-ranging views in the archaeological community. Estimates vary from the 1200s to the 1500s AD. The first written mention by the Spanish that specifically separated these people from the generalized term of "Apache," used to identify all Athabaskan speakers in the Southwest, was in Fray Alonso de Benavides's *Memorial* of 1630. It took an additional two centuries to find mention of Navajos north of the San Juan River as some fled from Mexican troops to the Bears Ears. That was in 1823; by 1850, Americans were noting that there was both an "Upper San Juan" and a "Lower San Juan" Band that planted crops on both sides of the river.[1]

The lands north of the San Juan in the area of our concern were terra incognita to most, buried in the mist of time in terms of a written record, except when white travelers and later settlers ventured forth. Fortunately, there are remnants of information in Navajo oral history that retain some of the names and events of those who lived in this region and beyond. In keeping with the emphasis of this book in letting

Navajos tell their own story, there are two sources, in addition to the interviews I conducted, that have proven particularly helpful. These sources were from a full generation or more earlier than the interviews, and were therefore closer to the past occurrences under discussion. The first was part of the Land Claims cases where the Navajos attempted to establish what had been their ancestral territory. Armed with tape recorders and interpreters, Richard Van Valkenburgh, working for the Navajo Tribe, conducted a series of interviews that ended in 1953. His "Synopsis of Statements Regarding Navajo Residence North of the San Juan River" provides information about people, places, and events that would otherwise be lost. This is also true of the second source, the Doris Duke Oral History Project, much of its materials having been gathered in the early 1960s.[2] I depend heavily on these two sources of oral history to discuss the four main topics of this chapter: (1) early life along the river, (2) neighbors—Utes and Paiutes, (3) the Fearing Time and Long Walk era, and (4) the arrival of white settlers.

Early Life

Assuming 1850 to 1890 as the time period encapsulating much of this discussion, one can see a growing Navajo dependence on livestock and agriculture, as earlier hunting-and-gathering practices slowly faded. These activities were still important, but it became increasingly difficult to sustain an expanding population on diminishing natural resources. Favorite places for hunting included all of the mountain ranges—the La Sals, Abajo (Blue), Henry, Carrizo, Sleeping Ute, and Navajo Mountain, along with Black Mesa, Bears Ears, and Elk Ridge, as well as the Dolores River and Dove Creek areas.[3] Deer, elk, mountain sheep, and antelope supplemented the Navajos' diet of corn, mutton, and goat meat. Mary Jelly recalled going with her family to many of these same sites to gather plants:

> A variety of wild grains grew abundantly in the area enclosed within the area of Ute Mountain, Carrizo Mountain, and Navajo Mountain, encompassing an area with a diameter of at least 90 miles. We went so far as the La Sal Mountains to the north. These grains included tł'ohdeeí (pigweed), tł'oh ts'ózí (narrow leaf grass), tłoh tsoh (big grass), tłoh dehł gai, haaz che daa, nidi'głiddie, ostse (tansy), dił tałi,

and numerous others. Most of these grains were dried, ground, and made into broths, cakes, or a paste for consumption. Other plants that we gathered included gad (juniper), tłoh a ziihipai (a tea), chaaz tezhi (wild carrots), tł'ohchin (wild onions), waa' (bee weed), and daa'w'oozh (berries). I am very familiar from personal use, stories, and traditions about the foods derived from these wild plants as related to me by my parents and elderly Navajos; it was common knowledge and practice among Navajos of times before my birth that these foods were essential for survival in addition to our hunting and agriculture.

While taking trips to pick plants for food, we also gathered them for herbs. These grew in abundance in this entire area which we regarded as the significant extent of our range. The area around Cahone and Little Cahone Mesas are still used for gathering plants for herbs, although they now grow in less abundance. There are shrines located at various points, on or near this area, to denote the intensive use of herbs by Navajos who lived, and those who now live, there. These shrines are used for offering a gift in blessing the earth from which the herbs and other plants were taken. Usually, a turquoise or white shell bead is placed at the site, accompanied by prayer and the use of corn pollen. One such shrine is located at the easternmost tip of Little Cahone Mesa. I recall clearly how my family and I went to this mesa's point to offer prayers and a sacrifice during a curing ceremony. This is the same area on which a corral was constructed as part of the entirely enclosed Little Cahone Mesa, much used by the Navajos for pasturing livestock. Another type of shrine comes in the form of a juniper tree. There are three such trees in the vicinity of Little Cahone Mesa that have been struck with lightning. Stinking Spring (Tóhnił Ch'ooni) was a source of water first used by Navajos for domestic purposes and livestock until about six years ago when it was struck by lightning. Since then, it has not been used for anything but a shrine.[4]

Piñon nuts were a seasonal staple that required more travel and the construction of temporary shelters, as the nuts often flourished annually in different places, depending on yearly temperatures and water cycles. Stored under proper conditions, this food was a welcomed addition to a diet when green plants were not available. George Littlesalt remembered that one autumn they were plentiful in the La Sal Mountains, and so his family went there for the harvest. "When they arrived, they built two houses, one for them to live in, and one for them to store their belongings in. They were brushy huts that were made out of cedar or piñon trees, used to stay in at night and also to safely store their bags of nuts. At that time, piñon nuts were not sold to the traders, just picked and eaten for food. The only corn patches that we had were down toward Fort Defiance. If the corn did not ripen in the fall, the people depended on the nuts for food."[5] The Utes living in the area were just as aware as the Navajos, so conflict between the two groups erupted, a relationship that will be discussed shortly.

The temporary shelters that Mary mentioned were widely used for hunting and gathering during short stays in an area. More permanent structures such as the male and female hogan required a fair amount of work, remained solid homes for years, and were cool in the summer and warm in the winter. The older male hogan (ałch'į'adeez'á) was conical and generally smaller and an older type than the female hogan (hoogaan nímazí bijááá hólóígíí), which was round and often octagonally shaped. During an interview in the 1950s, Hashk'áán Díil remembered how these structures were built before metal axes were plentiful. Speaking of these early hogans he said:

They were made in the old days the right way by performing the Blessingway. When I was a boy, we had no metal axes, so we burned down a tree and trimmed it with a stone axe. We used to make them out of a black stone we found around Bluff. One end was chipped off, two grooves were pecked in the sides, then placed in a forked stick, and bound with buckskin. When we went to build a hogan after cutting the wood, there were two kinds: the "forked stick house" and the "piled stick home" ('tsinditlin or hooghan dah diitł'iní). The "forked stick" was male while the "piled stick" was female. Of course, the old timers also used hogans with stone walls and dome roofs of wood. The old ones did not have a door like we do today. They put posts on two stone slabs at the base of the eastern poles, then a piece of wood across the forks of these door posts from which a door mat was hung. In the very old days, these door mats were made of buckskin and yucca splints because we did not have cloth. My mother and father told me that if I looked around north of Bluff, I would find lots of old Navajo hogans in the Blanding and Dove Creek areas.[6]

Just how ubiquitous were Navajo hogans? Old Lady Sweetwater, who lived four to five miles east of the Aneth Trading Post, gave an interesting account of just what she could reckon. Her mother's mother had eleven girls and two boys, which gave the area in which they lived the name of "Many Girls" (At'éédké Łáni), and a number of farms had developed along the river extending from Aneth to Soldier Crossing, approximately a four-mile stretch. Old Lady Sweetwater recalled,

> We didn't stay in one place all the time, but kept moving because we had a lot of sheep. I used to herd sheep all around here (Aneth) when I was a little girl and even after I had some children of my own. . . . My brother and I were figuring up the hogans, windbreaks, and shade houses my family built and there were about 60. That is why they call that ridge "Many Hogans." . . . About 30 years ago (1928?) there was a big snow and the storekeepers paid the Navajos to bring them wood. The Navajos sold them logs from old hogans in this area so that is why so many of the old hogans around here have no wood left on them.[7]

During this pre–Fort Sumner period, there were certain areas where Navajo camps and scattered settlements appeared because of available water, rangelands, and resources. The areas around Aneth, Montezuma Canyon, Montezuma Creek, Recapture Creek, McCracken Mesa, Comb and Butler Washes, Elk Ridge, and Bluff were some of these sites. The San Juan River, during high water times of the year, could be crossed at certain locations such as Pretty Cottonwood at present Mexican Hat, the juncture of Chinle Creek with the San Juan River, White Rock Point outside of Bluff, the mouth of Recapture Creek, the spot where Montezuma Creek meets the river, and Soldier Crossing upriver from Aneth. These areas of settlement north of the San Juan River fostered their own local leaders or naat'áanii, some of whom had strong personalities and significant herds of livestock. Some were medicine men revered for their power. The role that many of these individuals played has been lost to history, such as Mr. Heavyset (Hastiin Dííl), Owl (Né'éshjaa'), Rope or Ropey (Hastiin Tł'óół), Warrior (Hashke), Mud Dancer (Chaashzhiní), Hastiin Joe, Bunion (Kéwosi), Buffalo Rope (Bi Ch'idí), Blue Goats (Bi tł'ízi Dootł'izhi), and Spits It Out (Di ja i). White Sheep stated that many of these men lived permanently north of the San Juan River before and after the Navajos were taken to Fort Sumner. But there

The Navajo Land Claims studies provide some of the earliest recorded oral history about Navajos living north of the San Juan River. This photo, taken by Richard Van Valkenburgh in April 1953, is of old hogan remains that date to about 1850. It is located along Alkali Wash, a tributary of Upper Montezuma Creek in San Juan County. (Courtesy Utah State Historical Society)

was one person who seemed to dominate in prominence above all, and that was K'aayélii (also spelled K'aa Yélii; One with Quiver or Carries Arrows), who lived in the Montezuma Creek area during times of peace and around the Bears Ears during the turbulent Fort Sumner period; he will be discussed later.[8]

Ute/Paiute Neighbors

The Navajos were not alone in this land north of the San Juan River. During the historic period, the Utes lived predominantly to the east and north while the Paiutes lived to the west in the Monument Valley–Navajo Mountain region and southwestern Utah. According to many Navajo accounts, they were not present in substantial numbers in southeastern

Utah, which differs from what these two Numic-speaking tribal people believe. There is sufficient proof of their existence throughout the San Juan area. Indeed, their accounts claim that this land belonged to the Utes, who allowed Navajos to occasionally hunt and gather in this region, but generally kept their traditional enemies south of the river. The truth is somewhere in between, with all three peoples using the area. Since the Paiutes were the smaller and less belligerent of the three, they will be discussed first from the Navajo perspective.

To the Navajos living along the river, the Paiutes occasionally wandered into the area, destitute and looking for food. Some say that it was not until after the Fort Sumner period that they came in from the Douglas Mesa and Navajo Mountain area; they had no sheep or goats and only a few horses. White Sheep was definite in stating, "The Paiutes were not in the country north of the San Juan River when I was a boy. They came from somewhere in the west before they turned up around Navajo Mountain and Douglas Mesa, from where they moved, then crossed to the north side of the river."[9] White Horse agreed:

> They first came from Willows in Wide Meadow (K'įį Bitah Hóteel), far to the west, across the Colorado River between Dził Binaa' Łigai (Mountain with White Eyes—unidentified) and the Henry Mountains. There were no Paiutes in the country north of the river when I was a boy. Those who lived in Allen Canyon came from Douglas Mesa and Navajo Mountain country. A Navajo named Black Rock (Tsézhin) ran them north across the San Juan River, so they went for rations at Rabbit Brush Water (K'iiłsoii Bitó, most likely Navajo Springs near Towaoc). That is where rations for the Utes were handed out.[10]

Jimmy Holiday stated that there were Paiutes who lived and farmed at Dark Water (Tó Diłhil), located on a mesa fifteen miles toward the Bears Ears.[11] As the country became more settled, a community of Paiutes and Utes north of the San Juan River lived around Bluff and in 1923 received lands from the government in Allen Canyon.

Of far greater concern to the Navajos was their more aggressive neighbor, the Utes. This tribe is differentiated by anthropologists as the Northern and Southern Utes, both of whom the Navajos interacted with, but they were primarily involved with the latter. The Southern Utes were further divided into three bands: starting to the east in Colorado were the Muache; moving west in Colorado and northern New Mexico, the Capote; then in southwestern Colorado and southeastern Utah, the Weeminuche. All three bands were traditional enemies of the Navajo, although there were occasionally brief alliances and friendly family interactions. This was particularly true with the Weeminuche, who traded, enslaved, and intermarried with the Paiutes of Monument Valley and Navajo Mountain and were the closest neighbors to the river Navajos in Utah.[12] From the Ute perspective, the San Juan River was a porous boundary between their territory to the north and Navajo land to the south. To show just how porous, there is no doubt that small Navajo groups lived north of the river before the Long Walk and that the Utes lived and operated well into today's Navajo Reservation. For instance, in April 1939, Utah historian Charles Kelly interviewed a Navajo elder named Hashkéneiniihi Biyé (Son of Giving Out Anger) living in Monument Valley. As a young boy in the early 1860s, he fled with his father, Hashkéneiniihi, to Navajo Mountain to avoid the U.S. military with its Ute allies. "At that time, I was five years old and my family was living at Kayenta. Monument Valley then belonged to the Utes, and the rock called El Capitan (Aghaałą́) in Arizona was the dividing line between Utes and Navajos."[13] This places the boundary some thirty miles south of the San Juan River. Much of this to today's Navajos is not recognized.

For those living along the river, beyond occasional trade and brief alliances, the general tenor of the relationship was war. The Navajos speak of three conflicts, one of which occurred between 1841 and 1842 and another around 1858, with the third and most traumatic one—the Fearing Time—occurring in the 1860s.[14] The first two wars are not clearly defined other than Navajo informants saying that they took place before Fort Sumner, the third and most devastating war. A number of brief glimpses that combine the first two give a view of events leading up to the final one. Regarding neighboring Utes, White Sheep said, "They used to come down into the Navajo country from Ute Mountain, but they had no homes there."[15] When asked about the Navajos who lived north of the San Juan River before the Fort Sumner era, Tsék'izí stated:

We had three wars with the Utes from Sleeping Ute Mountain. The first war was Sh'ak'ai na sal [Van Valkenburgh's note: "Navaho name for Ute band or chief?"], which refers to "Boiling." This war was down on lower Mancos Creek. The second war started when a Navajo was trapped by the Utes. They sent two women on horseback to ride in front of a Navajo man to get him to chase them, leading him into a trap. This happened around Burned Out Place (Hodiltł'i'), which is now Dolores, Colorado. The third war started when one Ute stole another Ute's wife but blamed the Navajo. This was when Washington sent a lot of guns to the Utes to fight the Navajo. [Van Valkenburgh's note: "This apparently was in 1863 when the military armed the Utes and used them as mercenaries against the Navajo."] The Navajo had only bows and arrows to fight with, and the Utes started to push them towards Tsékooh Télí [Van Valkenburgh's note: "unidentified"] beyond the Bears Ears to the west and even towards Navajo Mountain.[16]

Eddie Nakai, referencing what he had heard from elders, noted,

These raids took place approximately 15 years before Fort Sumner and were frequent. The Utes who made these raids did not live in this area, but farther east on the Dolores River from where they made their raids. I was told they used to live beyond Silverton, Colorado, but the white settlers in that part of the country pushed them out because they were being attacked. This moved the Utes down into the Dolores River area and from there they raided into the Bears Ears country. My grandfather, K'aayélii, was of the Bit'ahnii Clan, born at the Bear Ears, and died in the Montezuma Creek area. He did not go to Fort Sumner but stayed at Bears Ears. All of the mountains where our ancestors used to hunt had wild game that belonged to them, as did the hills and streams. This country is mine and I feel it is like my mother, because it has hidden me, hidden my relatives in times of various conflicts, and saved them, which causes me to sit here today and tell you of some of my old ancestors like K'aayélii.[17]

Billy Antes agreed: "The real old timers, our great-grandfathers and grandmothers, lived up around Dove Creek, Cortez, and Dolores, Colorado. On account of the Ute wars, they had to leave that country. The Ute came in from the north to attack the Navajo."[18] Lucille Hammond, who lived near the Ismay Trading Post, shared what she had been told: "Horses were sometimes stolen from the Utes, who would also steal from us. One time, they chased some horses into a deep canyon and kept them there. The Utes sang songs against the Navajos, and when the Navajos asked for their horses back, they did not get them. These Navajos went home and performed their own songs and prayers against the enemy so that when they returned where the horses were, they came out without any trouble."[19]

The Fearing Time and Long Walk Era

The decade between 1858 and 1868 was known to the Navajos as the Fearing Time (Náhonzhoodáá'). The entire population came under attack from the U.S. military, a host of Indian allies, and New Mexican volunteer units who scoured every nook and cranny to either enslave or bring in Navajos to Fort Sumner, New Mexico, where approximately half of the population remained incarcerated for four years (1864–1868).[20] It was a time of desperation for both those who were captured and those who escaped, imprinting in the tribal memory an indelible stamp of suffering and hardship. The Navajos on the San Juan River fled to less accessible and well-known areas in the hinterland, away from their usual haunts, so that the Utes could not find them. Ever vigilant against attack, some Navajos evaded capture, enslavement, or death, while others were less fortunate. Most Navajo families, even today, have stories about their relatives during this, the third Ute war.

While other histories of this era discuss broken treaties, raids, and specific incidents around Fort Defiance and in New Mexico, for the Navajos living along the river, it was a continuation of hostilities that had been going on between the Utes and Navajos for years, except now there was added support and pressure from the U.S. military. Locally, there were a number of smaller incidents that led to bigger consequences. A few examples from this rich body of oral history set the stage. Tomas (a.k.a. Tom Jones) stated, "We had war with the Utes before Ft. Sumner. That's how we got pushed south, out of the Dolores-Cortez country. They cleaned us out of sheep and horses, and that's why a lot of Navajo got caught south of the river from up in this country. This was when Washington gave the Utes guns."[21] Martha Nez blamed the start of hostilities on the Navajos: "It was said that the Utes would get hungry and come among our people. One time a few Ute women were picking sumac berries, and some Navajo men found and harassed them, culminating in the women's death. This is what started the war. The fighting did not begin with the white people, but the Utes. The people moved out of this area onto Black Mesa according to the elders."[22] Louise Big Mouth's father, Left Handed Man, agreed with this story. "He told of Navajos living in the Blue Mountains, Dolores River area, and La Plata Mountains. Some young Navajo men in this area killed a Ute woman which started the wars between the two tribes, causing a lot of Utes to be killed. This happened before Fort Sumner."[23] Sally Bailey's great-grandmother, Woman Who Shoots Arrows (Adił T'ohí), spoke of a battle near Bluff:

> She never told me how many years these raids took place before being sent to Fort Sumner. My grandmother told me about how she would get on her horse and then wave a red flag and run the horse into the midst of the enemy, shooting arrows, killing Utes and Mexicans. I remember one story she related of a raid the Utes made on the Navajo near Red Mesa where there is a big rim of red rock. The Navajos stayed on top of the mesa, but it had only one path to the top. They would roll big rocks down on the enemy when they tried to climb up. This site is near Red Rock Trading Post. After running out of water, the Navajos used "Enemy Way medicine" to kill the Ute leader, causing the Utes to leave."[24]

Initially, this hit-and-run warfare targeted Navajo patterns for obtaining food and sites for winter and summer camps, allowing the Utes to pursue their enemy in a predictable manner. For instance, all Native American communities in the Four Corners area followed the development of the annual piñon crop, knowing where the best pickings could be found. Those attracted to the area were subject to Ute entrapment. George Littlesalt remembered his family

> picking piñon nuts, while trying to keep their horses near, when some Navajos came up and said, "Where are the suspected enemies?" and were told, "No enemies, no enemies. Don't say that there are suspected enemies; there aren't any enemies." They continued to pick nuts. Just then, another man came running up and warning, "There are many suspected enemies a little way off from here." As soon as they heard it, they all resaddled their horses, and just as they started back to where they came from, one little boy said, "We have forgotten our little puppy

at the place where we had our belongings."

One of my late grandfathers by the name of Disjédii [no English translation] left with some of the Navajos for where they had been camping. He and another man were riding a big white horse with a bag of piñon nuts between them. Sometimes they would walk, leading the horse. After a while, my grandfather rode back to where they had their horses, even though he had heard there were enemies. The horses were scattered but he caught one; a lot of enemies, all dressed in red, could be seen from a far distance. He tried to hide behind a tree, but they already had seen him, and some of the Utes started to chase him on their horses. He outran them on his horse by going over quite a few hills. When he came to the top of one hill and looked back toward the enemy, they also were on a distant hill. Then he left the Utes far behind and rode across a sandy area on his white horse.

He caught up with a man who was running, and the man said, "It has become rough for me; the enemy are after me." Then the man approached my grandfather beside the horse, and my grandfather grabbed his hair and pulled him onto his white horse. They went on until it was almost dawn, before they slept for a few moments. Then they started out again toward Oljato. About twenty days later, word of mouth came that some of the Mexicans were scouting along near Mexican Water and also by Teec Nos Pos, near where Arizona, New Mexico, Utah, and Colorado come together today. Another place that the Mexicans were moving was Dennehotso, Arizona. There was a wagon train and pack horses, and they were driving horses stolen from other people. Some of them had left the wagon train and gone off in a different direction toward Oljato.[25]

Ada Black shared one of her family's stories that centered around Montezuma Canyon and the piñon harvest:

Navajos should not be afraid of the night because that was one of the few times that we were safe. The night cloaked us. This is what used to be said. The Utes were the first ones to fight us, then came the Mexicans to attack and scatter us, followed by Anglos and enemy tribes. There were even other Navajos who stole from us as the enemy hunted us down, gathered the people, and sent them to Fort Sumner. My maternal grandmother said that the whole problem, ending with

Navajos going on the Long Walk to Fort Sumner, began with our people stealing from the white men. This is the way she talked about it.

Ada then switched to her grandmother's point of view to tell the story.

I was a little girl living on Blue Mountain just this side of Blanding. It is said there is a timber line right next to the canyon where many trees existed, right beside where there are now houses. In the distance there was another line of trees in which there was a lot of smoke from campfires where others were living. We thought these were Navajos who had moved into the area to graze their sheep and horses. My mother, grandmother, and I left our sheep at my uncle's camp in a place called Díwózhii Bikooh [around Hatch Trading Post in Montezuma Creek Canyon] to gather piñon nuts. While we were out picking, we had just finished our lunch when a man rode up on his horse. In a very anxious voice, he asked why the older women were not on the alert. The campfires in the distant wood line, he warned, belonged to the Utes who were out to kill and capture Navajos. He directed us to go somewhere that was inaccessible, then explained that a Navajo man named Ashkii Łizhinii (Black/Darker Boy), who had married a Ute woman, later killed her. The Utes wanted revenge, searching for groups of Navajos picking piñon nuts and killing them in retaliation. This happened a short while ago.

Now the Utes had gathered in larger numbers and were about to run into bigger groups of Navajos. My mother's mother went to the horses, quickly saddled them, and packed their things, saying they would return to Montezuma Creek. By this time, as a young girl, I was really afraid. The man who warned us said the Utes were about to ride this way and that we were all in the open in plain sight. I went to climb onto a horse, but was so badly frightened and weak that my mother grabbed me, placed me on her horse, and away we went through the woods and down the steep canyon slope. The whip was constantly on the horse. The two women were on foot, running behind the animal. My great-uncle appeared on horseback, coming from where he had been tending the sheep. He relieved me of my hard labor of controlling the reins of the horse, grabbed me off the saddle, and placed me on his horse behind him. My grandmother then laid blankets on the empty horse, mounted, and my great-uncle whipped it down the trail. It almost felt like flying, riding on the back of his horse. We were down in Montezuma Creek when some of the things tied on the horse fell off and I was thrown. He told me to stay right there because my mother would catch up soon, then rode away. Mother was still chasing the horse that her grandmother was on, but eventually reached my great-uncle. Mother and grandmother were so exhausted from this flight that they just collapsed upon reaching camp.

Two days later, close to Blue Mountain, the Utes killed my uncle. The enemy then followed a trail that led them to our camp. The Navajo men joined together and fought across a large brush fence, but when the Utes attacked, there was no stopping them. They killed men and women but took the children and young girls as prisoners. Before the fight, the Navajos carefully planned to tie their horses away from the camp in a distant location. After the fight, some of the Navajos escaped and followed their foes as they moved on. At night, the Utes made camp, tied their horses at a distance, and built cooking fires. The Navajos watched and waited as their enemy clustered around the burning wood. At the right moment, they attacked, killed some of the Utes, recaptured their children, and stole some of the frightened and confused Ute girls, all under the cover of darkness. The enemy ran around as if they had been thrown in different directions at once. The Ute girls, who probably just followed the escaping Navajo girls, were frightened, so they took off after them. With this, the Utes went back to their country in the Cortez area but would later live around Blue Mountain.

"This is how my maternal grandmother used to tell about this time," Ada concluded her story.[26]

It soon became evident to the Navajos that if they remained in their current haunts, the Utes would ferret them out and capture them. Evading the enemy became paramount to those people who did not go to Fort Sumner. Old Man Bob (Tó Bii' Jiztį—People Lying Down at Spring) noted the effect:

There were no permanent homes because there were Utes raiding in this country in those days, so we were afraid to stay in any one place too long. . . . The leader of these Ute enemies was Bitsii' Ba' Łigai (Ute

Warrior with White Hair). His parents lived in the Dolores River area before Fort Sumner. . . . My mother told me that her family moved back and forth between the Bears Ears and Dolores River country, long before this war broke out. She said that there was a long period before this conflict started that the Utes would sneak out and kill a Navajo, then the Navajos would retaliate.[27]

Old Ruins, born in 1871, shared the story of his father, also called Old Ruins (Kints'iilnii), and his mother, Woman Who Walked Like She Was Crippled (Asdzáán Na'niłhodii; also called Crippled Woman), living north of the Bears Ears. Crippled Woman's mother remained west of the Bears Ears and north of the San Juan River. A raid by the Utes pushed her group across the river, until they doubled back to the Bears Ears and joined the noted headman K'aayélii.[28] Mexican Woman (Nakai Asdzáán) followed a similar pattern. "When I was about two years old, my family followed a man named K'aayélii. We did not stay in one place, but moved across the San Juan River to Montezuma Creek and Blue Mountain, then west towards Bears Ears, and eventually Nameless (Henry) Mountain."[29]

Not all Navajos were as fortunate. Woman Who Had Her House Burned (Asdzáán Kin Díílidii) was born at the Bears Ears, but with the start of hostilities ended up on Black Mesa in Arizona. The enemy, under the leadership of White Haired Ute, raided her camp, captured her, and sold her as a slave to a Mexican; she did not return home for two years until the soldiers released the Navajos from Fort Sumner. "It was told by the Navajos that this leader [White Haired Ute] looked for Navajos who had sheep, horses, or young girls that he could capture and sell to other people such as the Mexicans."[30] Her great-grandfather, Man Who Regained and Lost Horses (Hastiin Biłį́į' Nádláhí), received his name when Utes and Mexicans stole his large horse herd. After he obtained more livestock, the Utes again stole a large portion of them. Finally, his camp, comprising many hogans located on Long Point near the Bears Ears, came under attack. Utes from the Dolores River area raided the settlement, killing him and others.[31]

These types of occurrences were typical of the time. Exactly how many Navajos did not go on the Long Walk is unknown. Estimates vary as to their number, perhaps as few as two thousand or as many as eight thousand; no agent stood on the periphery of Navajo lands, counting

The Utes were determined foe of the Navajos and highly skilled in ferreting them out from hiding places. Of all the enemy—Anglo, Hispanic, Pueblo Indians, and some of the Plains tribes—that took part in warring against the Navajos, none were more feared than the Utes.

those who escaped and refused to surrender.[32] In the vicinity of Comb Ridge, the canyons, mesas, ridges, and hills offered hiding places from bands of marauders seeking targets of opportunity. The Bears Ears, as a prominent terrain feature, served as a general descriptor for an area that included Elk Ridge and canyons feeding from there that were used by the Navajos. Many of these features parallel part of Comb Ridge.[33] Oral history accounts suggest that there were fairly peaceful relations between some members of the two tribes and that it was the Utes living farther to the east who hunted for those in hiding.[34]

Piecing together the story of those who either already lived or fled to this region is detective work. What emerges is a fascinating story of perseverance in the face of fear and uncertainty. A number of Navajos lived along Comb and Butler Washes before the conflict began. White Sheep (Dibé Łigai) told of his family in this area. His mother, Yellow Woman (Asdzáán Łitsoi), was born at Sweet Water (Tó Łikan at the foot of Comb Ridge where Highway 163 passes through today) and was a mature woman when she went to Fort Sumner. Her husband, Mr. Heavyset (Hastiin Dííl), was born in Allen Canyon at a place called White Spotted Reeds (Lók'aałgai) but did not go on the Long Walk, remaining with his family in upper Comb Wash, where he is buried today. His mother, Blue Coat Woman (Asdzáán Biéétoh Dotł'izhí), was born at the mouth of Comb Wash at a place called Beautiful under the Cottonwoods (T'iis Yaa Hózhónii), where she lived before and after her return from Fort Sumner. White Sheep's paternal grandfather, Mexican Clan People (Naakaidine'é), died at White Rock Point along Chinle Wash. Other friends and relatives that lived in the Bluff–Comb Ridge area before the Long Walk included Giving Out Anger (Hashkéneiniihi), White Sheep's paternal uncle; another uncle, Mr. Rope or Ropey (Hastiin Tł'óół), named because he made braided ropes; two brothers, Mr. Wife Beater (Hastiin Be'asdzáán 'Atííłíinii) and Owl (Né'éshjaa'), the latter of whom acted funny and did not worry about things; and Small Man of the Tótsonii Clan (Tótsonii Yázhí) and Old Man of the Tótsonii Clan (Tótsonii Sání), both of whom were friends with White Sheep's father.[35]

Paul Goodman told of his family group and their association with the Bears Ears. His maternal grandmother, named Shoot or Dragging Something, was born on the south side of the Bears Ears, fifteen or twenty years before the People went to Fort Sumner. As a younger sister of Hashkéneiniihi, she remained north of the San Juan River during the Fearing Time. Her mother, Uses Club Downward (Yaago'Adįhaąii), and father, Very Small, were both born near the Bears Ears. His maternal uncle, Giving out Anger, married a woman of the Bitterwater Clan, making him an in-law by clan to K'aayélii, living on Elk Ridge at what is now the Kigalia (anglicized name for K'aayélii) Ranger Station. His settlement comprised five or six hogans located near a spring (K'aayélii Bitó) named after him.[36] A pattern begins to emerge from these oral testimonies. The first is the importance of relationships. Extended families shared a general area of resources; intermarriage was common. The Bears Ears, known as a good place to hunt deer, herd livestock, collect berries, and obtain seeds and nuts, served as a magnet that drew Navajos to its resources.[37]

The most prominent leader in the vicinity of Comb Ridge was K'aayélii. Born near Shonto, Arizona, about thirty years before the Long

Walk, K'aayélii belonged to the Within His Cover (Bit'ahnii) Clan. He wintered in the Montezuma Creek area, where he had a racetrack located about two miles southwest of the Hatch Trading Post. In peaceful times there, he used to race horses with the Utes.[38] As a naat'áanii, he established his camp during periods of conflict near the Bears Ears. The people accepted him as their leader, adopting his policy of not provoking the enemy in order to avoid conflict, but he also had an uncanny ability to escape raids and ambushes. "These headmen . . . were good horse trainers. They trained their horses for hunting deer. They could ride them all day long and not wear them out. These old Navajos used to hunt in the Monticello area [Blue Mountain] when they did not have anything but bows and arrows, and used to get the game they wanted."[39] K'aayélii's sister, Woman with a Burned House (Asdzáán Kin Díílidii), lived in his camp behind the Bears Ears with other Navajos at Place to Escape from the Enemy (Naznidzoodi), a canyon that facilitated disguised movement off Elk Ridge.[40] Her husband, Mexican Man (Naakai Diné), was born in the vicinity of the Bears Ears, where the couple stayed during the Fearing Time. Her maternal grandmother (no name) was not as fortunate. Warrior Woman (Deezbaa') related how her grandmother fell into the hands of some Mexicans.

> My mother told me that when her mother was a young girl, she was among a group of Navajos who were captured by Utes and taken to some Mexicans where they were sold separately as slaves. She was kept in a crib log cabin in one room with a lock in the doorway so that she could not get away. There was a ladder that went up to the attic of the house, which she climbed and escaped to a nearby mountain. While she was approaching this place, it started snowing and so she got under a spreading piñon tree where she stayed all day long, while barking dogs and pursuers searched for her until they gave up pursuit because it was snowing too hard to track her. She stayed under this tree all night and the next day, then started out the following evening, eventually arriving south of the San Juan River where she recognized Shiprock. She had to break her way through the brush and undergrowth along the river, which she followed west to Douglas Mesa and then to Place across the River to Escape from the Enemy, where she joined the Kaayélii people.[41]

West of the Bears Ears is a site called "Lonely Tree" or "Navajo Woman Gave Birth to a Child." The family of Warrior Woman (Deezbaa'), who was born and raised on Elk Ridge, identified this spot where a pregnant woman was traveling. Wolves pursued her, so she climbed a lone tree to escape and did not descend until she had given birth while resting in the branches of the tree.[42]

There were also times when Utes, Paiutes, and Navajos cooperated. For instance, K'aayélii had Paiute men posted to watch for the approach of the enemy, so that his group could flee.[43] But perhaps the most dramatic, documented proof of Ute, Paiute, and Navajo cooperation occurred in September 1866. A group of Capote and Weeminuche Utes and a few Mexicans organized a ruse to trap a group of Navajos living in northern Arizona. The plan was to send word that the Utes wanted to live in peace and in close proximity to them. After the Navajos arrived, the Utes would kill the men, enslave the women and children, and capture the livestock. Upon hearing this, White Haired Ute refused, saying that he had friends among those Navajos whom he did not want to kill. A fight ensued, and the Capotes killed him, then fled. Following retaliatory strikes, White Haired Ute's sons went with other Utes to "the neighborhood of Rio Dolores, Sierra Salir [La Sal Mountains], and Sierra Orejos [Bears Ears]" to "join as is supposed the [Weeminuche] and Pah Utes who had made friends with the Navajos."[44]

Even with this slight leavening of apparent friendship, intertribal conflict with its fear and mistrust dragged on for another two years before the Treaty of 1868 ended hostilities. Those who had gone to Fort Sumner returned to the region, although many were slow to resume activities close to the Utes. As for K'aayélii, he continued to live and hunt in southeastern Utah after the conflict subsided. It is unclear when he died, although in 1953 a relative named Tsék'izí (Crack in the Rock) claimed it was fifty-five years previously and that he was buried "five miles up the west side of Montezuma Creek from where it meets the San Juan River."[45] No mention of his death is made by settlers who entered the area around 1880, and so it may have been earlier.

In 1868 the government signed a treaty with the Navajos living at Fort Sumner that released them to return to a greatly reduced land base to serve as their reservation. In reality, many went back to where they had lived before the war and continued with their livestock operations. Even as treaty negotiations were underway, the Navajos registered their fear of the Utes, recalling how effective they had been in fighting and capturing the Diné. Agents and the military strove to allay their fears, hoping that they would become sedentary farmers and livestock owners and that tribal frictions would subside. The San Juan River had long been a popular magnet for Navajo agriculturalists in the past, but there were lingering concerns of having Utes for close neighbors, and so many were slow to return along the river. And rightly so. The Utes were still aggressive toward the Navajos and were not truly responsive to government control until 1895, when they received an agency with the Muache and Capote at the eastern end (Ignacio, Colorado) and the Weeminuche at the western end (Towaoc) of their reservation in the corner of southwestern Colorado. As peaceful relations grew between Utes and Navajos, the latter had family groups interested in moving north to the river, while those who had initially remained returned from the hinterlands. It appears that it was during the 1880s when the greatest influx of Navajos moved into southeastern Utah along the river. There were reasons for this population increase. Expansion of reservation boundaries through presidential executive orders or congressional legislation in 1884, 1892, 1905, and 1933 encouraged settlement of these additional lands. In 1903 William T. Shelton established the Northern Navajo or Shiprock Agency, bringing further control to the area. Other conditions encouraged Navajo expansion. For instance, as the Diné tailored their resources to fit into the dominant culture's economy, wool, sheep, and arts and crafts became popular with Anglo clientele. Off-reservation trading posts operating along the border drew Navajos eager to sell their products; others sought employment as herders or itinerant laborers, beckoning them to the north and off the reservation. Finally, advancing technology and improving travel conditions increased social and economic stability. Aneth and Montezuma Creek started as white settlements in 1878 with Bluff following not far behind in 1880. Thus, the northern Navajo frontier assumed different qualities as the Diné received a new compliment of neighbors.

Mormon Entry

The first white settlers established in Aneth and Montezuma Creek were a mix of Colorado farmers, traders, and settlers.[46] But the real influx of Anglos was the arrival of Mormon pioneers who founded Bluff in

1880 after a six-month tortuous trip from southwestern Utah over the Hole-in-the-Rock Trail. Their arrival brought fledgling forms of government, law and order, and relative economic stability, all of which was enmeshed in qualities and characteristics of interacting with Native people different from many frontier towns. Agriculture, livestock, trade, and resource competition created a two-way bittersweet yet dependent relationship between the settlers and their Navajo neighbors. Compared to their Ute neighbors, the Mormons generally got along well with the Navajos, with both groups benefiting from peaceful relations.

These settlers sent an advance party the year before the main body arrived in Bluff. In 1879 there were already established in Montezuma Creek a number of non-Mormons from Colorado, who greeted the exploring party. Two Latter-day Saints families remained when the advanced guard left to determine a satisfactory route for the main group. From this beginning, a small protective structure named Fort Montezuma began to grow on the banks of the San Juan, with its greatest influx of settlers during the next two years.[47] Tódich'íínii (Bitter Water) recalled this earliest effort:

> Way back when I was little, there were no Mormons living around Bluff. At the mouth of Recapture Creek, a Navajo named Little Mexican (Naakai Yázhí) had a big farm that the river washed away. There were other farms near there owned by Tomas, High Chest (Hastiin Yidii), and Yánaal'a' (Servant), around Bluff on the San Juan, while Hastiin Joe had one about four miles west of there. There were four "outfits" living right around Bluff when the Mormons moved in. Long ago, Big Mustache (Dághaa Tso) had grazing lands all the way from the mouth of Recapture Creek to about 20 miles northeast of Hatch Store, where he ranged his horses. When I first saw the Mormons, they were at the mouth of the river and had ox teams, six animals to a wagon, with children riding inside while the men and women walked. [Van Valkenburgh's note: "Apparently this was the group of Mormons who attempted a settlement on the San Juan River about 5 miles east of the mouth of Montezuma Creek in 1880."][48]

Mormon arrival in the San Juan area in 1880 established a relationship that was generally peaceful and beneficial to both Navajos and Anglos. The San Juan or Bluff Cooperative was a welcomed trading spot where wool, blankets, livestock, and employment offered goods useful to Indian customers.

White Sheep remembered the main body of Mormons coming into the country when he was about ten years old and living in the upper Comb Wash region near the head of Arch Canyon.

> That was when the Mormons came in. They were just about out of clothes. They had ox teams so some rode and others walked. Hastiin Joe, Old Tótsohnii (Big Water), and Tall Mexican (Naakai Nez) saw them first up by the Bear's Ears. When they camped, some Mormons came out and asked the Navajo if they had any clothing or shoes. We traded them some stuff for green coffee beans and sugar. Then they asked if we had some corn, and we answered yes. Next they wanted to know where they could find a level place to plant corn, melons, and squash. They went down Comb Wash, around the end of the ridge at the San Juan River, where they had to pick a way to get around Butler Wash, so that they could reach the future site of Bluff City. We helped the Mormons get started, then they began to crowd the Navajos out, saying, "This is Mormon country. You Navajos do not belong here." I left there between 60–70 years ago.[49]

Regarding the Mormon settlement of Bluff, Hashk'áán Dííl (Big Banana/Yucca Fruit) said,

> At the time the Mormons came in, it was like a dream. There used to be a forest of thickets growing where Bluff is now. They chopped away a small place, moved in, and initially lived in tents. They were very poor, but when spring came, they put in a small farm and built a fence made of cottonwood limbs around it, where they grew corn and watermelons. Some used wagons pulled by oxen, some had horse teams, and others just dragged their stuff stacked on logs that their stock dragged along. The women and children either rode or walked and they had no sheep with them. The Mormons just came in and did not even ask about a piece of land, even though the Navajos had lived there a long time before. We did not give them any land, but they just moved in.[50]

Hashk'áán Dííl saw his first white man when he was a boy.

> I saw the Mormons moving into Bluff. A long time ago when they and the Navajo could not talk to each other, we just gave them our own

names. When they first came to Bluff, they were poor even though they had oxen and wagons and some horses and cattle. They had no sheep, but the Navajos did—goats, horses, cattle, and burros—a long time before the Mormons arrived. They built cabins in the ground and covered them with dirt, then started to plant corn and watermelons in little patches of land they cleared. When they got their harvest, they traded these to the Navajo for sheep. The next year, they grew more corn and watermelons and brought in some "green" coffee, cloth, and sack tobacco with a yellow band and a red spot on it, cigarette papers with a picture of a corncob on the package, baking soda, sugar, and salt in sacks.[51]

Maimi Howard, whose family lived across the river from Bluff at that time, remembered Navajos that were hired by the settlers to build more permanent housing.

They helped clear the land and quarried rocks from the nearby cliffs for these white men to build their homes. That is how the white men built houses that were bumpy and looked ugly. They slaughtered cows and pigs to keep the Navajos working for them. I have seen this, too. Kumen Jones (Dághaa Chíí—Red Beard) already made friends with the Navajos, so they worked for him. Those two rocks [the Navajo Twins] that are standing in Bluff are medicine, too. When a person licks it, the couple will have twins. During this time the white people made a red drink and the Navajos drank it. This was when I was about six years old.[52]

Once Bluff was established, it became home to a variety of trading posts, the San Juan (or Bluff) Cooperative Store, and a number of livestock operations, all of which brought services, products, and employment that drew additional Navajo people to the edge of the reservation. A number of its residents spoke the Navajo language, which became a desirable trait for those involved in the barter system. Some formed lifelong friendships with Navajo neighbors, while others appreciated the consistency of care that Navajo shepherds provided in caring for livestock. While there certainly were times when friction arose, culminating in fights and even bloodshed, relations were generally pacific, and friendships endured.

The Navajo people living along the San Juan River had three close neighbors—the Paiutes, Utes, and Anglos—all of whom interacted from their own cultural expectations. The Utes were the most problematic—before, during, and after the Fearing Time—but even then, there were moments of friendship, intermarriage, and alliances that made an otherwise dark picture somewhat lighter. All three groups provide context for the Navajo experience as it unfolded along the San Juan River.

CHAPTER TWO

Singing the Land, Living Its Teachings

The Power of the Chantways

Florence Begay sat with her son, Norman, in her home in Aneth. Norman, a returned Vietnam veteran, translated his mother's words, focusing on her but also glancing across the room and out the window at the San Juan River as it glided between its brown banks. Florence was an accomplished medicine woman, knowledgeable in the healing plants of the region as well as the teachings gained from the ceremonies in which she and her husband participated. Occasionally she sang a phrase or two from one of the songs to punctuate her thoughts. Next, she would move to the window to point out a terrain feature across the water or on the horizon and tie it to an event. Her gray hair, pulled back in a hair knot (tsiiyéél), hinted of the traditional life that she lived and a belief system rooted in the stories and teachings of the past. She wished to relay them to the next generation.

One thing was certain. Everything she taught tied into the lands surrounding the Four Corners area. Her focus, characteristic of so much in Navajo life, came from the songs and prayers derived from sacred narratives that encompassed the emergence of the Navajo people through the three or four worlds beneath this one, as well as later events. During this time of premortal and later mortal existence, the holy people laid the foundation for Navajo life, all of which was associated with specific geographic places.[1] Following the emergence, these experiences occurred at sites well known and accessible to Navajos, giving rise to the reason that anthropologists refer to the People (Diné) as practicing a "land-based" religion. Every story, moral teaching, historic or mythological event, or supernatural power may be tied to a specific mountain, rock formation, body of water, desert space, plant or animal, weather phenomena, or other aspect of the physical world.[2] What these powers may be, how they are controlled, where they can be found or appealed to, how they may be offended, why they exist, and how to call forth their aid through ceremony, are encoded in the myths or stories about the holy people who invested the world with these elements to assist the Navajos. In Mary Blueyes's words, "When the stories of the mountains are told, it is like telling about all of Mother Earth and its people. This belongs to the Navajos; these stories are told clockwise starting from the east."[3] There is nothing random in this universe—it is all part of a well-designed plan that, when followed, leads to healing, happiness, and well-being (hózhǫ́).

Mountains of Power

The first and primary mountains of the Navajos are Blanca Peak (Sisnaajiní—Black Belt Mountain, in Colorado), Mount Taylor (Tsodził—Big Mountain, in New Mexico), San Francisco Peaks (Dookʼoʼoosłííd—Never Thaws on Top, in Arizona), and Hesperus Peak (Dibé Nitsaa—Big Sheep, in Colorado), each having its own powers. The teachings, stories, prayers, and songs about them are extensive, too lengthy to cover here. Two illustrations of their powers and pervasiveness follow. One medicine man (unidentified) put it this way:

> The blessings that are of immortality are associated with the Sacred Mountains, and that is what we live by. Now these mountains that were placed in a circle are our home, and we are to live within the circle. They [holy people] made prayers about Blanca Peak. From the lip of the hole from which they emerged they made prayers about it. From right there the prayers began, prayers associated with the Emergence. It is called a home built with Soft Goods (as a rug or skin). It was

on Soft Goods that the prayers were made. . . . In accord with these prayers, all came into a condition of continued existence.[4]

Charlie Blueyes, from the Tódahidíkáanii (Hanging Water) area south of Bluff, illustrated how pervasive and interconnected these mountains are to daily life:

Sisnaajiní, which is a home [for the holy people], sits right over there. This is what my elders have said. It is made up of white shell, and prayed to when taking some of its earth (dziłleezh) for putting together a mountain soil bundle (dahńdiilyééh). Another mountain is Tsodził and is made up of turquoise while Dookʼoʼoosłííd is composed of abalone and Dibé Nitsaa is made of jet. These represent the Navajo home/hogan. Dziłleezh is gathered from these mountains and used to ask for rain when there is none. The prayers are said from here. When mountain soil is used, the rains come with prayers that are offered in a ceremony. A mountain soil bundle is also used when a person is sick or to bless livestock. The animals are what life is about, so people ask for them to be blessed through the powers of mountain soil. When prayers are offered through its power, rain comes and nurtures the land, which in turn feeds the livestock, giving us meat, and meat is our life. All living plants have pollen, which keeps us alive, and from the sheep, life is renewed. The same is true with cattle. Who would give birth in a dry place? This will not happen. Plants around here are given an offering called ntłʼiz (sacred stones and shell). From the rains brought on by the offering come many lambs or calves. On the tip of these plants are horses, cattle, and sheep. When one eats certain plants, one can have a baby. When a woman cannot have a baby, she can collect some herbs and drink them to help start the pregnancy. This helps her to conceive.[5]

While these mountains are mentioned in every ceremony, there are also local, less prominent sites that tie into the overarching plan set in motion by the holy people. These are accompanied by their own teachings that are harmonious with those found in the more prominent narratives. Every Navajo community has its own stories and sacred sites where people can appeal for help and that are just as important and powerful as more distant ones. This is key to understanding how Florence saw the world from her home along the San Juan River.

Take for instance the mythological story of the Navajo Twins, Monster Slayer (Naayéé'neizghání) and Born for Water (Tóbájíshchíní), whose mother, Changing Woman (Asdzáá Nádleehe'), and father, Sun Bearer (Jóhonaa'éí), through a supernatural union, created these two powerful warriors. As they grew in maturity, these youths became curious as to who their absent father was. During this time, monsters inhabited their world, killing and eating the Navajo people. The Twins set off to meet their father and obtain his assistance in destroying these monsters. After a journey fraught with hazards, trials, and obstacles, they visited their father, received the necessary weapons, returned to earth, and set about killing their malevolent foe. This lengthy story is filled with teachings, provides the basis for elements found in many ceremonies, establishes the pattern for warrior manhood, and identifies articles and procedures that destroy evil.

To Florence, this was an important role for a male Navajo. She outlined the plot of the story, abbreviating many of the details:

First Woman stood with First Man at their home on Huerfano Mountain (Dził Ná'ooditii) and saw a cloud on top of Gobernador Knob (Ch'óol'í'í). It looked like fog, tending to move along the ground. There, First Man found a baby girl. He brought her home and the couple raised her. As she grew up, everything about her had to do with four, and this is how that number in the Blessingway (Hózhǫ́ǫ́jí) originated and how the twins arrived and ordained to kill the enemies [monsters]. Before their journey, they were blessed to overcome the many obstacles in their way. When they arrived at Sun Bearer's home, their father did not recognize them, so he claimed they were not his relatives, but they insisted otherwise. Once Sun Bearer became convinced of their claim, he offered many riches found in each of the four directions. They had no desire for any of them, only the arrows needed to kill the monsters, but their father was a hard man to convince. After four days, he relented and let them take four different types, giving rise to the lightning we have today. He said that the weapon was not carried alone, so the oldest brother was given the lightning arrow while Born for Water received hail with the instructions to set it in a bowl while his brother went against the enemy. He was told to take care of the hail and that when his fire was burning, the head of the lightning arrow would start to burn if his brother was having a hard time. When the fire burned high, he was to put some hail in the fire to decrease and calm it. This was his job because he was named after water; he was to take care of the home setting. Together, they destroyed the enemy.

Take, for example, the déélgééd living at Red Mesa (approximately twenty-five miles from Aneth), where the sand was turned red with its blood. This monster killed people with its breath and ate them. There was also a pair of flying monsters called tsé nináhádleehí living on top of Shiprock (Tsé Bit'a'í). This male and female monster were so big that when they were flying around, they could see a person walking on the mesas at Mesa Verde. Once spotted they would fly to their prey, scoop it up, dash it against the jagged edges of Shiprock, then feed the remains to their two young. Monster Slayer placed blood from the déélgééd into some intestines and went out in an open area for the birds to see him. The female swooped down, carried him to the top of Shiprock, and slammed the warrior against the rock. Blood spilled all over, causing the bird to think it had killed him, but he had hidden, unharmed, in a crevice. Monster Slayer asked the young birds when their mother would return, and they answered that when the female rain covered Gobernador Knob she would be back. She would be the first to return, and when the male rain and lightning fell on Roof Butte (Dził Dah Neeztínii), the father would also arrive back at his home. Monster Slayer waited with the young birds, singing chants that gave rise to another five-day ceremony called Lifeway Male Shooting Branch (Na'at'oyee Biką'jí). When the birds returned, he shot and killed them with arrows. Their feathers dropped to the ground below, with the Jackrabbit selecting two for himself. This is why today they look like they have feathers for ears.

Monster Slayer now told the young birds that from that day forth, they would live on the mountains and in the trees and that the people would have use for them. Twirling one young bird above his head, then releasing it, he assigned specific responsibilities. The bird became an eagle, charged to be a messenger of good news for the five-fingered beings [people] and to share his protective and healing powers through its feathers for their benefit. To the second, the owl, Monster Slayer commanded that it also be a messenger, but not of good news. The owl was to work with his cousin, the vulture, in the realm of death, and so he received no healing power. He was told to warn the people of any danger, of hardship and sickness, and of the possibility of death if they did not get prayers or ceremonies performed to block an evil force. Unlike the eagle, who took his place on the mountain with the understanding that he had power over the earth, the owl was to dwell in trees and predict the future of the people by the sound it made.[6]

As Florence looked about the room, her eyes fell upon Norman. He had followed the trail established by Monster Slayer when the Vietnam War loomed in his immediate future. These teachings had kept him safe. Speaking of Changing Woman, Florence recalled:

> She raised the Twins to kill off the enemies [monsters]. The same ceremony that protected them is performed when a Navajo man goes off to war and is preparing to fight. All of these war rituals started at Tó Nts'ósíkooh Taah Yili, which means Mancos Creek meeting the San Juan River [Mancos Creek, Colorado, is approximately sixty miles distant from Aneth]. You did not get hurt over there, no scratch on you. Your father had this belief, and this protected you as you went overseas. It was the same when you were working on the police force. This belief was what your father had because he had this power and understood the origin of the chants. That is, he protected you. You didn't go over there on your own. Your father had a lot to do with it. This was done for a number of other young men, and they all came back. What Monster Slayer did to kill off the monsters is reenacted to protect individuals today. That is why ones who had this ceremony performed on them came back from Vietnam. It is like that.
>
> When a person goes into the service, there are other places where a protective offering can be placed. For instance, the highest peak around here is used. This is where the medicine men put ntł'iz. Also, where the rock meets the sand, or along the San Juan River, or near a tree that has been struck with lightning, or where there is an echo can serve as well. The emotion that Monster Slayer experienced is the prayer. According to medicine men, you have to know what happened to Monster Slayer and then imitate those things in that prayer. They have to know the story to obtain the power, and learn what to say and how to perform the ceremony. All of the five-day ceremonies that came from Mancos Creek are used for and about surviving. All the singing, five-day ceremonies, squaw dance singing, storytelling—everything starts from

The two first dancers in this Edward S. Curtis photograph are Monster Slayer, in the lead, followed by Born for Water. Known as the Twins, these two powerful deities represent the essence of manhood and protection from evil, and were the holy beings who made the earth safe for the Navajos to live in.

there. This is where the lizards, the coyotes, and other animals gathered together and formulated many of the songs. That is where the whole thing actually started.[7]

Speaking of this meeting, Jane Silas, an elder who lived in Aneth, felt that this was the time when the songs for the Blessingway

derived from a certain place to here. It was performed long ago at a ceremony where "all" gathered. Each was instructed to leave individually and secretly. When darkness fell, they spread a blanket on the ground, a sacred ritual, while singing the sacred hogan song (Hooghan Biyiin). Just when they were ending the sacred song, "The Old Coyote" himself entered the hogan, saying, "Huh, ah-zih, ah-zih, ah-zih. This is how you are supposed to sing it. I have arrived from the 'wrong' path, not knowing that the Blessingway path was here all along." He kept saying "ah-zih," so finally they asked Coyote "What are you saying? Why don't you just start singing the song." Then the coyote began singing, "This is the path, the path to Blessingway." He sang until he finished the song. He then asked the others to "follow/pick up after me." The group encouraged him to continue singing, but the coyote stopped and asked the others to sing. So the others sang all the songs of the Blessingway. That's where it began when Coyote introduced it. Every sacred ceremony and sing now is based on the experiences and doings of Coyote. Whatever was spoken then has turned to sacred songs for our people. Sacred songs are wherever we walk.[8]

There are many ceremonies that branch off from the main stalk or story derived from a particular event or part of a myth. Florence spoke of a main branch, the Iináájík'ehgo or Lifeway, which is subdivided into male and female versions of the Flintway and Shootingway, as well as the Shaft Branchway and Hand Tremblingway—six total. Each of these ceremonies has the ability to maintain life and restore an individual to normal after a traumatic accident. Part of the story that outlines how this type of curing first occurred tells of Monster Slayer traveling in the local area with three companions, who at one point were in the form of beautiful women but were actually buffalo. Florence said:

Monster Slayer walked with them over the mountains that we see over there, in the Dolores [Colorado] area near Montrose. These are the trails of their prayers and chants and the experiences of Monster Slayer. These women had names like Tsididin, Biyałhi Įtsooi (Yellow Under[?]), and Deegháįłʼaah (Someone You Can Send Far). He followed them and slept with them until he learned what they were. From this experience came the ceremonies of the Lifeway. In them, buffalo hooves are used as rattles. This was one of his experiences, and through these ceremonies (Hoof or Claw way ceremony—Akéshgaan) one is made whole again. The same is true with the Enemyway ceremony (Anaaʼjí). When all of these ceremonies were made from him, he started to die. People wondered what was killing him. He did not eat, just laid there, could not swallow water, and his complexion turned dark. There was this thing called Dǫʼtsoh (Big Fly—legendary messenger) that had great knowledge of everything. He performed the hand trembling ceremony for Monster Slayer. When he finished with this divination, he explained that the Enemyway ceremony was needed. The holy people asked him how this should be performed, and he showed them.[9]

Origin of the Utes

Near the Mancos River stands Sleeping Ute Mountain (Dził Naajiní— Black Mountain), home of the Weeminuche Utes. With a few notable exceptions, the Utes, who speak a different language and have a different culture than the Navajo, have historically been their traditional enemy. This mountain and nearby Mesa Verde are central to the Navajos' explanation about the origin of these people. Therefore, it is not surprising that Owl, the harbinger of bad news, and Coyote, a well-known trickster of the Navajos, are paired with Sleeping Ute Mountain when explaining the origin of the Utes.

Coyote's firstborn child was a girl, after which he had a number of boys. As this female matured, the trickster began to take interest in her, and true to his nature, saw nothing wrong in having a sexual relationship. The mother coyote did not agree, so Coyote started to scheme. He went to his wife and told her that he would die soon and that in the future, she would meet a man to whom she should give her daughter in marriage. Coyote also gave explicit instructions of how he should be buried. Not long after, he was found lying on the ground dead; just as he had proposed, the family wrapped the body in blankets, laid sticks and leafy branches on top of the grave, then more blankets. Following the burial, the people left for a vertical column of rock at the foot of Sleeping Ute Mountain to begin their journey to the north. Coyote informed them, however, that they were never to look back. As the family departed, the last son turned around long enough to see his supposedly deceased father jump out of his grave. One of the older children told him not to say something like that, since he had been warned not to look back, but the youngster insisted he had seen his father run into their home.

Coyote's plan unfolded. As the mother with her children continued their journey, they met a man whom they did not recognize. They had been instructed that if this should happen, the mother was to give her daughter in marriage to this stranger with the promise that in return, she and her children would have a good life. Acting on her deceased husband's wishes, she surrendered the girl to the man and continued on her travels. Soon, the daughter had a child by the stranger, only to learn that he was her disguised father. The young woman was enraged, seized the baby, stomped it into a badger's hole, and fled home to her family.

On Mesa Verde lived an owl husband and wife who heard the cry of the baby from a long way off. The male owl flew to the crying infant, brought it home, and with his wife, decided to raise the baby. When Coyote's son reached maturity, he became very good with his bow and arrow, causing his owl father to grow jealous and increasingly at odds with this offspring. Eventually, the parents of the young coyote man evicted him, ordering him to return to where he was found. For four nights, owl man visited him and the last time, the Holy Wind (Nílch'ih) came to advise the coyote to give the owl biyeel (his offering or payment) to his stepfather, which the coyote did. This was done by putting a piece of white shell (yoołgai) on his fingernail and flipping it to the owl, preventing the bird from pestering him by giving the first owl biyeel. This event occurred where the rocks stand near Ute Mountain (Chimney Rock and the Ute's "toe"). Florence Begay explained:

The teachings of the origin of the Utes describe a powerful people associated with trickery and misbehavior (Coyote) and death (Owl), qualities assigned to their historic relationship with the Navajos. As with every traditional story, it is tied to specific geographical locations and events that serve as a mnemonic prop to remind the people of what happened in the beginning.

He then had a vision of where he used to live, with branches lying in a circle, and when he went back, this is what he found. He also learned that his mother was there weaving and that he should call her mother and shake hands, but once he arrived, she ran from him and said a ghost had returned. She told all of the people around her, who became angry and started to chase him away. As he ran, he cut arrow shafts from four different types of wood (tlintz'iz), ash (dahba'), serviceberry (tsé' ésgízii), and didzééh (elk berry plant), which he stuck in the ground along the way. They soon turned into Utes, the Arrow People, and that is why they are found in the Dolores area and all of the surrounding mountains. This story also describes the origin of the owl biyeel and why the Utes, like the owl, "have very short necks (stocky)."[10]

The Utes claim Ute Mountain as their mother, and when they die, they will go back into it. A great Ute warrior is buried in this mountain, covered with trees and branches and blankets of clouds like Coyote once was.

San Juan—Old Age River

Florence explained that relatively close to her home sat the origin of other complex, five-day ceremonial myths. Where the Mancos River empties into the San Juan River is called Tséyaató (Water under the Rock) and is the place where Monster Slayer used to hold meetings and a site where later, Navajos came from all directions to grind corn and sing together. The first woman he ever slept with was called Asdzáán Ałganí (Lady Who Makes You Skinny), whom he took to the top of Chimney Rock (Tsé Yit'ayi'ai—near the southern end of Sleeping Ute Mountain). When they reached the summit, he learned that she was not a young, beautiful woman as he had first seen her at the corn grinding place. At her home, she turned into an old lady so that all he could do was to think about escaping from her. Looking in every direction, all he saw were rocks, and all he felt was hunger and thirst. Monster Slayer began to sing his medicine songs in the direction of his homeland, which helped deliver him from the old woman's clutches and which now are the chants used in the five-day healing ceremony of the Lifeway Female Shooting Branch (Na'at'oyee Ba'adádji).

In another story that starts at the same holy river junction, there were two men, accompanied by Monster Slayer, who sang beautiful songs. They became enticing to two young sisters who were non–sunlight struck maidens (Doo Bi'deedlaadí). They went with the men and spent a night together. These old men turned out to be bears, and so one woman fled to the mountain called Dził Dah Neeztínii (highest peak in the Lukachukai range) and climbed over it. From her many experiences came the Mountainway (Dziłk'ijí hatáál). Her younger sister ran down to the San Juan River–Mancos Creek junction, singing songs given to her by the Holy Wind as she traveled. One of the old men pursued her, but she escaped, giving rise to the Beautyway (Hoozhónee'iji) songs she sang as she fled. There are two other five-day ceremonies that originated in this area. In addition to the Lifeway Female Shooting Branch already mentioned, there is also the Male Branch, which started on top of Shiprock. The Mountainway deals with the mountains and bears, the Beautyway with the San Juan River and snakes, and the Male and Female Shootingway with Chimney Rock, Shiprock, and lightning. Thus, the land in the Four Corners area is associated with many sites named in the events of major Navajo chantways.

Florence also had a close association with the San Juan River. This body of water is one of four that surround, protect, and empower Navajo lands in a ceremonial sense. Starting with the east, there is the Rio Grande, considered to be female; the Little Colorado (south)—male; Colorado (west)—female; and the San Juan River (north)—male, each with their own personality. The San Juan River in everyday parlance is called Tooh (river, body of water) and in the past as Utes' River (Nóóda'í Bitooh), since the north side was considered their territory.

But in the metaphor-rich language found in the songs and prayers of ceremonies, it is known by terms that often magnify or accentuate its qualities or functions as found in the underlying story. Thus, it may be known as Old Age River (Są́ Bitooh), Male Water (Tooh Biką'ii), Male with a Crooked Body (Biką'ii Bitsíís Nanooltł'iizhii), Decorated with Abalone Shells (Bikáá' Hodiichíłí), and One with a Long Body (Bits'íís Nineezí). It is a powerful river described as an older man with hair of white foam, as a snake wriggling through the desert, as the home of the mythological creature Big Snake, as a flash of lightning, and as a black club of protection to keep invaders from Navajo lands.[11] The sparkle on the surface, to some, represents the shine of lightning. Prayer and pollen invoke the spirit within, which may be connected to protection through "singing the ways of the snake."[12]

Medicine man Perry Robinson explains why this body of water is called Old Age River. Its origin goes back to the time when Monster Slayer and Born for Water had killed most of the creatures that had been plaguing the Navajos.

> The Twins traveled throughout the land killing other monsters until they thought their job was finished. They were mistaken. Four evil beings remained—one was located near the site of Navajo Dam in New Mexico, another at Navajo Mountain, one at the crossing in Salt Canyon, and another along the Gila River. These enemies continued to harm and kill people, and so needed to be exterminated before the Twins could say they had completed their task. They set out for the first one, The Old Age People, living in the east on the San Juan River near what is now Farmington, New Mexico. When they arrived at their home, they found an old man and woman sitting outside, waiting. Monster Slayer asked if the elderly couple killed people, then said, "Before I slay you, tell me why I should allow you to live." The old ones motioned to them to sit down and listen to the story about the growth and development of humans, who are born and mature into puberty, become adults, then decline in old age. A man and woman will have children and then grandchildren along the way, but eventually become fragile and die. Their eyes will fail, hearing will go, as everything in their life slowly grinds to a halt.
>
> "That is how we kill people, but through them there are also a lot of their relatives, which they created, left behind. When their first child is born, there was only a man and a woman. Soon that first baby is joined by brothers and sisters, then there will be aunts and uncles and a growing network of relationships. That is how you establish your ground. By the time one becomes an old man, there will be many grandchildren and great-grandchildren, maybe in one, two, or three generations, but four will be the end of that story. By then, a person should be ready to die. Before going, however, there will be good talk about your relations, and people will point at you and say, 'That is my grandfather over there. That is my god. I walk with that god today,' because a lot of good things have been accomplished."

The Twins thought about this and felt it was a good thing. Even though Old Age killed people, Monster Slayer allowed them to exist. This part of the story also explains why the San Juan River, where this event took place, is called Old Age River (Sá Bitooh).[13]

The reason for these names and how they are thought of bear examining. As the Navajos emerged through the four worlds, their language became increasingly sophisticated and enriched with holiness. Those levels have been maintained and are used according to the audience listening. For children a simplified language is employed, while on the other end of the scale, ceremonial language not only depends on high Navajo linguistic skill, but also uses sacred names provided by the holy people so that an individual, animal, or object will be recognized according to the title given around the time of creation.[14] By using this name, it calls forth power and the assistance of the gods. Many of the characteristics of a disease and what it takes to cure it are embedded in the terminology used to describe it. For instance, Barre Toelken, folklorist and student of Navajo culture, lived with the Yellowman family in Montezuma Canyon for a number of years, spoke the language, and used many traditional practices. At one point, he contracted a severe case of pneumonia, and so Yellowman had the illness diagnosed through divination and then paid for a medicine man to perform a Red Ant ceremony. Toelken shared the story:

> I was being treated for red ants in my system which I had no doubt picked up by urinating on an anthill. Sometime after the ritual, which was quite successful I must point out, I had occasion to discuss the treatment with the singer (medicine man): Had I really had ants in my system, did he think? His answer was a hesitant "no, not ants, but Ants." Finally he said, "We have to have a way of thinking strongly about disease." I now take this to be a ritual counterpart . . . as ways of thinking and ordering they seem consciously symbolic (but not the less "real" to the users) and much more akin to what I call artistic modes of thought than they are to anything we can classify by our normal concepts of genre.[15]

While this type of language provides a "strong way of thinking" about the intangible, it is also the connecting link to the holy people, another "intangible" but very real power in Navajo life. Words are a controlling power that bridges the physical and spiritual worlds to make things happen that are not understandable in physical terms.

Returning to Florence, she spoke of crossing the San Juan River and the need for protection. The north side of this river places the traveler in enemy territory. Before going to the far shore, a person offers a prayer asking that the spirit of the river wrap its protective shield around the traveler before entering the land of the Utes and the white man. She recalled how Navajos prayed against their enemy:

> The prayers were a tool to defeat evil or to hide behind for a safe journey. They would say, "I will be protected with your long body and then put corn pollen in the river." When you cross it, you call it by One with a Long Body (Bits'íís Nineezí). Its holiness is called upon to help the traveler obtain goods and enjoy safety. In the past, a prayer was always said before crossing the river. If there was no prayer, you could not swim or wade. When you crossed the river, sometimes undercurrents forced you to swim, so prayers were said, coming or going. The river was holy when crossing, but today people do not do this anymore, and that is why many things are not going the way they should.[16]

Charlie Blueyes agreed: "This water can hear you and knows when corn pollen is offered it when you are going for something like buying a horse. It is offered to water and asked for assistance. The river is also used for shielding purposes, like when a person says harsh words to you and wishes you to die. This is when you put corn pollen into the water and ask for protection, and the water will listen."[17]

To Tallis Holiday, leaving an offering on the shore of the river helped him achieve his goals after he crossed. "When a person comes to the river, he offers his corn pollen for a good journey and prosperity. 'I will receive many things with this small amount of money or trade items.' The people pleaded with the river's holy being. A long time ago, the river was the boundary to keep the enemy out."[18] Florence noted, "The ones who are very old are probably still doing this as a tool to ward off evil or to hide behind. In addition to protection, rain, grass, and other good things come to the person who beseeches."[19]

Charlie Blueyes believed that one half of the river belonged to the Utes, and the other half to the Navajos. "In the Enemyway ceremony, the prayer stick should not cross the river. This is what has been said. Before entering, you tell it that you are going to cross and are traveling for goods. You put corn pollen on the edge of the river because it is holy. If a man said bad things to you, you could give the corn pollen to the river and maybe it would kill him. The river hears you. Some gamblers do this when they go to Towaoc and they win."[20] Sally Manygoats believed that "now that this practice of prayer for protection and assistance is no longer performed, the land is dry, rain has decreased, accidents have increased, vegetation is short and withered, livestock is dwindling, drowning is prevalent, and harmony is scarce. When people paid respect to Navajo boundaries, life was safe and happy."[21]

Stories of Life: The Bears Ears

Boundaries separate sacred from profane space.[22] The land bounded on the south by the San Juan River, the north by Elk Ridge and the Bears Ears, the west by Navajo Blanket and Lime Ridge, and the east by Bluff holds tremendous meaning for the Navajo people. Snakes, lightning, arrowheads, wind, bears, Ancient Puebloan sites, witchcraft, and the river are not unconnected physical entities, but powerful religious and philosophical things that lead directly to sacred teachings. Power, prayers, and protection are their theme. Take for instance Comb Ridge. This rock formation extends for one hundred miles from Blue Mountain in the north to Kayenta, Arizona, in the south and has served as a physical barrier, a delineation of Navajo territory, and a spiritual boundary of power.[23] There are over a dozen different teachings about its origin and powers that include mythological bears, snakes, and holy objects. Ada Black from Bluff, among others, recalled, "Comb Ridge became a shield and boundary at the time the monsters were killed. The rocks were red and made into a ridge. It starts close from the Bears Ears. My maternal grandmother said a long time ago the boundary was made here."[24] When asked why there was a need for a boundary, she explained that after the monsters were killed, the People still feared they might be harmed. The holy beings created the boundaries to be shields through ceremonies. These protective powers "will probably be used in the future. These are very powerful and when a person makes a prayer offering there, it will serve as a shield."[25] No single power dominates. They are all connected, each stemming from a different ceremonial belief and practice.[26]

There are two stories that explain the Bears Ears' (Shashjaa') origin and its protective powers obtained through mythological Bears. One of these stories is that of Changing Bear Maiden and is the basis of the five-night Evilway (Hóchx̨ǫ́'íjí) ceremony that exorcises bad spiritual forces besetting a patient. Mary Blueyes, who lived within sight of the Bears Ears, shared the story.

A long time ago there was a young woman who was at home making white baskets. She had four brothers who were very good hunters who brought deer to her, which she prepared and tanned. As a highly skilled woman, she took good care of their home, making it a good place to be until one day when Coyote, the trickster, came by. He said he wanted to be her husband, and although she had no desire to marry him, said that whoever killed Big God (Yé'iitsoh) could become her lover. This was at the time when the monsters were eating humans.

Coyote said there would be a sweat bath that day, heated by rocks warmed in a fire. He invited Yé'iitsoh to join him. The giant asked Coyote how he could run so very fast, so Coyote explained that he had a ritual that he performed that would help the monster with his speed. The ritual is called jadeenideesih and had to be performed in a sweat lodge. Coyote and Yé'iitsoh entered into the dark hut, with Coyote carrying hidden deer antlers. He broke them, then told Big God that he had chopped off his thigh but that it had already healed. Coyote instructed him to do the same and so he cut off his thigh and chopped the bone, expecting that he would be as he was before. Yé'iitsoh commanded it to heal immediately, but Coyote, before rushing out the door, asked since when had a bone broken like that become as it had been previously. Then he fled.

Coyote went back to the young woman and told her that he had killed Yé'iitsoh and so became the young woman's husband. When the brothers came home from hunting, they asked why the smell of Coyote's urine was everywhere. At first they thought it was coming from the burning firewood, and so they threw it out. The brothers said that if they had broken the tree limbs up higher, the coyote would not have sprayed them. They started the fire again, but the smell was still there. Then they found Coyote hiding under some of their things.

He came out and admitted that his brothers-in-law were smelling him. Then the sister took one of her brothers, and after telling him to wash his hair, said that she would comb it. While she was doing this, however, she bit his neck and killed him. She had obtained from Coyote the ability to change into a bear, and so she killed two more brothers the same way.

The Holy Wind warned the youngest one that when Changing Bear Maiden transformed, her heart was hidden in a cluster of oak shrubs where a squirrel was making noises. The sister told her brother that he looked like a mess and that he should have his hair washed, after which she would brush his hair. As she combed, he watched her shadow, which showed she was now growing long teeth and was about to bite his neck. He jumped up, sprinted away, grabbed his bow and arrows, then ran to the place where her heart was hidden. He shot an arrow into it. As Changing Bear Maiden ran after him, she dropped dead.

The youngest brother carved up her body parts so that they could not reunite, and tossed her breast into a piñon tree, which became piñon nuts. Another part of her breast, the glands, were thrown into some yucca plants, which became its fruit. He threw her ears and jaw into the distance, and they became the Bears Ears formation. It is said there is a ferocious bear who lives there to this day. For this reason, no person is to go there. This is how a young woman became a bear and how her brother saved himself by killing his sister.[27]

The other ceremony, which is less well known and rarely practiced, is the Bearway. Medicine man Perry Robinson explains that long ago, the Navajo people were afflicted by an incurable disease. After much prayer, the holy people sent the rains as well as a large black bear that emerged from the earth to fight the evil-caused sickness.

People were singing protection songs as his head poked above the ground. He slowly turned around so that those he would be guarding would be behind him. His eyes and ears faced north so that he was able to see the approaching sickness and hear the prayers. Unfortunately, the songs summoning him were never finished. Now, only part of this animal is visible, but it still defends Navajo land from evil approaching from the north. He is a holy one, so that when a Bearway ceremony is performed, we sing "On the north side he lives to spot things." That is where the prayers are sent. If somebody asks me to perform a Bearway, my words go directly to the Bears Ears, where the prayers and songs start before moving on to other places. In the prayer he says that he has to face north so that he will have the people behind him for protection and that is why he slowly rotated in that direction—"that my children will stand behind me, and I will be on the opposite side, facing my enemy." Anything that we talk about in the prayers is set behind him, keeping the bad things beyond the Bears Ears in a place where they will not have the power to return. Herbs used in the Bearway are also collected in this area.[28]

In Navajo thought, most things come in pairs, so it is not surprising that the Bears Ears has a companion that assists in protecting. The Bears Ears is a male and looks to the north while its companion, whose location is unclear, protects to the south. Florence explained:

When the two are brought together they take care of the mountains. For this reason, they have the Shashchíín—miniature bears made out of special stones such as turquoise and jet, which are used when prayers are offered. The ones who have these are the ones who hold special prayers to ward off evil. This way their prayers are more powerful. One bear stands guard on one side, and the other bear guards the opposite side. For that reason, when a prayer is being sung, there is a part that says, "The Great Dark/Black Bear will stand guard; you will walk to protect/shield me."

This is why the bears are there. In this five-day ceremony, the chants name the bears and call on them for the person who is sick. When the prayers and chants are to be performed, one carved miniature bear is put on one side and the other one on the other side of the person, thus protecting both sides. The sandpainting is to represent Mother Earth and the heavens coming together, but the bears are there to shield and protect. That is why they are put on both sides of the door, north and south, during the prayers or a chant. The bears are mentioned in both and asked to walk with the patient and shield him or her. This is how it is said.

There are two stories about the formation of the Bears Ears. When looking at this prominence from the south, it appears very much like the severed head of Changing Bear Maiden with her ears resting above Elk Ridge. When seen from the east looking west (pictured here), a bear appears to be emerging from the ground, facing north to protect the Navajos from evil coming from that direction.

The Bears Ears also has plants that serve as an antidote ('iiníziin ch'il) against witchcraft. If a person is bothered by this evil, herbs and many different plants are gathered and crushed with a stone until thoroughly mixed, then are placed in water. This is then sprinkled around the home in a clockwise direction without completing a full circle around the home. When the medicine man finishes at the north side of the doorway, he goes counterclockwise back to where he started on the south side of the doorway. Inside the home is blessed in the same manner, but the outside is done first. When this is completed, one sprinkles himself and his family. With this we say, "Walk to shield/ protect me." When one is very sick or has something bothering them, you start off with the protection prayers to ward off evil things and then have a Blessingway. Start off with the plant medicine to work against the witchcraft, then the bear medicine, and finish with the Blessingway, which is separate from the first two.[29]

Holy People Next Door

Mountains, rivers, and formations like Comb Ridge and the Bears Ears are imposing on a large scale and can be seen in some instances for hundreds of miles. Yet there are also rock formations and other geographical features that play an important role in surrounding the more local landscape in which Navajos live and travel. Across the reservation there are seemingly limitless numbers of such places, each with their own stories and power, but often known only to those elders living in their immediate vicinity. Rather than cataloguing hundreds of sites spread throughout the region under discussion, Martha Nez shared her knowledge of the living landscape near her home at Tódahidíkáanii. As with the more substantial topographic features, power, prayers, and protection continue as an ongoing theme.

Martha was short, not more than five feet high, and at the time of the interview, in her late eighties. Her traditional hair bun, wrapped in a colorful head bandana, did not hide the white hair poking out around her face and framing her intense black eyes. Bent with age and slow to move, there was one thing not affected by poor eyesight and the maladies of old age—weaving. Each time Baxter Benally, my interpreter, and I came to her small house, she would be sitting on the floor with a rug beneath her at a loom, working on her next project. Getting up was a challenge. Her mind, however, was still sharp and recalled stories and events that she wanted to give to future generations. After sharing some of her personal information and a few stories, she began to talk about her surroundings, a place where she had lived for decades. Moving to the door, she pointed across the desert landscape.

Do you see the gray hill over there with a sand dune in front of it? There is a trail over it that goes into a box canyon. When you reach the other side, there is a rock sticking out of another rock. On the south side of this rock, there is a trail made by horses, some of which have left big footprints while others are very small. It seems like they went through there when there was mud, leaving their prints in stone. It is said that on the other side there is the sun on the rock. I did not see this, just heard about it. Some people say that it is Tééh łį́į' [mythological creature, a water horse]. It is these that left their tracks behind. I thought water horses were this small [seahorse] and the tracks were this big. Their tracks led quite a way, and some men have scraped the hoofprints to make their medicine. It is said it is put on horses. That is why they did this. Over there, where the rocks are standing near that site, sits a place called Tsé Dit'ódi (Soft Rock). This was a shade that had corn drying on top when the people moved. Someone went back to where two women were taking care of the drying corn and found that they had been turned to stone. He went up to the stones and asked if they were the two missing people. The rocks answered yes. It was from here the talking rock [echoes] originated. This is what was said. Some people say it was Coyote who started the echoes, while others argue that Coyote came later. This is why people there harvest great quantities of corn, melons, and squash. The two women became holy people. I do not know what clan or tribe those rocks are [Valley of the Gods]. This is why you do not sit at the top of a standing rock. This is what was said.

These are holy places, and a person should not abuse them. Some people say we don't have holy beings. If we do not have holy people, then why does the sun come up? Or why does it become night? We have holy beings no matter what we do. This is what I think. We also have the Holy Wind. A long time ago we had air talker; now the white people have the air talker. Even to this day, a poor individual will experience the presence of the holy beings and will get help through them. One time when I was very sick, in my illusion, I thought I saw one standing in front of me. I wondered who it was. It looked like a Yé'ii Bicheii. It extended its hands toward me twice. Then it turned around and left. I thought I should say something, but I did not. So, that is why I believe that there are holy beings. This is why my great-uncle told me that you should not speak something without thinking. The holy beings are all around. You are not supposed to say Ch'į́įdii (ghost). All of these have turned back into holy beings to include all of one's relatives that have passed on and are now sacred. Therefore, one should not use this word.[30]

Martha paused, trying to remember what she had heard of some other geographical sites.

> I asked about Blue Mountain and the Henry Mountains, wondering why they are usually skipped in the stories. The medicine men do not tell about them, but the hill right there [pointing to a formation close to home] does have a story. When Monster Slayer was busy killing the monsters, that hill served as his pillow. That is how it is mentioned in the story. It is called Tsétsoh Dahyisk'id (Hill/Pile of Big Rocks). It was from this place he planned his strategy to kill the tsé nináhádleehí. He killed it from there. That is another story that relates to that rock. It is like the Tó Ádindi Dahazká (Place of No Water) The other place is T'eeshch'ídeesgai (Ash Coming Out). The stories that relate to that place are not agreed upon. Some say it is a prayer stick and some say it is not. I do not know which is right. The black rock is tsidił—stick dice. It is said that old women, like me, were playing this game, because they did not have anything to do. They played all day and into the night and died of old age there, next to a small hill they lived in. We were told there were dice there, so we looked for them, but never did find any. That is another story that relates to that rock. The stories are not linked together smoothly.[31]

Just down Highway 191 from Martha's home lived Maimi Howard, who at this time was around eighty-two years old. Her world was just as animated as that of Martha's, but she had some of her own stories about the land and its teachings. It seems that when the Navajos started back from Fort Sumner, black-faced sheep were given to each warrior.

> My great-uncles lived near the Tsézhiin Íí'ahí (Black Rock), where they offered prayers to it as their medicine. Now there are only remains of their home. My mother died when she was still kind of young, but she had five brothers. When they were chased by enemies, they used this rock to cause them to starve to death. In the making of this powerful medicine, these people witched the black rock, and through its power, people starved. This is where we have lived, and there are remains of our hogans in the vicinity of that black rock. This is how powerful these people were.

My great-uncle, Naa'áda'í, used to just put a stick in the ground, and that was where the water started to flow. This is how they found drinking water. There is another spring behind the sloped hill, and it is called Nahat'áhí Bitó (Planning Spring). He did this to this spring, too. They were very powerful medicine men, and they are the ones who taught me. There is also a place where a man walked on the rocks when they were still soft. One can place corn pollen there and be blessed. Something had walked this way from where the juniper tree is standing. My father followed these tracks that had long footprints and a far stretch from foot to foot when walking. My father told me to take care of this land from Tsé Deinít'i' (Up the Rocks) to here. He told me I would have plenty of sheep if I kept this land.[32]

Harvey Oliver, who lived near Aneth, certainly agreed with this premise, that the land served to bless the Navajo people. Speaking of a rock mesa in the form of a horse saddle near Montezuma Creek, he mentioned a man named Many Goats who used to live there.

He used to make offerings to it, and thereby owned a lot of sheep, goats, cattle, and horses while also receiving a lot of rain. People have now made that place a forbidden, sacred area. Navajos used to put their sacred stone offerings on top of it just as they did at another mesa near Hatch that is considered sacred for the same reasons. From on top of these mesas, our people asked for wealth, horses, and livestock. It was a place from where you could talk to God. Today, no one goes up there to pray nor leaves special, sacred offerings like they used to. Since nobody does this, we have drought. Also, "life" [oil and water] is being pumped out of the earth. It helped the earth function in its natural way, but now it is being removed. All of these natural things cycled themselves, returning back to rain, and so this was what our people prayed to. This is what our forefathers told us long ago. People prayed for horses on these mesas.[33]

Certainly enough examples are provided here to show the power and protection gained from the land in the Aneth–Montezuma Creek–Bluff area along the San Juan River. As Florence pointed out at the beginning of our visit, "The songs/chantways start here." What, then, are we to make of this expansive landscape so filled with stories, teachings, helpful possibilities, and deadly consequences—spiritual and physical—that it seems every foot offers some impact to the Navajo experience? Most important is that a physical site on the land becomes a mnemonic device for the teachings it holds, bringing together the sacred and profane in a visual memory-jogger that reminds one why that place is important and how one should act toward or think about it. To the person who understands, that mountain, rock, or river ties him or her to the holy people in a concrete way.

A chantway is a complex series of songs, prayers, and stories whose teachings and required actions can extend over one to nine nights or one to nine days. Some require the memorization of extensive songs and prayers that must be said perfectly, or if there is a mistake, use another series of prayers to erase the error. A system of learning things correctly must be emplaced to help the learner to acquire knowledge and the initiated to recall it. Perhaps one of the best ways to explain part of the process is to think of a technique used today to memorize a series of either related or random things, whether they are objects, actions, or pieces of information. Let's say that a person is given a list of ten objects that must be remembered in order. They picture the first one as he or she is knocking on a make-believe door, the second object as the door is opened, the third as one enters a room, the fourth as they remove their shoes, and so on. When asked to repeat the different objects, the individual goes through their mind's eyes, recounting the fabricated events that involve each of the objects. Memory is tied to meaning and produces recall. In a sense, the memorization of Navajo chantways follows the same process with the protagonist moving across the landscape—from one specific topographic point to the next with a series of events occurring at each one. The same is true in blessing a sick person, which follows a defined pattern by starting with the feet, then ankles, knees, hips, shoulders, elbows, wrists, neck, and head. At each point on the patient, there are words, songs, and prayers that must be said. Singing the land has its own starting and stopping places that recount the narrative and that help the medicine person maintain sequence as events, formulas, and ceremony produce the healing.

Another important aspect found in Navajo religion is the separation of sacred from profane space. Whether climbing a mountain, crossing a river, praying at a volcanic neck, or leaving offerings at ancient hoofprints, the person seeking help has a clear understanding of a special spot where mythological events occurred. Here, different actions call forth, beyond daily life, the necessary assistance. Holy people respond, the request is answered, and faith in the teachings is reaffirmed. Within the chantway, specific sites hold the power, encapsulate the incident, and designate what must be done to enter the realm of the sacred to receive access to assistance. At the same time, boundaries are established that fend off evil, define enemy territory, strengthen the power for good, and provide peace of mind and well-being (hózhǫ́).

A final point in this discussion is to recognize the high concentration of important chantway sites found within a hundred-mile radius of the Aneth–Montezuma Creek–Bluff area. Starting with the place of emergence near Farmington, New Mexico; then moving to Hesperus Peak, Mancos River, Sleeping Ute Mountain, Chimney Rock, and Mesa Verde, Colorado; Huerfano Mesa and Shiprock, New Mexico; Red Mesa, Arizona; and Comb and Lime Ridges, Valley of the Gods, and Bears Ears, Utah, there are over a dozen major geographical places that are central to major narratives important to Navajo religion. Add to this the San Juan River, which runs through three states, and hundreds of less well-known sites that dot the region, and one can see how this land-based religion illuminates the importance of physical sites. The ceremonies—Lifeway Male and Female Shooting Branch, Blessingway, Flintway, Beautyway, Mountainway, Bearway, and Evilway—are rooted in this topography in both major and minor ways. In many instances, as Florence pointed out, "this is where the songs start."[34] Perhaps there is no area on and off the Navajo Reservation that has a higher concentration of deeply significant sites that involve major Navajo chantways.

CHAPTER THREE

Learning from the Waters of Life

River, Rain, and Teachings

He Who Teaches Himself (Natí'nésthani) stood on the shore of the San Juan River, discouraged with life and looking for a new beginning. He had failed in his passion of gambling, been rejected by family and friends, lived in poverty, and felt generally unsuccessful in meeting daily challenges. His diet of wood rats and rabbits, clothes of worn yucca sandals and cape, and brush hut that barely kept out the cold brought no happiness but only a desire for change. The river offered an escape to a new and better world, so Teaches Himself began hollowing out a large cottonwood log in which he could float south for a fresh start. What he would find symbolically and economically revolutionized the Navajo way of life from hunting and gathering to one of agriculture—corn, beans, and squash—soon to become staples. The river he now gazed upon became an important part of this venture. Washington Matthews (1843–1905), an army doctor and budding ethnologist, first published this sacred account in 1897, long after the Navajo people had become successful agriculturalists.[1] This lengthy tale of woe, followed by a launch into the unknown, presents a mythological explanation of how the holy people not only introduced the Navajos to a new way of life, but also ordained it as a central focus for economic and religious beliefs and practices. On his own, Teaches Himself would have failed. Four times he tried to fit in a cottonwood log hollowed out by fire, four times he struggled to make his plans work, and four times Talking God (Haashcheh'ééyálti'í) warned him that he would perish if he tried to float in this craft. Finally, the young man listened, followed the holy being's instructions, performed the necessary ritual, and provided the requested offerings so that the gods would willingly create a log hollowed by lightning. Now his safe travel was assured.

Before departure, the holy people prepared a traveling companion, a turkey, for the young man. They put about the bird's body "black cloud, he-rain, black mist, and she-rain. They put under his wings white corn, yellow corn, blue corn, corn of mixed colors, squash seeds, watermelon seeds, muskmelon seeds, gourd seeds, and beans of all colors."[2] Through their supernatural powers, the holy people transported man and fowl in the log to the river and set them afloat to start their adventure. It was not always smooth sailing, but the gods provided protection for both craft and occupants, even when they came in contact with hostile Puebloan people or were dragged into the river's depths to the home of the Water Monster (Tééhooltsódii—One Who Grabs in Deep Water). One of the holy people—Water Sprinkler (Tó Neinilii)—went into the deep water to search for the lost man imprisoned in Water Monster's domain. The gods

> spread a short rainbow for him [Water Sprinkler] to travel on as he went to the house of the divine ones under the water. The home consisted of four chambers, one under another, like the stories of a pueblo dwelling. The first chamber, on top, was black; the second was blue; the third yellow; the fourth white. Two water horses [tééh łį́į́'— Deep Water Pet] with blue horns, stood at the door facing one another and roared as Water Sprinkler passed by. He descended from one level to the next, but found no one until he came to the last chamber, where he saw the Water Monster; Frog (a big rough frog); Beaver, Otter, a great fish, and the captive Navajo.[3]

The Water Monster and its offspring inhabit rivers, lakes, and seas. The main Water Monster resides in the ocean to the east (Atlantic) and is chief of the water people there.[4] Others live in homes within the depths of a body of water; a spinning, funnel-shaped whirl is an entrance into their chambers, where they drag their victims. Outside their homes are water horses serving as guardians. Water monsters have fine fur like an otter and horns like a buffalo, while their young may be spotted with various colors. Some people say they look more like a buffalo or hippopotamus. Water animals such as beavers, otters, muskrats, fish, frogs, and turtles, as well as waterfowl, live within the domain of the Water Monster and are not eaten by many traditional Navajos, although otter and beaver skins may be used for clothing and rattles. A turtle shell with pebbles can serve as a rattle or without the stones as a ceremonial container for liquids. Even a sheep, an animal free from most restrictive taboos, cannot be eaten if it has drowned in the river. It belongs to the Water Monster.[5]

The Water Monster that Water Sprinkler now faced refused to release his captive, and so the would-be rescuer ascended to the surface, where he obtained further assistance from Black God (Haashch'ééshzhiní). The two descended into the depths and confronted Water Monster, who again refused to release Teaches Himself. Not until Black God produced a bow drill and started fires in Water Monster's home did the leader of the water world relent, begging for the three to leave immediately, which they did.

> Before they had quite reached the dry land, they heard a flopping sound behind them, and looking around saw Frog. "Wait," said he. "I have something to tell you. We can give disease to those who enter our dwelling, but there are cigarettes, sacred to us, by means of which our spell may be taken away. The cigarette of the Water Monster should be painted black; that of the Water Horse, blue; those of the Beaver and the Otter, yellow; that of the great fish, and that sacred to me, white." Therefore, in these days, when a Navajo is nearly drowned in the water, and has spewed all the water out, such cigarettes are made to take the water sickness from him.[6]

The Diné have a deep respect for the power of water, lightning, and other natural forces. Another story, similar to Matthews's recording, relates how Monster Slayer visited the home of Water Monster and demanded the return of all the people who had been drowned, struck by lightning, or lost in quicksand and marshes. The guardian of water had no desire to let them go, so Monster Slayer set the water on fire and forced their release. The people were ecstatic over their newfound freedom; Water Monster only grumbled that he would "take some of your people once in a while," thus explaining what happens to those struck by lightning or overwhelmed by drowning.[7] The Waterway (Tóee) ceremony removes the effects of this kind of damaging experience for an individual who has experienced near drowning or dreams of it. The mythological basis for the ceremony explains how a man visited Water Monster to beg release of a drowned grandson, with both ending up covered with green slime. Finally, they were released. Frog, Turtle, Otter, Beaver, and the Thunder People performed a bathing ceremony that cleansed the captives from the limiting effect of the slime. This ceremony is still performed today.[8]

Teaches Himself continued on his journey, the gods watching after him until he reached the end of the San Juan River, where they bid him farewell. Alone, he longed for companionship and the better life that he sought, but this seemed to be what he had asked for. Suddenly, from the east, he heard gobbling and soon spied his pet turkey that had followed him faithfully throughout his trials along the river. Soon the bird joined his friend, and when Teaches Himself bemoaned the fact that he needed food while recognizing that he now stood in a beautiful place to grow plants, the turkey took action, moving in the four cardinal directions, shaking his feathers, and dropping the seeds the holy people had placed within. Right behind him went his master, planting the seeds in a pattern that became characteristic of how Navajos in the future would organize their gardens. Following this activity, the man and bird separated, never to see each other again. The Navajo soon met other people, married one of their women, and taught her how to prepare his garden foods and plant different crops. They returned to her family, where she reported to her father and others

all she had seen and heard: of her distant view of the beautiful farm under the rain, under the black cloud, under the rainbow; of her near view of it—the great leaves, the white blossoms of the beans, the yellow blossoms of the squash, the tassel of corn, the silk of the corn, the pollen of the corn, and all the other beautiful things she saw there. When she finished, the old man said: "I thank you, my daughter, for bringing me such a son-in-law. I have traveled far, but I have never seen such things as those you tell of. I thought I was rich, but my son-in-law is richer. In the future, cook these things with care, in the way my son-in-law shows you."[9]

Teaches Himself had further adventures and learned a great deal about hunting deer and the witchcraft of his father-in-law before he returned to his people and shared with them the good things he had found. His experiences and knowledge are expressed through many traditional practices.

This narrative is important for a number of reasons. First, it describes the introduction and underscores the importance of agriculture for the Navajos. This point is highlighted by the contrast and comments made about the purely hunting-and-gathering lifestyle of the people he encountered and then joined through wedlock. Second, it establishes not only the procedure for planting and raising crops, but also the preparation, cooking, and consumption of agricultural foods. It also assigns those tasks to women, while Teaches Himself learns hunting skills from his father-in-law. Third, the role of the gods in protecting, guiding, and rescuing this Navajo remains center stage throughout the narrative. Whether it is the preparation of the craft and the turkey for a journey into the unknown, the pueblo people trying to capture his log, the Water Monster holding him prisoner, the witchcraft practiced by the father-in-law, or the return to his people, the hero benefits from the companionship of the holy beings because he follows ritual procedures. The Holy Wind (Nílch'ih) is constantly present, whispering instructions for how to avoid danger. Fourth, the importance of the San Juan River, not only as a vehicle for change with its powerful creatures that reside within, but most importantly as a facilitator of agriculture, served as a constant supply of water in a desert environment. While Navajo people were experts in raising crops in a land where this commodity was often scarce, the river provided a continuous source that was generally accessible. Of all of the seeps, springs, rivers, and lakes that the Navajos had access to before drilled wells opened a new era in agriculture, the San Juan River drew the largest populations to its banks to grow food. He Who Teaches Himself could testify to those pioneering efforts.

Attracting the Powers of Water

In this story, the river is treated as a solitary element under the control of the Water Monster and its minions. The Navajos, ever observant, realized that there were many other powers at work that made the San Juan River possible. Starting from its origin in the San Juan Mountains in Colorado and accepting flows from numerous tributaries, the river receives its chief contributions from the mountains. There is the observable side in which melting snow, summer rain, and cloud formations produce and then send the water cascading down their slopes and tributaries to feed the river. In the northern area, Mount Hesperus is often mentioned in Navajo songs that appeal for water. Like all of the mountains surrounding Navajo lands, it has the ability to bless the people, but it is more. Mary Blueyes explained that each has a tó'ása' or large water bowl within. "All of the mountains are called this and have them, because they are filled with water that flows from it, causing vegetation to grow. From the mountain comes springs, a part of its entire makeup; people also refer to the mountain as a forked hogan."[10]

Rain is an important element associated with mountains and river flow, something that Navajos prayed for and summoned through ceremony. Harvey Oliver, who lived outside of Aneth, understood this sentient universe. "We started traveling by land. We prayed to the holy people and asked them for rain. The earth can hear us. The water can hear us. The heavens, sun, moon, and stars all hear us and everything we say. Our people offer them corn pollen or the small sacred stones in payment for rain or other things we want. It answers 'yes' by giving us the rain we requested. The same is true with the wind or air, 'wind so and so,' calling it by name, 'do this or that.' That's how we do it."[11]

Mary Blueyes, as a medicine woman, dealt extensively with plants for healing and understood the Navajos' dependence on rain and cooperation. She told a story about Hummingbird (Dah Yiitįhí), a drought, and how the animals obtained relief from the elements.

A long time ago, the earth was parched, so the creatures held a council and performed hand trembling to determine where water could be found. Hummingbird joined in even though it knew the secret of where to find moisture. The bird sat in the meeting and remained silent, yet later would fly to a small seep where rocky mountain beeweed (waa') grew in abundance. It also rained frequently in this area. The bird sucked the juice from the plant, so that when it farted, the smell of it drifted among the other animals. Mouse (Na'ats'ǫǫsí), a creature that feeds on wet roots, recognized the smell and knew where the bird flew to find water and rain. The other creatures were unable to discover it because the hummingbird flew too fast. These birds are often seen flying near springs and sucking the moisture out of flowers. The animals needed to find this place and so they performed a stargazing ceremony that indicated that the rains fell on the Bears Ears. They went to that place, made an offering of sacred stones, said prayers, and brought water to the land. Also, when a person catches a hummingbird, corn pollen is placed on it, and then this "shake off" is put on a horse, making it very fast. This is called dahyiitįįh baa nanoogaad (hummingbird shake-off).

There are other ways that medicine people encourage the rains to come. A man named Furry Hat (Ch'aa Ditł'ooií) used to hold ceremonies to encourage storms. He first made a forked hogan, then covered it with green branches from cottonwood trees and willows, which he placed upside down against the logs. All of the branches were upside down so that the top of the tree was pointing down. Inside the structure, he performed the ceremony to bring rain. The people also put ntł'iz in certain places on the mountain. Yesterday, there was a man called Honágháanii [clan name—The He-Walks-Around-One People] who put corn pollen in the water. I asked him where he put the pollen, and he said in the spring. A moment later, it rained on us. Tádidíín is corn pollen that is used in prayers for blessing, but there are many other types of pollen, one of which is called water pollen (tó bitádidíín), used for inducing rain. This pollen comes from rain puddles and tree pollen that collects on the edge of the puddle. It is gathered and used as an offering and blessing. There is probably rain here among us, because from the ocean comes the fog, which moves inland before it rains in the mountains. Navajos also use the ceremonial basket made by the Utes. Many families get together for the purpose of obtaining rain. The women put down white shell on a piece of cloth that is spread out, while the men put down turquoise, adding to it tádidíín dootł'izh (blue corn pollen), tééh bitádídíín (deep water pollen), t'eeshchííh (red ash), and abalone. This is performed through the Blessingway ceremony as many people gather for this event. When there is a ceremony with the

Tó 'aheedlíinii Clan, this ritual is done for them. The elements on the cloth are divided four ways. One part is placed to the east, another part to the south, and the same to the west and north, all on an open plain area that is within walking distance or on the highest point in the vicinity. My father was a medicine man, so I have seen him do this. I went with him to many of the ceremonies that he performed.

He conducted a rain-making ceremony using the mud bowl (hashtł'ish 'ásaa'), which is also used in the Enemyway ceremony. This small mud bucket/bowl carries water that is then sprinkled about to help attract rain. Sometimes an Anasazi bowl is used. Turtle shells and abalone shells and other things from the water were also part of the rain ceremony. The shell was used to hold the kétłoh, an infusion made with water and herbs.[12]

Jim Dandy explained further this ceremony for water and its connection to mud dogs or mudpuppies (tsilghaááh).

When the people want rain, they use this ceremony combined with the squaw dance, a part of the Enemyway ceremony. The same thing here, when you call for rain, it is going to rain. There is some rough play that goes along with it, and so the people involved often end up aching and sore. The men strip down to a loin cloth and then have cedar applied with some herbs put on their bodies along with red hematite (chííh) and a little white clay, which represents female rain. I participated in this ceremony many times when I was young. It was fun, but what happens is a form of prayer, following which it rains heavily.

One time we hadn't had rain during a long dry season. There was a squaw dance that I participated in where we performed a little prayer before going out of the hogan. We dug a big hole that we put water in to build up the mud so that there was lots of it. Then we ran after the people, caught them, and threw them in. One time my sister was making fun of me as I was on horseback. For some reason as I rode that horse, I felt so light. The ceremony makes you feel quick and fast and you think faster and feel stronger. When you grab somebody, you can really hold on to them and drag them to the mudhole. We took her, even though she was dressed really nicely, wearing beautiful jewelry and fine clothing, and threw her in the water and mud. What that does

There are a number of different ceremonies and practices that can attract rain in a dry, desert land. Here, as an additional part of the Enemyway events, a large hole was filled with water and mud, a spot where onlookers are tossed in to become mudpuppies, who are associated with and can summon rain and moisture.

is make her a mudpuppy. Once you go into the water, you become one and have the power to control moisture. When you get out, then your job is to get others into the water and to make them mudpuppies.

Following this they have a prayer. People line up, lie down on a blanket, and roll back and forth as others sing. This is a blessing and helps someone who is having a hard time to be healed. We become the medicine, the holy people more or less, helping that person to get better. We do it by getting as many helpers as possible so that others can line up and receive the blessing. Let them go and bless them; put a little mud on them and they are blessed. They usually have this ceremony the last day of the squaw dance. It is a lot of fun to watch and very exciting. When there are a lot of people who want to be blessed, they may stand in line for a long time. The last time that I participated, about ten years ago at Cow Spring, I took my children so that they could become mudpuppies. It was a lot of fun.[13]

Jim paused in his account, shifting from what took place to explain how this ceremony began and the meaning behind it. After all, to an outsider, it would seem to be a nuisance to the bystanders who get thrown into the mud pit. As with many other things in the Navajo world, the entire process originated with the holy people at the time of creation and their desire to assist the Diné. Speaking of the first two mudpuppies, Jim continued:

> One time, they were people and belonged to the leading Water Monster. They played the game in heaven where they became holy people and received the responsibility to send rain to the earth. As water babies and controllers of moisture, one remained in the sky and became a cloud, while the other went to earth. They work together to create and send rain that blesses the land. When one prays for water in this ceremony, that person is acting like them, summoning the clouds and bathing in the mud. This is where you find the mud dog people.
>
> When it rains really hard, mudpuppies and salamanders, which are treated the same, may be found, for example, on top of Comb Ridge in little rocky areas where water suddenly settles and water creatures appear. They are seen swimming with fish, tadpoles, and little frogs, all of which bring rain. During the ceremony, you become like them. That's the significance of these water dogs as they come forth and bring the rain that blesses the people. These creatures are symbols that hold power, and so that is why they are not to be killed and should be just left alone. Whenever Navajo people see them, they are not played with and their babies are not killed.
>
> These creatures are always found in muddy areas. The other day I found a big one in my yard. It had been in the water for a long time. It was yellow and kind of striped like a zebra. When you find one you say a prayer and put them away in a safe place. You don't want it to be around; I usually tell my kids not to kill them or frogs. They are the water people, so we have to respect them.[14]

Meals, Medicines, and Materials

Not all water animals had the same restrictions, yet each had their own story and power. Florence Begay remembered as a young girl:

> There were a lot of beavers living on the banks of the river. These beavers chewed down trees young and old, then threw them in the water. They must be very strong and have sharp teeth. The people killed

these animals so that the medicine men could use the skin for medicine bags. The groin skin and flesh were dried in the sun and used as incense for healing during a sing, while at other times, people used to roast and eat beaver meat. It is known that the Ute tribe favors beaver meat, but Navajos only ate it occasionally.[15]

Isabelle Lee also remembered a lot of beavers in the San Juan River, their busy work of felling and dragging trees into the water, their loin parts being used in ceremonies as incense, and their skins being worn during a ritual. She quipped, "A man named Mr. Wide Water (Hastiin Tó Nteel) used to kill beavers. His wife probably still has a supply of beaver loins," indicating more than a casual desire for them as a food source.[16] Ada Benally believed her forefathers ate the meat when other foods were scarce and used the trees they chewed down for firewood. For teething babies, the Navajos believed that the infant's first set of teeth were lost as the second set came in. The teeth of a beaver were rubbed over them to make them sturdier and last longer, while its nails and genitals were used in ceremonies.[17] Old Mexican, another longtime resident of Aneth, believed that when a person contracted smallpox, they should swallow a piece of beaver fat, then rub some of it over their body from head to foot.

> When the female [beaver] gets fat in the winter, you kill them and keep the chunks of fat in a steer horn. It will keep a long time. It is soft and does not need any warming. Anyone can keep it. The gall on the liver is dried and used to cure mouth sores. You cut off a piece and pound it up and put it in a half teaspoonful of water. After it has soaked you swallow half and wash your mouth with the other half. Keep it a long time in your mouth, until it has soaked in.[18]

The San Juan River also had an abundance of fish, but many elders indicate that they did not make much use of them. Some were forbidden to eat food from the river, perhaps because of a legend about the Anasazi, who enslaved the Navajos and were punished by being turned into fish.[19] Isabelle Lee was one person who refused to eat them. "There were plenty of fish, and boys would go fishing and eat them, but I never did. The fish they got were huge, deep fried, and delicious they would say, arguing that 'fish is clean meat because they are not scavengers,' but I still wouldn't eat it."[20] Neither would Florence Begay, who was told not to eat fish. "You can't eat fish after you have had a Waterway (Tóee) ceremony."[21] Even the smell was bothersome to some people.

Life along the river was usually good with its natural vegetation, continuous source of water, and wild and domestic animals drawn to it. Until the Bureau of Reclamation completed the Navajo Dam near Farmington, New Mexico, in 1962, the San Juan River flowed uncontrolled, subject to the precipitation that fell in the mountains, filled its tributaries, and gushed or trickled between its banks. A generally peaceful river, many Navajos have fond memories of using its resources and living by its flow. Ben Whitehorse, whose family had lived in the Montezuma Creek area for as long as the historical record exists, shared his reminiscences as a boy.

> I remember the San Juan River as a narrow stream on the far side of the wash. From the present location of the bridge on up were allotments of land named "Náhoodleeł" (Restored Vegetation), along which lived a variety of plants and animals. There were turtles with shells on their backs, raccoons living among the clumps of cottonwood trees, and groups of wolves living nearby. Many different kinds of plants used as herbal medicine grew along the banks, made possible by abundant rain every year. It hardly snowed down by the river, but in the higher elevation, it snowed a lot. In the early spring, the melting snow seeped into the ground, and with the rain we received, there was enough water to provide abundant plant life. In the spring one could see the vegetation rippling in waves across the meadows every time the breeze blew as the livestock grazed about. A variety of medicine plants could be found here, while some, such as pine leaves and branches, had to be procured from the mountains.[22]

Cyrus Begay added to Ben's memory of a fruitful land and explained how "Restored Vegetation" received its name.

> Our environment was good because it rained a lot. The river rose, causing some erosion of the banks and washing away the roots of trees and other vegetation. This debris accumulated in certain parts, creating dams higher than this hogan and causing the river to take an alternate path. Before too long, the riverbed had widened. Just this side of Montezuma Creek is a placed called Restored Vegetation. This

spot was formed in two years, after the river had switched to the other side, giving it a chance to grow a thick assortment of green vegetation. It was beautiful. But after a few years of occasional flooding and storms, subsequent erosion took its toll on this environment, removing its prosperous nature. I returned to Aneth after a lengthy absence only to find there was nothing left in this riverbed. The floodwaters had washed the trees and vegetation—everything—away. It still looks the same with its banks widened due to water erosion. The people in Aneth moved up onto the surrounding mesas, McCracken Mesa, and over to Recapture Canyon, but the people from Blanding kept them from going any farther. That is its history.[23]

Sally Lee recalled, "During that time there were lots of firewood and cottonwood trees with plenty of vegetation along the river. We used it all for firewood. Now it is gone, so we have only wet juniper trees. We also got firewood from the Blanding area. People carried their firewood on their backs, so if a person got two bundles on their back, they would have a big pile of firewood. If it was cold they would stick their hands out to the fire; it seemed like they could not get enough heat."[24] She remembered having two homes, one built by her mother and father and another by her older sister, but no one else lived close by. She grew up there, held her puberty (kinaaldá) ceremony, and married her husband all at this one location. Her entire life seemed to revolve around this area where "there was lots of vegetation all the way down the river. The sunflowers, the ones with yellow flowers, were high, and the sheep grazed among them. We had a lot of sheep at this time, and so we herded them through this place we called Sunflower (Ndíyílii). All of this was along the river, where planted fields placed in selected spots always provided excellent harvests. Eventually, the water eroded the soil along the riverbanks, and the places where we had our fields were no more."[25]

What Is in a Name?

Life on and near the river gave rise to the penchant of providing names to specific and more general areas. In Anglo society, locations are identified by street addresses, businesses, homes, or places where events have occurred. The Navajos have just as great a need to be specific but, as discussed previously, they use rock formations and water sources, as well as where individuals lived or events took place. The San Juan River was a magnet for people, so it is not surprising to find a wide range of site names in a relatively small area. Jane Byalily Silas, beginning with the river, shared just how extensive this naming could be:

> The river has been flowing since I remember. It was very narrow, with fields of agricultural plants all along its banks. Plants such as sage, juniper, "ch'iltsoh" (big plant), and round willow plants that grow in the wash beds were used as medicine. There was also a plant that grew by the river that a new mother drank right after giving birth. It helped heal and restore her back to health. People with internal ailments drank it for healing too. My family used to have our own garden spot until water erosion destroyed the fields, homes, trees, and plantations. We then moved away. Just below us they called Broken House (Kints'iil), and up the river is Black Water (Tó Łizhin), across from which is the mesa called Sweet Water (Tó Łikan), and up farther is Sumac (Chiiłchin) and Ridge in the Water (Taa Yii Sitáani) and Rabbit Runs (Gah Háásalii). They used to chase the rabbits into that canyon and catch or kill them. My husband joined in these rabbit hunts. Then around this rock point is Water in the Midst of a Rock (Tsé Ni'tó) and Rock Points Upward (Tsé Yadiiti). Further down they called the place "Ahizhnél'į" (To Look at One Another), so named because the trail goes up a hill. If two people met each other on horseback, they looked at one another while passing. Below this place is called "Łį́į́' Ałghaná'nilii" (Reclaiming the Horses), so named after an incident that took place. Long ago a woman named "Asdzáán Naakiiyí" (Twin Woman) reclaimed some horses that were taken away by enemy Utes and others. She whipped and scolded these rustlers. Our people live around these areas, unlike the white men who come and go, one after another.[26]

A plethora of names cover the landscape, far too many to deal with systematically by spatial arrangement. Besides those places identified due to strictly physical characteristics such as Rough Rock (Tsé Ch'izhí) on McCracken Mesa, White Rock Point (Tsé Łigai Deez'áhí) three miles southwest of Bluff, Gap in Rock (Tségiizhí) near Navajo Springs in Comb Wash, and Greasewood Wash (Díwózhii Bikooh) or Montezuma Canyon—there were other, more colorful names, attached to experiences. Just outside of Montezuma Creek lies To Look at One Another (Ahizhnél'į), a steep, narrow trail that forced those ascending and descending to look at each other as they closely passed by; below it is Reclaiming the Horses (Łį́į́' Ałghaná'nilii), where a Navajo woman took back stolen livestock; Scrambling to Own a House (Kin Bí Tájoozhjéhí) near Aneth; Ledge Pecked Out (Bitát'ah Ha'izlá) near the mouth of Butler Wash where it joins the San Juan River, and is an old section of road going to Bluff where Navajo Jim Joe lived; Looking for Horses (Łį́į́' Hanitáadi), a big point on Comb Ridge where one could see for a long distance to locate missing animals; Wagon with the Rear End Up across the river from Bluff because of the steepness of the trail; and Wind Up One's Ass (Hajilchii' Hááyolí), a narrow crevice through which one ascends to a mesa top near Tódahidíkáanii (Hanging Water). A family used to live on top in the winter, and so they hauled their belongings up the narrow defile, which was as wide as a person's body. It was so tight that the wind blew up behind one's back as they brought up their possessions.

Many of these names are tied to personal experience and may be known to only a few local people, so it is not surprising that one site or surrounding location may have had a whole series of names that changed as new people or events entered the scene. Take for instance where Montezuma Creek community stands today. Without going into detail, it has been called Among the Prairie Dogs (Dlǫǫ Taha) because some Navajo families transplanted a colony of these animals to serve as a food source; Restored Vegetation (Náhoodleeł) near the bridge, following the initial destruction of its natural habitat; Red Water (Tó Lichííh); Clay (Glashii—a type of sandstone used in ceremonies); Thin Ash (Tsiidtaaha—from burned sagebrush) because of the fine ashes left behind; Farm Went Back to Weeds (Naho Ditlo) at the mouth of Montezuma Creek, which was also known as Greasewood Wash Joining In (Díwózhii Bikooh Idiglinih), and because of the trading post and traders living there—Flew Back Out (Ch'ínát'a'—post name given by trader Joseph Hatch Jr.), Put Your Hand Out (Ch'izh Dílni), Black Hat (Ch'ah Łizhinii—trader William Young), and Mussi (Mósí Yázhí—Little Cat, because trader Wilford Wheeler's mother had a face like a cat). The Navajo ability to pick out qualities or characteristics that easily identified a place or individual was a strong cultural ability.

This same process of naming sites went on all over Navajo land. Ada Benally, whose hogan was south of the Saint Christopher's Mission near Bluff, illustrated again just how prevalent this practice was.

> We lived across from here at a place called "Kinbinaashii" (Against the House); just above this place was "Hóóchxǫ' Adahadeitiin" (Damaged Trail Coming Down), which was impassable by wagon and could be used only by donkeys and horses. Up on top it was called "Tsé Awozí Dahsitánígíí" (Marble Rock Ridge), then farther on was "Łibá Deez'ááą́" (Gray Point), my birthplace where I grew up. "Tsinyaató" (Water under the Tree), "Béyóódzin Bitó" (Paiute's Water), and "Séí Adáágai" (White Sand Dune Coming Down) are some places we've moved around in a wagon. Behind this hill was a place called "Tsinaabąąs Tł'aa'háá'áí" (Wagon with the Rear End Up), where the road came down, receiving its name for its steepness.[27]

The Vicissitudes of Farming

Daily life along the river, whether involving livestock, agriculture, weaving, or ceremonial practices demanded hard and efficient work to be successful. Farming was particularly water intensive and required astute observation and effective techniques to get it out of the river, onto the land, and then down the rows of planted vegetables at just the right flow. While many of the early white settlers living along the stretch of river from Aneth to Bluff built water wheels that dumped hundreds of gallons down a sluice, the Navajos did not have that benefit. Grading the ditches, installing headgates to control the flow, pushing the water to the end of the planted area, and managing the effects of the rise and fall of the river at the beginning of the ditches were all dependent on the skill and judgment of the Navajo farmer. Just as He Who Teaches Himself learned, the San Juan River was not always beneficent.

Navajos cleared and prepared their farms in April. Ditches from the river snaked across the floodplain, taking advantage of the natural slope in the land and direction of flow of the river. The Indians dammed arroyos and worked the water over the fields in a process repeated once or twice during the summer.[28] Alluvial fans extending from the mouths of intermittent or continuously flowing canyon streams such as Recapture, McCracken, Montezuma, Allen, and McElmo on the north side and Desert, Lone Mountain, and Tsitah Creeks on the south side of the river, encouraged settlements and farming at these locations. Irrigation systems were also easier to put in at these places because the banks were lower, the soil was rich, and the water was not as turbulent. Actual planting began in early May and continued through the first part of July, when the "first fruits of the slim yucca burst open." The Navajos planted corn, then melons, then squash, and finally beans, based upon which had the longest maturation period. The gardener placed anywhere from five to fifteen seeds together, if planting in hills; those seeds that did not germinate were said to have been "eaten" by those that did. Men used a digging stick to create a hole approximately four to six inches deep, as women followed behind and placed the seeds.[29] Of course later, shovels, hoes, plows, and other Anglo-manufactured goods increased efficiency and gave rise to larger agricultural ventures. Since livestock was an equally important part of their economy, the Navajos spent a lot of time ranging away from the plots planted on the river, returning occasionally to weed and water as necessary or leaving less mobile people like elders or children behind.

Once the harvest was in, it was often stored in large, underground bell-shaped holes dug beneath the ground. Isabelle Lee remembered, "Corn was our main source of food. Ground corn, sliced melons and pumpkins were dried, then either placed in a bag or ground to be used in the winter. Pumpkins were peeled and cut into strips before drying them in the sun, after which they were tied together, then boiled in the winter. It was prepared as a side dish along with cornmeal mush."[30] Old Mexican explained further:

> The ears of corn were as long as my arm. It had rained again, and that had helped a lot. We stayed till the corn was ripe, and then shocked it, and after that we husked it and laid it on the brush for a couple of weeks to dry in the sun. When it was dry, we made a square with four poles, put blankets around it, and spread a sheepskin inside. On top of that we piled the dried ears and then hit them with a pole. That was the way we shelled it. When we got through shelling, we had eighteen sacks full, each over a hundred pounds, and besides that we had some left unshelled that we gave to the others. Some we stored on our farm

Corn was the most significant plant for the Navajo people. It was not just food, but its pollen served as an offering to the holy people at sunrise and sunset and in sacred events. It also acted as a symbol of the clan system, a gift from the holy people during the emergence, and a token of peace and friendship. But it does not always come easily, as Old Mexican explained regarding his trials during irrigation, drought, and flood.

at Sweetwater, some we brought here to Wooded Hill Point and stored it in the valley, and some we took along when we moved back to the river.[31]

In 1947 anthropologist Walter Dyk published Old Mexican's autobiography, providing a history of a man who lived in the Aneth–Montezuma Creek area most of his life. Living from 1865 to 1933, he proved to be a tireless worker who left a detailed account of his daily activities, particularly between the last decade of the nineteenth century and the first decade of the twentieth. Emerging from his life story were three major themes— acculturation into the Anglo world, problems in marriage, and the difficulties of farming on the San Juan. We turn to this last topic for a personal perspective of what was required to wrest a living from this water.

For a brief time, he resided at Sweetwater at the base of the Carrizo Mountains and Wooded Hill Point, approximately ten miles south of Aneth, before moving to the Aneth–Montezuma Creek area, where he stayed for the remainder of his life. In Old Mexican's opinion:

> Irrigating was the hardest work of all. I didn't have time to rest, but had to walk around all day and watch the water closely, so it would go where it was needed and not settle in one place. This woman of mine was a pretty good worker. She would come in the field and help me, and when it was time to cook she would go back to camp and prepare the meals. We hadn't got mad at each other again. I irrigated two days and was about half through. That night I didn't have much water in the ditch, so in the morning I let some more in. Then I went to camp and ate some breakfast. When I got back to the field, the water had all gone into one place, and had worn a deep arroyo over the land. I had to put a dam across to level it off. I dug a hole with a shovel, where it was dry on top, to see if the people were right, but it was wet underneath and they were wrong. We got the field well cleaned of brush and limbs. My woman got a pitchfork and raked up the field and set fire to the stuff she piled up. I let the water run another day and night and a half a day more, and then turned it back into the wash. It took me thirteen days to dig the ditch and clear the land and irrigate. . . . When the corn got high, I had to hoe again. But there weren't many weeds this time. After I finished, I irrigated again. Then the corn started to grow. I surprised the other people by the way I worked my farm. In the spring, they had said, "That's no way to work a farm." [His neighbors thought his ditches were too big and that water was not soaking in.] But in the fall, I surprised them, when my corn was higher than theirs. Some had put in their corn earlier than I had, but their corn didn't get very high.[32]

Old Mexican's struggle to raise sufficient crops from the land continued. Always looking for new opportunities, better land, and access to available water, he moved to the Montezuma Creek area, where he established ownership and went to work. The efforts that this new undertaking called forth were characteristic of what other hardworking Navajos along the river went through.

In the fall I thought about getting another farm, one by the river, where there was plenty of water. I picked out a place about two miles above Montezuma Wash then stepped it off to see how big that farm was going to be, and how far up the river the ditch would have to go. This field was about two and a half acres. The ditch was four hundred steps long from the river to the farm. There was also another place I was thinking about, up near the mouth of McElmo [Creek], where there was good soil. There was a wide strip there, larger than the other. I measured off a place that was two hundred steps long and one hundred and fifty wide, counting every step of the left foot only. I learned that from the whites. This field was 6 acres long and four wide. I wasn't thinking about my wives. I was thinking about my mother, sisters, brothers and brother-in-law, and I was picking out land for them. Lots of people were living around both places, but I was the only one who ever thought of putting in a farm there.[33]

Help was on the way. Various Indian agents, government specialists, and visitors to the Shiprock-Aneth region encouraged the federal government to send qualified farmers to assist with better equipment, improved seeds, and new agricultural techniques to Navajos living along the San Juan and at other sources of water. This story is told elsewhere.[34] Suffice it to say that starting in 1905, James M. Holley served as the government farmer stationed in Aneth, undertaking such projects as building a riprap protective barrier to prevent the river from eating away at the tops of Navajo irrigation ditches, improving road conditions as well as new construction, and building a government farmer's station on the terrace below the Aneth Trading Post. The Navajo men who performed much of this work were compensated in agricultural implements. Forty-five days' labor netted a worker a wagon, five days a scraper, and one day a shovel, ax, saw, or some other tool. Four positive results came from this type of labor. The road improved transportation between Aneth and Shiprock; the Navajos worked as a team, creating community cohesion; the dispensing of tools ensured greater agricultural success; and the people looked more and more to the government farmer and the Shiprock Agency for advice, leadership, and equipment.

Floods—Too Much of a Good Thing

In 1908 Holley returned to the life of a trader, with J. H. Locke taking his place, but he lasted only a little over a year. W. O. Hodgson replaced him, remaining as government farmer until 1914. Midway through his tenure, Hodgson witnessed one of the two major floods on the San Juan, the other being in 1884, both of which were all-encompassing along the riverbed. There were often annual floods, but nothing approached the scope and violence of these two. Little of the Navajo perspective was recorded for the first, but the flood of 1911, which required over a year to recover from, was well-remembered. Starting in mid-July, abnormally strong rains began to cover the mountains of Colorado and lands of the Four Corners area. Canyons and rivers that fed into the San Juan River placed heavy streambed loads and large amounts of water into the flow going past Shiprock. Agent William T. Shelton noted that he had crews, two weeks at a time, shoring up the banks of the river with cottonwood logs, since all of the brush used for riprapping had already been consumed. Still, he was optimistic. In October the precipitation intensified as one two-hour storm dumped 4.8 inches of rain. The weather bureau later reported that between September 1911 and March 1912, twenty-seven inches fell, twice the normal amount for even the wettest areas.[35]

Old Mexican, that faithful recorder of events, said that he was on his way to the annual Shiprock Fair and had stopped at the trading post in Aneth to camp for the night, when

> we heard a great noise. It sounded as though there was lots of water in the San Juan, but it was in McElmo Creek. When I got up in the morning, I saw the water all over my farm with mud a foot deep covering the alfalfa. It had flooded the whole flat and drifted over my entire crop, blanketing the whole thing. Even the orchard was covered with mud half way up the trees. It enveloped everything and left nothing. I had had a log cabin there, and the water was half way up the door. My mother had been watching the corn, and she was on top of the hogan with the water all around her. She had been alone when the flood came. It killed the orchard and the alfalfa. The corn was the only thing that was saved. It was kind of up on a hill.

I took my mother's hand and led her over to the other side of the flat, away from the water, while my younger brother came and got the sheep pelts and stuff that was left. I got some wood for my mother and he went back and got more things. We were getting tired. In the meantime, my mother fixed us something to eat. In the evening I went back to where the wagon was. I was kind of sore all over from packing our belongings back and forth in the mud. My younger brother said, "I'll go on tomorrow. Before I go, I'll have to get some wood for my mother." I stayed with my two sons at Aneth that night. The agricultural things that I had saved that summer to take to the fair I just broke up and fed to the horses. I thought there was no use taking it, my field was all covered up and washed away. The lower field had been flooded too, a long time before. Lots of sand had drifted on it and young trees had started there again.[36]

Two days later, problems persisted. Old Mexican had finally arrived at the fair, but circumstances were not any better there.

The next day it started raining again. The fair ground was full of stuff. They told us, "Take all of the stuff out of the grounds today. It will get wet." They asked me where my things were. I didn't say anything about it. After the people got all of their possessions, one of them missed his beads. Lots of things were missing that day, rugs, rings, and bracelets. The river was getting high, rising every minute. Everyone was hollering to help get all of the children on top of the hill and to load up the wagons. They got the wagons and loaded them up with bedding and food for the children and hauled them to the top of the hill, where the boy's school now stands. Then they started putting up tents on the flat.

The next morning, they sent a message from Blanco to Shiprock, saying the reservoir up there had broken. The storekeeper rode around, telling the people, "The water is coming. Hurry and move up higher. Get on top of the hills." Shelton was with the school children. The water had already covered the campus of the old school up to the horses' bellies. And here came the rider again. "There is another message. Hurry and get on top of the hills. There is just lots of water. They are afraid it will wash all the towns away along the river, Blanco, Fruitland, Bluff City, and Shiprock."

All of a sudden, the people hollered, "The water is here!" One after another the adobe houses fell in. Then there was a big crack, and the bridge fell over. The water made a great roar. Two fellows were watching the water right close by the bridge when it fell over. That kind of scared them. As soon as the bridge fell, my younger brother and some other men started riding down the river to notify all the people that high water was coming. They didn't have time to stop at any camp. They just hollered as they went by and shouted across the river. They passed Aneth, and my younger brother kept on to Bluff City to tell the Mormons. He and the others left toward noon, and my brother was the only one that made it into Bluff City toward evening before sundown. The water got there just as the sun was setting. The river rose and kept on rising that night. The Mormons just built fires along the bluffs to watch the river. Only one of their houses had water around it; the others were higher up. Some of them stayed in their houses. They talked as though they weren't scared. That was all right.

Early in the morning the water started going down. They postponed the Night Chant. They said they would have it two days later. They had already started it. They had only one more night to go when the flood came. I do not know how the people got their prizes. I didn't get anything. I didn't even get a match stick. After they quit dancing, we all started home. The road along the river was pretty muddy. We could barely make it.

When we got back, we found the river had split the farm in two. We turned our horses loose to the stack of hay. My mother was there, and some corn was lying in the sun to dry. The next day we went out to where the farm used to be. We took a shovel and investigated to see if it was any good, but there was nothing but gravel that had drifted in. It was not worth working again. Just a little patch of corn was left. My mother told me to help her get it before we left. We got a wagon load and a half. That was all that was left. We stayed there that night, and the next morning we went back home to Montezuma Wash. That was the last good farm I had. When we got home, we started harvesting the corn up at my stepson's place.[37]

Martha Nez recalled specific details that impressed her as a ten-year-old child. She remembered that the new steel bridge that had just been built in Shiprock and another at Mexican Hat were destroyed by the rampaging waters, how people had flocked to the fair to participate

This dramatic photo, taken by William T. Shelton after the 1911 floodwaters started to subside, shows the destructive power of the San Juan River at the Shiprock Agency. Large areas of farmland, barns, outlying work facilities, living quarters, classrooms, and a newly installed metal bridge were inundated in a matter of hours and then swept away. All of this occurred during the fall Shiprock Fair, where Anglos and Navajos had gathered for days of activities. Fortunately, the students were safeguarded, and loss of life was minimal.

in a Yé'ii Bicheii dance, and how the river took the cornfield along the bank just before the fall harvest.

> In Shiprock, two horses were near the river when the flood came with the water rising up to the back of the animals. One of them was hobbled and tried to stay afloat by throwing its head up. The owner of the horse then got three medicine men to perform the lowering-of-the-river-prayers, and to this day some people blame this incident for the lack of rain. These medicine men conducted a ceremony called Níłtsą'ayiyadahast'i'—the prayer to talk away the rain. These medicine men put sacred stones (ntł'iz) in the river. They said their prayers, so the river went down. The horse was saved by this. From this day forward, there has been little rain. It was after this that the river became dry, and it was about two months later that it returned.[38]

Mary Jay recalled,

I have seen the river flood twice [1911 and 1933]. We were living across it at a place called Glance at One Another on the night of one of these floods. We had to move higher up on the mesa and herd our sheep to a ledge for safety. That night the water swept away most of the things in its path. We salvaged some belongings by throwing them on top of our summer shelter just before leaving. The second flood occurred while we were living a little beyond my children's homes here [Aneth]. There is a deep bend in the river, below the present school, where we saw many drowned animals along its banks. Among these animals was a white horse still tied in its harness as well as dead pigs and bags of white flour that looked like dead sheep lying all around. The floodwaters had brought them from somewhere. I hear people argue about when and how it all took place, but I personally witnessed it myself.[39]

An Anglo perspective of these same events is found in a patronizing newspaper account that belittles Navajo efforts, but captures the medicine men's view of the river's action being that of a living entity. As the water peaked, a man from Taos named Robb heard a "great cry" coming from the bank of the river. He went down to investigate and saw "a big bunch of Indian braves had gathered together . . . and were hard at work weaving a spell to defeat the will of the river devil. Wildly waving their bodies in rhythmic motion while their legs took them through the mazes of their mystic dance to a weird chant, they proceeded to push the river back into its bed. At least they thought they did, for it was about this time that the agent found the flood subsiding."[40] Robb ended his observation by assuring the reader of the sincerity of the Indians and that it was not a show for spectators. Still, he exhibited little cultural understanding of what was taking place.

Government Farmers of Aneth

In 1914 a new government farmer named Herbert Redshaw assumed the responsibility of helping the Navajos in Aneth. This distinctive immigrant remained there for eighteen years until his retirement in 1931; probably no Anglo outsider had a bigger impact on the People in this area than Redshaw. Family members described him as a "typical old

English man." Dressed in bib overalls, broad-brimmed hat, and sporting a mustache, he stood over six feet tall. His steel-gray eyes, large feet and hands, and raw-boned build gave him a commanding presence, while a corncob pipe filled with George Washington tobacco jutted from his lower jaw. As smoke curled around and colored his hat brim, one man quipped that it took more matches than tobacco to keep the pipe operating.[41]

To the Navajos, he was "T'áábíích'įįdii." An exact translation of this name is difficult, but an approximation is "His Own Devil." The Indians did not apply this epithet with rancor. Redshaw moved slowly and swayed slightly as he methodically swung his arms and walked; his name gives a feeling that he moved like a dead man returned to life. Another possible derivation could come from his cussing while working on a project that was not being done right, telling the wrongdoer to "Go to the devil."[42] Whatever its origin, the name is now applied to the Aneth Chapter, the place that Redshaw struggled to develop.

Much of his life there was filled with the day-to-day humdrum of farming along the river. He lived in the government station surrounded by forty acres of alfalfa fields and gardens, many of which Indians planted and maintained. The produce he divided among needy Navajos at harvest time. His red barn and red fences became a landmark to travelers, while his irrigation system proved ingenious. Not only did Redshaw use the waters from the more easily controlled McElmo Creek, but when those started to decrease, he also drew upon the San Juan. His primary ditch lay four feet wide and two feet deep with a main headgate that returned much of the water directly to the river, along with a smaller stream to flood his fields. By using this system, he alleviated the problem of accumulating silt. Redshaw encouraged families to settle nearby as he made the government station a center of activity. He held community meetings under the cottonwood trees along the banks of the river and encouraged the Navajos to settle on the floodplains.[43] By the early 1920s the government farmer had succeeded in having twenty-five families living along an irrigation canal that supplied water from the mouth of McElmo Creek.[44]

Redshaw diligently taught Navajos what he considered the proper method of agriculture. He spoke enough of their language to get by, but for formal occasions, he used Eddie Neskaaii from Shiprock. Harvey Oliver, a Navajo who worked for Redshaw for five years, explained his teaching style. "He would look at it [the garden plot]. He did not just walk around but he told us how to put watermelon seeds in the ground by counting them. Count the corn or the onions, this is what he said. There were distances between each onion that you should be aware of. He told me to learn all of this."[45] Oliver did learn, and by the end of his work with Redshaw, his salary had increased from one to five dollars a day. This did not include his carrying the mail to the Ismay Trading Post for ten dollars a round trip.

Older Navajos at the time of these interviews still talked about how Redshaw had one of the first automobiles in the Aneth area. Among other things, it served as the only motorized "school bus" that each fall brought the children to the Shiprock Boarding School. Part of this process started with a census number on a metal tag that he hung around each child's neck. In a few instances, he provided English names, ensured the boy or girl received immunizations, and filled the agent's requests for students. Then the farmer squeezed as many as he could into his black government Ford, cranked up the engine, and chugged across the reservation, making the required number of trips necessary to get all of the pupils to Shiprock. He also visited the children periodically during the school year and brought them home in the spring. Whether coming or going, it was not a free ride. Many of his passengers remember having to stop along the way and shovel dirt into the potholes and gullies that dotted the road.[46] He seldom missed an opportunity to improve the country and teach a lesson about work.

Sometimes, however, Redshaw was the one to learn a lesson. He often took a couple of Navajo men with him when he drove the reservation roads. More often than not, he would get stuck in sandy washes or muddy ruts, so he had his companions get out to push the vehicle free. The Navajos chuckled about fooling Redshaw by getting behind the car as if they were really trying to release it when, in reality, they were doing nothing. Eventually the government farmer caught on to the prank and carried a fifty-foot rope with handles that had gloves nailed on it for pulling. He attached the rope to the front so that there was no mistake about who was not working.[47] In 1931 Redshaw retired from government service and moved to Ucolo, Utah, for fifteen years before passing away. Navajo people often visited his home, sought his advice, and enlisted his help when the government pursued livestock reduction in the 1930s. This Englishman proved to be a constant and faithful friend to the Navajo people. There would be other government workers and large farming projects along the San Juan River, but none of these undertakings won the heart of the Diné like Herbert Redshaw.

A final event for those living along the San Juan occurred in June 1920, when rumors of a flood that could inundate the people caused many to move away to higher ground far beyond the river. What prompted this exodus—whether started by a man struck with lightning who later prophesied of the event or by a gloom-and-doom minister preaching about the flood of Noah's time—the reaction of people living on the northern end of the reservation was immediate.[48] John Knot Begay remembered:

> The people in Shiprock and surrounding areas had been warned about a big flood. The San Juan River was to overflow badly. Consequently, many families moved to the tops of higher hills and mountains. At that time, we were living in Montezuma Creek. The rumor did not bother us; we stayed where we were and nothing happened. The people who moved to the mountains left their wagons at the base of hills and filled them with heavy rocks to weigh them down. All of this was silly, but the people cannot be blamed for wanting to save themselves and their belongings. A very wise elder who lived in our area told us nothing of the kind was going to take place and for us to remain where we were.[49]

Margaret Weston recalled similar events:

> I remember one time when they said a flood was coming. Some moved up to the mountains, but we stayed here. We took some belongings and crossed the river at the point of this hill here and camped on the other side for a couple of days. While we were there, a Christian man came to visit us. We asked him, "How close is the flood before it reaches us?" He said, "There is no flood, they are lying to you." He boiled some herbs he had with him and gave it to a lady who was sick. We then moved down to the cornfield by the river. Shortly afterward, we moved up on the red rock ledge close to the edge of the river. Everybody had moved away from there, so we were the only ones living in the area. We found a bank wide enough to live on by the river and used a boat to bring our things to the other side. Once the river lowered, we brought the sheep across by the boat, while the horses just swam over in a herd.

I think the boat was there for everyone's use. I rode in the boat when we moved across, which gave a funny, scary feeling. Someone had to guide its direction. About a year later, the people were finally returning here, but until that time, we were the only ones there. I don't know who might have lived farther down the river.[50]

Whether flood, drought, or something in between, the San Juan River affected the pulse of the people, dictating both hopes and fears as it flowed toward the sunrise. He Who Teaches Himself as well as his pet turkey would have appreciated what had developed since he floated the river in his hollow log. Agriculture had become more than a crutch for survival; it had served the Navajos as a major tenant of their economy. No place was this more evident than along that body of water. The holy people had set in motion one of the most important elements of traditional Navajo culture, and it had served the people well.

CHAPTER FOUR

The Power of Plants

Medicine People Speak

The river Navajos had a strong dependence on wild plants for a variety of uses. Their world was circumscribed by employing them for many reasons in different circumstances. This is a broad topic that crosses over into every aspect of life, whether looking at religion, sexuality, economics, food, medicine, or social events. This chapter explores general beliefs about plants and the teachings behind healing humans with them. In each instance, the perspectives of medicine people are presented with the caveat that their views are based on how they were taught through traditional means. Their insight has not been verified by the scientific process, nor should it be. Indeed, these two views are often worlds apart—one demanding evidence through physical contents, the other depending on what and how the holy people ordained a plant's use. The interview process through which this information was obtained included fieldwork conducted by nonbotanists, the identification of plants in photographs, and a study of the oral tradition—hardly anything that the scientific community would accept for validation. For these reasons, the emphasis here is a cultural explanation of what these highly experienced medicine people—primarily Mary Blueyes and Gladys Yellowman—shared. Their environment was a pharmacopeia. Indeed, while there has been a fair interest in studying and cataloguing Navajo use of plants, there are still huge gaps in understanding all that was used as well as a cultural explanation as to why.[1] The intent here is to open the door to a broader discussion of these two questions.

Martha Nez, a neighbor to Mary and Gladys, first shared her experience in using herbs to cure the sick. Like most herbalists, Martha recognized a spiritual aspect in healing, but like a white doctor, there was also the necessity of receiving payment. Her account provides a personal context for what it means to be a medicine person.

> The Navajos used herbs, and the patient got well. There was one person who was good with plants, and people were interested in his stories that went with the herbs. This man did not like it and told them that they offered little money for his teachings and told them to leave. Arthritis was all over one patient who was in horrible condition. The medicine man received a beautiful turquoise necklace and one hundred dollars, so he fixed a cure for him. Another person came from Gallup, New Mexico. He said he itched in his crotch and on his legs, and although he had gone to hospitals and clinics, there had been no change. The medicine man gave him some herbs, and sometime later he returned, cured of the itching. Someone else came with a problem in his urinary bladder. He reported how he had tried to get well in hospitals and by using Navajo herbs, even going to the Hopi for help, but there was no change. He handed the medicine man a turquoise bracelet, saying that was all he had left to give and had no money. The herbalist left to gather medicine for him and returned with many plants that he gave to the man, who then departed. About three days later, he was back, saying the herbs almost killed him, and so he was returning them. His condition remained the same.
>
> This young man then came to me and asked if I would make herbs for him. The other medicine person told him he probably got his sickness from a woman, but this patient kept insisting that he did not. The pain came without any apparent cause. The medicine man kept insisting that something must have caused him to have an ache when he urinated and that he had given him the appropriate medicine for it, yet the herbs just gave him more misery. I told him I had not treated anyone with this kind of illness, but I had been told there was a plant for this situation that was used for little children when they had urinary tract problems. The plants did not grow near here so we started off to find them. He gave me a bracelet. I offered one plant corn pollen and dug up some of the neighboring plants. When he left, I told him

that if it cured him, to tell me. Many days later, he returned while I was herding sheep. He said there was nothing wrong with him now and left some money for me. My husband was there, kept the money, but told me this. I do not know how much he paid us.

People who lived a long way off were the only ones that came for our help. There is a man ['Awéé' Ádílíní—One Who Acts Like a Baby] who lived near the chapter house. He and my father belonged to the Kin yaa'áanii (Towering House) Clan, so he called me "sister" and said he needed assistance. His wife's hands were all bent and misshapen, and the joints in her legs did not work. He took her to the hospital, but that only helped a little bit. I told him he had great prayers in his peyote meetings, but they did not cure her, even though he tried again and again. I said he was too stingy. He laughed and told me not to say that. I asked him if he was serious about my treating her. He said yes, so I told him I had to be paid before I gathered any medicine, and that if he paid me only a little, I would not do it. He went out and got a concha belt that was nice and wide. I think it was because he could not stand the way his wife was. I told him to bring her in. I had some herbs that I was drinking and heated some up for her. He told me that I should pray before administering the medicine, but I responded that if he wanted to pray, then he could do it. He had big, long, beautiful prayers and seemed to enjoy showing them off. I said that I did not have any prayers, but that I would do what I usually did with herbs. I gave the woman the medicine to drink and told her it would make her queasy, then he asked to drink some; I told him this medicine was not for males. When a healer administers herbs to a sick person, he always partakes of the medicine. The plants did their curing, and now she looks okay. Some of her fingers are still crooked, and she opens and closes her hand again and again, but now she can walk, whereas before she could not. The doctors told her she had arthritis. Why they could not cure it, I do not know.[2]

The Holy People Ordain Plants

Mary and Gladys were adept at plant identification and use. Given a specific ailment, they could say where the plant to cure it was found, how it should be processed, when to administer it, and the expected results. Both were as competent as any druggist, but unlike the man behind the counter, there was never any mention of ingredients or, for the Navajo patient, any recounting of a story as to why it was used. Mary explained, "I do not know how the use of the plants came about. No one will tell us how they were first used. All I know is which plant is which and how it helps. Who told whom about the plants and their use at the beginning of time, I do not know."[3] In some instances, a medicine man or woman has to experience a certain sickness and be healed by another medicine person, who blesses and then transfers his or her knowledge to the patient. The healer is paid for this transfer of knowledge, freeing the patient to help others with it.

While the Anglo "customer" may inquire as to the composition of a pharmaceutical medicine, the Navajo patient depends on the wisdom and teachings passed down through medicine people. When asked for an explanation, there often is none—only that this is what they learned from another practitioner. There was rarely a specific story to explain its origin of use. However, Perry Robinson, a highly knowledgeable medicine man from Black Mesa who uses plants extensively, set the stage as to how the holy people organized their "pharmacy," how each plant received its qualities and accompanying responsibilities, and how the plant kingdom is a living, responsive community. He learned this from his grandfather as he sought to understand the way peyote, a foreign transplant from northern Mexico and now southern Texas, fit into the medicinal world of the Navajo.

> One time I asked my grandfather how peyote came to be, what was its story? He said that after White Shell Woman left the people for the last time, Talking God ordered all the medicines in the [mythological] White World to come together at a place called the Holy Mountain Hogan (Táálee Hooghan), a large medicine house [rock formation] on Black Mesa, northeast of Dilkon, Arizona. Everybody came, even the little plants. If any of them were useful, they were told to be there. They all sat in their ranked order in a circle, where they introduced themselves, told where they came from, what medicine they held, and how it could heal others. Just as the meeting started, one plant entered late. Everybody looked over to see Peyote trying to find a spot. He was a young man who stood by the doorway as he surveyed the filled-to-capacity hogan, searching for a seat. Talking God, sitting in the place of honor to the west, commanded, "Make room for him. Let

him sit by the doorway." Peyote looked, then said, "I want to sit in the west and be the main person." The twelve primary medicine people in charge did not think this was right and felt he would be sitting out of order based on the type of plant he was, so denied his request. "You can't make your way to there. You're not part of that group but belong to a different one. Go ahead and sit down."

"No," he said, then began arguing with those present. He became very angry, demanding, "If I'm not part of this group, I'm not going to be part of any group. If I can't sit over there, I'm not going to stay." The other plants begged him not to go, not to talk like that, but he just turned around and walked away. Sage sat in the north and was urged by the other plants, "Go get him. Bring him back. Put your arms around him. Talk to him. Have him return." The messenger caught up to the young man and grabbed him, saying, "Hey, brother, come on, friend. Let's go back in there. We are all in the same group here. We are all medicine people." Sage, because of his size and shape, was the only one of those plants that could put his arms around Peyote without being hurt. This is why sage is the only medicine plant that has a relationship with peyote and is now part of the Native American Church ceremony.

Peyote refused. He turned to the medicine plants watching him and said, "All of you, you think you're high medicine people, but one day people will forget about you. One day most of you will be forgotten and become extinct. When that happens, I will return. That will be when traditional teachings and medicine will end. People are going to lose their way of doing things, their hair buns, their moccasins, how they used to dress. Next will be their language, and they will forget how to speak Navajo. Then they will become like western [Anglo] people, and that is when I will come back as the only medicine." He turned and walked away to the east. Although everyone encouraged him to stay, he would not, so they left him alone. Still, the people insisted on giving him a name and so bestowed "The One That Came with the Earth" (Ni' bił hodeezliní ni' bił hodoolką' tsíłkééh naat'áánii) and even though he said all of these things, he still became part of the cactus people. His name indicates where he lives now—in little humps in the ground, visible at dawn and located in Mexico. That is where he was headed, and so that is the name he received. It is also the reason why peyote never became part of the regular Navajo medicine group.[4]

Charlie and Mary Blueyes, two accomplished herbalists, lived south of the San Juan River near Mule Ear (Tsénąąshch'ąąii—Designs on the Rock or Decorated Rock), a volcanic neck. Their three-room plastered house with windmill outside was surrounded by miles of sand dunes and sagebrush. Mary, a short, gray-haired Navajo elder, wore a kerchief around her head, a long calico dress that went to the top of her socks, and a silver bracelet studded with turquoise. Her gentle face, creased with age, was pleasant and usually wore a smile. Charlie was a perfect match—short, close-cropped silver hair and always ready with some humor. Both were in their seventies, had faced many challenges in life, and at this point, were willing to share their knowledge with the younger generation. When it came to discussing herbal medicine, Mary was the more informed, Charlie often deferring to her. She began by explaining the very real relationship she had with the plants she sought.

> People come to me for herbs. I go out and gather them. Before I start, I need corn pollen to give to the plants. You give corn pollen to only one plant that is the representative of the same plants that you are going to pick. You address it by its sacred name and present the name of the person it is going to heal because they are sick. You talk to the plant like an individual, since it is alive and survives on air, and give·it corn pollen, then you go to another one of the same species and dig up the roots or break the leaves to be used, gathering what is needed. By giving an offering to the plant, it provides its healing power in return. Just having the plant will not work; it needs to receive an offering.[5]

Five miles away from the Blueyes was the home of Gladys Yellowman, a powerful force for good in the Tódahidíkáanii community. Her mother, Maimi Howard, visited often and was the teacher of sixty-five-year-old Gladys. Gladys said:

> I asked my mother about the plants, and that is how I know the medicine. I saw her gather them, asked about their names as she collected them, and she would tell me their names and uses. She told me the plants came in fours, and I said I wanted to learn this. My mother used to know many plants, so people came to her for help and got well. Many people came far and wide to get herbal medicine, and some asked what the plants were and she would tell them. Others

knew part of her plant medicine. A man named Guy Manybeads now knows my mother's knowledge of plant medicine because he gave her turquoise beads and money. He said this would be his medicine. I wondered what was so powerful in it and wanted to do as she did. That is how her knowledge was passed on to other people, but now old age is bothering her.

The Navajos have great respect for their medicine. When a person is sick, he will come to you for help and you become the shield between him and the sickness when you are providing the herbal cure. This is why women who know herbs really treasure their medicine, but for those who do not know about them, they will probably think of it as a waste of time. When you are working with herbs, a prayer is said. I have helped people get cured of their illness, so this is how I am known. I make medicine in exchange for money. All of my children know the herbs because they have seen me gather them, and if grandchildren find a plant that I use for medicine, they bring it home, telling me they have found my medicine.[6]

Medicine men also went to great lengths to gather plants in specific spots. Mary Jay recalled family members traveling long distances to get healing herbs.

Our land flourished with vegetation. We had a lot of juniper trees growing here that darkened the mesas to their points. Sunflowers grew tall and thick and covered the ground everywhere and were so high I was not visible when I walked through them, herding the sheep as they grazed on Rocky Mountain beeweed (waa') and gray greasewood (díwózhiiłbáí). My father taught me about all the important medicine plants, while my uncle, Red Mustache (Dághaa Łichíí'ii), taught me some of his. I learned both of their medicine plants. My uncle was a medicine man who sang in the Blessingway (Hózhǫ́ǫ́jí). My father's main occupation was being an "herb man" or a real "medicine man." He traveled far distances to collect plants, riding his horse to Criss-Crossed Mesas (Tsé Ałnáda'ooztiin) and all the way west to Navajo Mountain. His trips took many days at a time, sometimes months. He would return with many sheep and goats that he earned along the way. No one would ride their horses that far today.[7]

Mother Maimi Howard and daughter Gladys Yellowman illustrate three important concepts as herbalists and medicine people. First is the passing of plant knowledge to the next generation. Second is the guarding of that information, given to only those who respect and understand its importance. Third is that it is not just a matter of physically healing a person but also a contractual relationship with the holy people who preside over the use and growth of the plants.

Plants as Food

Having lived in the Southwest for centuries, the Navajos were experts on using wild plants for food. For an excellent rendering of a large array of dishes that can be served up from desert and mountain plant life, see Charlotte J. Frisbie's *Food Sovereignty the Navajo Way: Cooking with Tall Woman*.[8] The families living along the San Juan River, no doubt, had a similar diet. Jane Silas commented:

> There were plenty of plants, such as wild onions, turnips, rhubarb, and "aza haleeh." Much of this grew in abundance in various places. Some were used as food and dried, then mixed in as ingredients. The wild onions we dug up since there were no regular onions. Cliffrose and sour berry bushes (chiiłchin—sumac) grew in the canyons and so gave names to places like Spring in the Sour Berry Bush and "Ha'ashgeedi" (Dug Up). The river was very narrow back then, and the banks were thick with these bushes and cottonwoods. It has all been washed away except for a few old tree stumps that are still visible today. People used to live under these cottonwood trees and kept their horses inside corrals built there. They would gather there and lasso horses to tame. The people survived on sumac berries and grass seeds, with women and children doing most of the collecting. They ground them and made bread or mush. Indian rice grass (nididlídii) that grows around here was also used. My maternal grandfather used to gather this. He would look like he was carrying a large bundle of wool before processing it by burning the stems and winnowing the seeds. It was then ground and mixed with milk and tasted very good.[9]

Fernandez Begay further explained, saying, "Plants such as beeweed, sumac berries, and rabbit thorn (haashch'é'édą́ą́), which is almost like sumac, bitter and eaten with white clay (dleesh), were popular foods, three of the main ones we ate. Juniper ashes were used in corn mush and in any other thing made with corn. Yucca (tsá'ászi') was another, with parts of it cooked in the ground, then cooled; it tasted very good."[10]

John Knot Begay remembered people gathering some "tł'oh she" (grass plant) along the side of the field to use for food. It was prepared by crushing and threshing out the black seeds, then sifting it in the wind to separate the edible part from all of the stems and leaves. The seeds were put in bags for storage, later ground and made into mush or used as an ingredient for stew or other foods. Corn was ground and cooked with fat.[11] Gladys Yellowman used many different types of wild plants in cooking. An abbreviated list follows: juniper seeds (gad bididze') were shelled and made into a mush or bread, but were also used as beads for warding off sickness. Piñon nuts were ground and made into tł'ish. A solution of water and Chiricahua pine needles (ch'oh) or ponderosa pine needles (nídíshchííʼ) became shampoo for washing hair and was said to make it grow long. The roots of narrow-leafed yucca (tsá'ászi'ts'óóz) were also used for shampoo, while its tender growing stalks were put under a fire, and once cooked, tasted like corn. They were also fried and then the stalks sliced like fried squash, which tasted like tender young squash. Acorns from an oak (che'ch'il binaaʼ) were used once they turned brown, so that the fleshy part could be removed and mixed with cooked, dried corn. The buds of both the prickly pear cactus (hosh nteelí) and canaigre (chąąt'inii) were made into jam, while the canaigre's roots were used in dying wool but also cured mouth sores; when one chewed on its roots the sores would go away.[12]

Mary Blueyes added that in the early spring, wild onions (tł'ohchin) were abundant and dug in the red sands behind Spotted Rock. Once harvested, they were mixed in cornmeal or made into a gravy. Beeweed was boiled for a long time and the leaves eaten, but even then it tasted bitter, no matter how much boiling; before the flowers came out, the leaves were more tender. This plant became important when other sources of food were hard to find. Trader Stewart Hatch, who owned a store in Montezuma Canyon whose Navajo name mentions grease-wood, remembered the benefits of that plant, which grew so high in areas that it was difficult to herd sheep because they disappeared in the tall thickets. "Greasewood is awful good wood. It grows for a few years, then dies and dries, but others keep coming. Navajos really value it, es-pecially for cooking. It does not have any smoke, and it is hotter than other wood. With a little greasewood, a person can make bread or cook a whole meal, just in a little place, without smoke."[13]

A lot of other items could be added to the Navajos' wild plant shopping list, but suffice it to say that even though agriculture served as one of the main staffs of life, collecting undomesticated edibles from nature was an ongoing task that bonded the People to the land and a

Used to heal everything from baldness and smelly feet to stomachaches and also extended as an offering to the holy people, wild plants can be used for every occasion. Many medicine people bemoan the fact that much of this knowledge has fallen into disuse, and that therefore some of these plants feel unappreciated and so are no longer available.

view of life made possible by it. Charlie Blueyes summarized this dependence and philosophical outlook:

> There are different varieties of plants, each species with its own name. We walk among them and use them. Every place has plants, and that is beautiful, and many we use for food. Mother Earth made this food for us with the help of Father Sky. A long time ago, they became mad at each other, each arguing that one was more important and independent of the other, and so the rains stopped, the lands dried out, and the plants and animals suffered. Neither side would give in to the other until the Holy Wind helped to work through the arguments and smooth the feelings between them. This same Holy Wind is the

air in us that makes us move and gives life to those things around us. The air moves everything, including the plants that grow everywhere. People grow up on plant juice. Livestock eat certain plants, which makes their meat taste good. A person grows up on this livestock. I do not know how you grow inside the womb, but we grow there and develop. Between man and woman, their juice comes together, and a baby starts to grow with the help of the Holy Wind. Then we become a holy being when we start to move and function. Baby boys and girls were once part of a plant that developed into a five-fingered person. When someone tends the sheep, the sheep will watch its caretaker. It will eat, eat, eat and get fat upon plants. When it is butchered, you will have juicy, fat mutton ribs in a big bowl thanks to the plants. Cattle also bring forth money and many other good things in the same way sheep do, all thanks to plants, as long as the person tending them is not lazy. If one does not care to help the animals, they will not help you and produce good food. If one is lazy, why should they give you something that is good? Even your sister or brother will not give you anything.

In some ceremonies, mountain soil (dził̃leezh) is used for blessing livestock. They are what life is about, so people ask for these blessings through the soil taken from the four sacred mountains. When prayers are offered through it, rain comes and nurtures the land. Feeding livestock brings us meat, which is our life. Since all of the plants have pollen, that is what keeps us alive, and with the sheep, life renews itself. It is the same with cattle. Who would give birth in a dry place? This will not happen. These plants around here are given sacred stones (ntł'iz) and they give you many lambs or calves. On the tip of these plants there are horses, cattle, and sheep. Sheep are made of plants only. The plants are in the sheep. When you eat this, you will get a baby. When a woman cannot have a baby, go get some herbs and let her drink them to help with starting the pregnancy. At first, she may not be able to have a baby, but soon, she will be able to have one. This will cure it.

The San Juan River (Tooh) is making its way down to the ocean (Tónteel) and is forever going that way. Water comes from the mountain and has everything in it—plants, all living things, and wealth like money and gold. The lumber that comes from the mountains and desert is nothing but water. It came from water just like the plants that grow around here. It is like this, my grandson. We did not come from anywhere else, only the earth. Our flesh is the dirt.[14]

Homes, Tools, and Childbirth

In addition to food, plants played a significant part in other aspects of daily Navajo life. A sampling of some of these uses illustrates the wide variety of types of plants and the many ways they assist the people. Starting with the earliest form of traditional Navajo home, the male hogan (ałch'į'adeez'á), Mary Blueyes described its origin.

> The people used to use a forked tree as the main post for a male hogan. A log is placed in the fork of another trimmed tree with other logs leaned against this tripod. Long ago, there was our creator called Bi'éé'łitsooi (God in Yellow Clothing). He made the negroes, Navajos, and other tribes, as well as sheep, horses, and many types of animals. This is what my father used to tell me. The creator would just blow on them and they would come to life. Someone asked what Navajos would use for their home, and so the people decided to hold a meeting to discuss this. Many of the other tribes were already stacking rocks to build their homes, while the Navajos had made a forked hogan that we could lie in. It was decided they would live in that kind of home, which would be called Saa'ąh naagháii bik'eh hózhǫ ("long life, happiness").
>
> The fire was built and the first fire poker carved, along with bedding composed of juniper tree bark and grass. These male hogans are now becoming extinct even though there are ceremonial songs that teach about them.[15]

Ponderosa pine (nídíshchíí') was used to make cradleboards. For smelly feet, a woman ground sunflowers (ndíyílii), which were then placed in water before bathing the offending part. The bark of the cliffrose ('awééts'áál) in the past was used as a diaper and bedding for a baby because it was so soft. Blue spruce pine (ch'ó deenínii) was used to protect the hogan and patient within against the influence of ghosts during a five-day Enemyway ceremony. Mary Blueyes told of how the use of this plant started.

> When the earth was young, the growth of the people was in its beginning stage. At one time, all of the humans and animals lived together peacefully. However, as time progressed, some of the animals, like bears and wolves, became enemies of the people. One day, Wolf

was making arrows out of blue spruce for Bear to use, when Coyote came by. Wolf told him that he was making weapons that kill, which made Coyote curious. He would not sit still but just looked at the arrows and kept asking if that weapon would really move. In his mischievous, naughty way, he kept saying that the arrow was going to move as he fidgeted uneasily. Wolf tired of his behavior and let the arrow begin chasing Coyote about. It followed him in a small area at first, then went a longer distance. Coyote tired, so he crawled into a place called Tsé 'Ahazhini near Mancos, Colorado, where the arrow followed and then stuck in the ground. To this day, it is still protruding out of that place and is the reason blue spruce is put on the hogan of a patient (hooghan bik'ida'alt'oh) for protection.[16]

Piñon pine (chá'oł) had many different medicinal uses, but its sap was used to waterproof pottery and seal a flat rock that served as a cooking pan. When a stone was to be used as a skillet, it was first smoothed by removing any bumps before piñon leaves were scattered and burned on it. Next, the rock was coated with piñon gum, and then sheep grease was applied to the prepared surface and the rock heated. Watery corn batter was poured on the hot surface, turned once, and came off of this griddle paper thin. It was then folded and eaten plain or with something in it. Piñon tree gum was a medicine for women who injured their breast and was also used on a sheep that injured its leg, the wound being coated and then wrapped with a cloth. Mary did this with two sheep and believed that the piñon tree was very powerful.[17] Margaret Tso Weston commented on one of the most prominent uses of the piñon tree, which was its nuts. Sold in large quantities to trading posts, and a welcomed addition in many Navajo recipes, it was harvested in the fall by entire families who traveled long distances to where they were most plentiful. Margaret said:

> I remember going to Cortez by wagon with my grandparents and aunts to a place they called "Biishdíílid" (Burnt Into) to pick piñons there and along the way. We would pick them in the late fall when it was cold. Many of those trees are now gone, replaced by bean fields. My grandmother and I walked and picked. I became so tired, my grandma had to pull me along as we kept hiding from the white men, cowboys who rode their horses out on the range. When we did not show up at

This Navajo woman lived next to the San Juan River, enjoying the shade of cottonwood trees along its banks and her summer shade in the background. Many of the elders mention their use and love for the cottonwood trees, a delightful break from the searing sun and intense heat. Next to this woman are two pitch pots fashioned from woven sumac and then covered with melted piñon pitch. Once the gum solidifies, these containers are leakproof and are said to keep the water inside sweet.

the overnight camp one evening, our family members came looking for us, but we were walking off the road and so did not see each other. Grandma and I spent the night huddled under the pine trees. Early the next morning we went out on the road again and were reunited with our party. Everyone was saying, "We could be kidnapped by the cowboys, we could be in danger." We sold the piñons to the trading post at a high price.[18]

Sheep had plants to meet some of their special needs. Snakeweed (ch'il dilyésii) was used when castrating lambs or calves, by crushing it, putting it in water, and having the animal drink some of the solution, while the rest was applied to the injured area to facilitate healing. Gladys Yellowman remembered, "When sheep get eye diseases, the long stem that sticks out of a yucca plant is cut and burned. The ashes are then crushed, mixed with salt, and put in the diseased eyes. The sheep and goats get well from this. If this happens to a human, berries from a plant called black alder (k'ish łizhin) were squeezed into a glass bottle and the liquid put into a person's eyes so that they could see again. My father used to use this and he had really sharp eyes."[19]

There are dozens of plants used to dye wool for weaving, such as rabbit brush (k'iiłtsoii). Rabbit brush is also a medicine given to sheep after they graze over the hair of deer or some other wild animal, which could cause the sheep to become uncontrollable and run away. When deer rub their antlers against a tree or shrub and break off plants, that spot was given ntł'iz and the plants were gathered. If people were careless as to where they put deer hair or bones and the sheep walked among these remains, it had the same effect. To cure this, rabbit brush (k'iiłtsoii ntsaaígíí) was mixed with blue flax (dinéch'il 'áłts'óózígíí) and another plant called 'na'asch'il, which spreads on the ground but closely resembles cliffrose. These are added to silky sophora (dibé haich'iid), which has red blossoms that the sheep really like to eat from top to bottom. That is why it is called the plant the sheep digs up. This mixture was then added to the plants the deer rubbed against, ground, mixed in water, and then sprinkled on the animals to curb their wild behavior. Some of these plants were also used in the Evilway ceremony for a young man or woman who has become unmanageable due to someone working against them so that they get out of hand, or for a person who injures himself when working on a deer hide or when hunting.

Thinking about and categorizing plants includes not only the plant's physical properties and appearance but also its sex and spiritual essence. Mary and Charlie agreed there were two types of the same plant—a male and female—that work together when providing medicine. Charlie pointed to a cottonwood tree and admonished, "You have to look with your eyes to see it. The female cottonwood has beaded earrings (seeds), while the male is without. All plants come in twos. For example, Mormon tea (tł'oh 'aihii) comes in twos, one gray and one green. Spruce and juniper trees are also like that. One type of juniper has leaves that are prickly while another does not. The same is true of medicine plants. When making herbs, you have to have both male and female plants."[20] Mary chimed in:

Douglas fir (ch'ó deenínii) has sharp needles that feel like they will cut you, and so these trees are male, while spruce (ch'ó) has softer, limp needles and is a female tree. Now we just see them as trees. The plants are also different. My father said there are four groups or species of plants. When you are making herbs for a woman, the plant is given a white seashell, some particles of sacred stones, and then corn pollen. As you are praying to these plants, you tell them who you are picking the plants for and say their name and what area of the person's body needs to be healed, and it is for that purpose you have come to get it. Plants are tended by the holy people who send them rain. This is the reason for the prayer as you thank them for the plant, ask them to heal, and ask for the well-being of that person. When this woman gets well, she will have prayers and songs. This is what you say. The same procedure is followed when picking medicine for a man, but instead of a white shell, turquoise is used, along with ntł'iz and corn pollen. The plant that receives the offering and prayers is left alone by going to the other plants for leaves or part of its roots. It is said that the holy people look upon every living thing: one stem, one person, or one animal, and take care of these living things through rain. Men will make babies, but the holy people are everywhere and we breathe the Holy Wind in and out, and that is what gives the baby life. We live only because of the Holy Wind, and this is probably true also of plants, while water is a main element for keeping it alive.[21]

The World as a Pharmacy

Many of the frailties and much of the sickness that are a part of human mortality are dealt with through the Navajos' knowledge of plants. Literally, from before birth to after death there are herbs and medicines to meet most needs. Gladys Yellowman continued the topic of determining the sex of a baby before conception. A plant called asa'ashk'azhi (unidentified) and barrel cactus (hosh sidáhí) will help the mother desiring a baby boy. This cactus is very small, grows in sandy areas, and does not come in bunches. If a girl is desired, a white seashell is used. Mary Blueyes added that her grandfather said that a small plant with red flowers that influences a baby to become a girl is "over there in those hills" and is called bich'i'i'at'eeke—to become a girl. Gladys Yellowman recalled:

> I picked some and just chewed it to get a daughter. At the time I had three sons. It worked. These plants are found in the Mexican Hat area. A person can use this same plant to get more brown lambs. Another technique to conceive a boy is to take a good turquoise stone and rub it on another stone, then take the powder and mix it with water before placing it in the woman's mouth. For a girl, a seashell that looks like it was turned in from both sides and folded inward is grated on a stone before putting the powder in her mouth and swallowing it.
>
> When a woman gives birth, she is not supposed to have intercourse for some time. If she does, there are plants that can heal it as well as heal urinary problems, coming in contact with menstrual fluid, or being unable to stop her menstrual flow. It is always administered when a woman gives birth, and so it is used in three different ways. It has cured me. When a woman's womb gets sore, the medicine is to find a juniper and a piñon tree growing from the same spot. They are given ntł'iz as you offer a prayer, then their leaves are added to elements from scrub oak (chéch'il ntł'izí), Gambel oak (chech'il), mountain mahogany (tse'esdaazii), aromatic sumac (k'įį'), and sumac (chiiłchin ditł'oi). Juniper and piñon trees also have sticky pitch, which is given to a female who is sick. There was a woman who came to my house when I was not there. She said she had two children and that both times she had intercourse soon after their birth. I did not want to help her because I might not get her well and told my children they were telling

me of a frightening thing, but they said she was really pleading. I gave
the woman herbs, although her womb was probably already spoiling
since there was some awful stuff coming out of her. She gave me a
blanket and some money after I helped her with medicine, and today
she is still alive. As you can see, plants are very powerful.[22]

Gladys, with many children and grandchildren, had an extensive
knowledge of plants to remedy childhood illnesses, but many of which
also worked for adults. Mint (tólchiin), for instance, is used for children's
fevers. The plant is placed in cool water, given orally, and then the child
is washed in it. Adults use it in a sweat lodge and in cooking. Another
plant called 'azee'nidoot'eezh (String of Plant Medicine) cures sores in
the mouth. There are two different types—one has red flowers and the
other blue flowers. They are put in cool water and can be used by older
people. Rock lichen may also be ground into powder and put into the
baby's mouth, healing it quickly.

Many plants are medicine to the Navajos, who have passed them down
from generation to generation. These were my mother's medicines.
Now I am doing what she has taught me. These plants are healing,
so my children do not have sores in their mouths. Another solution
of various plants—'azee'dithit, 'azee'tigaii, te'eze', 'azee'ntx'inii,
'azee'ntx'iniitsoh—is gathered and mixed in water to speed the
mending of broken bones and it is consumed until the patient gets
well. Wild onions are used not only to season food, but also when a
child has gas pains in their stomach; desert sage is put on a person to
quiet their fever. Ponderosa pine cones (ńdíshchíí') are burned and the
ashes put on a child's sore. The pitch is also used for infected areas or
in a balm when the skin gets very dirty and raw. A little bit of pitch is
mixed with grease and applied to the chapped area. This same mixture
is used for colds as well as pneumonia or whooping cough. A spoonful
is given to the child, who swallows it to open their air passage.[23]

Mary added to the list of herbal cures that Gladys shared. She
mentioned that aspen (t'iisbái) has a gray powder on its bark that is
rubbed on a young woman's face during the kinaaldá ceremony. This
prevents rapid aging of the skin and wrinkles in the future and encourages straight posture. Bottle plant is used for people who have a urinary

tract infection. One is not supposed to blow in it. The top looks like deer antlers. It is said that if a man is a deer hunter perhaps hauling à deer on his back or tanning a hide, these activities may start to bother him in his bladder area. This plant is boiled before use and is hollow like the urinary bladder, which is why this is medicine for this type of problem. Mary told of when her brother, 'E'eesheezh, almost died from the pain in his urethra.

> People gave him some herbs, but they did not work for him. The pain in his crotch area did its work. His urine was coming out another part of his crotch toward his hip, but there was a man who gathered only one plant that is found in the mountains, and it healed my brother. I know that plant and have used it. This herb not only works for urinary problems, but also for a woman who is in her menstrual cycle and her blood does not stop. Spreading fleabane (azee'na'oostádii—medicine that unwinds) is used for a pregnant woman who drinks it until she gives birth. It is like when a person lassoes a horse. The rope either goes around the leg or the neck. If a father was lassoing an animal when the baby was inside the mother, the baby might get choked by the umbilical cord. To prevent or undo this, the mother drinks this medicine, since if it is not done, the baby may strangle.[24]

At the other end of the spectrum, there are plants and ways to cure baldness in both men and women. Mary explained:

> One time my head really itched, and I wondered what I could put on it. There is a plant called te'etsoh bilizh halchiní (smells like urine) that looks like rabbit brush and grows in patches of dirt on rock around here. I brought it back, boiled some, and washed my hair with it, making the itch go away. It is said that te'etsoh bilizh halchiní will help you keep your hair. The black marks made by the water running down a rock face (desert varnish—tsé naajiin) are either removed by scraping downward or are given corn pollen. Some people use this on a girl who is having her kinaaldá. Other things that are used for this purpose are moss and small plants called hazéédą́ą́' that are boiled with te'etsoh bilizh halchiní and then used to wash hair. Finally, there is one's firstborn baby's initial urine, used to wash hair to prevent it from falling out.

Another plant, Gaillardia (wóláchíí'jich'il—red ant medicine), has a yellow flower, red roots, and is bitter. It has only one stem and is gathered during the mating season of the deer. This herb is used when a person has peed on an ant, because it will put pain in the urine, or if a child swallows an ant or steps on the ant's home and gets stung many times. Once there was a family eating their meal when a child swallowed an ant and very soon became sick. A man gave the powdered herb mixed in water to the child, and after drinking it, vomited the ant out. It can also be applied externally to an ant sting. There are other plants that are also good for this. They are called ch'ildijé'ii (sticky plant) and another is rough leaves (bit'ąą' dich'ízhígíí). These plants grow on rocky surfaces and together are collectively called red ant plants (wóláchíí'jich'il), but they are also used as medicine for sheep who drink the potion and have it sprinkled on them.

Indian paintbrush is called hummingbird food (dah yiitįhí dą́ą́') and is used with other red medicine plants for nosebleeds. When a person uses this plant for medicine, the hummingbird also knows it and will fly around him or her. The plant is put in water and drunk, but if the nosebleed continues, a mountain sheep's horn (tsétah dibé bidee') is ground into powder and put on hot coals. The person with the nosebleed hangs his head over the smoke until the blood stops.[25]

Mary recalled her grandfather teaching that with the plant called Mormon tea, there would be one branch growing out of the ground away from the main plant. "First, give that plant corn pollen, then pluck the one that is sticking out to cure diarrhea. You can do this with either the regular green or the grey Mormon tea."[26]

Yucca roots, on the other hand, are used as a shampoo in daily life and also in preparation for ceremonies. Before digging it up, one should know the direction the root is growing if it is to be used in the Blessingway. The length of the root is the width of four fingers. It is crushed, soaked in water, and then used as a shampoo. At night, the medicine man says a prayer called 'ach'ą́ą́h sodizin (protection prayer), which wards off the sickness known as naatah naax-niihor naalch'ili. The prayer asks that whatever evil mist or thought a person had sent toward the patient would be blocked and go away. The next morning was the time the yucca root was brought in and the washing of the hair took place, after which the yucca root was taken out and placed in a shrub so that the person with evil thoughts could not steal it away. The used yucca root is kept for four days before returning it to nature. Another sickness called Niichaad (parts of the body swell) is also treated with yucca.

Medicine men performing intense ceremonies that cast away evil, prevent harm, or cure its effects used a number of different plants that repulsed the evil and cleansed the patient. Some plants used in certain ceremonies served as purgatives to induce vomiting to rid the patient of ill effects. Ada Benally recalled that these agents, known as "ilkoh," are used in healing ceremonies such as the five-night Evilway (Hóchxǫ'ííjí) and Lightningway (Na'at'oyee): "The medicine man makes a trip to the mountain to get some pine branches, which are then mixed with other local plants to make the 'ilkoh.' These plants are powdered, mixed together, and then boiled for the people to drink at the healing ceremony. The sick person drinks the solution and afterward vomits, making him feel better. This process continues for four days until the end of the ritual. It will heal him."[27] Gladys also spoke of curative herbs, saying, "There has to be a ritual done for the making of a medicine to ensure it has the power to heal. When a person was sick, people gave them water, but the medicine men had cures for each sickness that they knew of in their way. They dug up many different roots, which were crushed and shredded, then put in a large bowl with water. The sick person drank this juice while the medicine man performed the ceremony. The plants used for medicine can be found on the Navajo Reservation. This is how my father knew the plants."[28]

Some medicines could be highly dangerous if not handled properly. Take for instance jimson weed (ch'óhojilyééh), which is used when someone has internal injuries.

It is not to be eaten in just any way because it is dangerous when not used properly. The patient drank its juice when added to water, then lay down and hallucinated as the plant healed the injury. When one is finished hallucinating, another plant medicine is consumed to help with the cure. The root from a plant called the Virginia creeper (bit'ąą'ashdla'ii—five leaved plant) is a vine plant that climbs trees or other vegetation and is found along the San Juan River. It is used in Lifeway ceremonies and may be given to a woman who recently had a baby, or for injuries such as when a horse throws a person, has a heart problem, suffers from incessant coughing, or is sick with tuberculosis. I

Just as a pharmacist knows what shelf or drawer to go to for a certain medication, Navajo medicine people understand where on the land a certain curative plant can be found. And like the pharmacist, the herbalist spends years learning the lore, classifying according to need, observing results, and sharing this knowledge with other professionals.

made some for a woman and she stopped coughing. Another lady who went to several different hospitals was not recovering from her case of gonorrhea. I gave her some of this herb and now she is well.[29]

Plants can also cure misbehavior. At the time of creation, some of the mountains were acting unruly, wildly rebellious, and needed to be quieted. Mary told of the holy beings giving them mountain tobacco (dził nát'oh) comprising a variety of plants found only in the mountains to settle them down. When a person goes insane and acts crazily or inappropriately and rebellious, this mountain tobacco purifies their thoughts and physical body, just as it was given to the mountains. "One is called dá'ák'ǫǫzh (they are sour) and there are many more that I do not know. Its purpose is to restore a person who has been promiscuous or abnormally lustful. There is much to learn about these medicines. It is a wonder why we are told all the mountains do not belong to us when they are in our prayers."[30] Another plant called 'asbídí daa' (dove beak plant) helps a person who accidentally swallowed some menstrual discharge when washing clothes by hand. The discharge affects the bone structure, which this plant is believed to heal. There are also medicines that work against witchcraft. Gladys stated that mountain lion bile ('atł'izh) is poured on some corn, which is then ground. A very small dose is given to a person who faints, to ward off the effects of a bewitched potion. There are also plants used as an antidote to witchcraft that are called 'iiníziin ch'il.

> Some people make it according to a medicine man's prescription, while others know this themselves, and so they make their own. This medicine is found in the mountains and is the root of a plant. The potion is composed of two ingredients, just like a man and a woman. In some cases, the potion may have four ingredients, but all are in powder form. Red-blossomed plants and berries of all kinds are used. The very first plant to begin with is called nji'ahi (butchering). The seed of this is the very first ingredient to be collected. I pick it in the summer at Tsé Alnaazt'i'i. This potion is made only during the time of a kinaaldá ceremony. When all of the ingredients are gathered, it is tied to the girl, who will run with it during the whole four days. After the cutting of the corn cake, the potion is then distributed among the adult relatives, because it is powerful. The 'iiníziin ch'il probably has some sort of ritual when it is made, but I do not know what it is. This is just one way of making a potion for medicine.[31]

Going full circle to where we started with Perry Robinson's explanation of the plants reviewing their role in the healing of humans, it is fitting that we end with peyote. The religious beliefs that accompany its use, the lifestyle that has grown around it, and the Native American Church that depends on it have been thoroughly discussed elsewhere.[32] Yet it is also considered a form of medicine with healing properties that can do things in a way that traditional plants do not. The Native American Church is popular among the river Navajos, and so a brief experience here is included, although according to many who strictly follow traditional healing practices, it is not a medicine for them. John Joe Begay described his first experience using hallucinogenic peyote buttons.

Until fairly recently, there was no mention of peyote and such things as a peyote meeting. It came from the plains Indians or the Hopi. At first, they sneaked the peyote to the Utes at Cortez. Then a man called "Big John" brought some to me where I used to herd sheep. He asked me if I would eat some of what he had. I asked him what it was, and he told me it was a plains Indian medicine [peyote]. I said, "Maybe it is not good to eat," but he said, "No, no. I eat it myself."

The cactus button was dry and hard. He kept at me to eat it. He gave one to me and I crunched on it. A little while later my body felt weird. I thought maybe I ate a dangerous thing, but perhaps it was real medicine. I felt like I was dying, the end of me with no way back to the living and nothing to stop it. I gave up fighting its effects and completely surrendered myself to it. People said this medicine could kill. There were fifty peyote buttons boiled in a large bowl filled with this medicine, which I drank entirely when it was just cool enough to swallow. This was between noon and one o'clock. I felt like I did not have any thoughts, did not know which way to go, so just walked around and around. The hogan was on the incline of a hill but I was told to get in a shade house nearby. I walked and walked and eventually my body felt alright again. I saw what was killing me, looked at it, and was healed. If I had not taken the medicine, this witchcraft thing would have killed me. This medicine is real.

After that, I ate the medicine again and again, but once I got well, I did not take it anymore. I do not eat peyote now and have no way of getting it. At that time there were people near us who brought in peyote from some place. Now there is no talk of new shipments of medicine. There used to be a man from Tall Mountain who had a constant supply of it, which he got from the plains Indians and Utes. After I got healed, I did not touch it. I almost died but it healed me, so it is real medicine.[33]

The end of the traditional story concerning peyote prophesied that when this plant returned and was put to use, much of the traditional knowledge would be lost. Now, many of the elders agree that the old ways are fading into the past and that the up-and-coming youth live in an entirely different world. Isabelle Lee commented on the gap between her and the latest generation.

I never went to see a white doctor as I was growing up. When we caught a cold we drank herbs, or pounded and then mixed them together before boiling them. We placed some hot stones in the mixture to produce steam, covered ourselves with a blanket, and inhaled the vapor, the same way we did in a sweat bath. This usually cured us. Recently, I started seeing the doctor, but as a child, I never did. Besides, there were no doctors around, and I had never heard anything about them. We only used herbs for our medicine. The plants were always here; it was our grandparents' medicine. The younger generation does not know the simplest use of plants, even the most common ones available like Mormon tea or tumbleweed, and what they can do. People everywhere are like that; they have forgotten or don't know, except for a few elders. Some who have turned to Christianity have thrown their knowledge away. We were raised on these foods, and we were always healthy. People of today are forever going to the hospital because of the food they eat. When one of us got a cold back then we drank homemade herbs, juniper or sage, as our medicine. Who would think of using such plants or herbs these days? Nobody. Our natural medicines are growing out there and are going to waste. It's no wonder we are suffering from sickness. People prefer white man's medicines more than ever before. We had plenty of plants for medicine, but not anymore. Who would use them?[34]

The Navajos, indeed, are losing a source of knowledge that has existed for centuries and brought great benefit. While some elements of traditional culture fly in the face of western beliefs and customs, the use of plants and alternative practices to western medicine are far more palatable to outsiders. Revitalizing this knowledge is still possible, but much of it is fading fast. The elders who spoke here are now gone, and so it is for the present generation to gather what they can and renew the view that nature is their pharmacopeia.

CHAPTER FIVE

The Making of a Medicine Man

David Kindle and Hand Trembling

Controlling intense supernatural power generally falls in the realm of men who understand the relationship between the holy people and the earth surface (human) beings, learning what is necessary to call forth those powers to promote healing. This is a complex interaction that delves into ceremonies that can last for a few hours or for as long as nine nights or days. Entire books have been written about some ceremonies including songs, prayers, sand paintings, and ritual actions, along with their causes and effects. Approaching the topic of medicine and healing from this aspect requires detailed, technical analysis. Another way of examining this fascinating topic is through the life of a practitioner, which is the method used here. Two chapters are devoted to this discussion—this one looking at a medicine man's philosophy in different aspects of this sacred calling using hand trembling as an example, and the next in examining his teachings about a number of ceremonies. No attempt is made to compare and contrast this person's knowledge with that of others or to suggest this is a complete rendering of topics such as hand trembling or the Windway ceremony. Instead, it is an inside perspective from one individual based upon what he understood as a highly regarded longtime practitioner.

Who is this person and how did I come in possession of his teachings? In August 2017 archaeologist Kevin Conte and I drove to

Helena, Montana, to obtain a series of transcribed interviews that Dr. Robert W. Putsch III, retired clinical professor of internal medicine, had conducted in the mid-1970s with medicine man David Kindle.[1] This was the culmination of a number of discussions between Putsch and me over his work and his desire to have these materials preserved and published; it was also David Kindle's and his family's wish. Everyone understood that much of this thinking and ritual knowledge was disappearing, and that to make it accessible to future generations was paramount. There was a lot of work to do to bring this to fruition, and since I was involved in other projects, Conte agreed to organize, research, and write a first draft, which was no mean task. I greatly appreciate all that he accomplished and draw heavily on his excellent organization and work.

What follows is not a total rendering of everything that David Kindle shared. Whenever possible, I have used his words, but occasionally those of Putsch, for contextual discussion. Kindle was very open in providing his knowledge, an approach that not all of his family appreciated, since Navajo culture generally frowns upon talking about sacred and ceremonial beliefs and practices unless there is a transfer of wealth to indicate to the holy beings that their rules and knowledge are valued. Kindle, who approached Putsch to record this information, was as much concerned about loss and preservation at this point. His intent was not to obtain fame and glory; indeed some of the material he wished not to be made available until after his passing, since he named names and incidents that might bother people. At the same time, he did not want to be vague. Putsch honored every request expressed by Kindle and remains close to his family and their wishes to this day. At the time of the interviews, by Kindle's calculation, he was eighty-one years old, placing his birth around 1894. He lived in the Shiprock area all of his life, with stints around the agency and at Hogback, and much of the rest of his time in sheep camps west of Shiprock. In general, he lived in an area approximately forty miles southeast of Aneth and along the San Juan, so for our purposes, he is being included as a river Navajo.

David Kindle—A Life of Teachings

David Kindle, like so many medicine men, began by introducing himself in a manner that teaches values as well as outlines his earliest life. His intent that listeners live a good life forms the basis for his sharing. On

February 21, 1975, Kindle and Bob Putsch sat in the Kindle family's winter sheep camp, where Kindle explained his early years and how he started on the road to becoming a medicine man. He wanted the doctors and nurses in Shiprock, as well as his people, to understand Navajo medicine by having Putsch record and share this information so that it did not disappear when he died.

Remember this will be kept for us in future days. I am not playing with this story; I will record it so I am not wasting it on you. I will tell you a little bit about myself and how I stand, but not go into detail. What I want to record are my teachings. I was born eighty-one years ago. At that time just about everything was hard to get because there was nothing. It is simple to live life today. The only kind of blankets we had were woven. Sheep and goat skins were sewn together and used as quilts and as bedding. Our homes were cribbed and forked roof hogans. There was one door and no chimney, just a large opening in the roof so that when it snowed it covered the fireplace. But firewood such as piñon and cedar were available. Since there were no chimney pipes, fires were built in the middle of the hogan with about three uncut logs touching in the center where they burned. People kept warm during the winter by using this wood just like coal, and if they were big logs, the fire lasted all night. We smelled like smoke.

Materials such as baby diapers did not exist, so we used the bark of the cliffrose. This softened bark was braided and placed as bedding under the babies, who were then wrapped in goat skins.

It seemed like everything came about because of the Anglos. How it was before then I do not know, but at that time, we did not live a good life until we came in contact with them. Then good things came about. There were no shovels and axes until the time we call "To Where the People Moved Back" from Fort Sumner. That is when we acquired shovels, axes, hoes, and picks used for planting. Before then, sand used to wash out from rocky areas and made a nice place to plant corn. After people moved back from Fort Sumner, there were shovels to dig irrigation ditches. Four Navajo men lived at a place in Arizona called Cove in the Corner. They were named Within His Cover Clan Silversmith, Tall Edge of Water, and Yellow Bottom. They began walking from there to where red water from Cove flows. They said, "Let us walk along it. Perhaps there is somewhere that the land could be cultivated with this water." So, they started along the San Juan River until they reached Vegetation into Water, where they found enough water amid the greasewood to cultivate cornfields. This began farming in this area, and people began living the good life, bringing good food like white, yellow, blue, striped, and gray corn. About sixty or seventy years ago, the first Anglos came to live on the reservation among us at Shiprock. Two missionary ladies called Tall Woman and Bed Bugs [probably Mary Eldredge and Mary Whyte] moved into the area. From then, people began planting wheat and hay, creating a good life without poverty. Before that, the ways of life are embarrassing to tell about. While I was growing up there was barely enough food to eat.

I started realizing things when I was five, so it was about seventy-six years ago that I began remembering. There was hunger then. It seemed like we were barely living. I don't know how we got clothes, but I believe we used shaggy sheep and goat skins, which were very warm. That is how I grew up. It is not a good life to tell about because it was not a good life. They used to talk about the Anglos, but I never saw them. I did not see one until I was sixteen years old. They would look for little boys to go to school, so the Navajos hid them, and that is why I did not get an education. My parents used to tell me that I was smart and that I did not need to go to school. They took formal education away from me.

My grandmother was called Many Horse Rock Woman, and my grandfather was He Who Plucks His Whiskers, while my mother's father's name was The Fat One, and a nephew of He Who Plucks His Whiskers. He stole my mother, who had secretly become Whiskers' mistress; they were related as kin by clan. Her paternal grandfather married her. Before my mother married, she used to live with a man called Gáanaanééz, which was a good marriage. He was my father, and my older brother is the son of He Who Plucks His Whiskers. The Leader (Naat'áanii) and I were born when Gáanaanééz was still married to her. My older brother was born first, with three years between us and my little brother, Naat'áanii, who is three years behind. We did not have any sisters by the same parents; there were only the three of us. There was a time when I lived alone with my mother, who had a great deal of teaching in her. She really talked to me even though she was always sick. One minute she would call me her baby, then the next minute she would hit me, saying she did not know how long she would live. It is a good thing she did that because she wanted me to lead a decent life in later years. I was hit a lot when growing up, and she would kick me out of bed at dawn. There was a strap hanging up for spanking me, but it was there for me to live a good life and do something beneficial. It disciplines one's mind just as a fire poker is used to enforce discipline and teach. The poker stirs the red-hot coals and when one is hit with it, they receive energy to move about. A strap is another teaching tool that gives one energy, a stable foundation, and strength for life.

I do not remember how we grew up as babies, but I do know how my mother raised me. She used to teach, "Why should you sleep late?" as she got me up very early. "You need to grind the corn for me." Then I was told to card the spinning wool, and later, I learned how to do a little weaving. This is how I grew up. There were no young men my age nearby. We were not raised the way boys are now. Houses were located fifteen, twenty, or perhaps thirty miles apart. There is an old man that lives at Cove. He, just like me, has white hair. He is the only one I grew up with; I used to herd sheep with him for my grandmother. I did not see him until six or seven days ago after a long time had passed, perhaps sixty-five years. He is the maternal grandson of the one called Chatterbox and is of the Saltwater Clan. I remember the name he had as a child—Pretty Boy—but I do not know his name now.

I was sixteen when my mother died. She had told me to try to do my very best and to remember her in the future. She left me three or four horses and about thirty head of sheep to take care of as well as the cornfield at Many Horse Rock. The land I gave to a clan brother, even though she had told me to have it. She also cautioned me to not join up with bad boys and run off somewhere. "You will run around without shoes, with your knees poking out of your torn pants, and wearing a shirt ripped up to your belly button; your bedding will be torn and ragged. If you are smart, you will have nice woven blankets to sleep with and live in a good way." Indeed, my mother was smart. For example, squaw dances are fun but not the place for a person to stand around half naked in torn clothes. "You must have nice shoes and clothes and a horse with a decent saddle blanket, reins, and saddle. If you do not listen to your elders and are not smart, you will go on foot while other people travel on horseback to the squaw dance. Yé'ii Bicheii dances are fun, too, but not for those who sleep until noon and

Physical health and knowledge was stressed to Navajo youth in preparation for life's rigorous pathway ahead. Early morning runs, cold ice baths, attention to detail, and the ever-present traditional teachings established a pattern for future well-being. This young woman's puberty ceremony, the kinaaldá, encapsulates these values.

are not dressed up. Finally, you should have herbal tea for vomiting, so you will have a clear voice and others will listen to you. If you do not do that you will choke on your mucous and people will make fun of your singing. The young men will laugh at you, the young ladies will laugh about you, as will the men and women. You better have herbal tea on the fire, then young men and women will listen to your singing. People will say, he is the maternal grandson of so and so, or he is the son of a well-known person, and his uncle is so and so." These are all things my mother taught. What a smart thinker she was. She taught like a man, saying, "If anything happens to me, don't run away, take care of yourself with whatever you will live by in future days. Look for this and don't just take off; please my child." She died during the Shiprock Fair, when harvesting the late corn was taking place.

After her death, I felt lost and kept returning to Many Horse Rock. She had told me to take care of the cornfield, improve the irrigation system, and put in small check dams. I began watering the fields and herding sheep for my maternal grandmother, who lived at Trail Over the Rocks, traveling back and forth to the cornfields. Then a clan brother named Tall Man from a separate family came to see me. After he left, I started herding sheep again, until one afternoon my older brother was waiting for me when I returned home. He was well dressed in a coat, black pants, white shirt, and looked just like what my mother had described, saying that in the future I would dress well, just like him, but I wondered where he had gotten those clothes. He spent two nights, after which another brother called Tall Man (Diné Nééz) came by on his horse to visit. We talked awhile until my older brother said that he was going back the next day to Hogback, where he would work on digging out an irrigation canal. This was about sixty-six years ago. Tall Man said he wanted to go too, and I wanted to go with them. My brother warned that our maternal grandmother would probably say no to my leaving, so I said I would not ask her, but just run away, which was most likely the only way I would be able to go. That settled it, and so my brother, who had come to visit, returned home. The next day while I was herding sheep, it seemed to take forever before noon arrived. I returned with the sheep, and by late afternoon my brother arrived on horseback. We just laid around in the shade for a while, then went to some large rock potholes with warm water in them and went swimming.

Earlier that morning, I had hidden my new striped blankets far away. They would have cost about four dollars at that time, which seemed expensive to me. As we left, I picked them up on the way. When I ran away from home, my tracks showed that I had one good and one worn out shoe. I came to where The Road that Leads over the Rock meets the road that goes to Mitten Rock, then to Where Red Ochre Is Dug, and by late afternoon came to a place called Nearby. By the time we reached a mesa close to what is called The Nose, we arrived at my maternal grandmother's home. She was called One Who Cannot Hear. We stayed there overnight, then left the next morning, reaching Tall Leader [Shiprock Agency] in the afternoon. Once we came to the river, something screamed out [a whistle blew].

There was a trading post across the San Juan to the east with a canyon in between. I had never been there before and learned that the trader's name was He Who Pulls One Up. This was the first time I ever saw an Anglo. We ate there and left again, arriving at Hogback at noon. Since my brother knew the way, we reached my late aunt's house, where I started to learn about what Anglos had introduced. It is embarrassing to tell the kind of life I had led previously, where only cornmeal and milk was our food to fight hunger. Some people had good homes with lots of sheep and plenty of food so that when someone got hungry, they would butcher a sheep, even if it was evening or after dark. If the children were hungry, a sheep was killed. This is how my tracks led to Hogback, even if they did look like I had two different shoes with one side worn out, which was embarrassing. Now it is known how my tracks lead from here thanks to the Anglo ways. I walk in oxford shoes, wearing long pants, shirt, and white brimmed hat. This is when I got my first hat and I began to live.

After my mother died and was buried, I found a new mother at Hogback—work. Work took care of me and became my means of life. Who became my father? The government because it has everything. It provides a good life so that one can have shoes and clothes to wear, and good horses to ride at a time when there were no automobiles. An Anglo job is a good thing to hold on to. When you live the Anglo way of life, it is good. This is how I look back at this time. If I was not smart and had joined the bad boys, I wonder what kind of life I would have had. At eighty-one years of age, I am telling you this story with the hopes that young people will live by it. The good things that Anglo life offers should be taken seriously, so that one does not make a fool of oneself. What is called good food is breakfast, afternoon lunch, and dinner with good things like a bed, chairs, fine blankets to sleep on, and nice quilts. You will enjoy this life. One should not fool around with oneself or with life. It is like crying about what my mother had taught me a long time ago; life is too good to waste. Here I am sitting with white hair and wishing I was only fifty years old and a young man, that is what I am thinking as I am telling this story. I just got into the midst of the good life when I became old.

My children who are a generation behind me and my maternal grandchildren who are two generations behind me will teach their children by talking to them of all the things that I have just told you with the hope of making a good life for them. It was good for me to live a harsh life up to the time that I got my first job at Hogback. From then on, life was good and I was strong. When I began work, I received $45 a month while employed by the government for five years, then my pay increased to $75 a month, then to $90. From that time forward my earnings grew and the government became my main source for obtaining a living. Today there are all different kinds of resources available to us. Life is the most beautiful thing and the best ever.

There are many roads to a good life. From the east to the west, roads lead off; all along the ocean from north to south, roads lead in those directions. These roads are the shoestring to material goods. Money causes that to happen, and it is what built these roads. One can go to the end of the world with money, which is the primary thing that accomplishes much, but it can also cause bad behavior by becoming everything. The greatest life that one can have is in money if it is handled well, but one has to think about it. It is available from outside beyond the hills, where the valleys are. There is money in the valleys, where the roads are, where the mountains are. Money is the most precious thing around. When I say that it is bad, what I mean is that it is up to each person and how careless they get when it is available. It is up to the individual. There are gambling games, women, bars for alcoholics who spend their money on whisky and wine. Anglos know how to use these things in their livelihood, but one should leave them alone. Hold on tight to that which will benefit your life, my grandchildren and Navajo people, wherever you are. In the mountains or on the plains or in the valleys where all kinds of vegetation grow, there is money and valuable possessions, precious objects, food, by which one can make a livelihood.

One goes through life with their teachings. My mother told me that if I was smart, that I would have children after I had obtained a wife and home, but I was not to have them first. Mother did not have the strength to push on living, so there were things that I had to learn myself. Today, too many people fool around with their life. Young men are going from woman to woman. One's body will not be strong from that kind of life, and that person will not have a strong stable home. A lady might also live that same way. She may not have a husband or children or a loom, weaving batten, weaving comb, spindle, stone grill, or a grinding stone. If one is not smart, one will have nothing. When one walks with clear direction, then they will have all the things needed to exist. Lefthand Curly Hair once spoke in front of me like this, as did Ayokin and Very Tall One. They were great teachers. Old Police from Cove understood how to speak well, as though he knew about every toenail, and then there was One Who Killed a Man, who did not speak up too often because he was quiet. Tall Red House and Old Beadway Medicine Man also carried the good life in them. There was another man called Bizhóshí who was like that, but he was competitive.

All the things I have said are some of the least important items in life according to Lefthand Curly Hair. Indeed, a woman causes one to have a good life. She is the greatest life-giver one can have. There are belts and earrings, but those are just things. The Very Tall One said that too. He was also called Tall Within His Cover Clan. My maternal grandfather from Tooh Dah Astání (pond) or Bí'iil'aashí had teachings as a Red House clansman. He agreed that one has life because of a woman. When one does not have a wife, one does not have two pairs of shoes. The men said one will only have the pair of shoes that one is wearing. That was their way of teaching.

To hold on to a piece of land, one has to have sheep and cattle and a sheep corral at their home. That is how one carries on life. Our family land is at a place called Salty Water. I will tell you a short story about it. A man named Slender Policeman used to live here. His teachings, thoughts, and words are what I am repeating. He taught that in the future we should all hold on to our sheep's leg, so that the sheep will not disappear from our sight. You will keep them standing here and below Tsé Bit'a'í (The Rock with Wings—Shiprock) and farther down from there at a place called Tódík'óóz (Bitter Springs). From Tsé'élkáá' Nideetiin (Rocky Surface Road), down to where the soldiers trail came up and down, along the river where the Mexicans beat them down, to where the potatoes grow, to where the canyon is grayish, the land should be cared for and held on to. This is your land. Do not argue with each other with bad language. We should not rub each other's elbow, neither the ones living along the river nor the ones living around each other in this area. You all shall remember me like that in the future. Thank you for listening to me as I spoke my words.

Hand Trembling Picks a Disciple

Kindle's admonition for peace and fair treatment were central to his personality as a medicine man. He first started into the use of powerful spiritual forces somewhat by accident during a ceremony undertaken for his wife, Amy, who had become unexpectedly ill. Several medicine men had gathered around her as she lay sick and motionless.

> There were a few elders sitting about, one of whom was Dishnoozh, who performed Lifeway ceremonies and was at that time singing a Lifeway song. Others there included my uncle Fat One's Son, Slim Policeman, Man Who Couldn't Walk, and Water Beneath Oak Tree. The one who cooks for me [Kindle's wife] was ill, and so these men were sitting around discussing the situation. "Why is she ill, what is causing it, and what can be done about it?" they asked, as she walked around in a stupor that appeared like drunkenness.

Kindle and his daughter, Daisy, looked on while the men performed a ritual, but Amy's condition continued to deteriorate. Daisy noticed her father's arm began to suddenly shake while he felt a flutter in his heart that then spread down his arm to his hand. At first he tried to keep his arm down and under control, but as the trembling continued, he attempted to hide it, all to no avail. The shaking became so exaggerated that he sat on his arm, trying to still the movement. One of the medicine men spoke up and said that Kindle should go along with what the spirit was doing and see what happened.[2] He let it go, the shaking continued, and directed him to go inside the hogan, where he began to dig into the ground. Something told him that witchcraft and a lot of evil spirits were close by, just outside the door. Kindle continued describing his impressions, but his grandfather laughed away the idea of witchcraft, then asked, "Who would really be doing witchcraft around here?" Kindle followed his impressions, saddled his horse, and rode all the way to Shiprock with his hand still shaking.

The divinatory power that controls hand trembling, Tiníléí, a supernatural Gila monster, told Kindle that someone had bewitched his wife and that something of hers had been buried next to something "not good" under some rocks in a nearby canyon. The force guided Kindle to the location. Afraid that someone might see him, he was reassured by this presence that he would not be observed. On horseback Kindle headed toward Shiprock, ascending to the top of one of the huge rock wings that emanates from the side of the formation. After tethering his horse, he continued up the steep slope, asking which way to go. At first, no answer came, but a second time he learned he needed to go over another hill, where at the summit, he continued on a path that led under some rocks to a grave. His first urge was to dig into it and remove whatever item of Amy's had been buried there, but the hand trembling told him that he was not spiritually strong enough to withstand the power. In Kindle's words, "It seemed like it was telling me that it would kill me if I disturbed it and that I should not take it out." He learned that Amy was in the "Devil's stomach" or literally inside the stomach of a ghost. The person witching her had taken a piece of cloth that she had used when menstruating and had placed the blood-soaked material inside a corpse. Kindle learned that she could only be healed through a restoration prayer and that there was a medicine man who lived in the Many Farms area who should sing over her. Then the hand ceased its trembling and Kindle returned home.

He hired the medicine man from Many Farms, who sang over Amy for four days, followed by a second person who sang over her again. This time she got better. Hand trembling told Kindle that four individuals had ganged up to curse her and that they did not want her to live. The power also indicated that two of these individuals would soon die, and that the third would commit suicide, but that the fourth would live longer and that Kindle would see all of this come to pass. The following summer the first two died. The power told Kindle the third would commit suicide when he was attending a squaw dance. During the dance, this third man took off running and shot himself with a rifle. The fourth one was still alive, but Kindle had no idea who it was.

Speaking of this incident, Kindle said:

> One thing I learned is that if the hand points upward, the patient will be alright, but if it points downward, that is not good. If I got the impression that the patient was not going to live or get better, I would not tell them so as not to burden them with despair if I was wrong, which sometimes I am. When Amy was very ill, my hand pointed upward, indicating she would recover. It said that although she was sick, she would not die, would continue to get well, and in the future would walk in a good way. After this message, my arm just fell down and stopped trembling. She had a small Blessingway ceremony performed, followed by an Evilway. There were very strong prayers offered on her behalf, then a Protectionway ceremony with a há yá'át'ééh (it is good for one) ceremony to "secure liberation ceremonially by prayer." This is where the patient repeats the prayer along with the medicine man word for word. The hand that trembles can tell what bothers the mind. When the heart bothers someone, the hand shakes very roughly and cannot stop trembling, which seems to assist in the cure. In the past, the Blessingway used to be used for healing. So, it is speaking the evil spirits out of the person. All of these ceremonies were performed. Medicine men who are elders and conduct ceremonies, those who know crystal gazing, and Anglo doctors help me. All are beneficial, so I do not rely solely on Navajo ceremonies.

Kindle also used hand trembling to determine the cause and cure for his sick daughter Daisy. She had suddenly become ill with vomiting, headaches, and loss of appetite with no apparent reason to indicate a cause. Just as a sick person in Anglo culture might go to a general practitioner to narrow down tentative reasons for an illness and then turn to a specialist, Kindle began a broad spiritual search to determine what was wrong. While at his winter sheep camp, he invited Bob Putsch to record his prayers one January night in 1974. Kindle began by running fresh pollen down the length of his arm in a lightning bolt pattern, then praying on behalf of his daughter.

I am not asking a vague question about the future; I'm asking about this person. She does not know what is making her ill, so I am asking you about it today. What is it that is making her sick? What is causing her illness? It is for this reason that I am asking these questions and making an offering of beautiful corn pollen. Jóhonaa'éíí Nilíínii (One Who Is the Sun Father), I am making this offering of beautiful corn pollen to you. Today you will reveal the answer clearly to both of us. I am using you to discover the cause of her illness. There is nothing on earth that you are unable to do. We walk in your sun stream on this earth, and you know everything about our lives. You know what it is that may be ailing us, what is making us sick or maybe killing us. All this you know. It is for this reason that I made an offering to you. This is the purpose for which I am using you today. Who or what will make her well? There are the medicines and religion of the white man; perhaps she will get well using their medicine. There is also the medicine of the Hopi. Tell me, who or what will make her well? Once we have received your aid, well-being will come to this woman as she goes forward in life. Sun Father, I have prayed well and asked that the cause of her illness be known this day. It is in this way that I have prayed and sought your good help for her well-being.

This ended Kindle's first prayer. As mentioned, the Sun views everything that takes place on this earth and so will have seen and understood the cause of the illness. After a short pause, Kindle appealed to the holy being Gila Monster, who controls divinatory powers, the conduit through which an answer is received. As images and impressions of possible causes went through Kindle's mind, his hand indicated to him if what he was thinking and praying about was correct or if he was going astray from understanding what actually happened. His mention of a rock crystal, a technique related to stargazing, is another form of divining the truth. Beams of light and images within the stone are often part of learning an answer. Kindle commented:

Now this thing called crystal gazing, some elders know how to do. It happened for me just once. I tried in vain, but it does not work well for me. Hand trembling is not a plaything for entertainment and came to me suddenly. Well-being will come of this. I am addressing you, Black Gila Monster, as you lie sunwise with your body extending in four directions and resting just under the sacred mountain. Let that which shines on you shine on me. Move me with the black wind with which you move. Move me with the white wind with which you move. Move me with the yellow wind with which you move. Give me knowledge with your little winds, which give you knowledge. Shine on this thing with your rock crystals that you shine on us and by which you know everything. You will shine on it with your rock crystals, and by that you will make the answer known to me. Dark Gila Monster, I have asked you well as you lay to the east, resting sunwise under Naatsis'áán (Head of Earth Woman—Navajo Mountain), the sacred mountain. You said that if a person on earth offers corn pollen, you will tell them the correct answer, and I have made an offering to you this day; it will be the price for your telling her. It is said that you offered to tell the people and to help them when they made this gift to you. That is why this patient and I have used you here today. The gift of beautiful corn pollen has been made. This woman does not know what it is that is making her ill. I, too, do not know the cause of her illness. You, Gila Monster, know. It is said that you would offer to help the people someday. That is why I am using you today. The answer will be known to you today. Today we will learn what is bothering the patient. That is the reason I made the offering. There are all different kinds of animals that live in the sea; perhaps one of them is bothering the patient. There are a variety of different lizards on earth, each with different names. Their names are known to you. Then there are snakes of all varieties and names. Their names too are known to you. The different animals that live on earth are known to you, as are the different animals that live in the mountains. Their names and these animals are all known to you. Perhaps one of these is bothering her. I am asking you about this.

Putsch commented on this foregoing process, noting that in following translations, there was a seeming discrepancy. Both the translators were highly proficient, and yet when comparing directions used in the prayer, they were not the same. After questioning both translators and a third person, the mystery was solved. Putsch explained:

There is a set of prayers that are addressed to the moon and the Gila Monster, but there was a complex set of word changes that occurred when doing so. In those prayers, the Gila Monster is addressed in "the place where you are"—a sacred place—"in the west underneath the sunset" while David said it was in "the east underneath the sunrise." The second translator interpreted it as "to the west underneath the sunset." A third interpreter explained that, as in most Navajo ceremonies, the proper movement during a ritual is in a sunwise direction. Depending on the time of day, the Gila Monster would be moving sunwise and be located in the east in the morning or the west in the afternoon, following the same trajectory as the sun. One of the interpreters, however, changed the wording because he felt that there should not be an exact translation of the prayer, since to do so would be offensive to the holy people.

Kindle continued addressing the powers:

There are medicine men who sing the Holyway. These sacred ceremonies have different names. All of them are known to you. Furthermore, there are the Enemyway and the Evilway that can be used to make the patient well. I am asking you about these also. It is said the problem might arise from some physical injury. Perhaps that is what is bothering her. Is it a fever? I am asking you what it is that is bothering the patient. This is the reason I made an offering and need your help. Who or what will help her? White man's medicine or perhaps Navajo or Hopi medicine? The patient seeks her well-being through your assistance, and that is also the reason that I am using you. The cause will be made known to me by following after you; the knowledge will be revealed. This is the reason I have used you. You will be my lead, my holy one who will make it known to me. I have prayed like this to you, and you will tell the patient correctly. By your good help it will be known to the patient.

Kindle's approach may seem at times somewhat demanding, but what is being expressed is an almost contractual relationship between a medicine man and the holy beings. This covenantal transaction is based in two-way respect that operates on proper words in prayer and song, appropriate sacrifice as specified in the story that outlines the procedure, and a knowledge of the symbols given in response to the request. The holy being receiving the petition, if satisfied that the requirements have been met, gives an answer that tests the knowledge and understanding of

Divination is performed by both men and women. In this picture, a medicine person uses hand trembling to receive impressions as to why this woman is sick. The answer: she had come in contact with a lightning-struck tree, later requiring the Holyway ceremony called Lightning or Shootingway. The patient—sitting upright with legs extended—is using required ceremonial posture.

the recipient. This pattern of inquiring is an underlying theme in many of the mythological stories that serve as the root of the healing ceremonies. Perhaps the best-known example, out of many, is that of the Twins— Monster Slayer and Born for Water—when they visited their father, Sun Bearer. Their ability to prove their identity, obtain weapons to kill the monsters, and utilize the power they received was based in answering questions that required symbolic thinking. Hand tremblers and crystal gazers obtain their answers through the same means, drawing on their knowledge of the stories, sandpainting figures, natural phenomena, places, and events that teach a principle and provide an answer. The holy being giving the response tests one's knowledge and ability before rendering feedback. By Kindle offering a number of possibilities as to why Daisy was sick, he was opening up to the holy people his thinking so that they could indicate to him the cause. From there, one of a number of Navajo ceremonies known to cure a specific malady will be selected. This may require more than one, depending on the various symptoms involved and the effectiveness of each. Sometimes the same ritual will be repeated using a different medicine man. As with any healing process, whether involving Anglo or Navajo medicine, there are no guarantees that the first procedure will be totally effective. Hand trembling and other forms of divination are the gateway of diagnosis to begin the healing process.

Kindle also directed questions and reasoning with his daughter. Here is part of his conversation with Daisy: "Things seem okay, however, I wonder how it is? It seems that your head is hurting here to your eyes. Then there is also trouble behind at the back of your head. The pain appears to extend to your eyes and across your forehead. Finally, there may be pain or illness that has settled inside your abdominal area, which adds to your headache. It does not seem to be a severe injury, but might be the reason that food does not seem to agree with you." Next he returned to the holy people inquiring if elements healed by the Shootingway chant were bothering her and whether the image of the sun should be remade for her.

> It seems that whatever it is that makes her vomit is also causing the headache, so that should be treated first. What is making your body ill? Is it the operations you had in the past, those that the Anglos performed on you? Is that the main problem, the operations? You will likely improve in two days or so, once the medicine men have treated you. Your reason for not wanting food will suddenly be gone. However, it seems the reason you don't want food is your stomach, which causes your head to hurt. The first thing I thought of to cure this problem was Anglo medicine; however, the power said no. The Gila Monster said that Navajo medicine ways were how it really started, and so white man's medicine is not very good for this illness.

A conversation with David Kindle, Amy, and Daisy further assisted in diagnosing the cause and cure. Amy questioned Daisy, "Didn't you touch the lambs that were struck by lightning over there?" and Daisy responded, "Remember we carried them and dragged them around." Kindle by now had determined that the Male Shooting or Lightningway (Naʼatʼoyee Bikąʼjí), used to eliminate the effects of lightning-struck objects, must be performed. Regardless of how long ago the "injury" may have occurred, if an individual has come into contact with something hit by lightning, it can cause the symptoms of intense headaches, sleep-lessness, and general illness that Daisy was exhibiting. But before this ceremony could be performed, Kindle believed a briefer ritual, the "Remaking of the Sun" should be accomplished. "That is what is really bothering you. It is bothering your head. Then there is the need for the Lifeway (Lightningway), which is making you very ill and hurting you." In the separate ceremony of Remaking the Sun, a medicine man creates a sandpainting that portrays the sun. During the ritual, which lasts about four hours, the power of the sun is invoked in healing the patient. Kindle felt an urgency to see that this was done soon. Next came a lengthy dis-cussion about who would perform the healing rites. Snow-packed roads, medicine men attending a funeral, reputations about their effectiveness, and general availability were all considered. Although Nakai Chee Begay was most preferred, his attendance at a funeral for a very close relative and the subsequent four-day limited activity led to their second choice of Allen George, who met many of the above criteria. In Kindle's mind, the Making of the Sun ritual was paramount and must be performed immediately. Allen, a Lifeway singer, knew the main ceremony of Lightningway/Shootingway and the separate ritual of Remaking the Sun. Another important preparation to help Daisy was for her to inhale, smell, and sprinkle corn pollen in preparation for invoking the assistance of the holy people. A brief discussion took place between Kindle and Amy as to when preparations for the smoking should begin. Following these procedures and ceremonies, Daisy returned to good health. No further information as to how long the process took was given.

Asking the Right Questions, Following Impressions

Kindle became increasingly adept at using the power of hand trembling and confident that even when a sickness or injury reached outside of tra-ditional Navajo ceremonial healing, he would know what to do. He gave the impression that this was a special, additional skill that he received through traditional power.

> Whatever the illness, I am able to determine what it is and what is necessary to cure it. To this day, even though I am getting old, I am able to do that. There might be some people who do not believe in it or consider it inappropriate, but it works and we continue to use it. I

not only can understand what Navajo ceremonies are needed for an illness, but there are also sicknesses and injuries that are better handled through Anglo medicine. This ability came upon me, appearing on its own, and it is with me to this day. One time I was out herding sheep on foot when a car drove up. The people inside said, "Our boy, our son is dying. Despite having various ceremonies performed on him, he seems to be getting worse. Hand trembling needs to be done," I was told. Just his clothes were brought to me to pray over. They lived a long way away, perhaps fourteen or fifteen miles, but I did hand trembling on him. "How did this happen? Perhaps the horse did something to him; I wonder what the horse did to him." I determined it had hurt the boy; however, the illness was something the Navajos could not cure, but the Anglos could. I told them the doctors are the only ones who can determine what's wrong, but we must hurry. I knew Anglo medicine was needed, so that is what I told them. As the sun was going down, they immediately took him to the hospital in Shiprock. Later I was informed that the horse had thrown him, causing his sickness. I wished I could have said that the Navajo Lifeway ceremony should be done, but I realized only Anglo medicine would be of help. The parents sent the boy to either Window Rock or Gallup, where doctors took X-rays before they performed surgery the following day. His intestine had "twisted" [ruptured], so it appears that nothing could have been done with a ceremony. The Anglo doctors straightened his intestines out and he is still alive and well.

There are times that hand trembling does not work. I have misdiagnosed an illness on several occasions. It is good if done correctly. Now no one is learning these things, and so what will happen, what will it be like in future days? There is a big need for the practice to be relearned. It seems now that somewhere there is a person who cannot stop shaking. How can one like that be cured? There used to be a healing song for the purpose of curing those who shake. Now it is no longer available for anyone. It is only here in my mind. The Anglos who are our friends, the government is responsible for us. They know how things will become with the new ways of the Anglo. It is in vain trying to do anything. Our children can live in a good way by using it. Navajo medicine is also useful if done correctly; however, Anglo medicine is more advanced. We are behind in that technology. Anglo doctors know everything about our body, much more than we do. Hand trembling is not advanced, but we still use it.

Navajo people recognize that there are real benefits to using Anglo medicinal practices combined with traditional herbal and ceremonial remedies. The approach to illness may require different means, some physical, others spiritual. Therefore, it is not surprising that David Kindle, through hand trembling, appealed to the holy people to determine the best course of action for a particular patient.

Perhaps a year or two ago a man came to see me. I told him he had appendicitis and it meant to kill him and that a Navajo ceremony would not cure it. I directed him to go to the hospital immediately and only then would he be saved. He went that night, and they performed an appendectomy. Now he is alright and works for the hospital. I can't remember the Anglo name he goes by, but he is educated and understands English. It was with hand trembling that I diagnosed him, and he is not the only one I did this for. It has worked in many instances where my diagnosis has come true. Hand trembling does not lie, but it is rather about me trying to guess the correct answer in an attempt to determine the problem. That is when I may not receive the correct answer. If my thoughts are good and I ask the right questions, I know the necessary answer, telling me specifically what the issue is. Crystal gazing works in the same way for those who practice it. Others are now performing Peyoteway ceremonies. Perhaps it is true for these ceremonies as well. Hand trembling, however, is an ancient practice going back to our beginning, as is crystal gazing. There used to be Wind Listening, which also dates back to the time of our beginning, but there is no one who does that now. It seems crystal gazing is somewhat disappearing as well. There is only one type left called Enemyway crystal gazing. Those who still practice crystal gazing should teach about it. That is what I am doing now on hand trembling. There are specific songs and prayers that go with it, and so I hope that those who know these things will pass them down. Hand trembling uses and respects corn pollen as its path. Without an offering of corn pollen, it is just entertainment, but when it is held sacred and used, then hand trembling gives you what you are seeking. It seems the use of corn pollen and the songs that go with hand trembling are disappearing, as are our ceremonies. This is what I think about.

One might ask what the experience has been for members of the Anglo community who have encountered hand trembling by medicine men. There are, of course, those who are nonbelievers. For those who have worked extensively on the reservation and rubbed shoulders with medicine men practicing divination, many do not dismiss its effects, ranging in acceptance from staunch believers who are unable to explain how it works but have witnessed some amazing events to the other end of the spectrum and those who categorize it more as faith-healing or good guessing. Bob Putsch shared two accounts of what he has encountered. In 1974 Dr. Taylor McKenzie, who was the first Navajo medical doctor and would later become vice president of the Navajo government, discussed with Putsch a case he had in which he observed, as a Navajo but non–medicine man, the effects of hand trembling. Putsch related the incident, in which we will use the fictitious name of Henry.

Taylor asked me if I knew a Navajo legal aide named Henry. He apparently came with his wife to see Taylor, both wanting to discuss a problem he was experiencing. About a year ago, he began to notice that he could tell what was going to happen in the future.

I guess he did this thing like going along in the car listening to music or something when all of a sudden, his hand would start trembling. It happened once when he and his wife were on their way to Gallup. Next, he saw things and began having visions. He was worried about what might happen to him. The DNA office [Navajo legal services] had been having a lot of trouble, and he had come to talk to Taylor about what was going on.[3]

Henry decided that the office was witched, so he discussed it with the person in charge, who eventually gathered all of the Navajo people employed there and brought in a medicine man. The healer decided that the site had truly been cursed. Henry told Taylor that was why there were so many difficulties for a lengthy period of time at the DNA office, but that they had taken steps to have the problem fixed. By doing so, Henry felt that he had prevented some bad things from happening and that he had the ability to foresee future events. Both he and his wife were quite concerned about it. Taylor was sitting there, trying to explain to them what was happening, but he supposed he should have sent them to David Kindle or someone like that. Henry's wife had been quite worried about him, but she had also noticed that these things really had been taking place. She came along with him and sat there, afraid about his being crazy.

I asked Taylor whether he knew anything about how Henry had discovered that his hand was trembling, if it had been around the time of a ceremony, if he knew anything about the wife's family, and had there been any troubles they may have had or experienced with hand trembling. He said that she was college educated and he did not know much about her family, other than that her parents were Navajo. I then discussed the fact that some people are quite afraid of hand tremblers or fearful of having the sign of hand trembling appear in themselves. For this reason, the ceremony is used at times to either prevent someone from having to go on to accept the power and become a hand trembler or to take care of problems caused by being a hand trembler. I pointed out that Henry was probably having considerable internal conflict about what was happening to him, especially in light of his legal training and the fact that both he and his wife had college degrees. Also, difficulties that one or both of them might have with fears of hand trembling or problems that their families have had with hand trembling, creating considerable difficulty for both of them. For this reason, I suggested that it would be appropriate for him to have Henry talk to some medicine men about what was happening to him.

A second example that involved Putsch more directly was with a patient he had at the Shiprock hospital in his earlier days there. He recorded the incident in 1977. It is particularly interesting, as both sides of Anglo and Navajo medicine were brought to bear on a very sick Navajo woman, and the diagnoses were starkly different. The technical, scientific explanation delineated the physical problems couched in the world of specialist doctors. To an outsider, unschooled in the language and functions of modern medicine, it could be bewildering. On the Navajo side, steeped deeply within their culture, it was a spiritual issue that needed to be corrected within their recognizable Navajo realm. Putsch, as an observer in both worlds, shared his observations.

> We had a patient who was the mother of one of the workers at the Shiprock hospital. She had terrible microvalve disease, a rheumatic heart disease problem that involved her having her microvalve operated on. She'd had her sternum split, had heart surgery, and fought a lengthy struggle with diabetes. Eventually the repair to her valve became restricted, with the doctors unsure she could survive a repeat surgery. Today there is medicine to remedy this.
>
> She was always at risk for strokes, and in fact, had one that wiped out her ability to produce normal speech. As far as we could tell, she understood commands like "sit up" or "do you need help out of bed?" She would say "yes," so the staff thought she was receiving messages normally, but had lost her speech ability. She also had a problem called "polycythemia," which is when the number of red blood cells in a body reached a point that the patient would have abnormally thick blood, which was partly related to her heart failure and other troubles, including her stroke. She was a complex old woman.
>
> Some family members approached me after we had worked on trying to sort out her problems as best as we could. They wanted to take her home to Lukachukai to see a diagnostician and have a ceremony performed. Fanny, her daughter, asked if that would be alright. I said yes, and then Fanny asked if I would like to come and bring my wife, Poo, and I agreed. Would I be willing to go in our car? At that point, I thought, "Oh man, I just got caught. I have been invited to a ceremony just because they want to use my vehicle and gas," which was not the case, but it seemed like it at the time. The family was actually

convinced, as it turned out, that she had been bewitched in the past by some neighbors, and they did not want anybody to know whose vehicle it was. In that country, one of their cars would be recognized immediately. But if my car showed up, it would be a wholly different deal.

The sick woman had been seen by two diagnosticians, one of whom I had gotten to know pretty well because he was always doing hand trembling on patients, going around the ward performing this service. His name was Chííh Hąą (Ochre on Him). He did hand trembling for her, then drew a picture of the camp and said, "You have a summer house here where there is a fence and a little dry creek that runs near it. The reason for the fence is that the family put it there because some of the neighbors had cursed her before." Another hand trembler saw her while she was still in the hospital. This man was very polite, coming from the checkerboard area and was dressed like a fancy Native American cowboy in a dressy western outfit. The family said they wanted to see more hand trembling performed, and so they hired this man. He said that someone had shot something into her neck and that was how they cursed her. Our group—me; my wife, Poo; the grandmother, Fanny; and Allen Brady, her husband—got into the car, with Allen carrying a gun. I asked him why he had brought it, since he had never had one before.

We drove to Lukachukai and met with Carson Tsosie, a school bus driver from Red Rock, Arizona, whom I had met before. I had not been aware that he was a hand trembler until then. I also learned he was a crystal gazer. It was one of those times when I watched a diagnostician use more than one technique, as he started with crystals, then went to hand trembling. Carson began with the grandmother by removing her top and going up, down, and over her, looking for trouble through his crystals while chanting. The content of his song I could not tell you. Next, he threw her hair over the front of her head and sucked out something hard, giving her a big hickey on the back of her neck, then spitting out a small piece of bone into a napkin. He said that was what they shot into her neck and why she had trouble talking. He repeated the same procedure on the front of her neck. Allen, the son-in-law, looked at me and asked if I had seen what had been removed, reminding me that it was just what the hand tremblers in Shiprock had told the family—that something had been shot into her neck.

Carson then excused himself in English to Poo and me saying, "I'm going to act a little crazy." It was the first time we had heard any English. He put down his crystals and started hand trembling. Unlike other diagnosticians, he did not put pollen down his arm and bless it, but just started whacking himself in the head as his arm began jerking; he excused himself, went outside, and vomited in front of the hogan. We could hear him. He then went around the hogan, vomiting each time he passed the door. When Carson reentered the hogan, he announced that he could see that something was wrong, that those who had witched her had done things up in a nearby canyon, and that we had to go find it. Again, my car became the topic of conversation.

We all got in the car, with Carson Tsosie sitting in the front with me, and Allen with another man in the back, both with guns. Carson had told Poo, Fanny, and the grandmother to stay behind, that he would leave his medicine bundle exposed with the crystals out, and that they should keep an eye on the stones to see if one of them started glowing. If it did, someone should pick it up and blow on it because something was wrong where we were going. Carson implied that this was a dangerous outing as we left for the canyon. When we got out of the car, he used his crystals again to find his way up behind a rock, where he located a stick-like drawing. It was obviously a woman because it had breasts. He spent a lot of time cleaning it off the rock, then did a blessing. He found a bottle of pills from the public health hospital on the ground underneath the rock, started a fire, blessed everything, and cleaned the whole area. While we were doing this, we heard a bird singing. Carson said, "There is something wrong back in camp."

We returned to the women by 3:30 a.m. to find a frightened Fanny. The neighbors whom everybody accused of witchcraft had shown up at the camp about 1:30 in the pitch-black morning. They knocked on the door, Fanny answered, told them that everything was alright, and essentially invited them to leave. Carson said, "They know that she is here, that we are removing the curse, so it is not safe for her to stay. She needs to go back to the hospital." Fanny, distressed over the situation, asked Carson to check her out, so he went over her with the crystals and reassured her that she had no symptoms of witching. What an experience. We barely made it back to Shiprock in time to brush our teeth and return to work at the hospital.

When Putsch was later asked if all of the events and "coincidences" he had witnessed during the entire episode were by chance or did they really happen as they appeared, he responded:

> I can either come to the conclusion, if I wanted to be a confirmed skeptic, that this was one of the most elaborately orchestrated hoaxes I've ever seen, like a good show on TV. Carson would have had to stop up there and take care of that rock drawing on his way down because he came down the same road we did. Or these circumstances are evidence that hand trembling really does work. My only bias is this: if you are caught up in this world and you do not do it for your mother or grandmother, you are going to be in deep trouble if she doesn't survive. You just do what you need to do! And I've heard it from almost every family I've ever taken care of. Somebody dies—and you better have done everything you possibly could.

David Kindle and similar Navajo diagnosticians live in a world of power. They understand how to interact with the holy people and use their teachings to help others, while at the same time they work against those who wish to cause harm. They assist those who have made mistakes and need to correct a problem to obtain hózhǫ—a state of well-being. Following a diagnosis, they can prescribe what type of cure is most helpful—one from Navajo healing ceremonies or one emphasizing Anglo physical medicine. But Kindle's understanding and powers did not stop with divination. As the next chapter shows, he also performed the Windway ceremony and participated in other rituals, all based in the traditional knowledge that he shared. Thankfully, his insight has been preserved.

CHAPTER SIX

Practices of a Medicine Man

Framing the World through Stories, Songs, and Prayers

D avid Kindle, as a knowledgeable medicine man and diagnostician, had a broad understanding of different Navajo ceremonies.
He knew that once a patient's illness became apparent, the
next step was to determine the most effective cure to meet the need
as outlined in the origin story of that remedy. The connection through
the story explained the way the cure came about, performance of the
ceremony, required materials, songs and prayers, length, time of day
performed, seasonal restrictions, location, and level of participation,
among other things. The complexity of these philosophical underpin-
nings, when combined with the number and type of rites, suggests that
Navajo religion is one of the most sophisticated and involved of all of the
North American Indian belief systems. In this chapter, Kindle opens the
door on a number of different ceremonies, with emphasis on the sacred
narratives from which they were derived along with a short discussion
about what is required for a cure.

Kindle, speaking with Robert Putsch, set the stage with his understanding of the beginning.[1]

These stories were passed down from men a long time ago. Some of their words I will tell you so that you can put them down for use in future days. A long time ago these medicine men began their teachings as chanters who sang, but now they loan us their words for days to come. Navajo people will learn them, and their medicine will be available again. People used to know these teachings, but they have been forgotten. Some men say they are relearning them, but really none are. We were training apprentices as medicine men to follow our teachings, but now I feel these practices are really gone. Perhaps by tape recording them, it will be a good way of learning in the future. A long time ago, when men wanted to learn, they would sit beside a medicine man who smoked mountain tobacco and taught the songs and prayers. The teacher and the apprentice would rehearse them in their mind to learn them well. Only someone who really loves you will take the time to teach you in this way, and give you what he knows. I learned from Slim Policeman [Amy Kindle's father], who said to me, "In future days when I get to old age, you must take care of me." I agreed, so in return, he taught me and counted on me to keep the prayers and songs safe.

Broadly, what Kindle learned are the songs and prayers that emerge from each of the sacred narratives. They are memorized and internalized, then used to heal the patient through a ceremony. But songs and prayers are also part of everyday life and may accompany the most mundane activities, whether grinding corn, building and maintaining a home, traveling to a trading post, or preparing food. In the Navajo world everything from animals and birds to rivers and mountains to plants and tools have their own songs, prayers, and powers. For example, Kindle gave a brief discussion about caring for his livestock and the songs that are sung during different times of the day. "In the Navajo way, we have what are called sheep songs. When one knows them, even if the sheep do not look good and are not pretty, when they come out of the corral they will be blessed. It is just as true for horses. They will become beautiful when they reproduce. There are just four sheep songs, each one representing part of their daily activity. The first one is about the livestock leaving the corral, then spreading out on the land, returning home, and finally going back into the corral." These songs protect and direct the sheep in their daily travels and implant in them their goal of assisting the shepherd and his or her family. The corral reflects a number of similar values associated with the hogan, which has entire rituals and procedures as prescribed by the holy people. Like the hogan, the corral is round and made of wood, the entryway faces east, the gateposts represent wealth derived from soft and hard goods, it is a place of prayer, and it is visited by the holy people.

A few lines from these four songs underscore their importance while providing an example of how they work. The first song of releasing the sheep from their home (dibé bighan) mentions that White Shell Woman and her white horse are present, the shepherd and animals are shielded from harm, a corn pollen (blessing) is in the shepherd's mouth, and they are part of an assortment of horses and sheep that walk and graze across the land: "With me it is beautiful." The second song amplifies the good things that happen as the animals are accompanied by "White Shell Woman on her turquoise horse with me," ensuring protection. The holy person's mount has changed from white, color of the east and the morning, to blue, color of the south and midday. Song three is sung as the shepherd returns: "With me it is good. . . . The corn pollen is coming back with me; a variety of material goods return with me [what the sheep will bring in the future]; a variety of horses [future] come back with me; and a variety of sheep, all of which is protected, that I might succeed." The fourth song repeats these images as the animals enter their corral with the dust floating in the air like corn pollen. White Shell Woman on her turquoise horse, a red flicker bird, a mirage stone, and corn pollen, each having been mentioned in previous verses, have given their protection, and all is well. "A variety of hard goods return with me," as the sheep and herder are safely home. Kindle ended by noting, "Here my song is in place," then turning to Putsch, who had been recording them, and saying, "Through the days for me these songs will be present. Material goods and things of value will favor me. White Shell Woman will favor me because these things are preserved and protected in a place, even though far away [preserved in a library]. My songs have been recorded and now will be safe. Through the days, into the future, my songs will be available to be heard. May material and valuable goods, white shell and other valuables favor me, that I may possess them. May my prayers and songs stay with me always. It is like that."

Anatomy of Sickness

In Navajo thought, both a physical and spiritual component can cause disease and illness. By providing a traditional teaching about how a particular malady first appeared, it presents something concrete, making the cause understandable. Whereas Anglo medicine discusses an illness in terms of bacteria, microbes, and blood cells, often difficult to comprehend because of their complexity, especially when combined with a reaction to medicines and procedures, the Navajos provide a story, metaphor, or image that is both understandable and believed in a very real sense to be the cause of the sickness. These are two different approaches to the same problem. Kindle, in discussing the origin of sexually transmitted diseases, illustrated their origin and traditional cure from a Navajo perspective:

A long time ago in Arizona there was a big male Gila monster who used to live like humans. One day he saw smoke in the distance and decided to go and investigate why it was rising from Coyote Canyon. As he walked along on his journey, suddenly lizards came out from wherever they lived onto the path to meet him. There were all types— some that were long, had green stripes, and ran really fast. Others were small and gray and lived among the rocks and greasewood; there were also tree lizards as well as tiny ones that sit on the tips of plants. One of them was a dark-skinned man who was very fat and led this group of very handsome male and female lizards whose faces were colored red. Once they had gathered around him, the Gila monster asked where they were going. "We are on our way to hunt and you are invited to join us." He decided to go with them over to White Rock, where the sagebrush protrudes. Once they got there, they heard the deer talking from within the tall brush, but the man could not see them. "Where are they, my grandchild, my son-in-law," he was asked, but he still could not spot any. Many of the lizards broke off in pairs and entered the sagebrush. The man saw no deer, just lots of flies, so he killed nothing. The Holy Wind told the young man to hurry and look for a gray rabbit. As he was running, he startled one that darted under a rock. The man reached in and pulled the rabbit out, then was directed to tear it down the middle, leaving behind part of the skin attached to some meat. He sat there watching the carcass and a host of flies gathering on it, then started swatting at them four times.

Finally the boys and girls approached. "What are you doing my friend? Why are there so many flies? This is what we call deer," they said. "Thank you for helping us." The leader instructed one of the boys to go back to their home. "We will butcher here and haul all of this meat today," he said. They began to butcher as a large number of flies began to swarm. The gray lizards lived inside a well-built underground wooden structure, but just outside they built their fires. These were the origin of the smoke the male Gila monster had seen. The gray lizards continued to butcher and haul all day long as others were cooking near their home. Some of these female lizards were real pretty, and everyone referred to the big lizard as their in-law even though they did not know him. He ended up having a sexual relationship with one of the pretty lizard girls.

The man took his kill and joined them, but Holy Wind warned him not to eat any of the food they prepared. Even after he was served some, he tried to avoid eating it, but there was stew slathered with lots of fat, which looked appetizing. "I would like to taste some," he thought, and so he put it in his mouth. After swallowing, he became sick and infested with maggots that began eating his groin area. After four days he could barely walk because of the syphilis he had contracted. His buttocks and groin became swollen and inflamed, caused by the lizard girl he slept with who was eating flies. Germs reside in flies and maggots, and since the lizards were eating them as their staple food, he contracted the sickness. Holy Wind told him to pull a particular herb out of the ground, boil it, and drink the juice. He set off to find one of these plants that grew near Tohatchi in the Chuska Mountains. After locating one, Holy Wind told him to pull off some of the petals from the plant's flower and continue his search. He descended toward a place called Gray Checkered Juniper, where he found more of them. This time, Holy Wind directed him to dig up the whole plant with its roots, because he would need it in the future. He then boiled these roots, drank the broth, killed the maggots, and flushed his system by vomiting. Holy Wind told him he was now himself again.

Kindle further explained his beliefs:

Syphilis and gonorrhea did not come from the Navajos, but from Blacks, Mexicans, and Anglos, yet it was initially introduced in the past by the lizard people. It is a bad disease that attacks the kidneys and eyes; that is how it kills. If someone has been infected many times with syphilis or gonorrhea, when they have children it will harm their eyes, kidneys, and urine. This began with the flies. The germs are in

In June 1968 David Kindle attended a conference with medicine people from a number of tribes in Denver, Colorado, to discuss the topic "Can the Red Man Help the White Man?" This picture was taken at that time. His willingness to share much traditional information was part of that answer—for both cultures.

the maggots that come from flies, which introduce the disease into the body. When the Navajo people were in captivity at Fort Sumner, these diseases spread, but it all started with the lizards. The stories tell us that this is how syphilis began. Many died at Fort Sumner from this sickness. I don't know if there is anyone left who knows how to treat it. Blindness also came to us. This illness makes groin sores as the maggots work against us. So flies are very dangerous, as are the birds that eat them. We used to say that lizards are not good and that snakes can spread cancer. Crows and eagles are also dangerous because snakes are the eagle's food, just as flies are the lizard's food. Cancer is dangerous, which crows and eagles can carry. Now you see Anglos handling eagles, who in the future can be infected with cancer. This is how Navajo stories are told and how I know it to be.

Smoking as a Restorative

Kindle continued by discussing the traditional value of tobacco.

Around Shiprock, the Monsterway ceremony, which came from the War Twins when they first visited this area, was practiced. What I am about to tell you is just the main part of the story and not the detailed version. When the Twins traveled to meet Sun Bearer for the first time, they received help along the way from different holy people. One of them was Caterpillar, who gave them a small wad of medicine to counteract the effects of a poisonous tobacco that Sun Bearer would use to test the identity of the two boys. After the Twins had passed all of the necessary trials, had confirmed that Sun Bearer was truly their father, and had received four types of sacred arrows that they could use to kill the monsters on earth, they smoked mountain tobacco as part of a final purification before departing. Sun Bearer counseled them that if they killed something, they could lose their minds if they did not follow the proper procedures. One of these was to use mountain smoke to purify themselves as part of the ritual to remove evil influences. Smoking took away any harm, returning them to a peaceful composure. This is when the tobacco ceremony began, which is connected to many, if not all, of the first ceremonies.

Sun Bearer further explained to the Twins that Big God (Yé'iitsoh), the first monster they would kill when they returned to earth, was actually their older brother and his son. He was sad as he put lightning arrows of jet black flint in their hands, a gift from the heavens, and told them, "Just as soon as you return from killing the giant, smoke mountain tobacco immediately. When you do this, your mother will ask why you are smoking mountain tobacco. You must not tell her. You will just do it four times and your mind will begin to be healed. In the future, how you smoke mountain tobacco will be remembered and the ceremony will become useful. It is a present from Mother Earth; you will gather it from the top of Sleeping Ute Mountain, Mount Taylor, the San Francisco Peaks, La Plata Mountain, Huerfano Mesa, and Gobernador Knob. Plants collected from these places will fix a person's mind when troubled. In the future, when a man or woman talks and acts crazily, even though they have not been drinking, they can be cured with a good way of thinking that restores the mind to normal."

Sure enough, when the Twins killed Big God they returned and smoked mountain tobacco. Their mother asked for some, saying, "What a sweet aroma. Lend me some, my children," but Monster Slayer remembered how he had been counseled and so told her not to ask for it. "I will not talk about it." Four times she begged to try some until finally, she took one puff, then rolled over. After gaining her mental stability, she puffed twice and rolled over again. After inhaling four times, that was enough. Smoking mountain tobacco and singing its song began to cure her mind, and so it may be used by both men and women to heal their minds. No one over here now knows the mountain tobacco ceremony. I am the only one around who still sings the mountain tobacco song, and I no longer have the tobacco that comes from Blanca Peak, Mount Taylor, San Francisco Peaks, and the La Plata Mountains. I only use what grows locally that can be picked at Sleeping Ute Mountain or the Moqui Buttes. It has big, wide leaves and is strong but is hard to find, while thin tobacco is found in areas where sheep graze.

Deer eat the roots of the plant found in the mountains, and if it chews part of it or some other plant and lets it drop out of its mouth, this should be dried, ground up with other ingredients, then smoked as mountain tobacco. Deer, because they are associated with

the mountains and eat medicine plants found there, are part of what
is mixed and served as medicine in the mountain tobacco. They have
chewed on the piñon tree, young juniper tree, mountain mahogany,
and cliffrose. These are all used and are part of the story of the creation
of various types of animals. A thin plant called Rat's Ears, which smells
like rat urine and is hard to get, is also used and has a separate song. I
spent one summer with a person named Lefthand Man, and he taught
me what I know about smoking mountain tobacco. I only have a small
part of his knowledge. He also taught me the Enemy Monsterway.
Each time I talked with him I learned more and was able to put it in
order, which I have with me now. My hand trembling is separate from
that. Over here, wild game is what bothers the mind.

Young boys and girls as they mature have many impressions
placed in their minds, some of which are not good. By the time they
reach adulthood, there are thoughts that are harmful and need to be
straightened out. Only with mountain tobacco smoke can these things
be removed. In the Blessingway ceremony, when one smokes mountain
tobacco, the mind is helped, and Mother Earth will continue to provide
it for our use if we use the ceremony. The Blessingway begins and ends
with this tobacco.

Before continuing with Kindle's teachings, there is another version,
often cited, as to how the use of mountain tobacco originated. When the
Navajos began to live in their present location, the holy people created
the mountains of Navajo land from materials brought from beneath
this world. Each mountain had its own personality, and like many of
the holy people, their own trials and triumphs. They were situated and
dressed in clothing that indicated their direction of white shell (east),
turquoise (south), abalone (west), and jet (north). At one point, Mount
Taylor went crazy, cutting off her dress of turquoise and doing strange
things with her hair. The other mountains became upset, and so the gods
placed mountain tobacco on their slopes so that they could smoke the
plant and settle down. The plan worked, ensuring that the mountains
would remain quiet to this day. This story is applied to today's youth,
who are wearing strange fashions and unacceptable hairdos, and who
act irresponsibly when compared to traditional Navajo values. The elders
warn that if they continue to do this, they will not reach old age with
white hair (snow) as the mountains have because they have remained
unsettled.[2]

There are a number of different types of sacred tobacco used in healing ceremonies to cure certain ailments such as water tobacco for a near drowning and sheep tobacco to settle a flock, but mountain tobacco, sometimes comprising as many as eighteen different plants, is the most common. Mary Blueyes discussed its origin and use as another explanation to accompany that of Kindle. She offered:

> It is said that one time the mountains were acting out and emotionally in trouble, seeming to have gone crazy. The holy people directed that they smoke some mountain tobacco to settle them down. It is called dá'ák'ǫǫzh taa', which I use to help patients, and there is also bidahochii, another type of smoke. There is one called Dibé Nát'oh (sheep tobacco, Lambert Locoweed). It was given as an offering to the four sacred mountains, which settled them down. That is what happened, before they started out in the Blessingway. Whenever a person goes somewhat crazy, acts strangely, loses their mind, or wanders off unknowingly, then they should smoke mountain tobacco to return to a peaceful, orderly life. Just as with the mountains in the beginning, they will settle down. The young man or woman becomes better again. The ceremony uses a buckskin from an unwounded deer, upon which the tobacco is spread. A man will give a prayer, use a tobacco offering, and provide the smoke that heals his patient, who becomes better and will walk about feeling well. It happened to one of my granddaughters from Chinle. She used to walk off, rambling around until someone brought her back. A man named Hastiin Ba'aaztaanih performed the mountain smoke ritual for her, using a buckskin, and she became well. Now, she walks about with no problems and has two children. That is how it is done, so many ceremonies include this smoke.[3]

Medicine Pouch and Tobacco

Before delving deeper into different ceremonies, it would be helpful to continue Kindle's teachings about the deerskin used to hold ritual objects. In Navajo thought there are two types of deerskin—one that is taken through hunting an animal by using a weapon such as a bow and arrow or rifle. The deer—before, during, and after it is killed—is treated with great respect, its hide being used for clothing, tools, and barter, while its meat is viewed as medicine because of the plants it has eaten.

The second type of hide is from an "unwounded" or "unharmed" deer, the buckskin (dook'aak'éheji) being without holes or puncture wounds. It is highly prized and used for ceremonial objects, pouches, and medicine bundles. In the old days, these deer were pushed to exhaustion by a relay of runners, or later by men on horseback, before they were captured and smothered by a bag with pollen placed over its head before strangling it with a rope. The hide remained unblemished.

Mountain plants, deer that live upon the mountains and eat those plants, and this animal's association with mental and physical healing are all interconnected. Kindle shared part of a lengthy story, not always as clear and straightforward as desired, but that outlines a general basis for the origin of how this practice of obtaining the first unwounded buckskin came about. He began:

> There are parts of the story that are missing, so I will have to fill them in, but it will not alter the theme. The area called Where It Fell Over was a difficult place to survive. The people hunted and made meat jerky, but still struggled to find enough food. One man walked far and wide on foot, but found that everything that could be eaten was disappearing. Suddenly deer tracks appeared going in a clockwise direction heading east. He located the deer lying under a piñon tree before it bolted off to the east. The next day the man spied deer tracks again and followed them, circling around the animal twice. He went north, where he found a small juniper tree with a deerskin beneath it. He put it on and began to walk with the Holy Wind (Nílch'ih). It is said he became a deer and continued to travel alongside other deer. This is our story for teaching young boys. To the south, behind a small juniper, he found a deerskin, which he tied to his hair and walked along with the deer before returning home.
>
> The next day there were more deer tracks. He followed them and found one lying under a rock. From behind it, he donned the deerskin and began moving so quietly that he was able to sneak up on it until the animal realized what was happening and ran off to the west. The man gave up and returned home. For four days, he pursued the deer in each of the cardinal directions.
>
> The last day he continued his search by following deer tracks to the north, where he found a fallen tree beneath a cliffrose bush. From behind this plant, he dressed in the deerskin again, approaching very closely, but this time, he prayed over the yellow part of a ripened yucca

stalk, which through spiritual power he shot internally into the deer, overpowering and killing it. He found the dead animal with blood flowing from its mouth and nose as it lay in the shadows of a fallen juniper tree, having been bewitched by the arrow. To this day witchery exists because of this event. He was now called a holy man because the ceremony had begun here.

Kindle suggested that the bow and arrow that the hunter carried fell to the ground and were useless. It was supernatural power, not physical arrows, that killed the deer, leaving the hide "unwounded." Anthropologist W. W. Hill, author of *The Agricultural and Hunting Methods of the Navaho Indian*, a definitive work on this topic, describes ritual hunting in this manner.[4] The Witchway of hunting was used to kill a large deer by a single individual. "The chanter went to a broad-leafed yucca and obtained two or three new shoots from the center of the plant. Then he removed some dirt from the deer tracks and placed it upon the leaves. On the dirt the hunter put four pieces of iron ore, over which he said prayers and sang. When he finished, he knew that the deer was dead." He then followed the tracks, located the animal, and butchered it using certain ritual songs that others should not hear. This procedure closely follows the story outlined by Kindle, who appeared to be describing one of four types of witchcraft, this one being known as wizardry. The foreign object "shot" into the deer or person is referred to as an "arrow" and leaves no mark on the body; it may be removed from a victim by a medicine man sucking it out after reciting certain prayers.

Kindle continued: "The hunter took the hide he had obtained to a little sandy hill, where he found a doorway that opened for him. He entered and found a clean, beautiful home with a man sitting in a corner preparing to do a sandpainting, but who refused to speak to the hunter." Most likely the man resting on the floor was the over-spirit representing the deer or Talking God, who controls these animals. Eventually through pleading and showing respect, the relationship warmed, and a discussion about how to make medicine pouches began. They considered various colors used to prepare the skin—white clay, yellow ochre, and red ochre—then the holy being told the man to cut out a bag for tobacco.

Here he was introduced to how to make a medicine pouch. On one side he drew the sun, on the other side the moon. He sewed it up, then put tobacco and a prayer stick inside. Just then the spirit man picked up the pouch and examined it. He looked at it on one side, then turned it around and looked at the other side, asking, "Who instructed you, grandson?" and receiving the answer, "No one. I made it just like that on my own."

"You did a fine job, and only you know my price. You think that I do not go anywhere and just sit here to take care of my children. Do not say you are in a hurry to smoke." He then made plans and set a date for a ceremony, putting his hand inside the medicine bag to withdraw a prayer stick with a single notch that smelled like tobacco; this prayer stick now became his price.

"Okay grandson, my medicine pouch is outside under a juniper tree. Bring it in." The hunter went out and returned three times but could not find it. The old man urged that he had left it under a juniper when he prepared it. "I saw the medicine pouch. It was there a little while ago. There was something that had softened the bark of the juniper and pushed it inside. Now get it." On his fourth attempt, the hunter found the medicine pouch, brought it in, and placed it beside him. Now the old man told the hunter to sit backward, as he smoked the mountain tobacco, lifting it to the Sun, then puffing it four times. A change began to take place. The bundle, called pine squirrel medicine pouch, was not very pretty, but contained coal, white clay, yellow ochre, and four different prayer sticks colored black, blue, yellow, and white, each with its own number of notches. They also had inserted in them eyes that were dark with white in the middle.

Thus, with help from the holy people, the Navajo received a medicine pouch with prayer sticks and materials to summon powers that would otherwise be unavailable for mankind.

Killer Bear

Navajos often relate to many of the different ceremonies as being part of a main stalk of corn that branches out to connected teachings and rituals. Kindle's rendering of a little-known story and ceremony derived from it offers a good example of how it is tied to other rituals associated with the powers of the mountains and their creatures. Little has been recorded elsewhere of this ceremony called Bearway, a ritual that "sits within" or may accompany the well-known Mountainway ceremony used

Pictured here is the anatomy of a ceremony. Prayer sticks surrounding this large sand-painting summon the holy people, who are depicted in this multicolored representation made from charcoal, sand, and crushed minerals ground to a fine powder on the small rock slab to this medicine man's left. Next to it are medicine pouches made from unwounded buckskin. The gourd rattle, with sacred stones within, creates sounds that connect the heavens with the earth and is used in Windway, Nightway, and Featherway ceremonies. The singer sits on the west side of the hogan with the sandpainting opening to the east. The holy people recognize him by his headband and turquoise.

to cure people bothered by mental illness, fainting spells, and delirium. Healing powers and teachings come from specially ordained animals, with bears being in charge of those creatures found in the mountains and serving as a medicine doctor over plants growing there. In Kindle's words, "It is said that Bear has told us, 'I am in charge of the plants that are in place on the mountains. Only I am in charge of them.'" Bears are holy beings who serve as earthly representatives of the gods and share a complex relationship as both physical and spiritual overseers of what occurs during the annual cycle in their domain. Sometimes exhibiting qualities of love and wisdom, other times of warlike ferocity, the bear becomes emblematic of human nature, both good and bad.[5] Kindle's story of Killer Bear (Shash Agháani) was the basis for a ceremony that healed the patient by removing stress and strains and placing them on a path of mental health.

His story begins with some of the Bear People leaving Mount Hesperus (Dibé Nitsaa—Big Sheep), Colorado, and traveling through southeastern Utah, into New Mexico, and finally to Arizona. They began their journey by following Little Stream Canyon (Tónits'ósí Kooh), where the water talked to the Bear People, saying there were places they needed to go and important things that were going to happen in the future. They traveled through Little Canyon to a dome-shaped rock that looks like a hogan [Church Rock] near the road [Highway 191] between today's Moab and Monticello. There they spent the night. The next day of travel took them to the north side of the Carrizo Mountains and Teec Nos Pos (T'iis Názbạs—Cottonwoods in a Circle), where they camped for a few days by a brook flowing from the mountain. This water also spoke to them in their dreams, urging them to continue their travels to the west to Ugly Canyon (Bikooh Hóchxọ'ó), then on to Canyon with a Pointed House (Tsé Nit'ááh Hooghan). At each of these stops there were "houses" or places to stay, all the way past the Lukachukai (Lók'a'jígai—Reeds Extend White) Mountains to Tsaile (Tsééh Yílí—Where the Water Enters a Box Canyon) and Sonsola Buttes (Sọ Sila—Stars Lying Down), which has a body of water nearby. This place is now called The Lake That Sits There but used to be known as The Water That Breathes and Moans. There were no streams feeding in or out of it.

Once the bear couple reached it, they dug a trench that drained the water to the south, into other rivers and eventually the ocean. From the sea came a Water Monster that looked like a water horse (tééh łį́į') but also had the qualities of a cow with its wide nose, big nostrils, and little horns. This creature took up residence in the waters of the lake, where it gave birth to a little boy. One day the bear couple heard a baby crying on top of Sonsola Buttes nearby. The Water Monster had left the infant in a circular enclosure made of juniper trees, the kind used in the fire dance during the Mountainway ceremony. This is the beginning of the Tóee or Waterway ceremony because of the boy coming from the tééh łį́į', and the Mountainway ceremony with the discovery of the baby in the center of the sacred circle within the enclosure. Three different ceremonies—Mountainway, Waterway, and Bearway—have their roots in this one story.

The bears raised this baby until he turned twelve years old. By then he was a very accomplished hunter trained by his bear father, who knew how to track, stalk, and kill game, how to dress it, and the proper prayers necessary for success. The boy also learned prayers that helped protect him, which he used when later confronted by those seeking to harm him during four nights of terror. This geographical area around the Lukachukai and Chuska Mountains is important to the Navajos in the development of the bear way of hunting, since this is where the young man learned those techniques.

The bears' adopted son was very prosperous for four years, bringing in an abundance of meat every day. The family traveled and hunted about, staying in homes that are now mountains and rock formations. One day, when they had returned to the lake, the male bear went to its shore to get water but never returned. The female bear waited and waited, wondering where her husband had gone. She finally decided to follow his tracks even though the Holy Wind warned against it; she started her search, but also failed to return. The water had captured and taken them deep into the lake.

The young man missed his parents; one night he had a dream that told him to cut the water off that flowed from the south side of the lake. He moved to that spot, where he met another male and female bear. He lived with them for a long time, but as the male bear grew older, his ability to hunt declined. The old bear tried everything he could to obtain food, failed, and grew increasingly desperate; starvation stared at him as he continued to search without success. Finally, the old couple became so desperately hungry that they decided to eat the young man who had been so kind to them. Holy Wind came to him and warned, "You better leave because the male bear is really hungry. He's getting angry about his unsuccessful hunting, so he is going to come and eat you. Since you are not one of the Bear People, he sees you as a possible source of food. He's getting angry, stressed, depressed, and is ready to kill you. You had better go to Mount Hesperus and remain in those mountains. It is the only safe place."

As the young man set out on his journey, he knew that he must go but always had thoughts of returning to the man and woman bears. The Holy Wind persisted, warning not to go back, for they would kill him. Meanwhile, the male bear was tracking his potential victim. That night, the young man camped on a high plateau. Holy Wind cautioned to put fire all the way around him in a circle, because bears avoid flames and will not go over them. Bear appeared and requested, "Put the fire out. Let me come in, and we can go home. Let's talk about this." The man refused, keeping the fire burning around him all night, and in the morning again started his trip to the mountains in Colorado. The next three nights there were similar challenges but different solutions that prevented harm. For instance, the second night the man climbed on top of a rock with a small flat surface. The bear could not get up it, so he sat beneath and begged his intended victim to come down and go home with him, but he refused. The last night, the man crawled into a large crack in a rock, after putting fire outside of the entrance. Finally the bear gave up and returned home while the young man reached Mount Hesperus, where he became one of the sacred people who live there. The Colorado River that runs from behind the mountain and goes on to Moab, then joins with Green River, is also sacred, as is the mountain.

Each of the four times that the bear tried to break down the defense of the man, new sacred prayers and songs given by Air, Night, and the Fire People grew out of the experience and are now part of the Waterway ceremony because this young man had come from the water. He also took actions that protected him, and these prayers are now part of the Bearway. The same is true of parts of the story connected to the mountains, and so is part of the Mountainway. From the water to the mountain, the ceremonies came together. There are other elements of this story that are much more detailed and important for medicine people, but this brief summary shows how the land, animals, and ceremonies are tied together.

The teachings from these ceremonies help people to get through some real-life crises. The bear was physically trying to harm the young man; implied in the meaning of getting him to come home was also sexual abuse. The bear suffered from anger, frustration, and other behavioral disorders that led to the destruction of another person. Fortunately, the boy had been trained for twelve years by his adoptive parents to understand the behavior of bears and how to avoid problems. When the boy saw the bear's teeth bared, ears up, and claws ready, he recognized what was next and avoided it. Navajos today warn that one should not strike a child with a hand, which is considered holy, because it will knock sense and goodness out of the person struck, and those qualities will not return. The same is true when living with one's wife or interacting with other people. That person will become bad, not listen, and develop his or her own way of bear thinking. If a person returns, persuaded by the abuser, they are told, "You already knew what was going to happen and you came back anyway. So part of it is your fault." That is another teaching.

At the same time that some bears represent evil, other bears are protectors. The bear parents who raised the boy taught him how to defend himself through sacred prayers developed at that time. Everything that the boy learned helped him to overcome the problems that lay ahead. The sacredness of the bear is captured in the Bearway songs, whose prayers have become part of the Protectionway, developed as the young man learned to think like a bear. The prayer about protection includes "wearing black flint shoes to protect my feet, black flint socks going out from my toes to my knees, clothing of black flint that goes from my knees to my shoulders." Then the prayer declares, "Black mirage [flint] is going to surround me (dinoolyínii hiináanii) for my protection, all the way up to my shoulder." Next there is a black flint hat that protects the head, and finally there are twelve black feathers, which nothing can penetrate, that encircle the person. "In my hands are two rocks that are very holy. They will protect my hands. Everything that I hold will be against my enemy. Black lightning will go around me twice, lightning and thunder will encircle me four times, and they will protect me for who I am. My enemy will fall before me. Whatever the enemy tries to do against me will not work, and I will defeat him." This is how the prayer goes as a patient dresses himself with the entire image. Well-being and hózhǫ́ result.

Windway

Kindle took pride in having been taught the Windway ceremony by his father-in-law, who apparently had mastered a series of rituals and was willing to pass them on to his son-in-law. The training to learn this complex observance was extensive. Briefly summarizing the teachings, healing capability, and performance of the ceremony puts Kindle's comments in context without being inundated with the details of what could be a nine-day undertaking. There are two types of Windway ceremony— Navajo Windway (Diné Binítch'ijí) and Chiricahua Windway (Chíshí Binítch'ijí)—both of which belong to the larger classification of Holyway chants. There are no significant differences between these two curative chantways, the latter coming from the Navajos' close cousins, the Chiricahua Apaches. These rituals can last from one to nine nights and require an extensive apprenticeship and dedication for mastery. There are three elements that, according to anthropologist Leland Wyman, cause illness that these chants cure—wind in its many forms including whirlwinds, objects knocked down by the wind, and sites affected by wind; snakes that have bitten a person or crawled over an object; and cactus used for cooking. The winds are considered to be Holy People, personified with human attributes, who perform a variety of functions ranging from destruction to restoration. Different types of illness coming from these causes are heart and leg pains, headaches, stomachaches, eye irritation, and lung troubles, among others. If a singer or healer is unsuccessful in effecting a cure, it is because of a mistake in the ceremony or failing to observe a taboo. The ceremony includes sandpaintings, the number of which depends on the ritual's length. Representative figures of winds, snakes, and other images mentioned in the teachings summon the powers of these holy people, who effect a cure in the patient. For more detailed information about these two ceremonies, including the contents of the medicine bundle, the sandpaintings, and interpretation of symbols, see Leland C. Wyman, *The Windways of the Navaho.*[6]

Kindle, who was working with a patient at the time of recording, began by mentioning some additional ceremonies called upon for their different healing qualities specific to the man's needs as well as what his father-in-law shared about the Chiricahua Windway:

> Slim Policeman began to instruct me in the Evilway (Hóchx̨ǫ́'íjí) and the Chiricahua Windway ceremonies.[7] In the past, Lifeway ceremonies were done by the elders with a great deal of enthusiasm and may be used in conjunction with other rituals.[8] They traveled great distances for them. The ceremony would begin at sundown with singing and praying and the accompaniment of a rattle with deer hooves that continued all night long. My patient wants to have one performed before Chiricahua Windway. The Lifeway is usually conducted when a person has been in any kind of accident or has had any type of surgery performed. It usually takes four days, but is sometimes done in three. A long time ago it was completed in just two or three days. Some medicine men do not add the prayer portion immediately, but do the

The power of language is the means that summons the holy people, moving the patient through time to the first event portrayed in the sandpainting, and connecting healing forces that act upon one's inner being. Here, Talking God joins in with the medicine people to bless this child sprinkled with pollen. (Drawing by Charles Yanito)

singing first. Others prefer to wait several days between these ceremonies before beginning another one, while some immediately begin
the next one without waiting. My patient's health has been declining
ever since he was in a car accident, which was followed by surgery.
That is why he wanted to have this ceremony performed before he
had the Windway, which is not restricted to the winter months like
some of the others. It can be carried out any time of year. A rattle is
shaken all night long. This is made from a gourd with deer hooves
placed inside and the tail of a buffalo hanging from the bottom. There
are also different medicinal herbs that are mixed, then placed on the
patient while chants are sung.

The Windway heals a person whose mind may be affected in three
ways. There is Deerway, where things should be kept sacred, but were
not. For example, a person might be drinking and laughing when he
is butchering a deer. This affects his mind, and so a hand trembler
will diagnose this. Another type of sickness may be healed by the
Prostitutionway.[9] Whirlwinds bother Navajos. They run over people
and crush them, injure babies, and push people down. Anglo doctors
with their medicine cannot cure the sickness caused by these winds.
There are several offerings for them such as red charcoal, corn pollen,
green cattail pollen, white cornmeal, and yellow corn pollen. These
things are offered to the whirlwind, which is the price for being cured.
Navajos sickened by a whirlwind keep the stories of what happened to
themselves. The Chiricahua Windway is not the only ceremony derived
from the main story, which is also related to the Shootingway, Evilway,
Mountainway, and Navajo Windway, all of which share elements that
can help in treating the sick. It seems like I am only left with a small
part of it. Somewhere, sometime, a whirlwind will injure us, and so
sacred offerings accompanied by prayer are given for protection. When
the ceremony ends, the whirlwind's price is paid.

There are many different types of songs that are sung during
this healing process. For instance, the wind's song may attract four of
the spirit wind people—Black, Blue, Yellow, and White—as well as
four spirit snake people, and four lightning people who participate in
healing. The Sun and the Moon also take part and so have their songs.
With these elements, medicine men perform an overnight [or longer]
ceremony with sandpaintings portraying these holy beings. There are
thirty-two different songs offered to the Spirit Wind people, twelve

for the Snake People, as well as some for mountain tobacco. The Snake People put their songs in place for their role in healing. Because this ceremony occurs in a hogan, there are also songs for this structure. There are Sun and Moon songs that are sung first, spirit wind songs and prayers that follow with those that summon other holy beings, as well as Blessingway songs. During the ceremony, we smoke mountain tobacco for the snake people and pray, just as we do with the songs given for the Lightning people. There are also two Spirit Wind songs, two snake songs, and two lightning songs, each of which is sung consecutively and accompanied by the use of herbs.

I learned these things from Slim Policeman, who counted on me to keep the prayers and songs safe. The person who comes for help will have good restored, his sickness will be cured once the ceremony is completed, and he is taught what to avoid. This makes me happy to see a patient get well and is the reason that I learned these things. Evil ways are not good with life. Even when you get old and your hair turns white, if you go in the right direction you will be well taken care of with a place for you to sleep. In the future, people will talk well of you. They can only speak about what they know, so good things will be told about a person who makes good medicine. I did the things he asked of me and took care of my elders, and now I am old. If one does these things, he will be kept well with fat on his ribs. Slim Policeman taught me protection prayers and in return I took care of him.

Losing the Past

A recurring theme that threaded its way through a lot of the interviews between David Kindle and Bob Putsch was that many of the old ways— from ceremonial knowledge to traditional practices and etiquette to correct language use—were being forgotten, eroding the core of Navajo life. Kindle was not alone in this belief, as the last chapter in this book confirms. Here, he shared his thoughts about the fading past, providing sketches of some of that disappearing knowledge, perhaps never to be reclaimed. Short vignettes give a glimpse into what he felt.

During a mid-October visit, Putsch went with Kindle on a trip to Towaoc, Colorado. Their purpose was to gather plants from Sleeping Ute Mountain, a spot very familiar to the medicine man. They were joined by Kindle's grandson, a young man named Benjamin, who did not speak Navajo very well but had accompanied his grandfather on a number of previous occasions to gather medicinal herbs. He had recently been discharged from the army, was currently unemployed, and lived in Shiprock. Putsch recalled:

> After driving to the southern end of the mountain that looks like a Sleeping Ute, we got to its "foot," a large perpendicular rock formation. David pointed in the direction of Mesa Verde and noted that when the sun rose to a certain position during the year, it shone on the foot. This spot contains a medicine that Navajo males can use for virility since it is viewed as a Navajo penis. David believed that some rocks to the north of this formation were female genitalia, and this whole area was where men were supposed to come if needing help with sexuality.

He told Putsch that there was more to the teachings, but he did not know the rest of it, as it had been lost.

Another time, Kindle was teaching about the hogan, a central structure when performing ceremonies. He commented:

> I will tell you a story. It is for life that a hogan was made, because planning was done within. Everything came into existence from councils held inside. Medicine came about, and the holy people planted it on Mother Earth. We used to have medicine for everything, but we have forgotten it. Who is there to ask? A few people know it, but the young ones do not. There used to be medicine for stomachaches, toothaches, and many other ailments. No one knows these things anymore; the knowledge is disappearing. Now I wonder who makes those cures—no one—so we cling to the Anglo's medicine and hospitals. Our ceremonies are forgotten, and the old ways of healing are no longer practiced. There used to be what was called a protection ceremony. When there were ailments and illness, we would have discussions about them. The people no longer do that, and its accompanying songs are being lost. Those from long ago, from the beginning of our existence, are now gone.
>
> Squaw dance [Enemyway] songs nowadays are just made up, because that is all there is. There used to be descriptive names given to those songs. Squaw dances are similar to the Yé'ii Bicheii dance in that although to some extent the dance is for entertainment, there are

also strong prayers from within that are part of a story and ceremony. They are not just playthings for amusement, but a very strong form of education. In the past, the holy people placed Shiprock here for us to look at and lean on. Yé'ii Bicheii and squaw dances brought out the very best, when people wore their finest attire and rode their best male horse. It also brought youth, good young men and women, together. We used to look to it for good thoughts. The squaw dance controls our possessions and brought out the best in youth with them dressed in their choicest clothes and jewelry, sitting atop their horses, which were also dressed in their finest. These dances, as part of a ceremony, used to be like that. Now there are only vehicles.

We are going to a bad place. These teachings are no longer taken seriously and have become just a plaything. Strong thoughts and planning were brought about. Everything was taken into consideration, such as horses and sheep. The squaw dance was for life, but now it has lost those values and has become only entertainment. There are no more stories of the things I speak of. We used to have ceremonies where we might, in a small way, talk about our elders; no one does this any longer. There were those who had the stories and understood the ceremonies but kept them hidden so that now there are none. Who can we count on to continue the stories and lean on in the future? There were ceremonies for dogs and the Coyoteway, but there are none now. There were many other smaller ceremonies, which have been forgotten. Our elders used to have stories, but now there are many told that are untrue and just made up. Plants and seeds that we used have disappeared. It has been said that when there are no more stories, it will be the end of us. We have forgotten it all, and they are no longer in our thoughts. The loss of these teachings is ruining everything for us who live on Mother Earth. The holy people warned that this would happen; how will it be relearned and brought back to life?

I wish we could restart it. My hair has turned white. I used to sing very well a long time ago when my inside was in good health, but now it has deteriorated and is not good. Not only do I not sing as well, but it seems like there are things changing in me each year. There are fewer and fewer who are my age, so that those who knew the stories are no more. Even our language is being lost to the Anglos. It is all disappearing. I will live for horses and sheep as our elders used to instruct us. There used to be teachings concerning life's possessions, which we called the basis or foundation of life and the stories. Songs used to be formed on these foundations, but now you no longer hear them. If we try very hard, we can restart it. If our prayers, songs, and teachings as we know them disappear, then whom will we look to in the future? There will probably be no more. It is to the point where it can be and should be revived while we still have older men and women who know the ceremonies and prayers. I wish this could be done. This is my way of thinking, and I am saying it for the sake of my children. Somewhere in the future my grandchildren will listen to the things that I have shared. Our stories will be among us. They will hear it as the truth and know that it is real. I am hoping that some of them will use this as a pathway to life.

CHAPTER SEVEN

Daily Life along the River

Traditional Values at Work

As mentioned in the introduction, this book serves as a companion piece to *Stories from the Land: A Navajo Reader about Monument Valley*. While providing a good representative understanding of the life and teachings of the Utah Navajos, its operating principle is either to highlight certain aspects that are unique to one of the two geographical areas or to emphasize things common to both while avoiding repetition. For instance, the Navajo view of the creation of the world, the Anasazi, moviemaking, the uranium industry, and tourism were discussed in the first book, while chantways, water, medicine people, and boarding schools play a larger role here. Still there were many shared elements, some of which are discussed in this chapter. Topics such as raising children, traditional clothing, views of the body, and witchcraft were common in both geographical locations but are delineated more in this text. Together, the lifeways of the Navajo people, told in their voices in both books, present a rich tapestry of what it meant to be one of the People at a time when traditional values held sway. Part of that story is told here through the eyes of childhood.

Childhood—Learning for a Lifetime

Even in the best of circumstances, life was challenging for children. In traditional Navajo culture, childhood was a time of training, which could mean going without, making do with what was available, and being ready to perform an elder's wishes. While reality had the potential of being harsh for all, children were often loved but suffered through circumstances that forced them to understand sobering aspects of life and what it would take to succeed.[1] Compared to today's practices where a child often comes first and is perhaps pampered too much, many Navajo youngsters at that time faced starvation, death, and challenging work responsibilities. Some were also handed off to other family members who needed help with their situation. Central to all of this was the lecturing from parents, grandparents, and other relatives in giving advice for survival in a harsh land and tranquility in human relations. The following testimonials about childhood are heavily laced with these teachings, a testament to the lifelong impact they had on these elders. Consider the contrast between experiences and the consistency in instruction.

Ben Whitehorse was born into a prominent family who had lived in the Montezuma Creek area for a number of generations. His youth was typical of that of a good, stable Navajo family.

> As we were growing up, we were taught many things, such as getting up at dawn and not sleeping in. We were told to get up and look for the horses. "Take a snow bath. Break the ice on the lake and take a bath so that someday you won't be sick with a bad cold or be irritably mad when you're asked to do something. Go running at dawn. Challenging yourself will prepare and strengthen your mind and body to withstand anything you may encounter in your life." This was their way of disciplining and teaching. The young girls were taught in the same manner. In those days, there were no trading posts around here, just a small one at Greasewood Wash (Montezuma Creek—Díwózhii Bikooh), where white men brought in merchandise by wagon to sell. The people planted corn by the river in the spring after building irrigation ditches to water their fields. Our main source of food—corn, watermelons, cantaloupes, and squash— came from these farms. At harvest time in the fall, we stored these foods at our winter camps.[2]

Martha Nez remembered that in the early days, a lot of people had only a few sheep and some had none. "Hunger was among the people who lived mostly on plants. I did this myself when I was herding sheep. Some of those plant roots tasted good. This is how people survived. Navajo clothes were made from warm wool, so that when it was very cold, a woman could untie her belt and let another person crawl inside the dress so that both of their heads stuck out in one place. The clothes also served as a blanket."[3]

Mary Blueyes also had a hard life.

I had two older brothers and three older sisters when I was in the cradle at a time when the family had only a horse and burro. The sister of Naakai Yázhí wanted to raise me as a baby, so she took me but did not really take care of me. I lived in very poor conditions and had the primary job of maintaining the goats. My stepparents often told me the police would come and take me and other children to school. During that time, they were looking for children while I was herding goats barefoot because I had no shoes. They wanted me to care for the animals but did not want me to go to school. Since I did not have shoes, I went to places where gophers had dug out tunnels so I could put my feet in them. This was how I herded goats in the vicinity of Dahaz'áanii through heat and cold and hunger. There was also a place for me behind a loom to do weaving. The wool on the sheep or goat skin could barely be seen, but that served as my bedding, and I did not shake out the dirt. The skin was given to me in the fall and remained there for a long time. This was how I was raised and what I was aware of at the time. I suffered from cold and hunger as I grew up.

Next I went to my mother's home, where there was a man called Hastiin Yázhí who threatened to throw me off a cliff. This was over by the bluffs over there [Tódahidíkáanii area]. Maybe he was going to rape me; I don't know, but I ran back to where my mother was living. This is how I grew up, and later became Jones's father's other wife and moved with him to Black Mesa. My mother, one of my younger brothers, my son, and baby daughter died over there. When we moved back to here, I had a daughter who died after she learned to walk. My youngest brother also died. Our father had many children and they all died. Heartache was so very great with me that one time, I did not want to live, so I stopped eating. We moved about and went through Tsaile, but I just could not eat anymore even when others were picking piñon nuts. Jack Jones and my younger brother were still with us at the time my arm started to shake. I told people that this was happening from time to time, and they said it was because the hand trembling wanted to come to me. I was asked why I did not let it. When they went back to picking piñon nuts, I started to hand tremble again. It made the air spotted and bent my arm; the air [wind] seemed to stand before me, and this is how I hand trembled on myself. Soon after, I had the five-day Windway (Níłch'ijí) ceremony performed on me, became well, and started to eat, feeling peace throughout my body. There were several times I almost died, but I lived through these experiences as days went by. When we moved back this way, my younger brother died at a place called Tsinyíł'áádi (Forest). That was the last of my younger brothers and sisters.[4]

Ella Sakizzie provides a beautiful example of how her life intermeshed with her parents' teachings, underscoring what was of value in times of struggle. Note the constant undertone of preparation for independence and adulthood.

As a child, me and my older brothers were taught by our parents, who forbid us to do a lot of things. They told us to get up at dawn to run, that we could not sleep in, and how to perform our responsibilities around the home. This included caring for the hogan and how to make a living. There were no off-reservation jobs and automobiles as there are now. Teaching the meaning of life to the children was most important, a priority. We were taught how to care for the livestock, fetch the horses at dawn and water them, drive the sheep out to pasture at sunrise before it got too hot, return them to the corral at high noon, and then let them out again in the evening. Sheep were our main source of livelihood, and there was plenty to learn from having a flock—how to care for them, process them as food, and prepare wool for weaving.

Our mother would say, "I'm not teaching you these things for nothing, for I will not be here for you forever." My father said the same and it is true. "I will not live for you forever, because someday I might kick the bucket, then I will not be with you. Therefore, learn to take care of the sheep; take care of the horse, for he will be like a 'father' to

Children learned early the value of livestock as part of the "life of life" that would sustain them through good times and bad. But it was more than just a physical relationship—it was a joint partnership in which man and animal took care of each other if they were, in turn, taken care of.

bring you food, while the sheep will be like your mother and father and support you. Its meat will be your food, its wool will be used in many different ways, but it will be up to you. If you are willing to learn how to card, spin, and weave with your hands, then you will have all that you need and want. You have to force yourself to learn these things, but if you do not care, then you will be begging for handouts from other people and taking your children here and there. Only you can make it possible to own valuable necklaces, concho belts, sheep, and horses; these will give purchasing power to increase your prosperity. Your wealth will not diminish or die, for this is the 'life of life' and 'strength of life.' It is the 'life of life' because these animals are alive— they drink water and consume food just like us. You will lose some to predators and sickness, but you will continue to thrive and survive with the rest. It will become your way of life for as long as you live. Know their identity and learn all you can." This is what my parents taught me.

Their teachings became my reality and way of life. I have sheared sheep, woven wool, and made rugs to sell or trade for merchandise and money. I wove their wool into beautiful saddle blankets to decorate my horses, causing them to be overly excited, happy, and proud, so much that they would not stand still. "If your horse wears ragged old blankets, he'll be sad and will tend to be lazy with his eyes half closed," my father used to tell me. I believe him, because I've witnessed this to be true, and that was the way I was taught. It is the meaning of true living.[5]

Navajo teachings were comprehensive, ranging from a relationship with an ant to one with a person, and from plants and rocks to livestock and weather, but nothing was more central than the home, the "womb" of the family. Even its physical construction embodied what was important to understand. In making a hogan, the placement of the log had to be done clockwise with the root or growing end as the starting point. Spaces within the hogan were divided by gender and the accompanying division of labor, while inside the log wall structure was located the four sacred mountains with their blessings. There was nothing haphazard about how families were to live. John Knot Begay, who was raised in a traditional family, shared the insight he gained from his parents' teachings.

When we were growing up, we were taught to respect other people's property—home, livestock, valuables, and so forth. We were forbidden to touch what was not ours. People's hogan/summer shelters were left unlocked. Their belongings of turquoise, saddles, rugs, and buckskins were left inside. Everyone was forbidden to touch something that did not belong to them. Other people's valuables were considered "holy" with their blessing songs and prayers, so they had to be left alone. "Do not criticize or make fun of others, even if they're ugly looking, for they possess all of the unseen beauty that comes from many sacred songs and prayers. Leave them alone. They are human," my elders would tell us.

"Also, leave other people's homes alone. Each and every log that forms a hogan has its own name and its own prayer. Some are from male trees and others from female trees. They are all created in their own sacred way." Our present, modern houses are just as holy because they come from the same source. This is why our people have a special sacred song called Hooghan Biyiin, especially for the hogan/house. This structure is like our mother, when we sit inside our home the same way we were inside her womb before birth. Hogans that are built with layers of logs are female, while the type that is built with a pointed roof is male or the father hogan. The utensils used inside these dwellings are also considered holy. The firepoker stick is like our grandfather, so he is the "fire" that is "crisscrossed" with the air and every living thing on this earth that was made for us. The water is like our parents. It takes care of us and our needs. This is what I was taught, and I have learned to live accordingly up to this point.

Back then, we were constantly lectured. The whip was always available. They'd say to us children, "You, boy, be prepared and swift to move; don't be stubborn; be ready to do what you're told, for it will make you a better person in the future. But if you're lazy and sleep in, you'll be grouchy and irritable. And if your parents, grandfather, brother, or sister take off your blanket, you'll grab them by the collar and throw them around because of your anger. You cannot do this. It is forbidden." They would point their fingers straight into our eyes and say, "Those black pupils of yours are there for you to see with; that nose of yours is for you to smell with; the openings on the side of your head are for you to listen and hear with. Therefore, don't do what is forbidden! Leave things alone!" No one was allowed to talk back or ask why. Having been taught these things, one was expected to wake up before dawn and run. "When you get to the top of the hill, yell or sing aloud," they would say. "Your training and willpower will reflect your future self. It will pay off for the good. It is for your own benefit, not anyone else's." I grew up under all of these conditions and lectures.[6]

A final example of the training and teachings given by elders to inculcate Navajo values in youth is given by Jerry Begay.

I was told in your life's journey, you are now young and you will see older men and women. That elder person will be walking in a certain way; perhaps they are blind. You do not laugh about them or you might become their son-in-law. This is one area left alone. Wherever your life road takes you, you will be aware of this. I was told to be careful how I talked by being thoughtful and considerate about what I said because it will reflect on me so that I can lead a life that will be respected by others. "Take care of yourself and listen to the elders who have knowledge to share with you. It will help you progress through your life. You will get a wife and then have children with whom you will share your teachings. Life is not difficult if you have this knowledge to make better decisions. When you are with a group of people, do not laugh for no reason at all. A person may not like the laughing and carrying on and so may use witchcraft against you."

This is what was said and why a person does not carry on. Move with respect through life. I was told with these teachings that I would walk through life and to take care of my belongings, horses, sheep, and other things. This way, everything is in harmony. And it is the same with the home where there is a fire burning. It starts there, and everything else falls into place. One has to take the ashes out first, and then the whole home is swept. The fire is then lit, and the place is warm. I was told that this is how I should live.[7]

Wresting a Living from the Land

Parts of this sound advice and these words of wisdom were put to the test of daily life in the form of an intense food quest—either through farming, herding, hunting, or gathering. Some of the process was seasonal, while other aspects continued throughout the year. Chapter 3 discussed the paramount importance of corn in the Navajo diet, while chapter 4 examined harvesting wild plants. Florence Begay paints a picture of the scope and timing of these pursuits.

In the area of Kin Díílidii (Burned House—at the Mouth of Marble Canyon), there was a large field with plenty of corn from which Navajos procured pollen. They were careful in using it. Upon our arrival after school at Shiprock for the summer break, we would see green fields of corn already growing, which we hoed and took care of. When the squash flowers bloomed, we cooked them with our meat. The young corn, not quite ripe, was peeled, cooked, and eaten with a variety of other foods, meat, ribs, etc. It was similar to the way miniature corn is served in salads in restaurants today. I helped with preparing these foods. After five to eight days when the corn ripened a little more, we ground it and spread the cream corn on the husks for cooking, then after another ten days we made kneel down bread. This corn was ground with mano and metate. That was how we timed, step by step, the cycle for fixing corn. When it was time for gathering pollen, the women were out in the cornfields all along the river, shaking it into bowls. We had plenty of it, but now it is no longer like that.[8]

Jerry Begay remembered corn mush and the cantaloupes that were cut in strips, dried, and then boiled during the winter, something he thought was a tasty treat. Boiled cantaloupe and corn were mixed with different food in a variety of ways. There were different plants that had been gathered, like sumac berries, haashch'é'édáá, and tł'oh dei (tassel on plant), and if there was meat, he considered it a luxury, but he added that he was never hungry.[9] Mary Jim was not as happy with her lot, declaring that during this time, she consumed anything that was edible—"even the skin of a goat or sheep or horse. It was made almost like jerky. This is how we were raised, with the help of our grandparents."[10] In some areas of Aneth, peach trees flourished. Martha Nez recounts how people from the Oljato area came to trade for peaches.

One time there was a young man who came when my brother and I were by ourselves. The stranger had brought mutton to exchange for peaches and asked where our father was. We told him he had gone to the store. He took the meat—mutton jerky—inside, putting it away, and started eating our grapes. He asked us where we got them, and so my brother told him. He wanted to see the place, so we took him, he looked at it, then said he would spend the night there and that the next day we would get him a bunch of grapes. My father came home late in the afternoon with three one-hundred-pound flour sacks and filled them with peaches and a fifty-pound flour sack full of grapes. By the time the man reached home with his two pack horses, it had all probably turned to juice.[11]

While livestock was available to slaughter and eat, there were alternatives. Florence Begay told of capturing prairie dogs that were ground, broiled, and eaten. Cottontail rabbits were another source of meat for many because they were abundant, healthy, and fattest during the fall when the ground was covered with frost. The meat was fried at a low temperature and slow-cooked, giving it more flavor. Her family feared the big jackrabbits because they had a disease that caused internal blistering. The men hunted by chasing both big and small rabbits. Florence recalled, "Across from here there is a place called Hastiin Biwoo' Ádinii Náátłizhii (Man with No Teeth Who Fell) because an elder named Hastiin Biwoo' Ádinii (Man with No Teeth) fell off his horse during one of these rabbit hunts and was knocked unconscious for a short time. There, the hunters clubbed the rabbits while riding their horses. It was believed that these hunts produced rain, and so they were considered a sacred event."[12]

Mary Jay, after describing hauling large gunnysacks of corn in a wagon to the Aneth Trading Post, where it was ground into flour, told of the community's effort to hunt rabbits.

> Men owned bows and arrows with which they killed rabbits up in the mesas. They hunted in the deep snow during the winter and so dressed warmly. Moccasins of cowhide with the fur turned inward with the fuzzy side next to the skin extended to the knee as a wrap. Split yucca was used to tie it together or mend torn or worn moccasins. Sometimes they were able to run and catch the rabbits and kill them with a stick. Later, people would gather in the spring, when the corn was ankle high, to go rabbit hunting. They all went on horseback, swarming to and fro after their prey. One person followed them around carrying all the slain animals, dangling down the side of the horse and rider.[13]

Another source of protein, especially during the flu season, was horsemeat. Mary recalled:

We would kill a two-year-old pony since we had a lot of horses. Man with Many Children (Hastiin Ba'áłchini Łáni), who lived across the river, always butchered them for us. He would take the guts out and hang the carcass on a post, so that we could later slice up the meat and share it with others. It is a good remedy for colds. People are usually healthy when they eat horse meat, so we rarely heard of anybody catching a cold during the winter season. I have never witnessed a donkey being butchered, just horses. We ate beef, too, but it didn't cure colds so it is like sheep—has no curing power like horse meat. When children got sick, we also used herbs such as ch'il dích'íí (bitter plant) sagebrush plants. We pounded these herbs and put them into hot water, then used the green juice that came from it for colds. After giving the baby a bath in this solution, we wrapped it up in a cradle board, covered it with something, and slipped the herb juices under the cover to serve as an inhalant. If that did not work, we mixed sheep fat with cedar pitch and rubbed it on their body. It cured their cold right away.[14]

However, to Mary, fish and creatures associated with the river could not be eaten. "People didn't eat anything from the river back then. They used to say a thing called tééh łįį' (supernatural water horse) lived in the river. It was considered dangerous and people were afraid of it. Beavers built their homes along the banks, but the boys were scared of them when they used to go down there to swim. We were forbidden to go near the river or eat its contents. Even if a sheep drowned in the river, we were forbidden to eat it."[15]

Changing to Changing Woman

Much of individual and community activity revolved around recognizing different stages of life and ceremonial observation. The Navajos, as deeply religious people, brought spiritual beliefs and a codified standard of conduct for dress and daily prayers as well as individual and group interaction. Much has been written about their customs and so is touched upon lightly here, but by adolescence a boy or girl started to assume increasing adult responsibilities. For example, at a girl's kinaaldá, or coming-of-age ceremony, she was instructed primarily by her female relatives on proper behavior as established by the deity Changing Woman. Florence Begay remembered:

The first kinaaldá took place atop Huerfano Mesa (Dził Ná'oodiłii) with First Man and First Woman and their daughter Changing Woman. It was done in the Blessingway (Hózhǫ́ǫ́jí). It's for real. Females at the age of fourteen become a "kinaaldá."

The young woman is supposed to wear Navajo moccasins, dress up in her best traditional clothes, wear turquoise beads, silver bracelets, concho belts, and a blanket or shawl at all times. These things are encouraged throughout the ceremonial event. The same rules are applied at squaw dances, too. Women are required to wear this clothing even during hot weather and are not to put on coats, since those are only for males. All of this clothing was heavy, but women did not have sweat problems, even in hot weather, although wrapped in shawls while standing in lines to watch the events. Nowadays, people get too hot and stay under the shade of an umbrella.

The kinaaldá is kept in good posture, maintaining a straight back during these days. She is "massaged sacredly" and adorned with jewelry, which cannot be removed for four days, even as she runs at dawn. When it is time for her to come back to the starting point, she has to turn clockwise as people yell and make noise to encourage her. We were also warned not to look back while running, because if you do, you are going to die before your time. I was careful, so I obeyed, and sure enough, I am still here. As a kinaaldá, I had to wear my hair down. "Don't pull your hair back with your hand or you will become bald," I was told. I had to push my hair back away from my face because I was uncomfortably hot. Sure enough, I have lost my hair. I probably still would have it if I hadn't pushed it back. We were told, "Your hair is the rain (symbolically), therefore, don't cut it. Other parts of the body have their own story." We were told, "If you ever start cutting your hair, we will have no rain." I think this is true because we do not have much rain. Back then, men and women always wore their hair in a knot. It is considered "male rain" and so should not be cut. Everyone kept their hair long up until they started wearing pants and doing all the forbidden things we were taught not to do.

Later in the day, people helped the young woman to grind corn with stones for a big cake that was cooked in the ground and eaten on

One of the culminating acts during the four-day kinaaldá ceremony is when the young woman is shaped and molded into the image of Changing Woman as portrayed here. For a brief time, she holds the power to bless others—young and old—and is now eligible to bear children as a mother formed in the likeness of deity.

the final day. Nobody grinds corn by hand like that anymore, but just takes it to the mill. The girl is advised and lectured the whole time. "Don't slouch. Don't talk nonsense. Don't laugh or talk with a deep voice. Speak delicately. Don't eat sweets or sugar. Eat only cornmeal." I wished I could have some of the cantaloupe, peaches, and watermelon that the others were eating, but I had to suffer by myself. I tried to sneak a bit and got caught and chased back inside. The older women told me that if I ate sweets, I would lose my teeth, and if I sat with a hunched back that it would stay that way. I had to watch my language, could not bathe or wash, and had to obey all of the rules for the four days of the ceremony and then four more days after. These same basic teachings apply for a person who is having a sing done for them, too. I dreaded not washing and hurting my body from wearing the heavy jewelry whenever I had to have a Blessingway performed on me. We don't observe such things anymore. All my classmates with whom I grew up are dead now. My maternal grandmother was good at making all sorts of things, and so she provided much of the instruction. She used to make traditional woven wool dresses (biil), wove all kinds of rugs with different designs and textures, and cooked good corn foods with wheat, which served as a sweetener.[16]

During this four-day ceremony, as well as with most other rituals, the Navajo sweat lodge was used to cleanse physically, mentally, and spiritually those who were central to the activity. It was also used for daily bathing in a land where water was scarce. This sudatory, in the shape of a very small male hogan, might have fit ten people at a time and was available for use by both men and women, but was always used separately. Speaking of its use, Florence Begay said:

> The sweat bath hogans are built in sacredness through songs, as are the stones used for warming the inside. Everything is done sacredly. Sweat hogans become a center for teaching and learning holy songs, prayers, and ceremonial activities. You learn the prayers and songs for self-protection and self-healing of mind and body as you take herbs and medicine. These sweat hogans were used a lot and did not just sit idle. It was not used as a simple sauna bath because it had much more meaning. Females are not allowed to use the sweat bath with males, not even their spouse. If they do go in together, it can cause blindness and "iich'ąh" [curse or death because of sexual intentions]. The men have to throw out the tree bark they sat on and clean out the sweat hogan before the women use it. The whole process provides safety and protection against danger. Today, people don't use the sweat hogan as much as they did in the past.[17]

There were other forms of protection outside of the sweat house. Mary Jay told of how the women prayed for her well-being as they stirred cornmeal, holding up the sacred stirring sticks and saying "tse bee nááníshóóh" (brush it again on the stones), "and there was the long grass brush we used to brush our hair into a knot. We painted our faces with 'chííh' [mixture of red ochre and sheep fat] and owned a bag with sacred corn pollen and arrowheads in it."[18]

Daily Rhythm of Life

Once Florence and other girls had their kinaaldá ceremony, Navajo society considered them women and eligible for marriage. In traditional times, the family of a young man might have selected his future bride and made arrangements with her family for the transfer of livestock and perhaps some other forms of wealth before the wedding ceremony, in which both families participated. Following this, the new husband and wife set out to establish their life together. Florence recalled:

> I was married in 1933. My marriage was arranged for me, although I had not planned on it. James Owl and his wife came to propose that I marry their son. I really didn't want to, but it had already been planned and approved by my family and now we have been married for forty-eight years. We established our homestead across the river and had cattle, horses, and sheep, taking care of our livestock as it should be done, shearing sheep, raising lambs, and so forth. We had our winter and summer camps with our summer camp down by the river.
>
> It was rather hard to make a living at times. We hauled wood in the winter from off the mesa with a wagon and two mules. There was enough dried wood then, but now there are only green, wet trees. We had to herd the sheep to better grazing places and did not have ready-made grain. We actually had to hunt for good pastures to keep our livestock in healthy condition. Small dams were made to water the sheep, and in the winter, we had to break the ice for them to drink. In the spring, we moved down to the riverbank when the water was deep. We hauled our sheared wool in mule packs, then took the wool across the river in a boat to the store. Sometimes we transported the wool by wagon to Teec Nos Pos or Red Mesa, but other times the trader came by himself to haul it off. When it came time to sell the lambs, we had to slowly herd them to Teec. It took a long time to get there, so we brought along some lunch. We also herded them down to the river and ferried them across by boat to the trading post to sell. The river was at times impassable.

By March or so we would run out of food, so I would make a run to the store on my horse, pour all the flour I needed into a specially made bag, purchase a lot of canned foods, then pack it all on another horse. I would then have the horses swim to the far bank with me at a certain crossing place called Road by the Water (Tó Dah Ni'deetiin), which I used coming and going. I have made many trips this way. I had two girls at the time, but my husband was often off to work on the railroad with other men from around here, so I stayed alone and did everything by myself.

If we needed a ceremony, such as the Enemyway (Ana'í Ndáá'), we fetched two horses and notified the medicine man. These horses were used to ride up to the mountain to gather herbs to induce vomiting (iiłkóóh). We had five horses that we kept nice and fat and used only for traveling purposes such as going to squaw dances. They were kept separate from the other herds of stallions and mares, were very well trained, and could handle almost any type of terrain as well as swim the river with a person on their back. They were swift, traveled far without tiring, and were good for carrying the sacred stick for a squaw dance, even if it was to be held in Teec Nos Pos.

When it came time for a certain event, the people gathered these special horses in a corral to test them to see which one was best fit for the occasion. This corral used to be by Burned House (Kin Díílidii). Two people would then go up on the mountain to get the herbs and pine branches used in the sing, which were then brought to the summer shelter built for this occasion, where there was also a hogan. The herbs and pine branches were set on top of the summer shelter and brought into the hogan, a little at a time, for use in the ceremony. They were pounded and boiled in a pottery pot separately and labeled as Evilway (Hóchxǫ'íjí). The people drink this during the sing and then pay dollars to use the herbs. At this time, a variety of other herbs and sacred ground sand were distributed at a price.

Women helped in this medicine way too. Some of them could really sing. Often their grandfathers and fathers were medicine men who took them to ceremonies to participate, and so they learned quickly. My husband wanted me to learn from him and take me on his trips, but I didn't feel up to it, so I never learned.[19]

Jerry Begay remembered how people spread the word, gathered, and supported those who were having a ceremony performed.

> Some brought food to feed guests and participants; others might assist in making a sandpainting or chant during the ceremony. If a person sang along with the medicine man until dawn, he received a piece of fabric as a token for helping with the ritual. Those who assisted singing along also learned the songs, which helped them. People tried to support one another. For instance, when a person is exposed to lightning or where lightning has struck, they will become sick. The ceremony called Lightningway or Shootingway (Na'at'oyee—male, or Iináájí—female) is used to heal that individual. First an offering (yeel) of sacred stones and shell (ntł'iz) is given and a song sung at the place where lightning struck. Surrounding plants are picked to be used later to induce vomiting, which is part of making the person whole again. Somehow the illness caused by lightning threads its way throughout the person's body, but it is removed through this ceremony. Medicine men are very cautious in the way they conduct this ritual and treat it with respect. In this way, the holy beings see that these people are doing things correctly, and the healing takes place. Everything has to be treated with deference. For instance, my grandfather went hunting often, and when he killed a deer, the meat was eaten with care and the skin not wasted but carefully tanned to make buckskin. He also brought back the hooves, sawed off their tips, softened them through boiling, and then drilled a hole in them to make rattles, which he used in the Shootingway ceremony.[20]

Mary Blueyes was another person who was highly respectful of her traditional knowledge. As a medicine woman, she was particular as to where and when she shared her stories and information about plants and the holy people. As I interviewed her one day, she was hesitant to tell certain stories because at that time of the year, spiders were out of hibernation since the first thunder had sounded, snakes were stirring, and

> the frogs who live by the thunder were active. All the things move when the thunder sounds. These stories should not be told now, but only in the winter. The whole earth is a prayer. It is all prayer. It is

said that the breaking of each dawn represents a new hogan, while the twilight becomes a night hogan. The shoe game songs are not sung until winter and must end with the first thunder. Otherwise, the spiders and snakes are crawling, and the thunder is still with us. It then becomes dangerous because it will have no respect for you, so you may be struck by lightning. These old stories are not to be told. The only other time that they can be is for a few days in midsummer or when in the mountains. This is what my father said. This is how songs are sung and when stories are told.[21]

The reality of these beliefs became apparent when I asked her, during the summer, about the story of Changing Bear Maiden and her connection to the Bears Ears. Mary gave the above explanation, and so we went on to other topics. As we discussed medicine plants, she noted that she was short a few types and that she would like to go to the mountain to get some. I readily agreed, climbed into the pickup truck with Mary and Baxter Benally, my interpreter, and headed toward Blue Mountain some sixty miles away. After stopping for lunch on that sunny day, we proceeded to where she wanted to go for certain plants. She picked what was needed and returned to the truck, where we sat on the tailgate and discussed some of the things she was doing. Since we were on the mountain—a permissible place, she had mentioned earlier, to talk about the Bears Ears, which in Navajo thought is connected to Blue Mountain—I asked again. She consented, saying that the mountain would be there to witness, and so it was all right. When she finished, we continued collecting plants, and within an hour's time we had worked our way to a reservoir at the foot of the mountain. She started walking next to the body of water, giving offerings and prayers and selecting herbs, until we got about a third of the way around. In the meantime, dark ominous male storm clouds gathered overhead, the winds increased, and jagged bolts of lightning creased the sky. By the time we reached the truck, a heavy downpour of rain splashed over the countryside in a typical late-afternoon midsummer thundershower. I wondered how Mary was reacting to it all. Thankfully, she was pleased with the rainstorm that drenched us, explaining that it came as a witness that the holy people were happy with the telling of the Changing Bear Maiden story. It had transpired in the right way, the right place, and the right time, and so the water had come as a blessing.

Telling the story about the Bears Ears and Changing Bear Maiden in an accurate way was just as important as the time, place, and circumstance of telling it. Mary Blueyes, like the medicine person pictured here, understood the significance of doing things right and in tune with the holy people, who provided the blessing of rain as their recognition of what transpired. (Drawing by Charles Yanito)

Evil Personified

There is also the opposite side in the Navajo way, where things are done intentionally wrong, prayers and songs are used to curse and oppress, and the desired outcome is misery and death. Witchcraft ('iiníziin) is a powerful force within the belief system of the Navajo people and is credited for many different types of mishaps, against either an individual or a family or group. Knowledge of its existence is widespread, but if a person knows too much, they may be accused of practicing it, which in the old days could lead to their execution as a witch or, at the least, social ostracism. A number of excellent studies analyze the four different types of witchcraft—witchery, sorcery, wizardry, and frenzy—and explain their origin, variations, and use.[22] Here, the purpose is to provide Navajo testimony, not anthropological analysis.

Antisocial behavior contrary to Navajo custom and beliefs is one of the major causes that summon accusations of witchcraft against a person. In the following story, observe the lack of generosity and mean-spirited assault that preceded the death of accused practitioners. Around 1908, Old Mexican in the Aneth–Montezuma Creek area observed the effects of antisocial behavior as he watched an old man, his two wives, and his son get shot or chopped to death with an ax, with only one of the wounded women escaping—all because of their insensitive treatment of two boys in the family. The youths reported the crime and were quickly implicated. According to Old Mexican:

> These two boys were sent to reform school. The bigger boy was about fifteen; the other was younger. They were orphans, no father or mother, and had been living with their older sister and their "older brother," the young man who was killed.
>
> I guess the reason they got mad was because their "older brother" treated them pretty roughly. He used to scold them all the time, and whip them without giving them anything to eat, and he never bought them anything to wear. Even when he wanted them to go after the horses, he would get on his mount and run them over. We saw him do this. He never did any work himself; he just let the young boys do it all. And the old woman, their "mother," treated them the same way.

The young man had run over these boys with his horse that very day, and that night they got pretty mad, I guess, and killed them, while they were asleep.

The old man had been a witch. Once, while they were having horse races, he had trouble with another man over a bet. His son, who got killed, had been with this fellow and lost. They nearly had a fight there at the race track. A few days after they all returned home, the fellow who won became ill. He was sick all that summer and fall and part of the winter. They were having all kinds of medicine work done for him. One night, the singer [Ba'álílee—The One with Supernatural Power] and his son who was helping him went outside and looked at the stars. While they were gazing at them, they saw the old witch and his son and his oldest wife standing outside. They disappeared right there. A star made a bright light, and there they saw them, standing in a row, one behind the other, the old man first, then his son, and then his oldest wife. This star told them who was killing the sick man. The three fell right there. That showed that they were going to die soon and could not kill this sick man. Supernatural Power was the singer and he was stronger than the witch. He was praying over this man the time the soldiers came for him. These three were not there in the flesh, only their shadows were seen, their spirit, breath. If they had not seen that night the shadows of these three, the man would have died. That is the reason that about eleven months after they saw these spirits, the boys killed them. The gun they used couldn't even shoot when they wanted it to. Because the witch couldn't kill this man, his power turned back upon him and finally ended him. That is the way lots kill themselves off. They bewitch someone and fall.[23]

Often people practicing witchcraft, through supernatural means, slip into the skin of a wolf or coyote before venturing forth with their powers to disrupt the lives of others. They can travel at high speeds on foot but still might be accidentally discovered as they prowl about. Harvey Oliver in Aneth, although stating that he was not familiar with such practices, had encounters that led him to declare, "Skinwalkers do exist."

When I used to herd sheep near the base of Sleeping Ute Mountain, I had an experience with these things. It was near sundown and I was cooking supper when a black dog came out from behind a house. I was wondering what it was because nobody lived close by and there were no dogs in this area. It passed by me. This was in the fall and the animal had not shed its rusty colored fur. I stopped cooking and picked up my gun that was propped against the wall beside me. The dog saw me and started running with an awkward trot as his whole body seemed to vibrate. It did not act like a dog, so I shot at him but missed, the bullet splashing sand beneath him. I took another shot just as he crossed the wash, he spun around with a wound, and I later noticed blood stains. That was the first time I saw what is called a skinwalker.

Another time was when we lived farther up the river, where a large bunch of juniper trees grow. We owned a lot of goats, around two hundred at the time, and let them go up on the mesa to graze early in the morning. They would spend the nights on one of the mesa points where nothing ever bothered them. They were well-behaved, staying together as they grazed. One morning, my family decided to butcher one, so we went up to fetch it. I climbed the rocky side of the mesa because that is where they usually remained for the night, but they were not there. I then went to a rock shaped like a head, another place they frequented. I walked toward the place, noticing a hogan on my way. Suddenly I saw a coyote come out of the home before it came through the trees to my right near some rocks. As it got closer, I noticed it was not a coyote because it had an awkward trot and everything vibrated when it ran. Just as it passed me, I threw a rock and hit its stomach, causing it to take off as fast as it could possibly run before disappearing over the cliff. I did not check where it fell but only saw its tracks.

I continued in a hurry, looking for the goats so we could have some meat. They had traveled down into a small canyon and met me on their way up, so I herded them toward the water hole, then went to the cliff to look for the "thing," only to find that it had jumped off two levels of the cliff, then continued to walk along its base. I came to two huge rocks resting against each other, where I noticed a small black bucket underneath one of the boulders. I walked up to it and saw that someone had just taken a bath. This made me a believer in skinwalkers. Some people change into coyotes like that person who lived in the hogan. His tracks led that way, and after I discovered him, he died before the year was over. His skin was underneath the rocks where he had hidden it, but I pushed the rocks away.[24]

Oliver's account brings out a number of aspects common to Navajo witchcraft found in other narratives. One tenet is that once the practitioner has been exposed, he is vulnerable to having his power turned against him or is susceptible to some other type of death. What happened to this person proved to Oliver this belief. Many of these stories end with a death or an individual being wounded when in their "skin" and then appearing later, as an injured but normal person. A second aspect is the place and conditions in which the story occurs. He mentioned familiar locations—a rocky area, the boulders where the bath had taken place, and the rocks under which the skin was hidden. Navajo people often identify specific sites known to be frequented by skinwalkers. Charlie Blueyes mentioned Designs on the Rock, discussed previously, as a place where witches met to practice their trade.[25] Mary Blueyes was more specific:

It is not very good if you take part in those things. There was a man who told this. It began from a place called Standing Black Rock (Tsézhin Si'ani), where there is a trail that winds through that goes by Mr. Black Rock's (Hastiin Tsézhini's) place. The trail goes by that white bluff and is said to be the one used by skinwalkers. Then it goes to the place where the water meets. It is somewhere near this spot that there is a witches' meeting place called "home of evil ways" (ánt'į́įh ba'hooghan) where they practice witchcraft. Some people have gone inside the one at Tsé Naazhiin. Charlie's son, who was a police officer, told of how his police chief was dying. A medicine man performed crystal gazing for him, and learned that witches working against him had obtained some of his body waste (chłiin) through which to curse him and that it was located in their ánt'į́įh ba'hooghan. A group of police officers went there to get it back. They found an old sheepskin lying on the ground, got what they went for, and departed. On their way down a rocky slope, something was being thrown at them by what seemed like slings. The objects whizzed by, and one of the police officers fell down, so that the others had to carry him the rest of the way. Eventually, the police chief got better after having a ceremony performed; he is still living. So there are really such things as áńt'įįh ba'hooghan and skinwalkers.[26]

Depending on the desired outcome and the materials that a witch uses, there are a number of different types of places and means for cursing an individual. Mary told of placing an image or object from a person to be cursed on a rock where the sun shines the hardest in order to harm them. An Anasazi petroglyph can also be used to work against an intended victim. Reeds can be made into arrows and shot into an individual to sicken them. Witches also put an object from a person on a juniper tree, and as the plant grows, it affects the bewitched, especially if it is a growing child. Hair, spit, and fingernails from a person can be brought into a burial site or into the witches' meeting place, where it is worked against by the dead. Mary also heard that those who practiced witchcraft ate human flesh, which she called ch'ohdeeníní.[27]

Martha Nez's parents told her not to play outside at night and that during the day she should not go near hard-to-reach places or travel along the side of tall rocks and cliffs because witches have corpse poison ('áńt'įįh) that can be thrown on a person to kill them. Skinwalkers also may come to a home. She told of how one fall morning her mother and father said that something had visited them during the night in the family's hogan.

> That night, something was scratching the surface of the hogan. This thing pulled one of the halved logs out of the hogan and made a hole in the wall. My father told the intruder that there was a door and asked why it didn't use it. Silence. The next morning, we looked at the tracks, which were very close together but did not appear to be those of a dog or a coyote because the paws stuck out every which way. We were told not to walk on those prints that led to the cliffs and then up them and away to Tsé Łichíí Háá'áhi' (Red Rock Sticking Out) and into Lók'a'jígai. There was a man named Haa'dijaa'isani who lived over there. My family suspected him, but I do not know how they knew this.[28]

Her mother died that spring.

Margaret Tso Weston said that her parents used to scare their children about skinwalkers, but it became even more of a reality when she, as a little girl, was herding sheep.

> One windy day, I saw a strange animal that looked like a dog but had a skinny behind, huge shoulders, and walked funny. I said to myself, "This must be a skinwalker," since I was told they came only on windy days. I saw it as I came up on a hill, then the animal heard me and crouched down. As I watched this strange creature walk up a wash, a shiver suddenly ran up my body, so I started walking faster to get away from it. We were told that these skinwalkers' main route was up and down this very wash after they came across the San Juan River to roam around here. I believe they do because I have seen it, yet I have no knowledge of how they do it.[29]

The power of a human to slip into the skin of a coyote and then assume supernatural abilities such as running at excessive speed, cursing, and killing individuals, and wreaking misfortune of all types, is done through the reversing of beneficial songs, prayers, and actions. By doing so, they take what is normally good and transform it into a tool of destruction and misery. Their actions are secretive, their powers maintained and practiced only with other witches, as they work against others either alone or in a group. Harvey Oliver encountered some of these qualities when he was herding sheep for Ern Hall (Beautiful Singer—Biyin Nishzóní), a trader whose post was in McElmo Canyon on the Utah-Colorado state line.

> One evening I saw three dogs on a hill and one of them said "Hooo!" to me. They were skinwalkers. Another time, I was checking for some lambs on top of a mesa. The sheep used to climb on the rocky ledges, and I was checking to see if any lambs had been left behind. As I made my way through some huge boulders, I came upon two naked women laying side by side. They had yellow stripes around their ankles and on their chests, faces covered with red clay, foreheads with a white line across it, and feathers tied to their bodies. They were lying upright and

sound asleep. Resting beside them was a dog skin and a coyote skin. I quickly turned and left. I came so close to them I almost fainted. Skinwalkers can communicate with coyotes, dogs, and bears, and often come around a person's homestead to intermingle with house animals. Witches can also use a bear's skin for skinwalking. They can communicate with the earth, heavens, sun, moon, stars, and air. Nearly all our people have participated in this skinwalking. That's how it is.[30]

This last part of Harvey Oliver's statement, that "nearly all our people have participated," needs to be taken with a grain of salt. What he bases it on is unclear, but the practice and topic of witchcraft is frowned upon by most Navajos, who see it as the polar opposite of how one should act. While many of the People know bits and pieces of this lore, any move toward its use is considered evil and to be avoided.

A final phase of life along the river was the natural occurrence of death, not to be confused with witchcraft and its evil. Indeed, death is a highly sacred time and one that is treated with utmost respect bordering on fear. Depending on the stage of life in which a person dies, the circumstances, the place, and the individual and family's attitude, there may be a variety of different reactions and procedures followed.[31] Florence Begay shared her observations of a fairly typical, traditional funeral:

When a person died, it was not publicized and only the immediate family was involved. The deceased was washed and dressed in their finest clothing, whether they died outside or inside the hogan. Two men then took the wrapped body to the burial site, usually a grave dug by relatives. The body is laid inside, then covered with boards on top or placed in a coffin. Some take a saddled horse to the burial site, where it is killed and the saddle placed beside the grave. After the burial, the two men have to step over cactus and bushes with sharp bristles to get home. Women and children are forbidden to go near the dead; this was not a happy event. The two men who buried the deceased had to stay in a separate hogan by themselves for four days while family members would be in another, but no type of work or entertainment could be performed by anyone during that time. The dishes weren't washed. It was very strict. You wondered what was going on as people sat by the fire. No one lies down; everyone sat up until dark, and then they went to sleep. I have witnessed many burials. Everyone was forbidden to look around, to talk a lot, or to be loud. It was very sacred. It's not that way today.[32]

There are many more aspects of daily life for the Navajos that are discussed elsewhere. What becomes apparent for the few mentioned here—child training, clothing, food quest, witchcraft, and funerals— is that there is a rich cultural view based upon intricate traditional teachings that the People were careful to pass along to ensuing generations. The lifeways of the Navajos are unique; the elders wish to see that they are maintained and continued. By sharing their teachings, mothers, fathers, grandparents, and others ensure that they transmit the lessons and stories they have received from previous generations going all the way back to the holy people. What it means to be a Navajo is preserved.

CHAPTER EIGHT

Trading on the San Juan

Posts, Boats, and Barter

T rading posts servicing Navajos along the San Juan River have been covered extensively from a number of different perspectives.[1] These stores proliferated at this time because of the Navajo trade in wool, lambs, and weaving since these items fit into the economy of the dominant culture. No trader on the San Juan became rich through this barter system, but each of these "mom-and-pop" endeavors provided a living that kept families together and economic wheels turning. To give an idea of how many of these posts existed, by limiting the area to those along the San Juan River in southeastern Utah and a few miles over the southwestern Colorado state line, there were at least fifteen between 1878 and 1930. Starting at the Four Corners and moving downstream, there were the Four Corners Trading Post or (Oen Edgar) Noland's, "Burned House" (Kin Díílidii), Aneth, Montezuma Creek (2), Bluff (3), Rincon, and Mexican Water. Heading toward Colorado, there were posts in McElmo (3), Hatch, and Ismay, as well as ranchers and farmers who traded on the side for a little additional income. Each of these stores has its own tale, often with multiple owners who bought and sold with an eye for greener pastures, and a mobile clientele who traded for best deals and credit. In this chapter, the main emphasis is on the Navajo experience—how they viewed and named the traders, what they recollected about transactions, the overall role they played in family and community events, and a general evaluation. There are also the traders' views—how they worked with their customers, what their experience entailed, and some unique aspects of the trade. A composite sketch that outlines these centers of activity will paint a brief but colorful picture of this important institution in the transitioning Navajo culture.

The location of a Navajo trading post played a key role in its success or failure. The population it was to serve had to be considered in terms of the number of clientele; the amount of livestock owned; natural lines of drift or travel patterns including valleys, roadways, and river crossings; seasonal accessibility; availability of resupply for the store; and reservation boundaries. Equally important was a favorable community attitude. While almost every post on the reservation had to evaluate its location against this criteria, there were also many off-reservation posts that had their own considerations. The difference between those on and off was that of government control and supervision. The on-reservation stores were monitored by federal agents who examined pricing, treatment of customers, and terms of barter, while those off reservation established their own standards of conduct and cost of goods. In the early years, all of the posts in this study were off reservation, but with boundary changes in 1884, 1905, and 1933 the Montezuma Creek, Aneth, and Aneth Extension areas came under tribal and federal jurisdiction.

Trading Post Navy

Dirt paths and roadways that wended their way through the desert, over mesas, across gullies, down valleys, and around mountains were part of a typical experience for customers and traders alike for many posts on the reservation. One thing, however, that made the San Juan experience unique was the use of boats to cross the river. During the spring and early summer, when the San Juan ran high and could not be forded, traders solved the problem through "customer service" with a boat to ferry people and their wares to the post. In the spring, Navajos loaded their wool clip into large burlap bags ranging from six to nine feet long and sold it in exchange for basic foods like flour, sugar, coffee, canned products, and dry goods. In the fall, the big sale item was the lamb crop and to a lesser extent piñon nuts. Woven blankets and rugs, silverwork, and other handcrafted objects were bartered throughout the year. Of those stores mentioned above, almost half had their own ferry operation, sponsored by the owners or run by an entrepreneurial Navajo. The size of the craft could vary from a small dinghy to a large flat-bottomed vessel thirty feet long, twelve feet wide, capable of transporting fifteen to twenty men with horses across to the post at Rincon.[2] Some of the boats, especially the larger ones, were attached to a wire cable that spanned the river, ensuring all that was needed was a strong back and arms to provide the power to get across. Others less fortunate started upstream, estimated where the current plus manpower would land the craft, then rowed through the waves, hoping to arrive at the post's backdoor without too much excess labor. Mary Jay remembered this process:

> The San Juan River sometimes rose high, so people used to go across in a boat to sell their sheepskins to the trading post. The river ran wild at times. Nobody does this anymore. People sheared the wool off the skin when they butchered a sheep and took the skin and the wool to sell at the store. They also took cowhides to sell, but the traders refuse to buy them now. Since the river ran high, some people began building boats so they could cross whenever they needed to. My grandfather, named "Hastiin Tooh," used to be a good sailor even though he was a short man. He would row back and forth, bringing people across, then taking them back. Navajos used a place just above the trading post where they tied up the boat with a huge rope before the passengers stepped onto a flat deck. The pipe with a dock on the end is still there. According to my mother, the river used to be narrow enough to jump over, but I never saw it like that. Slowly the river became wider, until travelers had to use a boat to cross. Mother said that at one time the river ran dry so that people and animals nearly died of thirst, but I was not alive at that time. They had to dig up the riverbed to find water, and did this until the water returned. I remember most of my past history, but my mother used to tell me about what went on in her time, too.[3]

Martha Nez recalled crossing often in one of the boats at Bluff. "When there was a lot of water, that was the only thing used to cross. Sometimes the river would have sand waves, which made crossing a scary experience with water sloshing in, pouring over the edge of the boat. There was a man named Hastiin Johnny Yázhí who rowed it and lived nearby his landing place. Sometimes he was given five dollars for taking people's belongings to the other side."[4] Maimi Howard refused to even get into the boat, afraid that the sand waves would swamp it.[5] Sally Lee had a different experience when boating at Aneth.

> The river was slimmer at that time, probably about ten yards wide, but also deeper. The river settled the sand, but as it eroded, the soil along the banks fell into it, and water ate the banks away. It was not scary crossing. There were two people on each side when there was lots of water. The main run of the river had humps in it, looking like something was swimming in it, but the water did not get into the boat, which glided along beautifully. We used it numerous times to go to the trading post so that they could carry sheep over in it.[6]

Posts of this day followed a fairly standard pattern. Traders entering an area might have started with a canvas tent or two, then would begin gathering materials for a more permanent and secure structure. The next step could be a small store built out of cedar logs, often set in by digging a trench in the ground, inserting the trimmed and skinned poles vertically before chinking them with mud, and then crowning this two-or-three-room structure with a flat wood-tarpaper-dirt roof. Cottonwood was also a popular construction material found along the river. If very successful, a trader might have built an even more permanent structure out of quarried rock garnered from the nearby landscape to create a store sporting a half dozen rooms or more plus outbuildings for accumulating wool; a barn for hay, grain, and horses; an outhouse; and perhaps a utility shed.

While every post was unique in its own way, there were some standard elements found at each structure. It had to be near a source of water, easily accessible to customers; have a room for trading that had a large, open area called the bullpen that was heated by a potbellied stove; have high, wide counters behind which were shelves stocked with goods and under which were bulk items; have a pawn room if it was a larger structure; and have at least a second room where trader and family slept and ate. Taking one of the no-longer-existing posts at Montezuma Creek as an example, John Meadows provided a description of the store that he and his father, Billy Meadows, traded at for five years. By the early 1900s this site had seen a succession of traders behind its counters. The structure's genealogy started with Richard Adams locating the post near the confluence of the San Juan River with Montezuma

Creek. Around 1910 William Young ("Black Hat") assumed control and remained until 1916, changing the store from a crude shack of cedar logs to one lined with boards inside and out with mud poured between for insulation; the building formed the familiar L-shape covered by a roof of heavy tarpaper with a storage shed located to the west. The long side of the building was approximately thirty-two feet and the short stem about sixteen feet, with a fourteen-foot square bullpen surrounded on three sides by counters. The door faced east with windows on the north and south sides of the facility. When Young left the post, he was followed in succession by Oscar Hatcher from Durango, Jesse Foutz, Chunky Tanner, and Wilford Wheeler, after which it was vacant for a while before other traders bought it.[7]

This post provides a perfect explanation of the reasons for the site selection. The boundary of the Navajo Reservation at the outset was the middle of the San Juan River, which meant that the traders here were not under government control. The shore along the river was flat enough to have a dirt road, albeit rough, sandy, and subject to washout, originating in Bluff with each mile marked by stone cairns leading into Montezuma Creek, thence Aneth up McElmo Canyon and into the Montezuma Valley and Cortez, Colorado. A spur to this road went from the trading post through Montezuma Canyon and extended all the way to Monticello and Blue Mountain, allowing a limited number of Utes from this area and Colorado to also conduct business in Montezuma Creek. Thus, between the river, canyons, and desert lands, access by customers and resupply of goods were feasible. Approximately eight hundred feet north of the post sat a spring of potable water with a guest hogan not far away for Navajos staying overnight. Traders encouraged their clientele to camp at the post by providing firewood, lending cooking utensils, and giving a free can of tomatoes, peaches, or some other food item, as well as offering limited tobacco for a roll-your-own cigarette.

While Navajo customers came from all directions, the majority flowed in from the reservation, requiring a boat. Trader John Meadows and others remembered a Navajo man named Sneak (Biníí' Ditł'oi or Straggle of Whiskers on His Face) providing nautical services for the post. He received his Anglo name because he walked around quietly and appeared when least expected. Sneak captained the wooden boat owned by the store and camped on an island in the middle of the river,

This artist's rendering of the Aneth Trading Post in the late 1920s captures the essence of what transpired in the spring at many posts along the San Juan. Navajo herders drove their flocks to the near shore, where the sheep were sheared and the wool stuffed in a six-by-three-foot (or longer) burlap sack supported by a wooden frame to hold the bag open. It was then secured, placed in a boat that was either rowed or pulled across on a cable, and then weighed and purchased by the trader. Wagons or trucks transported the wool to major railhead cities. (Drawing by Charles Yanito)

where a large stand of cottonwood trees shaded his homestead and provided wood, which he sold to the post for fuel.[8] Meadows described the operation:

> When we were there, this old guy, Sneak, who was a great big husky Indian, operated an eighteen-foot boat. From side to side it was a little over four feet wide and bulged a little in the center. He had two places he could tie the boat on either side of the river. He'd pull it up to a little place where there was not as much current. When someone came in to cross the river with their sheep to sell or a little load of hides, or blankets or something, they would whoop and holler so that old Sneak would get them. He would untie his boat, load their stuff in, and start across. The water was pretty swift, and so he would go down the river for a hundred to possibly two hundred feet, land below the post, pull the boat back up with a rope, dragging it to the first anchor point at the post, and help unload the goods. On the return trip, the current took him downstream again, so that he would again drag the boat back to the starting point. He had a place to anchor on both sides. It was kind of comical but interesting to watch. There were times the sand waves in the middle were pretty high and ferocious, while near the banks it was calm. In the center of the river was the greatest, deepest, and swiftest flow of water.[9]

Opening Shop

The Navajo experience once at the post was generally positive. Since this has been covered extensively elsewhere, only a few snippets are shared here. Mary Blueyes and her sister were herding rams by themselves and had heard that the trader in Bluff often handed out candy to children.

> We got there, went inside, just stood there, and looked at him. He gave us a small bag of candy, then we ran out of the trading post and went back to where we were herding the rams. We were without shoes. . . . Later when I was older, I went to the Mexican Water post. If you got there in the evening, you would spend the night if you were a long way from home. The traders let you borrow a coffee pot and coffee, bread, water, matches, and firewood. If you did not have any blankets, they

let you borrow theirs. Back then the traders were really nice. Now they would not do this.[10]

Old Mexican shared a typical spring experience of clipping wool, paying accumulated debt, and obtaining supplies at the Aneth Trading Post around 1890.

> In the morning we started moving my wife's sheep to the river. I was planning to shear across from the store, at the mouth of McElmo, next to Aneth. We started shearing the following morning. My wife's relatives who lived by the river helped us. After we had sheared quite a bunch, I went to the store and got a wool sack. They had a boat to cross the river. I took the boat across and put the wool in it; after I got on the other side again, I put it on a burro and took it to the store. For this first full sack, I got seventeen dollars. The next day we sheared again, and for the second sack I got fifteen dollars and seventy-five cents. It took us two days to shear all the sheep. My wife killed a goat, and we ate that up. A little wool was left, which I took to the store the next morning. My wife and her oldest daughter followed me, and when they got there, they sold their wool and did lots of trading. They got coffee, calico, flour, sugar, and other things they needed for the camp.[11]

Trading was far more than just a business transaction about picking up supplies and paying a debt. Both trader and customer were invested in a relationship of trust (k'é). The trader had to determine the probability the customer would pay, amount of credit to extend, other places he or she was trading, family connections in the community, size and condition of their herd including number of expected lambs and tentative wool crop, skills in weaving and silverwork, and overall demeanor. For the Navajo customer, there were parallel questions of where the best prices were, how much credit had been extended and how much more was likely, the security of pawned goods and policies to redeem it, distances to travel, generosity of the trader not only in the store but in assisting during ceremonial events or family hardship, awareness of cultural practices, and social demeanor including the ability to speak Navajo. Theoretically, each trader had his own territory in which he served a particular group of customers, but everyone was free to travel and barter elsewhere, as long as they had not overextended their borrowing power with the intent of not paying off the debt and then looking for another place for additional credit. It was incumbent upon traders to encourage customers to keep returning, pay their bills, and foster friendship. Dependability for all involved was paramount, but there was at times an undertone of skepticism and mistrust between some of the customers and traders.

There were, of course, exceptions, but generally speaking, both sides of the bullpen honored their relationships. Jerry Begay recalled working with Ira Hatch (Tall Boy—Ashkii Nezii) at the Hatch Trading Post in Montezuma Canyon:

> I first saw him as a young man, but he remained for a long time and got old there. He worked well with the people and got along with them. He would give you a free gift on top of the things you had bought, putting the cost of food on credit. Hatch and his wife spoke very good Navajo and became more fluent over the years. He has a son there now who is like that, too. In the fall, the trader bought lambs so that one's credit was paid off. People would then go to the trading post and start their credit for the winter months based upon the anticipated wool that was sheared in the spring to again pay off their debt. Sometimes there was money left over that was put forward as credit, which started the cycle to fall when the lambs were sold at the trading post. In those days, people had more sheep and the weather was different. It rained constantly, causing the lambs to get really big and the trader to rake in the money. It sometimes looked like he may have robbed the people by profiting too much. When he started out, supplies did not cost a whole lot, with soda pop selling for ten cents, candy bars at only five cents, and basic food stuffs inexpensive. A big piece of pig meat was only a dollar, whereas today a piece not as big costs a lot.[12]

One of the single most important operating principles within Navajo culture is the establishment and maintenance of respectful relationships. This is true not only between people but also with the holy beings and everything animate and inanimate (according to the Anglo classification system) in the world. Everything has a spirit that can be appealed to for assistance as long as proper procedures are followed that show respect and appreciation. So it is not surprising that traders and customers followed the same pattern. Martha Nez discussed trading at Mexican Water and described how the storeowner, in this case John Lee, treated her and her family:

My brother and I were not yet ten years old, but when the trader saw how ragged we looked, he gave me clothes and my little brother a pair of pants and shirt plus popcorn. This is how it was; he really helped us by giving us food, so I was not afraid of him since he called us his children. Even people from Oljato brought in their wool here. His Navajo was excellent; he talked just like us and used to go to Enemyway ceremonies wearing a concha belt and turquoise beads. In his store, he sold coffee, sugar, and flour by the pound, which he just dipped out of large sacks. At that time, coffee was green, a small bag of it costing twenty-five cents, while fabric was one dollar for ten yards. When you buy these things in large quantities, they go very fast. In the past, food was bought in small amounts and it lasted. There was not a lot of variety of anything, but mainly food and blankets—what now costs a hundred dollars then cost twelve. The only meat they sold was pork, and for sweets there was canned jam and candy, but no soda pop. He brought these goods in by wagons. When we sold a small rug, we received two dollars, but if it was large, ten dollars. The price was very low. An old ewe was seventy-five cents a head and a big castrated ram was two dollars and fifty cents. The payment for the things that we took in was very low, but it was the same with what we paid for goods he sold.[13]

Maimi Howard had fond memories of a trader in Bluff who provided fresh food for the Navajos to eat. His name was One Who Grew into the Heavens because he was so tall; he slaughtered cows and pigs for a feast and involved a lot of the Navajo women with butchering. When customers came to his store, they received red water colored by a powder that came in a glass bottle. Although they were not sure what it was, the customers enjoyed the treat. Any money or supplies obtained at the store could be easily lost through constant gambling, usually card playing, going on outside. Navajos enjoyed this pastime, even though many were warned by family members to avoid its pitfalls. Still, they wagered against the holdings of other Navajos and the Utes, who were equally avid in the pastime. The storekeepers in Bluff spoke Navajo, and so they encouraged many to work for them. Even though Maimi felt "that white people all look alike," she had a good relationship with them.[14] This sense of cooperation extended to others, not just the traders in Bluff, according to Martha Nez.

Navajos would rise early in the morning to help the white people in Bluff. In the evening, the people would have their day's earnings in a sack. They chopped firewood for them, while many women went there to fluff up wool to put into a quilt. Even though stealing was not supposed to occur, it happened sometimes along the way. The women who carded would put wool into their clothes or hide it in the bushes. We used to do it because we did not have any wool to use for weaving. The children also assisted in doing this, but all of those who did have died. I am the last surviving person. I see this type of behavior taking place all the time around me and it seems to me these people die easily.[15]

John Knot Begay spoke of the larger community appeal of having a post nearby with a trader who cared about the people:

Back in those days, the community held many activities like Enemyway ceremonies and other events that drew Navajos in their homes near the trading post, while others came from miles around on horses and in wagons. The traders were very helpful to those in need. If some family sponsored an activity, they were given flour, coffee, sugar, and shortening from the store to be used for the event, creating a very good relationship on both sides. The trader also helped less fortunate people in every way possible. He bought their wool and lambs, giving them food and merchandise. This interaction between the two parties was an important means of existence back then.[16]

The posts served as economic "exciters," encouraging different forms of industry. Traders paid for services like road repair, delivering and chopping firewood, freighting supplies, building construction, herding trader livestock, and guiding tourists. Ada Benally, speaking of one of the posts in Bluff, explained how her family took advantage of different opportunities.

The people had a good relationship with the trader even though he did not understand the Navajo language and was there for only a short time. His name was Owl (Né'éshjaa') because he copied an owl's hoot, so us children were afraid of him. People used to sell their rugs and buy what they needed from him. He rarely paid in cash, which was hard to obtain. My father would work doing odd jobs once in a while earning 50 cents plus some food or hay. Navajos worked for a loaf of bread or potatoes or flour, so whenever the trader needed wood or someone to chop it for him, he asked the people who came to shop at his store. My father used his wagon to haul wet and dry wood from across the river for him.

The trader owned some pigs, so sometimes he gave the pig's head to the people. It had plenty of fat and meat, making it good enough for a meal. If there was money, it was all in silver coins, worth 10, 25, 50 cents and one dollar. The Navajos called it "white money." The trader used to sponsor holiday festivities where the children had fun and received candy. At Christmas, they invited everyone to a Christmas party where they donated food for the feast. Everyone gathered at the trading post and took part in cooking the meal, with each family bringing their own firewood. A few white men and a lot of Navajos participated in these activities.

Navajos did not sell things to each other, but only bought from the store, which also had a gas pump with a handle to fill a car tank. There was no electricity. For those who came from long distances, there was a guest hogan located on the small hill next to the present-day senior citizens' center where the flagpole now stands. The trader, Little Deaf One (Jééhkał Yázhí), was the first to hold these activities.[17]

Old Mexican mentioned another source of income that both Navajos and Utes took advantage of—to the point where it sometimes turned into armed conflict and decimation of the herds—and that was deer hunting.[18] Posts purchased cow, sheep, goat, and deer hides, which were shipped back east, tanned, and processed into leather goods before the age of synthetics like nylon and other coal derivatives. Deer meat was a staple for the hunting-and-gathering Utes, providing food, shelter, clothing, and other essentials. The meat was a welcomed addition to the Navajo diet, and hides were used for clothing, ceremonial articles, and various utility objects. By the end of the nineteenth century, the herds were under tremendous pressure from both Native American groups and Anglo factions ranging from sport hunters to cattlemen who saw these animals as competitors for livestock. Trading posts added to the fray by purchasing hides. Old Mexican gave a candid account of Navajo effectiveness in hunting and what sales were like across the counter:

When I got to where they [Navajo friends] had set the date to go hunting, they had already left, so I took my pack horse and rode after them and caught up with them by sundown on top of the canyon called Montezuma Wash. There we camped overnight. The next morning, we moved on to where we were going to start hunting. This was the same kind of hunt as the other, but this time we hunted the deer afoot and shot them in the thick timber. Silver was the leader. He was chosen by one of the men when we got to the place where we were going to hunt. Silver didn't know much about this kind of hunting though, and we all had to help him. He thought he knew all about it, but he didn't. He knew some of the songs, but he didn't know the one that came at the end. He didn't know any other kind of hunting ceremonial either. Ten of us went that year. We stayed thirty-three days and killed seventy deer, bucks and does. Before we started back, I went to get more horses and saddles and boys to help us pack in all the meat. When we got back, we had plenty of meat to eat.

A few days later three of us left again on another hunt. All we went for was the buckskins, not the meat. We stayed a month and killed sixty-seven head. We picked out the fat meat and left the rest and only brought back the hides. I had twenty-two hides for myself. I sold twelve and kept ten. I got fifty cents a hide for doe hides, before they were tanned. We didn't get much for hides in those days. There were lots of them. The buck hides I tanned and kept for myself. After I tanned them, I gave three to my wife.[19]

Name That Trader

Navajos have a penchant for giving names to individuals for any number of reasons. Shortly after birth, a newborn may receive a sacred name that is used during ceremonies and special prayers to the holy people. It is a spiritual identification, known only to the closest relatives and the gods. An additional name based on a child's qualities may also be bestowed, but it is used to denote pleasant characteristics for a playful infant. Everyone uses kinship terms to address close and extended family members. Accompanying these terms are role expectations that forge tight bonds of unity—father, mother, "little mother" (aunt), and so forth. A name can be given to an individual for something they did—whether

This happy Navajo man was in Allen Canyon and about to sell his deer hides to some Ute customers. In the past, however, there had been serious competition between San Juan Utes and Paiutes, Colorado Utes, and Navajo hunting parties seeking access to a limited and diminishing deer population. Old Mexican's report regarding his success in hunting on Blue Mountain suggests why, by the first quarter of the twentieth century, deer herds had almost disappeared.

good or bad— their clan, relationship to another individual, physical characteristics, or emotional or social qualities. The latter may be based on an incident. At times, an individual may have three or four titles, yet may not be aware of all of them since using proper names instead of kinship terms is frowned upon and considered boastful. It may also be offensive to the recipient if it captures an embarrassing moment. Navajos are keen observers and not averse to noting human frailties in others and then creating a name to identify that person.

Traders, immersed in Navajo communities, were ready targets for receiving a name or two, which were sometimes passed on to his store or the community around that post. As mentioned previously, Aneth and today's Aneth Chapter are named T'áábííchʼįįdii (His Own Devil) after the government farmer, Herbert Redshaw, while the name Aneth was bestowed on the community in 1895 by the Methodist minister Howard Ray Antes, who used imperfectly a Hebrew word that meant

"The Answer."[20] When pursuing the names of traders working at the Aneth post or any other store, there are some caveats. The first is that no one was keeping records at the time, as a procession of traders spent a few years at that site and then moved on. One might have been at a post for six months or six years. Not until there were boundary changes and until the federal government required an application and associated documents did a paper trail emerge. Second, that trader may have been given more than one Navajo name based on physical characteristics or an event, or due to groups of customers recognizing him in different ways. Third, there is the ever-present issue of oral history and the fallibility of memory. Given these concerns, what follows is how the Navajo people and some of the traders remember the succession of owners and how they were named. As correct or imperfect as this may be, these traders played an important role in their communities.

Jane Silas believed that the very first trader in Aneth was Logii, then Dezhch'ah (Open Mouth), Ghaan Agódí (Stubbed Arm), Atł'aa'ii (Buttocks, because his "crack" was often showing—Arthur Tanner Jr.), Ghaandílí (Big Arm—Ralph Tanner), Shash (Bear—Art Tanner Sr. because of his strength, also known as Hel-cotch-Ch'įįdii or Desert Devil), Ashkii Tį (Boy Who Wants to Go), and Naakai Yázhí (Little Mexican—John Hunt). Then there was a trader with a long nose whom they called Chịị Háá'áí (Club Nose). Another was named Ajaa' Yázhí (Small Ears). Dághaa' Chíí (Red Beard) was the last trader she knew. The store assumed the names of its owners, at various times being called Jaa Nididiłii (Wiggly Ears), T'áábíich'įįdii (named for Redshaw, who was not a trader but lived below the post on the floodplain), Ghash Dílí (Fat Arms), and Doo Yildin Da (The Despised).[21]

Below Aneth at the mouth of Marble Canyon stood a store owned by William Hyde. After the 1884 flood wiped out his post in Montezuma Creek, Hyde moved to this location, where he put in a ferry and trading post. Little is known about this point of activity that remained open for four years. This place is now called locally Burned House and was owned and operated by a trader named Silver (Béésh Łigaii) who "used to live there until he got mad at some people who then threw him out," according to Mary Jay.[22] Jane Silas added a few more details to the sketchy picture: "People used to haul in their wool and sheepskin to that place. Silver's trading post was located on this side of the river near the narrow point of the gray hill. There was another house beyond that, but

The Aneth Trading Post was ideally situated by being on the San Juan River and its travel corridor, next to McElmo Creek and Canyon, and was initially off reservation lands. After the 1884 flood wiped out the first post, a second one was built above the floodplain and continues to be the oldest continuing business in San Juan County. Note how the structure is built of local rocks in an L-shape—one side for trade, the other for living quarters—and how there is a clerestory cupola to let in light.

people used to shop at this store. Eventually, when the store was no longer in operation, someone burned it down."[23]

Some of the posts at Montezuma Creek remained open for a good length of time, so their ownership was remembered by other traders. For instance, Richard "Dick" Adams, known to the Navajos as "Batter" (Ahkali) because he limped around with a cane shaped like a baseball bat, wanted to improve the welfare of his customers. He was a kind man who generously gave away chickens so that every Navajo camp could start its own brood. He was equally generous with goats, selling them at low prices. In the 1920s Chunky Tanner did a similar thing, buying lambs in the spring only to sell them again in the fall in order to encourage Navajos to shop at the Montezuma Creek post. His wife sewed "squaw skirts" and blouses, which Chunky peddled on horseback, trying to attract customers, but with disappointing results. Business proved to be too slow, and so he eventually pulled out.[24] This post also provided a name that is now used for the entire community—Mussi (Cat). The area had first been known as Sagebrush Wash (Díwízhii Bitó), but when Wilford Wheeler moved there to trade, the Navajos who knew his mother and father gave him the name of Son of Woman Who

Looks like a Cat (Mósí Yázhí—Little Cat). Apparently, this woman's ears, face, and nostrils with protruding hair reminded her customers of a cat with whiskers, and so she received the name that now denotes the town.[25] Other traders included Yaa'nidi'ashi, who was replaced by Chííh Tsoh, who had a big nose and so received this name, Ka'li, Yeelii, Náá'tsohii (Large Eyes), Ch'ah Łizhinii (Black Hat—William Young), and Ghaandílí (Big Arm—Ralph Tanner).[26] As mentioned in a previous chapter, Montezuma Creek had a number of names, but those associated with the trading posts were Black Hat, Mussi, Put Your Hand Out (Ch'izh Dílni), and Flew Back Out (Ch'ínát'a'). This last name came from a store built by Joseph Hatch Jr. along the San Juan River, not far from the still-in-operation store in Montezuma Creek. The small sixteen-foot-wide by thirty-foot-long building, built in stockade style, was short-lived, the name remaining longer than the trader. Apparently Hatch would say to his customers, "I flew back out like this," as he described his travel to different places.[27]

Bluff had a number of different posts over the years, most prominent of which was the San Juan Cooperative Company or Co-op, run by Mormons who had their own governing board and paid dividends in the good years. A group of individuals owned this store. Names for the men behind the counters included Jééhkał Yázhí (Little Deaf One), Bilagháana Nez (Tall White Man, probably the same person as Hot'ahniisani—One Who Grew into the Heavens), Tł'ízíchǫǫh (Billygoat—June Powell), Bila'sighani (Skinny Hand, a Navajo), Dóola (Bull), Bidzaanééz Łigaii (Owns a White Mule), Bilagháana Bichiin (Strong White Man), Hastiin Bikin Názti'ii (Man with a String of Houses), and Hastiin Yííyá (Scary Man). Red Beard (Kumen Jones) worked for and with the co-op almost since its inception, was a skilled trader behind the counter, spoke some Navajo, and was a soft-spoken, patient man. Equally popular was his wife, Mary, who, like Louisa Wetherill in Kayenta, became known for her precise linguistic ability. Even some of her children learned the language.[28]

A Trader's View: Stewart Hatch

To fully understand the trading experience, one also has to stand on the other side of the counter and listen to traders who told what they saw. For that we turn to the Hatch Trading Post and the recollections of

Local photographer Charles Goodman took this interior shot between 1895 and 1898, when Jesse V. West owned the Aneth Trading Post. His helpers, Anna Ames and Gussie Honaker, lived on farms by the river. This is a rare picture of the inside of an old post before the turn of the century and gives a clear indication of the effectiveness of the clerestory cupola as well as the variety of goods stocked behind the counters that formed the bullpen.

Stewart and Ira Hatch, two brothers who worked in the store created by Joe Hatch Jr., another brother, in 1926. Located in Montezuma Canyon with access north to Monticello and south to Montezuma Creek, with a flow of traffic dropping off of McCracken Mesa to the west, and with easy access to Ismay and posts along McElmo Creek, thence to Cortez, Colorado, and beyond to the east, the Hatches were ideally situated. Although there had been a precursor near this site, the Hatch family remained in this community for over sixty years, trading with both Navajo and Ute clients. The Hatches knew many of the old traders, weathered the storms of change as other posts either died or morphed into convenience stores, and shared lifelong friendships with Indian neighbors. Stewart Hatch had a particularly sharp recollection of those halcyon days of the trading post before livestock reduction and lawsuits curtailed much of the old ways of conducting business. What follows is Stewart's candid explanation of the operation of Hatch Trading Post, which was in many instances typical of other stores in this area.

We serviced around twenty-five Navajo and twenty-five Ute families, all of whom had a lot of livestock, which justified a trading post and gave them a place to sell their wool, lambs, and rugs. Lambs were always the best crop. A Navajo would come in and say, "I've got 400 head of sheep, let's say 500 head of sheep, and I want to get credit." That helped me to figure out about how much wool he would have in the spring when he sheared his flock. If you gave him credit all winter, then he'd pay his bill in the spring after the clippings were weighed at the present market price for wool. He would subtract that from what he owed you, or if he didn't owe that much, then you owed him a little bit. Usually, it was the other way around, unable to pay their entire bill. After the wool season, as they called it, we would extend more credit on the strength of their lambs, six months away. They were a little more lucrative. Usually, the lambs paid off all their grocery bill with maybe sixty or a hundred dollars remaining, then traded outright.[29]

There was a difference between the livestock owned by Navajo herders and those of Anglos. Traders used the terms "Navajo sheep" and "American sheep." Those belonging to a white man were substantially bigger, having larger bones and receiving supplemental feed in addition to grazing. When sheared, an American sheep might have produced ten or twelve pounds of wool, while a Navajo sheep produced perhaps five or six. Traders had no dealings with American sheep. Navajo sheep had to forage where they could.

That is why most of the Navajos, back in those days, had their hogans where they lived in the winter and moved to a different range in the spring and summer. They kept their livestock right around that winter hogan area, so the grass got awful short and the sheep skinny with weight loss. In the spring, when the grass started growing, the stock owners moved to summer range with more feed and let the other grazing area rest. After they sold their lambs in the fall, they would move back to their winter hogan. They all had their own "shikéyah" (my land) or grazing territory. If a man had five hundred head of sheep, he would summer them at a certain place that did not interfere with his neighbor. The term means "my place"—literally, "this is where I put my foot down." They didn't argue about it or have any trouble back then about being friends. Now, it's altogether different.[30]

When a Navajo family brought their wool to the store, there were posts set in the ground to hold open the seven-foot-long burlap sack that the trader filled with wool once it had been slightly cleaned and weighed. Since payment was by weight—for both the Navajos and the purchasing warehouse before being sent back east—it behooved the trader to make sure he was accepting good wool. There was, of course, the possibility of accidentally getting sand, sticks, and other debris from the shearing corral mixed into the bag. There was also the possibility of putting materials in to increase the weight. Stewart recalled incidents where this intentionally happened, but it was not a frequent occurrence.

> They used to put in the corner of those wool sacks some wool and tie a string around it. This left an "ear" sticking out so that a person could grab onto that end and the same way on the other end, making it easier to handle. A lot of times, Navajos would put rocks in there instead of wool, adding a couple of pounds. But generally, people were pretty honest about the wool, even though it would not be sacked right. Often it was too loose, so the sacks would bend and you could hardly hold it, and when putting it on a scale, it would touch the ground. Most places, in fact about every trading post, opened up the sacks and graded the wool, removing anything that should not be in there. One time, I bought some wool, dumped it out, and found an old sheep hide with the wool sheared off with the skin wadded up. I guess a few customers tried to finagle around to get a little extra weight, but it was not really a problem. These Navajos were pretty good when they sheared, removing what they call tags. On the rear end of sheep there are a lot of little tags, maybe some turds or sticks entangled in the wool. They clipped them off, kept them separate, and placed them in a little bag to present to the trader who would give them something at a way cheaper price.[31]

In the fall, traders, with the help of Navajo shepherds, herded the lambs to a market town, usually associated with a railroad. Everything else going to or from a post went in wagons and later trucks, including supplies to the post and produce—wool, rugs, and other trade items. For the Hatch Trading Post, its two main destinations were Durango and Farmington, with emphasis on the Farmington Mercantile. Anglo and Navajo people who had their own wagons and horses would hire out to a store to deliver its goods and haul back its supplies. They would load the merchandise and then take two or three days to get wherever they were going. Experienced traders and freighters knew exactly how long it would take to make the trip, where to find water for them and their horses, and where to camp each night.

Transactions made across the counter were unhurried events. A Navajo would enter into the bullpen and for a few moments just quietly look around to see who was there, eventually greeting them. Shortly, he or she would approach the trader, maybe take some free tobacco from a container fastened to the broad counter or enjoy a canned treat, share some family and community news, and then begin to trade, one item at a time with accompanying calculations. Men and women followed this well-established pattern. Stewart felt that both Navajo and white women held their own in trading, but Ira Hatch had a slightly different take.

> The man did most of the shopping. A woman would finish a rug, and the couple came to the store, but the man had it rolled up, tied to the back of his saddle, and headed for the post first. The woman might be a mile or two behind so that sometimes the bartering over the rug was half completed by the time she got there. He would buy a shirt, trousers, and shoes, so that when she arrived, she received the remaining money. As for a white woman as a trader, my wife did as well as I did.[32]

It should be noted that Navajos generally have a well-developed sense of property ownership, and so not all women turned over control of their income to their husbands.

Saddle blankets and rugs were an important part of the trade economy. Indeed, Stewart estimated that his biggest income producer came from livestock (sheep, lambs, and cattle) and next from rugs.

> We bought thousands of Navajo rugs from all over the reservation. My experience, from the time we opened this place, is that we dealt in everything. We figured on rugs as our main business, then, of course, wool and lambs, which were most important in paying off their bills. Usually, a Navajo would not pay off their account with a rug. They never did that. They might trade it to you for groceries, buy a new shawl, material for clothing, or clothes for their children. New shoes were a good sale item, which for the women was what we called at that

Hatch Trading Post, built in 1926 in Montezuma Canyon, served both Navajo and Ute clientele living in the canyon. Pictured (left to right) Joe Hatch, his brother Ira (who was the primary trader), Father Joe Hatch Sr., and Anglo neighbor Hugh Rentz, who married K'aayélii's sister Carolyn. All three of the Hatches spoke Navajo fluently, had good relations with their neighbors, and bought wool, lambs, baskets, and rugs produced by their clientele.

time squaw shoes. These were high tops with laces. Not everything was on credit. Usually, you have an understanding with a man and his wife with two or three kids. The family has sheep, so the trader makes a deal with him for a little credit for the winter, because he has got nothing else coming in. It's kind of a sacred understanding that he won't abuse that account. About the only thing he'll buy is flour, sugar, coffee, lard, baking powder, and salt. Those are the staples along with a little bacon and canned stuff. On this tab, there are no shoes or clothing or anything like that, which was usually purchased through the sale of a rug. Ninety percent of the time, you won't lose it.[33]

In summarizing the percentage of items bought and sold at the Hatch Trading Post in the 1930s, not including the livestock, it would look something like this: 10 percent in baskets, 60 percent in wool, 25 percent in rugs, and 10 percent in silver.

Before Ira Hatch could purchase the store, he worked for ten years (1924–34) for an Englishman to earn enough money to get started. During that time, this trader used secco money, or specially made stamped coins tied to a specific trading post. When the Englishman sold out, he gave Ira $450 worth of dollars and change in secco, which he introduced into the Hatch Post–Montezuma Creek economic system. Although the federal government frowned on its use, suggesting that real money should be used, there just was not a lot of it around in those Depression years, especially on or near the reservation. No trader had to accept tokens from another post—it was strictly internal to each store unless arrangements had been made. According to Ira:

> I used tokens at Montezuma Creek during the Depression. If it was done correctly, you would have to be bonded before you used it, but it seemed very practical when there was no money. A medicine man could come to the store and get those secco dollars and carry them in his pocket instead of herding in his livestock. It worked well. They could pawn and give them that trade money and use it like cash between one another. Many traders did not accept it because of the inconvenience of exchanging it at different posts. There was one trader down on the San Juan River, Black Hat, who would take it. He would wait until he had a hundred or so dollars and then come to Hatch to cash it in.[34]

Another means of extending credit without exchanging dollars was through the pawn system. Historians have written a great deal about how this system worked, and so it will not be detailed here. In short, a Navajo customer could bring in an object of value and leave it with the trader for an agreed-upon time before redeeming it. This "live pawn" became "dead pawn" after the due date elapsed without payment. Technically, the trader could then sell the dead pawn for market value, but in reality, it was sometimes held for years, since family ties to post and object were as much of a social obligation as a financial contract. In a perfect world, the family would redeem the pawned item, meet all obligations, and the trader would have his money. Reality was different. Some families drew out paying their debt, leaving the trader holding a bill but still needing to purchase supplies to keep the store open. There was also the issue of security and safeguarding these family heirlooms from theft, requiring most posts to have a pawn room that could be locked. It is popular today to accuse traders of taking advantage of their customers to make money, but the historical records for posts in southeastern Utah suggest this was not the case, which is confirmed by a number of federal audits. In later years, when government checks or those earned through hiring out for employment came into the store, the customer would present it to the trader and then "thumb it" with the help of an inkpad.

While posts catered to the needs of males and females, rich and poor, there was one social class that required some special attention—the medicine man. In general, they were a wealthier lot in that they would be paid in livestock and material goods for performing a ceremony, pushing them above the normal Navajos' income. One item that the posts carried that was used in every ceremony was the woven "Navajo wedding basket." At least one and often a number of these baskets woven out of sumac were used for everything from acting as a container for a medicine man's bundle of ceremonial items, to holding cornmeal mush in a wedding ceremony, to serving an emetic in the Evilway ceremony, to accommodating herbs to bless and heal a person. This utility basket had a standard pattern that called forth a wide variety of interpretations and was used at certain times and in specific places in a ceremony. At the end of the ritual, the sponsoring family would give the baskets to a medicine man as part of his pay, and then he could choose whether to keep them or sell them at a post. He or the sponsoring family could also go to a post to buy them. At the Hatch store, there were both Navajo and Ute basket makers who sold their products, which were consistently good. Stewart explained, "The Navajo basket makers that I knew when I first opened up here were really good weavers. Their baskets were awful tight and nice and held water easily, but that did not last long when this group of elders passed away. No doubt, before my time, the Navajos were probably really gifted at making baskets. They looked around to locate sumac branches—not willow—which I always thought was being used. The strands of this plant may grow two or three feet long."[35]

To be acceptable for purchase, baskets had to be tightly woven and have good colors. The Utes used brown instead of red for part of the design, while the Navajos preferred red, but both used black—all of which came from packets of dye purchased for a dime. At the very center of the basket, where the weave started, there was a pinhole that the medicine man filled with a little piece of cloth to make the container leakproof. The color difference between red and brown was not an issue, but the store separated the baskets according to new or used—determined by cornmeal, pollen, or other material stuck in the cracks of a used basket—and by the clockwise or counterclockwise weave. To do this, there were four separate piles. Stewart commented, "Every time we bought one that was made in reverse [counterclockwise done for a specific ceremony], we kept it separate from the other baskets, and they'd come in and tell us they'd want one that was woven in reverse. Then we'd usually have a little stack of them, and they could pick out the one they wanted. We'd never get too many of them."[36] The Hatches bought baskets whenever they were brought in but kept them primarily for local trade. The price of a basket ranged from one to four dollars; there was very little profit in carrying them but a great deal of customer satisfaction in obtaining one when needed.

Another item purchased for medicine men by the post was a deerskin of an animal that was not killed by violent means such as a bow and arrow or rifle, but rather by suffocation or strangling. This unwounded buckskin (bįįh bikágí doo k'aak'ehii) was highly valued for medicine bundles, for ceremonial paraphernalia, and as a covering to place medicine objects upon. Preferred was the complete hide, skinned very carefully so that there were no cuts from a knife. Stewart explained what his customers sought:

> The first thing they looked for were the ears, although in certain ceremonies they could use the buckskin if the ears were not present. The tail was also desired, even if it was just a little hair. They liked to have hair on the tail and the ears. The first thing a Navajo does when picking out a hide is to have a medicine man with him to ensure the skin is good. So you show him one and he'll spread it out and look at the ears and tail, then he's interested and will examine the entire hide and how it has been colored. The fewer holes the better.[37]

Stewart, like many of the old traders, had a deep respect for the medicine men who came into his store. Although some traders had a superficial knowledge of what the ceremonies were about, others were generally aware of what was taking place. Very few denied the efficacy of what they observed when invited to attend. Stewart affirmed:

> Yeah, I kinda grew up that way. I've seen a lot of things that are hard to explain. For instance, there was a child that had been badly burned by hot coals on his knee that would not heal. The medicine man looked it over and performed a certain ceremony, which, with prayers and songs,

included burning a rabbit skin and making some powder from the singed hair that he placed on the wound. There was no infection and it healed quickly. That sounds kind of funny, but that's what I saw.[38]

In summarizing the role of trading posts for both the Navajo customer and Anglo trader, one can see that this economic institution lay at the crossroads of change and exchange between the two worlds. Each culture depended on the other to obtain what was needed to live; each encountered and then accepted or rejected those things that fit into its worldview; each modified its own views to accommodate the other; and each had a voice in shaping its response. Perhaps no institution played a bigger role in using friendly terms at a time when change was all about. The Navajos took advantage of what these stores had to offer.

CHAPTER NINE

Early Inroads in Acculturation

Shelton, Shiprock, and Students

W hile Navajo parents had their ways of teaching values to their children, the U.S. government, in an attempt to prepare the youth for entry into the dominant culture, used the boarding school as a tool of indoctrination for the rising genera-tion. The Indian Service, later Bureau of Indian Affairs (BIA), heavily recruited children living along the San Juan River as part of the newly established Northern Navajo or Shiprock Agency, which presided over a five-thousand-square-mile region. Under the direction of William T. Shelton, a ten-year veteran of the Indian Service who originally hailed from Waynesville, North Carolina, the agency assumed the responsi-bility for government programs in this heretofore isolated section of northwestern New Mexico. On September 11, 1903, Shelton arrived on site and immediately set to work establishing a school, which many children of the Aneth–Montezuma Creek–Bluff area attended. Before hearing their firsthand accounts, a brief description of the school, its growth, and its programs will establish a foundation for understanding their experience.

Launching the Shiprock Boarding School

Many Navajos lived in the area and watched carefully as the first log and adobe homes arose, soon to be replaced by larger, more permanent structures built of stone or fired adobe brick. The first two structures made of stone were a house for personnel and a day school for education. Other buildings followed—a barn, gas house, laundry facility, pump house, and administrative quarters. These were made, for the most part, with local materials, the rest being shipped into Durango by rail, then hauled by wagon to Shiprock. Shelton, as a fomenter of progress, took great pride in seeing the agency and school blossom. Just two years after its inception, the *Farmington Enterprise* published a lengthy article about just how successful the attempt to move Navajos down the road of acculturation had been. In it, the author noted that as soon as a person crossed the reservation boundary below Jewett, the roads were new, straight, and in good condition. A mile before the agency, the road merged into a wide, well-graded street, leading to a site where the buildings and grounds were artistically laid out with young shade trees. There were a large number of already completed buildings with others under construction. "The whole institution, when completed as planned, will cover about six blocks, which will be beautifully apportioned with a view both to utility and magnificence. Young trees have been arranged among the larger ones and walks and trivia among fine buildings, beds of flowers and shady nooks. In all, a picture which cannot fail to wean the wary red man from his customs of generations to those of a higher ideal and to habits more satisfactory and effective."[1]

The article continued to extol the virtues of each physical structure, separating them according to their functions as part of the agency or school. The stone home of the superintendent, eight adobe residences alternating as homes for white and Indian employees, a long log warehouse to hold goods to pay for Navajo labor, blacksmith and carpenter shops, a stable, and a camp house completed the agency space. A three-story brick building eighty feet long soon replaced the spruce log school, and was to be matched by a three-story boys' and a three-story girls' dormitory, a brick hospital, a school warehouse, and a barn to facilitate agricultural instruction. The main buildings were heated by steam, illumined by acetylene gas lights, and serviced with water from a pump that pushed thirty-five thousand gallons a day. Other facilities on the south side of the river included a warehouse, barn, and other buildings to facilitate the government program when the river proved impassable. The government school opened its doors on February 8, 1907, with 106 pupils attending, all of whom were boarding. Others were turned away due to lack of space.[2] As new facilities opened, more pupils were accommodated, with a short-term goal of raising the number to 150. No Indian children attended off-reservation public schools.

A year later, in April 1908, John L. Conway, a local newspaperman, visited the school and provided an interesting view, not only of its activities, but also of associated values during this Progressive era in history. After describing the physical facilities in which he observed intense orderliness of the environment with the buildings all aligned, the wide, well-kept streets, beautiful lawns, and flower gardens, he remarked:

> The regular routine during the school term is interesting as well as instructive. In the laundry, the children show no signs of sluggishness but hurry to and fro, changing the clothes from the washing machine to the rinse water, guiding them through the wringer and carried to the line to dry. Specimens of the neat work which the Navajo girl is capable of are to be seen in the sewing room. The playroom and dormitories present the same appearance that is noticeable throughout the entire place—cleanliness and order. Numbered books with the Navajo as well as the American name of the pupil neatly typewritten underneath are to be found in the washroom and in the dormitory halls where their school clothes are hung when not in use. . . . Each pupil spends half of each day in the classroom and the other half on the farm, in the garden or poultry yards, in the industrial shops, in the kitchens, sewing rooms, laundry, or wherever practical instruction can be given that is likely to be of use hereafter. The progress made by the pupils in the San Juan school so far is really remarkable.[3]

Conway went on to laud the students for their ability to carry on a normal conversation in English, for their hard work in the beet fields of Colorado, aptitude in trades, steady dependability, and high intelligence compared to other Native American groups. On a lighter note, there was time for recreation—but even that was part of acculturation. Shelton wrote that the boys had the run of the farm, chasing jackrabbits and riding in boats, but baseball, football, marbles, and tops were also

The Shiprock Boarding School, under the guidance of William T. Shelton from 1903 to 1916, became the flagship for acculturation of the Navajo people. Shelton, also called Naatáanii Nééz (Tall Leader), was a stern, no-nonsense, progressive champion, and his Navajo name soon became synonymous with the community of Shiprock. The school's administrative building here, with its rows of watermelons stretched out on a shady, well-manicured lawn, is ready for a large group of Navajos to descend on the agency for the Shiprock Fair.

popular. During inclement weather they played dominoes and checkers, sang school songs, and read books. The girls, on the other hand, sewed, beaded, swung on swings and hammocks, jumped rope, played basketball, and went for walks accompanied by an employee. Some even wove little Navajo blankets. The two sexes came together for chaperoned Saturday night dances and socials.[4] All of this was in stark contrast to the home life left behind and the worldview they were accustomed to. What follows are the reactions of Navajo children to this new world opening up to them—whether they wanted it or not. For some, it was a welcomed relief from the tough existence of reservation life with its many uncertainties, while for others, it was a place to flee in order to return to family and the familiar.

Today, it is popular to malign the role of the boarding school as a tool of imperialism and harsh treatment by insensitive bureaucrats who made their living through excoriating traditional culture (here Navajo), punishing the children who practiced it, and intentionally cultivating emotional trauma. There is truth to these allegations. However, the boarding school experience cannot be lumped into one black mire for all children. It was a multifaceted encounter that in many instances met the needs of participants. This is not to excuse the bad, but to suggest that many elders saw good in what they learned and how they were treated. Some did not. What follows is a wide variety of viewpoints and an understanding of some Navajos' perspectives.

Old Mexican told of when Shelton first arrived.

> During the winter the people said there was a white fellow surveying all around Shiprock and across the river. He had been to Aztec, Farmington, and Durango. That was Mr. Shelton, the first superintendent of the district. They said, "This fellow has been around, saying that he was going to put up a school." The people hated having a school close by. They thought, especially the old folks, that they were going to take all of their young children, and they cried. In the spring, we got word from Shelton, saying "All people, whoever wants bucks and sheep, come and get them." My mother and my older brother went, but I did not go so I could work on the ditch. . . . My older brother got a scraper and also a scythe and pitchfork. Some of them got garden hoes and saws. My mother returned after nine days with three bucks.[5]

Two years later, feelings had mellowed. Old Mexican reported that Tall Bitter Water, a community leader, said,

> About the school children, let the people who would like to put their children in school, and some of them want their children or their grandchildren or their relatives to go to school, let them send them to school. We would like to have more educated children on the reservation. Some places they have educated boys and girls. That is the way I would like to see you people do around here. We are not starting school just now. It has been started a long time. Some have been to Fort Lewis, who are already on the job. We used to talk like that way back, but that did not help us much. Some of the boys and girls are worrying about this, that they wish they had been to school. They sure have put up some good school buildings at Shiprock. The rooms are

in good shape. The children all wear good clothes. They even pack a napkin in their back pocket, and a handkerchief in another. They even have a clean cloth that they wipe their eyes on in another pocket. And they have lots of good things to eat besides, and lots of clean dishes to eat in. And in the place they live, there is no smoke. They keep the house clean. Over here, in our camps, the room is always full of smoke. That's why we all have brown eyes, and some have yellow eyes.[6]

Resistance and Reasoning

Each family had its own view of sending children to school, and at times, regardless of how they felt, government workers would descend on their home and insist that the children go with them. Margaret Weston and Ada Benally, like so many children at that time, feared the approach of a car or white men in a wagon, convinced they were on their way to Shiprock. Margaret explained:

In those days our parents didn't encourage us to go to school because they would rather have us stay home to look after everything. Suddenly we saw officers visiting the homes, asking the parents to send their children to school. They were taken against their will. The people spoke of Herbert Redshaw, the government farmer living in Aneth, as a leader of the community, keeping things in order, but he was the one who ordered the people to send their children to school, allowing the officers to take them. Some children absolutely did not want to go, so they kept running away and never went. There were different kinds of automobiles. One of them had a tent-like cover on top, the kind the old man used to haul the children off to school in. I was taken to school in one of these, the type that had to be cranked in front to get it started. I remember we cried because we didn't want to go and thought we were being kidnapped. When we were asked to go to school, my father and grandfather refused to let us attend, saying, "The white men are dangerous and will kidnap you," so we were scared. These Anglos rode their horses here and there along the San Juan River asking and looking for children that needed to go to school. Our kinfolk would hide us from them. They might have had a reason for their refusal because look at what is happening today—nothing but chaos. I used to hear the old folks say that education was not meant for the Diné. Our people did not want the Navajos to live the white man's way. We had a chance to be educated, but didn't go.[7]

There were a variety of reasons for parents keeping children out of school, a primary one being the assistance that would be lost in handling chores at home. Hauling water, chopping wood, cooking and cleaning, processing wool and weaving, child tending—the list seemed endless. But of all of the time-consuming tasks to maintain the home and family economy, at the top of the list was caring for livestock. In the dozens of interviews of Navajos involved with either going or not going to boarding school, the subject of herding the animals was paramount. When one considers constantly searching for grass and water, frequently moving between camps, letting the sheep and goats in and out of the corral twice a day and then moving them to pasture, maintaining them in the winter when snow covered their feed, dealing with lambing and shearing seasons, and moving the wool or animals to a trading post— one can see how child labor was important, even indispensable. John Joe Begay serves as a prime example.

> When I was a boy, there was talk of school. I was about six years old and volunteered to go. I only heard, "No, no. Herd the sheep. Herd the sheep." I said I would let the sheep roam and would run away to school and was told, "You shouldn't say such things." Regardless of outside events, I was not allowed to do this. It was all because of the sheep. They needed tending, so I was lectured that the sheep would come to help me, just like my mother and father, and that one day they would also take care of my children. I was held responsible for these sheep all the time I was growing up.[8]

The ability to perform tasks could be the deciding factor as to who could or could not go to school. The more skilled or able the individual, the more likely that the boy or girl would have to remain at home. Government officials asked Mary Jay to attend school at Towaoc on the Ute Mountain Ute Reservation, but her little sister started crying, insisting that she should be the one to go. Her parents decided to let the younger one attend, since she was not all that much help around the home, whereas Mary was much better at carding wool and herding sheep. There was little time lost. As soon as her sister dismounted from her donkey, the government employees "hauled her off" without further preparation.[9] Martha Nez did not go to school because her older sister took her place. A man was given to her by Martha's father, but she did not like him, and so he left. As children at that time, all they did was tend sheep and were told that they would have them for life; her sister, however, was to go to school so that one day she could return and help. Martha and the others missed out on any assistance. "Now all I say is a coyote must have gone to school because we never got that help. School only consisted of papers, and it did not deal with the facts of life, like hoeing, sheep herding, and so forth. All I say is there are many words there, but there isn't any food in the stomach."[10]

There were other parents who for various reasons wanted to have their children go to school. Ella Sakizzie attended at the age of five, along with her older sister and brother. Her mother was expecting another baby, Ella would have no one to play with, and her parents could handle the chores. She spent three years in the Shiprock school, then one year at the boarding school in Ignacio (Southern Ute), and another year at Towaoc, which completed her education. As an elder, she recalled, "Many years ago, we had to 'sacrifice' so much just to keep our children in distant schools. They were gone for a whole year before they could return home for a short two-month vacation! We had to cry 'tears of departure' every time."[11] Florence Begay also had willing parents when Redshaw showed up at their hogan door to register children. He told her mother and father that the children had to attend, and since Florence was the oldest and tallest, she was a likely choice. Some parents didn't want to send their children off and cried but, Florence remembered, "My father said to me, 'You are probably capable of attending school so it is okay with me. I will come to visit you often,' so I agreed and was registered."[12]

Finding children for school was often a challenge. The search for good summer range and water took families far and wide with frequent moves. John Norton recalled, "This was the time people moved from one place to another. There was a constant movement, seeming like we spent only a few days in one place, then moved again. The main site we returned to was our winter camp."[13] John grew up near Red Rock (Tséchii) close to Bluff, then later moved to Black Mesa to be with his mother's younger sister, then back to Red Rock. His mother and father visited Redshaw, who was always on the lookout for new pupils, for the purpose of sending their son to school. At this point, there were no cars available, and so John rode double on the back of his father's horse. They traveled through Aneth and spent the night at a place called Tó Nii' Tsékoh (Rock in a Pond). The next day they arrived at school, where "there were lots of children. I was turned loose among them." At the start of summer, John's father came to pick him up for a two-week break at home ("be back in two Sundays") before returning to school. Both ways, he sat astride the back of his father's horse, riding double, unlike the more fortunate children whose parents owned wagons.[14]

This went on for five years until a physician examined John and determined he was sick.

> Every so many days the children were weighed and diagnosed according to their weight. We did not have any doctors and not that many Anglos, so the facility was in poor shape because its program was just starting. Still, many people came to the clinic with sickness in their eyes to get treated. I was told that I was not gaining weight, so I was admitted to the hospital and given a special diet. I was still allowed to do other things, but this went on for almost a winter. I fell behind in school as my classmates advanced and then was told that when one of my relatives came to get me for our two Sundays off, I was to return home and not come back. Perhaps this was in 1923 or earlier. I remained there even though I was not aware of any illness. I felt fine and thought there was nothing wrong, but that was the end of my schooling.[15]

The School Experience

Redshaw worked extremely well with the Navajo people and was not averse to going out of his way to help them and make sure things were done right. He lived on the river in the government station and spent much of his time providing transportation for young scholars heading to Shiprock. He supplied the only motorized "school bus" that each fall brought the students to their destination.[16] Once the students arrived at school, they entered a new world. Daily routines unlocked the power of consistency and school expectations. Orderliness and government standards ruled the day. Florence continued her account:

Herbert Redshaw (T'áábíích'į́dii) and reservation doctor Benjamin Church stand in front of Redshaw's Ford truck with the government station built on the river flood-plain behind. The building was swept away by the 1933 flood. Redshaw's standard bib overalls and broad-brimmed hat stained on the rim by smoke from his pipe, as well as his plodding gait, were well-recognized features of this friendly government farmer.

In the autumn of 1922, I left for school and continued to attend for ten years. Mr. Redshaw came in a Model T automobile with another man, Hastiin Joe, to pick me up. I was wearing tennis shoes but dressed traditionally with my hair fixed in braids. When I got to the car, I saw some other students—Nora Sakizzie, Margaret Clitso, and Irene Mark—sitting inside, who, every now and then, would start crying. Counting me, there were four of us girls leaving that day that were taken to Shiprock to a school called Camp School. The new building, freshly painted at the time, still sits beside the trading post. Several children were already there when we arrived, then soon after, our hair was cut short and combed. We dressed in striped uniforms that were given to all of us, while our traditional clothes were put away. Two white women came to our school, and one day, one of them wanted to name me Florence, after a place where she was from.

At the school, we could speak our language and nothing was said about it. Two of our dorm matrons, one of whom was named Ida Yazzie, usually spoke to us in Navajo and taught us in Navajo what to do and not to do. They treated and cared for our lice-infested hair. Our food was prepared for us. We ate bread and had mutton that was roasted, fried, or boiled but always very tough and had a strong smell. Sometimes we didn't eat it, yet for some, it didn't make any difference and they ate it anyway. For breakfast we had no eggs but mostly oatmeal with milk brought in from the school dairy in barrels transported in a small wagon pulled by a horse. There were no refrigerators, so things were kept cold in a small storage box on the porch. An older man brought in coal to burn that warmed our huge dormitories heated by four big wood-burning stoves, but the rooms were still very cold. The old man kept busy all night long trying to keep the place warm, but by morning, he was dozing by the fire.

We did not do much because we were very small. The other school for older students was located farther down from our camp school. They probably did chores because there were many tall girls whom we would see every now and then on Sundays, but I remained with the smaller children. We had fun with jump ropes while the boys enjoyed marbles and baseballs. Nobody forced us to play, so we chose what we wanted to do, but the boys and girls remained separate in different areas. There were no other houses, just fields of watermelons all around and the Shiprock Trading Post. Otherwise, there was nothing but barren land. On Sundays we took walks to different places across a single bridge to play in the sand on the other side of the river, but usually we were forbidden to play in or near it because some people were said to have drowned there. Between 1924 and 1930, the river flowed full, probably because there were no dams to hold the water back. People contained some of the runoff by digging a well lined with rock walls, then putting something on top to cover it. In the fall, when the rains came, there was a lot of water, so we were forbidden to cross the river. Some people upstream owned a boat, which was the only way they could get across. The only bridge that existed at that time was in Shiprock. Horses are good swimmers and so they might try to get to the other side, but the river fluctuated a lot and could be very dangerous.

I suppose some children tried to run away from school, since I have heard about such incidents, but none of us smaller children did.

It was impossible for us, but the older children in the other school may have. Our parents taught us never to run away from school because it was dangerous due to the presence of wolves that roamed in our area. They came down from the Mesa Verde mountains. Cows and bulls could also be furious and mean. It never entered my mind to run away.

We had dances where the boys would ask us to be their partner, but the girls could also ask. We could not refuse a dance or we would be in trouble. Everyone had to dance. Halloween was also fun. We decorated our dorm with jack-o-lanterns and skeletons. Some children were afraid of these things because of traditional beliefs, thinking that ghosts came out at this time. We celebrated Christmas the same way with lots of decorations, listened to Christmas songs, and received a lot of candy and presents—dolls for the girls and balls, horns, and marbles for the boys. On Easter we all received a white dress to wear, and in those days, we were not picky about what we wore. The girls had high-laced boots and long black socks, but the youth of today would not dare wear something like that to a party. All the girls wore the same type of white dress with small pastel prints. These handmade clothes were simply fashioned with belts and sleeves, and although they were identical, everyone was so proud of their dresses. Pants on girls, however, was another thing. We were criticized if we wore them, and so all females wore dresses, never pants. This was in keeping with Navajo traditional beliefs that when women do start to wear pants, it is a sign that it is the "end of an era" and "a change in time," and that it will be a time when homosexuality increases among our people. Therefore, females should not wear pants. I wonder if this has been fulfilled.

There were a number of houses for the staff and the old hospital, which the BIA now occupies. The doctor, Mr. Needles, had his office there, as did the principal. Mr. Redshaw used to come and meet with the school staff. He received his name (T'áábíích'įįdii—His Own Devil) because he walked really slowly, his legs were stringy and tired; he dragged his feet and talked slowly, too. It was our fault that we gave him such a name; there was no use trying to change it, and besides, it fit his teachings and behavior. Still, he was very helpful and friendly and an excellent spokesman for our community. He helped the people a great deal as well as the children who were away at school, visiting us at Shiprock and giving us each twenty-five cents, which we thought

was a lot of money back then. He particularly visited with the Aneth
students as if he was our father. Our parents hardly came to see us.
Once in a while, my father used to ride his horse to Shiprock to visit me.
When he did, he brought piñon nuts, blue cornmeal bread, and mutton
at Christmas. He traveled on his horse a lot and was always prepared,
carrying grain for the animal. At the end of the academic year, school
employees loaded us in a truck where we sat on yellow army blankets
on the floor and headed home. Redshaw always volunteered to take
us back to school. In 1932 the officials shut our school down because
the water supply was gone. I believe the pipes that brought water to
the facilities were washed away due to a flood. All the students went
elsewhere. I left school for a period of time, then enrolled at Towaoc
in 1933, but because of my family's wishes, I was married in 1933.[17]

Margaret Weston echoed many of Florence's observations, and
though she did not attend school at Shiprock for very long, she felt like
it had been a positive experience. She mentioned the huge stove in the
basement being loaded with wood for warmth; the oatmeal, applesauce,
homemade bread, beef, pork chops, potatoes, onions, and milk—all of
which were products made possible through the students' efforts; how
the boys and girls were not allowed to be together; going to church on
Sundays, and taking walks with their "deans." The only difference was
that if the children spoke in Navajo or talked a lot, they were punished.[18]
John Norton told of strict enforcement of this discipline, similar to what
he encountered in his family. "The people that took care of the boys
were very stern people. We weren't allowed to talk in Navajo. We told
our elders so and so had talked in Navajo. We were taken inside and
laid down on a chair. There was a hose this long [two feet] and we were
whipped by this. We were told sternly that we should do things in certain
ways. It was the same at home."[19]

Cyrus Begay also had a positive experience but ended up running
away with a friend. Although he had heard of students being mistreated,
he was not. In his words:

My teachers used to tell me I was smart, quick to react, and polite.
There was only one time I got in trouble, and even then, it was not
my fault. The girl who sat behind me borrowed my eraser, and when I

All of the older children attending boarding school had various jobs to keep the facility running. Farming, cleaning, dishes, laundry, care of livestock, blacksmithing, dairy chores, the processing of food, and a host of other tasks were seen not only as necessary duties to support operations at the school, but also as a means of acculturating the Navajos.

turned around to get it back, the teacher suddenly slapped me above my ears. I almost jumped up to hit her, but didn't. The girl, Carmelita, protested that the teacher should not have hit me in the ear and suggested we tell the superintendent about this incident, so we did. He sent me to the doctor, who said my ear drum was slightly injured and warned that I might go deaf someday. I received a written statement to give to the superintendent, Mr. Easter. He fired my teacher. "Don't you know you're not supposed to slap anybody on the ear or eye? You better leave." This was all because of the eraser, but the teacher misunderstood. Our first superintendent, Shelton, was alright, but I think Mr. Easter was better. He was overly protective of the Navajos and punished those people who made the little boys cry. He even fired the agency workers if he saw them mistreating students and warned them to be careful.[20]

Cyrus enjoyed the food—oatmeal, pancakes, or potatoes with eggs for breakfast and meat with rice or potatoes for lunch—cooked by a Navajo woman who was assisted by schoolgirls.

This help, along with a multitude of other tasks, was part of the program to teach useful skills that would lead to employment and a better life after graduation, and it lowered expenses of school operation. The amount of work accomplished was impressive. There were many acres under agricultural cultivation, a haying detail, large herds of livestock, impressive orchards, canning facilities, laundry rooms, a blacksmith shop, and a host of other meaningful, supportive experiences. Cyrus's chores included working with cows.

> I used to milk the cows at the dairy every morning, along with six other boys. Some cows would kick as we tried to milk them, so we tied their legs together. Two of us also churned the milk for butter after breakfast. We prayed before we ate our meals. It seemed that people always wanted me to lead out in everything—whether at school or home—and that is not bragging. I can clearly remember the prayer, which was not hard. "God is good. God is great. Lord, we thank you for this food. Amen." Then we ate. Christmas and Thanksgiving were special times, when we decorated the school with ribbons and ate turkey for both occasions. In the summer we ate watermelons cut in four pieces, which were huge, out on the grass after supper. It was good.[21]

He also had time for play. In addition to the regular boys' games of marbles, sports, and exploring, he also took the opportunity to act out a current event. He attended school when World War I was unfolding. His brother had enlisted and was involved in the conflict, but Cyrus was not sure why it was taking place.

> I heard them [family at home] say it was because of land disputes and that Germany was involved. People are always fighting over land because of its riches and they wanted to own them. The Germans hold out their hand to reach for these minerals. As children we played war when attending the Shiprock school and pretended to be Germans. We used wild spinach stems, which Navajos used for food, for our

guns. In our play, we'd say, "I'll burn your hands off!" or "Shoot your hands off!" Our school uniforms were right for playing army, including our caps.[22]

Runaways and Rescues

Although Cyrus was generally happy with his boarding school experience, he also did not shrink from an adventure with a friend from Oljato, Utah—even if it was in the winter.

I went along with one boy to run away. We wore our school uniform—knee-length underwear, pants, cap, and coat. I did not want to go, but he insisted he was scared but was probably lying. We left after supper one Sunday and heard the other students going to church to the beat of the drum. We went along the river, which had floating ice in it, traveling through washes and over mesas. He wanted to cross the San Juan, but I did not. I decided to go to one of my relative's homes whose name was Noisy One (Ha'diłch'ałi) and lived close by. I told the boy to go ahead and cross the river, but that I was not going to be responsible if he drowned. We argued, then he went on alone, and I never heard what happened to him.

I finally found my way as I trudged through the snow on the ground. It was getting cold to the point that I thought I would freeze. Suddenly I saw tracks left by the wagon that took merchandise to Aneth. The land there is flat with no place to take refuge. Going farther, I finally found a small hole at the base of a sand bank and crawled into it, hoping to see the next day. Soon after, I heard an owl; I do not know where it came from, and I was too cold and shivering to figure it out, but somehow all of my discomfort stopped when the owl left. It must have been a man or woman.

I went to sleep without feeling cold and when I got up in the morning, I could see steam where I had been lying. I started running toward home. I was a fast runner and used to beat everyone at the fifty-yard dash. When I arrived home in Aneth, everyone asked me where I had come from. Ralph Tanner was the trader at the time and gave me coffee, biscuits, and bacon before I left with my sister. She loaned me a horse. I told her I slept warm last night and that I had a "visitor" who hooted four times. He helped me or else I would have frozen to death. Somehow I made it home safely, where I stayed for a few days before the police came to take me back to school. Many students, both girls and boys, have run away and were not so lucky, having lost a foot or half of a foot from frostbite.[23]

There is no doubt that running away from boarding school was fraught with danger. Even though one might have the impression that it was a common occurrence, the frequency and scope depended on a variety of factors such as the age of the students, conditions at the school and home, government policy, personalities of both students and teachers, environmental considerations, distance from home, and physical fitness. It was an individual decision being made by youth who were not ready to weigh all of the factors for the desired outcome.

Trading posts became another element that either directly or indirectly influenced the call for students. In the first quarter of the nineteenth century and into the 1930s, the spiderweb of wagon roads threading throughout Navajo country had nodules of trading posts that served various far-flung communities. These central points, located on strategic crossroads, worked as the gathering places for area activities. Just as Aneth and Montezuma Creek were likely locations for commerce, so was the Hatch Trading Post in Montezuma Canyon, where Navajo and Ute camps were scattered across the valleys and canyons that fed into it and were connected by roads. Very few traders, in general, could avoid assisting the government in some way in getting children to school. Ira Hatch was one person who tried to avoid that fray, but inevitably became drawn in to help with different aspects and to learn of events, good and bad, that affected his trading clientele. In his words, "I stayed out of that. You couldn't get along with them Indians and still help send their children away, and I can hardly blame them. The government would take them a hundred miles away, while the families had no transportation to see them. Sometimes the kids would run away to go home, which was one of the main reasons the Indians kicked against sending their kids to school."[24] Attempting to sit on the sidelines, he observed and later reported what he saw. Redshaw, who usually received good reports in working with Navajo students, was not quite as fortunate when recruiting those in Montezuma Canyon. Hatch reported that the government farmer had to be awfully careful not to offend the families sending students or they would refuse to let them go at all. Sometimes it took two or three days of arguing before they allowed them to leave.

But it was not just Shiprock that tried to fill its quota of students. In the late 1930s the Southern Ute boarding school in Ignacio, Colorado, extended its tentacles to Montezuma Canyon, taking Ute students and a "bunch" of Navajo students 130 miles east of their camps in the canyon. After they had been at the school for about a month, a seven-year-old, some eight-year-olds, and one nine-year-old decided to run away to home. Ira Hatch told their story:

> They slipped out sandwiches and anything that wasn't perishable that they could get their hands on for a week before they left. When they departed Ignacio, they were scared to stay on the main road because they knew they were in trouble and that the police would be patrolling around to pick them up and take them back, so they moved through the forest. In three days, they made it to the head of McElmo Canyon. This was the second year of school for the eight-year-olds and the first year for Billy Yazzie, the seven-year-old. His clothes were not sturdy enough to stand the trip. His shoes wore completely out with the soles coming loose, catching in the brush and grass, causing the child to fall down, but the group had made 120 miles in five days, even though traveling cross-country.
>
> Here is how they all made it. The first night they stayed at the old smelter in Durango. After the laborers left, no one was there, so they crossed the river and went into the building, which was unlocked. When they left Ignacio, they had taken a couple of army blankets, which were all they had to sleep on the whole night, so they bunked up, sleeping on one and covering up with the other, doing the best they could. The next night the group made it to Hesperus and the following to the head of Chokecherry Creek. There, they stayed on the side of the mountain in the oak brush so they could not be seen from the road. When they left the next day, Billy started falling behind about four or five miles out from their last camp. A mountain lion began to follow the group and Billy, in particular. The older ones, who were about a quarter of a mile ahead decided they had better sacrifice him, since letting the lion attack the whole group might cost them half of the boys. Billy hollered for them to wait, but they would not, and there was

little chance that he could keep up, even if he did join them. He looked back and saw the grass moving about twenty-five yards behind him, causing him to again yell for the boys to wait, but the lion was gaining on them, so they refused and just kept going. Billy had found a two-by-four and an old match case with seven matches when the boys had camped at the smelter. He remembered his folks telling him to build a fire to scare away wild game, so he got in an opening where there was some dry grass, struck a match, and then fed more grass into the fire along with some green brush to create smoke and smell. The mountain lion stopped following, enabling Billy to rejoin the other boys at the head of Chokecherry Creek, where they stayed that night.

The group found a pine tree with some lower branches on the side of a steep hill. The boys put down dried quaking aspen poles that had fallen over and made a walkway to the protecting shelter, then cut branches off of a spruce tree. They dug through the snow and down to the ground, where they made a bed of the trimmed limbs, creating a solid place to sleep under the tree. There was no other vegetation around it to break the wind, but they built a fire, gathered plenty of wood, and burned it down to a big bed of coals. The next night they made it to Point Lookout at Mesa Verde, where they found a Mexican with a herd of sheep, moving along the north rim. He kept them overnight, fed them from a big pot of beans, and made some biscuits. That was their first real food since leaving the boarding school. The man also took some fine wire and tried to reattach the soles of Billy's shoes, doctored his feet, which were badly blistered, and gave him a clean pair of socks. The next morning, the group went toward Cortez. At the head of McElmo Canyon, I was coming up the grade before turning toward the town to purchase some things for the post when I happened to see them heading to the canyon on a high ledge above Perry Major's property. The kids were running from one clump of brush to another to avoid being spotted. I hollered and they answered. I told them to come down and that I would take them to Cortez to get something to eat. I drove them in my pickup truck into town, where I bought each one a hamburger and cup of coffee. When they heard I was going back to my post that day, they decided to come with me, since some of them lived on McElmo Creek south of John Ismay's trading post, while others lived at Montezuma Creek. Their camps were down at Black Hat [mouth of Montezuma Creek and the San Juan River]. There happened to be a customer at my post from down there, so I sent some of the boys home with him. The next morning, Billy Yazzie's family arrived with an extra pony and took him home. Some of them eventually went back to school, but their parents were pretty hesitant about it because they felt that the school did not watch them closely. Those boys could have perished just trying to get home. It was a wonder any of them made it.[25]

Skills for Life—Yesterday and Today

Not everyone had as traumatic of an experience as these Navajo boys. Indeed, there were those who flourished, such as Maimi Howard, during the early years of the Shiprock Boarding School. Her home was on the south side of Tsé Yaandee'nílí (Rock Formation Coming Down), where there is a big black rock. There she had her kinaaldá ceremony at age twelve, then she left on horseback soon after for school. She remained very homesick for a year, but during that time, she informed her teachers that she knew how to weave. Many of the girls wanted to learn, so she taught some of them how, first instructing in basic designs, then moving to more complicated ones, which a number of her students mastered. They learned well and appreciated what she taught them. Because of her weaving, she eventually earned money to buy sheep and received more invitations to teach others.

Housecleaning became another acquired skill while Maimi was a student in the boarding school, leading her to work for William Shelton's wife. The superintendent recognized the skills and determination that Maimi had, so he enlisted her to first teach in the dormitory and then sent her to Denver, where she taught in the summer instructing non-Natives how to weave and entered her woven products in competitions. In her words:

I was invited to many places to weave, including Denver under Shelton's charge. My weaving won continuously in contests throughout this ten-year period. People were proud of me, even though I was a girl. My weaving took me places, and I did not forget how to do it over in Denver. While I was there, Shelton came to visit me and brought a pair of Navajo moccasins he purchased for me in Bluff City. He followed me to these different places. I had to take large amounts of wool like an old lady along with the tools to weave rugs. People got to know me and wanted me back to weave for them and to learn how a rug was made. It is a pretty good life to know this skill.

When I first met Agent Shelton, he was still kind of young, but later his hair began to gray; he was really tall. The agent was a very helpful man with the Navajos, generous, and understood the Navajo language. He had Diné employed for him, and he often worked with them. My older brother was among those he hired, as was my husband, who became a foreman of the Navajos with the job of going to the mountains for logs. After Shelton left Shiprock [1916], he returned only once and told me that he missed me. He was like a father to me.[26]

There was also marriage on the horizon. A Navajo man named Howard, who lived in the Tódahidíkáanii area, sent a message to Maimi through Shelton when she was working and eventually married her in Shiprock, where they celebrated and danced for two days and nights. The couple stayed there in a "borrowed" home until her father bought from the Mexican Water Trading Post a red wagon, since there were no automobiles around at that time. He hauled the couple's belongings back to property he owned where she could keep her sheep.[27]

The preceding stories have given a glimpse into the feelings and experiences of some elders who lived along the San Juan River during the early years of the Shiprock Agency when livestock and agriculture ruled, traditional values and ceremonies were intact, and Navajo culture was not deluged by elements from the dominant society. For those who grew up in this environment—whether they attended school or stayed home to assist their family—what they learned of the school experience established the way they thought formal Anglo education should be. Even John Knot Begay, who never attended, had regrets and opinions about where education was now taking the children and what their future would look like. What many elders saw going on in the system sixty to seventy years later may have had value, but it was moving the students in a different, not always compatible direction from the way traditional society had been. What follows are some of the concerns voiced by these elders in the 1980s and 1990s. John Knot Begay explained:

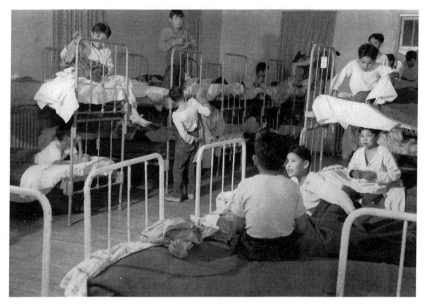

Not everyone who attended the Shiprock Boarding School tried to run away, but there were enough to give concern to school administrators and parents alike. Those who did escape were primarily boys with an adventurous attitude.

If I had gone to school and gotten educated, I could have kept my father's claim on his land at Red Rock. As it is now, the fence posts have fallen to the ground, and I see the white men's boundary markers posted here and there across my land. They have claimed it as theirs. I cannot communicate with them. I cannot tell them how I feel or explain what that land means to me. I want to tell them that it was all that I knew, my home, and where I grew up. "Won't you respect me and consider it as mine, too, my friend?" But there is a language barrier, which makes it difficult for me. Today, I see all the oil wells pumping away on my land and I'm stuck here in my helplessness. That's how my life is at present.[28]

Sally Lee echoed the sentiments of many elders:

I say that school today is not done appropriately. Ever since I became aware of school, it has changed and is different from that time. Children were taken away to school, where they stayed through the winter, then returned home in the spring. Whenever school got out, they rode home double on a horse and then would tell us how they were taught. Now there is no teaching taking place; there is nothing. At times I wonder, how will they live? I do not know and I do not know how they will become aware of themselves. I ask them, "What will you do when you get a husband and then have children?" I talk to them about my life and traditional teachings, but it seems they don't understand what I am saying and just don't get it. Some say, "Tell us about what happened," but they are not serious about learning. I begin to talk about it and they start running around, so I just quit.[29]

Ella Sakizzie agreed:

We are facing a crucial problem. Even though we have spent millions of dollars to build a school so that our children could have a "home"—a home to learn how to make a living—look at what is happening to it! Why, after all this hard work, do we allow our children to go down a way, to get drunk and maliciously vandalize our school buildings? How can anything decent be sponsored in a place like that? I have said this so many times, because I don't like what is happening. People are probably tired of listening to my complaints, but I am very concerned.

In my opinion, if the fathers and mothers of our community would only teach their children the meaning of "leaving things alone and respecting the teachings," then it would not be this way. Tell them also about the hardships involved when there were no schools in our area and that we had this school built here because we wanted to be near them, to watch them, and more importantly, because we love them. "Why do you do this? Why are you vandalizing the school? It would be better if you left it alone." I keep suggesting to the parents to say this to their children, but nobody does. They seem to think that I'm saying it for my own good.

It is even harder for drinking parents to say this to their children. It was different and better in the past, when our people didn't drink. They were more apt to discipline their children and teach them how to respect others. Today, some children are witnessing their parents' participation in such unsightly activities. These parents cannot communicate with their children anymore, let alone teach them. Our community is gradually getting better.[30]

John Knot Begay chimed in again, this time concerned with what the law now mandates against parents disciplining their children. The old teaching of "The whip was always near" is legally unacceptable in today's society. Many parents feel helpless against laws that remove corporal punishment as a form of behavior modification. Regardless of whether one is for or against, it was a part of traditional society—in both Anglo and Navajo culture—at the time these elders were children. Begay was frustrated by new court rulings:

> I attended a meeting recently where a judge stated that "your children can turn you in for mistreatment or verbal abuse." I feel that this favors what our children were doing and defending their violent behavior. As parents, we try to discipline our children, teaching them how to obey and respect their teachers. But this statement blocks our intentions to accomplish what we want for our children. Our disciplinary actions and manner of teaching could land us in jail if one of our children reported us! I said what I thought at the meeting. "I don't think our children should have that right," but the judge said, "It is the law." I don't believe this is correct because parents should have the right and the ability to lead their children in the appropriate direction. It is our responsibility to carry out what is necessary to help our children succeed.[31]

Harvey Oliver, speaking of the local Aneth Community School run by the Bureau of Indian Affairs, added, "They were planning to run a good school and to teach the right things, with not many false teachings, like it has now. It is not a government school. It is full of false teachings. The community workers want to change it back to Washington's (government) school, but the BIA is blocking it. It is hard to make it a good school."[32] While Harvey may not have had a complete picture of what was taking place in this facility or not have understood that the BIA is the government, it seems that he was hearkening back to the old days and old ways, when things were "right." Whatever the thinking behind his observation, it is fair to say that most of the elders interviewed in the late 1980s and early 1990s wanted more strictness and accountability for learning, as they understood what took place in the "good old days."

Much of the early, formal educational experience of the river Navajos revolved around the Shiprock Boarding School and the personalities of Shelton and Redshaw. Both men were sensitive to Navajo practices and so, unlike many other government-run schools of the time, they tried to accommodate where possible, given early nineteenth-century beliefs, compatible elements of language and culture. For example, traditional clothing was preserved, names were written phonetically in both Navajo and English, weaving was encouraged, and student protection was implemented. True, by today's standards there were still elements of "cultural imperialism," and though they were part of the belief system of the time, they were not tyrannically enforced. That is why the elders who now look back on those days are not filled with intense resentment but rather have a positive outlook about what took place.

CHAPTER TEN

From Anasazi to Autos

Change as a Way of Life

O
ne constant in life that never changes is that it is always changing. Whether using seconds, days, months, years, or centuries in a timeline, very little remains the same. A new item comes in, an old item goes out, a new idea becomes outdated, and physical things decline into a state of disrepair or entropy. Culture undergoes a similar transformation. The Navajo experience of the seventeenth century was far different from that of the nineteenth, not to mention that of the twentieth. What was once accepted as normal and contemporary became "traditional" a few generations later. Innovative ways of thinking and doing, as well as new forms of materials and technology, replaced the now-dated things of yesteryear; what was considered impossible became commonplace. From foot to horse to wagon to car to plane—change has been continuous for the Navajo people as their culture has shifted and new forms of tradition have been accepted. This chapter explores the speed of that change and the direction it has taken.

Some of the first topics in this book began with a traditional story about how the holy people and the Navajos first encountered some aspect of their world and the teachings that derived from it. This topic of change is no different. It may seem strange that when examining the introduction of the automobile, road improvement, the airplane, the CCCs (Civilian Conservation Corps workers), and off-reservation employment in the early twentieth century that we begin with the Ancestral Puebloan or Anasazi culture. These people migrated out of the Four Corners area by 1300 AD, yet are still relevant to the Navajo. For the Diné, the Anasazi provide a prehistoric example of what happens when one culture departs from traditional practices and grabs hold of anything new and innovative, only to forget about its important relationship with the holy people. A more complete study of how Anasazi sites, petroglyphs, pictographs, artifacts, and stories figure into Navajo culture to become a prime example of the problem of decreased spiritual activity and increased materialism and antitraditional thought is offered elsewhere.[1] Following a short discussion on change and the Navajo perception of the Anasazi, the emphasis will be on the introduction of new technology and practices and how they affected Navajo daily life.

Anasazi—Prologue to the Present

Briefly, the Anasazi were viewed by traditional Navajos as a highly gifted people who were blessed by the holy beings but then became so consumed with self-importance and their own physical abilities that they forgot the spiritual source of their greatness. The capacity to travel at high speeds including flying, as well as control of the elements, profaning sacred symbols and powers, excessive inventiveness, and haughty pride all led to their downfall. The gods, angered by this inability to show humility and frustrated by the abuse of power, destroyed the Anasazi in a number of ways including removing air to breathe, sending destructive fires, bombarding their homes with ice, drowning and flooding, and allowing them to destroy themselves with their own inventions. All that remained were ruins, artifacts, and skeletons, which for the Navajos were to be avoided unless a medicine person who understood how to eliminate the cursed effects of the attending spirits could bring their power into play. Among the Navajos, there was a wide range in practice from strict avoidance to little concern about taboos surrounding interaction with the long-gone Anasazi. Generally, if someone knowingly or unwittingly strayed over the line and became sickened, an Enemyway ceremony could be held and the offending spirit destroyed. The ruins and artifacts left behind by these people became mnemonic devices that reminded the Navajos of what happens when the holy beings are ignored, inventiveness leads to destruction, power is uncontrolled, and traditional ways are not maintained.

Anasazi ruins were reminders from the past of a people who were highly gifted but who went astray because they ignored the teachings of the holy people, leading to their destruction. Sites and artifacts were believed to still be connected to their past residents and owners, and so were avoided unless a medicine person knew how to deal with these foreign influences. (Photo by Kay Shumway)

So when Baxter Benally, my interpreter, and I sat in Harvey Oliver's living room one March day, we were interested in how he understood the Anasazi, whose remains are so prevalent in the Aneth area, where he was born and raised. It became apparent that he understood what had gone wrong with them but was not as concerned with the power they might gain over him.

I will tell you what I know. The Anasazi were the first people to be created, before the Diné and before the white man. They were the "holy people" but had human characteristics. I know they were like this because long ago I worked in excavating some of their dwellings [a real taboo for some] in Mesa Verde (Gad Deelzha—Juniper Forest). Their homes contained many artifacts similar to those of the Navajos, such as their cups made from mountain sheep horns and "bee yildehí (one you wipe with)," small woven front-piece used for baby bibs and cradles with head bows. I dug up an Anasazi from his grave. It was well preserved. Its skin was dark, just like ours, the Diné. I was not afraid of it. I was about eighteen years old then and excavated many adults and babies, some still in their cradles while the adults were in a sitting position. They seemed like they were Navajo since their culture and lifestyle appeared similar to ours; they probably spoke the same language, unlike the Hopis, as they falsely claim. The Anasazi were strong in spite of their small framed bodies and built their homes with large rocks in hard-to-reach places in the cliffs. They must have had the ability to fly, but then I never saw any of them with wings. They were normal like us.

During the excavation, I came upon one Anasazi in a sitting position. I had dug in the sand and rocks when I found his body and called over my boss, Jim Wood, asking him what it was. We looked at the remains, and noticed that his skin was dry and dark and that his hands and feet were like ours. His shoes were made from woven tree bark with leather soles while others wore sandals made from braided yucca plants. My boss said, "Let's leave him as he is and put some chemicals on him for preservation. If we pick him up now, he will shatter." A couple of days later, some people came to apply a glue-like substance all over the body. They let it dry for a day, before removing it. These Anasazi ate the same foods we did, such as corn. It is said that their extinction began when "they copied their body" on rocks in the form of petroglyphs as well as placing handprints on the cliffs and their pottery. The "holy ones" brought forth huge tornadoes to destroy them. From my observing their dwellings in Chinle and Spider Rock, the Anasazi lived very high in the cliffs. It makes one wonder if they had wings to fly up to these places. Some white men I worked with said the same thing. I was extremely amazed. It might be that the ground level was higher, but later diminished through erosion. My elders never told me the exact details about the Anasazi and their lives and were afraid to go near their dwellings. It was forbidden because if one went inside, there might be a spirit that could kill you. To step on their artifacts and in their homes resulted in death. I have handled many of their bodies, but I have never been sung on in the "Charcoal Way" (Hóchxǫ'íjí—Evilway; ant'eesh—blackening) or the "Squaw Dance" (Ana'í Ndáá'—Enemyway). I usually tell my people that I disagree with the belief that it caused death. People said the same about the white man, but we eat their food and wear their clothing and shoes. They don't kill us. It's a lie.

I think the Anasazi people were "holier" than any of us. It was also said that the Diné had some form of communication in the time of creation. There is a symbol or imprint of the Sun somewhere on the cliffs of the canyon near Beclabito, and one in Huerfano Mesa (Dził Ná'oodiłii), and Bloomfield (Naabi'ání) and other places. It was said that a person could walk up to this sun symbol and speak to it, which could then be heard in another place a long distance away. They were considered holy. This is where the white men picked up their idea of telephone, radio, and other far-reaching communication systems. The one we used was for "listening" [divination]. People could listen and hear beneath the earth. Dogs were considered to have this listening power also. Medicine men used ear wax from dogs to do this listening ritual. They applied the dog's ear wax on their ear to do it. Our people lived in a "holy way" and knew what they were doing. They said our medicine men traveled through these holy powers using sunbeams and rainbows and were capable of crossing oceans. That is how they went to see Jesus Christ's birth, and how our men brought back the wealth from other countries. That's what our elders said. These stories, especially the stories of Monster Slayer, are never told. Practicing the "talking to the rocks" communication is very rare now. It used to be that one could talk and listen to the rocks, but that is gone.[2]

What Harvey explained was only the tip of the iceberg about why it is important to understand what happened in the past with the Anasazi so that Navajos will not fall into the same pit today. Medicine man Buck Navajo believed that the same supernatural powers that the Anasazi had, and that the Twins used in destroying the monsters, were being unleashed by Anglos. "They can walk anywhere. They dig up the earth, walk underwater, walk in the heavens, and go up to the moon. For us Navajos, we cannot do this. This will kill us all in future times."[3] Fred Yazzie added more detail for clarity:

Just like now, Anglos are designing many things. They are making big guns and poison gas. Whatever will harm humans, they are designing. What happened during the time of the Anasazi I am relating to now.

When they placed designs on their pottery, they reversed the drawings, yet people did not believe they were overly inventive. That can lead to self-destruction. Now the Anglos are going up to the moon and space. Whatever obstacle is in their way, they will not allow it to stop them. Some are killed doing this, while others return from their quest. Do these people believe in the holy beings or God? . . . The Anasazi built with ease their houses in the cliffs. Their mind probably did all of this and this was like a big competition between them. They started to fly, then got jealous of each other.[4]

Isabelle Lee tied the future to the past, suggesting that Navajos were heading in the wrong direction because of their attitude.

It seems like the end will come soon because everybody's going the white man's way. Once our people leave our culture and traditions, we will no longer have an identity. No one partakes of the sacred corn pollen anymore. That's how the Anasazi destroyed themselves. They got carried away with their inventions, just like we are doing today. Our technology is overpowering the human race. The Anasazi "outdid" themselves, and that is where we are now, close to destruction. When it happens again, the world will end. We are drying out our earth by digging up the land and pumping up its water and oil, so it will soon collapse. I think the end is near. Our elders used to tell us, "When the end comes, it will take place in the wink of an eye," because this is how the Holy Creator said it would be. The holy ones exist in the fog that often covers our land. Some warning signs for the end are if a horse bears twins, if planted corn seed fails to grow, or if a baby is born with teeth and white hair—these signs mean the end is here. We will perish like the Anasazi did, dying with their babies in their arms. Likewise, the end will come in sudden death for us too.[5]

Chidí Arrives

With this understanding, imagine what it was like when a Navajo saw their first car or airplane. Elders who recall this experience laugh with a twinkle in the eye as they now accept what is commonplace. As with any people, first encounters are explained by what is already known and understood in their world, not necessarily what and how something is really happening or working. From foot to horse to wagon, here is how the first automobiles were seen and understood. John Knot Begay shared his initial encounter:

> I saw my first automobile when I was living with my grandmother, herding sheep for her. I was quite young, but capable of doing this. Randolph Benally asked me to go down to the trading post with him because he was going to chop wood for the trader and I was to get some things from there. We both got on the donkey and rode to the store. When we arrived at the brick house of Tall White Man (Bilagháana Nez), we saw a crowd gathered around something unusual and decided to investigate for ourselves. Everyone was excited and talking. This "something," an automobile, had small wheels, similar to those of a wagon. Hastiin Randolph stared in amazement and kept circling it. Someone asked him to turn the crank in the front, so he did, starting the engine with a loud noise. This was my very first time to see a car. It has become our main source of transportation, replacing horses.[6]

Jane Silas felt the automobile looked funny with its rear end higher than its front, making it look like a stink bug. The vehicle made funny sounds when someone cranked it in front to start it. "I was very scared to ride in it, but not anymore."[7] The first car that Mary Jay saw belonged to Herbert Redshaw. It had a black body supported by skinny wooden-spoke tires and a crank in front.[8] Ben Whitehorse remembered Redshaw's car, commenting that all vehicles were called "choo-gii" because of the sound they made. "I remember the first auto I saw was the one that Redshaw brought back here. It was covered on top with canvas and in front was a window, while inside were a couple of seats. It had a crank, which you had to turn to make it go. It made a sound, 'choog, choog, choog' when it started up. The wheels were thin with wooden spokes like a wagon wheel. Automobiles were rare and seen just once in a while."[9]

John Meadows also recalled Redshaw's car and the man who drove it. "He done a lot for the Indians, going around on the reservation helping them as he drove one of the first Model T touring Fords there was. It was a rag top, two-seater." Cyrus Begay was a student attending school in Shiprock who rode with Redshaw and recalled the road system they traveled.

There was only a wagon trail out of Shiprock coming to Aneth. Redshaw would always be equipped with shovels, so we fixed the road going either way. They were very rough and rocky, with rain continuously washing out the parts that were good. The first real road was just past Beclabito, New Mexico. You can still see the ditch where it used to be, extending through Teec Nos Pos and Mexican Water. This was the road that Redshaw and I took for special errands, then worked our way around on other roads. I helped him whenever we got stranded or stuck. The main wash from Montezuma Creek to Hatch was filled with cottonwood trees. Up on top of the valley walls were big greasewood bushes with huge stems. They grew higher than a hogan roof in some places. The horse trails went under and through these tangled-top bushes. They were that thick and high, but it is not like that now, being much shorter.[10]

As cars became more common in the 1920s, Navajos began to purchase them, but not without beginner's errors. Meadows described this early transitioning from horse and wagon to automobile.

The Navajos did not have much money, and so they stayed with their ponies for quite a while before beginning to buy cars. They finally got to where they'd get an old secondhand one from a fellow who would take them out for a ride and show them how to start it with the crank and steer it on the roads. They used to have some awful times with those cars because they had no idea how to control them or how they operated. Many times you would see them on the side of the road, pulled off of the main thoroughfare, working on a vehicle in kind of a backwards way. They very seldom understood what was wrong. Sometimes the vehicle ran out of gas and the owners would have the car halfway stripped before they realized what the trouble was. Those motors were all new to them. Some dishonest white people realized that a Navajo did not understand the mechanics of the auto, so they robbed them by charging far too much money and "fixing" things that were not broken, then presenting a bill of $20 or $30 for a whole day's work. The Navajos, however, shared information with each other and let things go until they got some guy who had learned a little about how to change a tire, add oil, and check the fluids so as not to burn out the engine. But in the beginning, Navajos had an awful time with their cars.[11]

Herbert Redshaw stands behind his famous 1917 Model T Ford. He conveyed hundreds of students over the years to their school experience in Shiprock. During these trips, he also had their assistance in mending roads and helping other motorists along the way over the windblown, muddy, potholed desert highways.

Gas stations did not exist, so some men, trying to make a few dollars even though they did not have a license, would buy a barrel of gasoline, drive it onto the reservation, and sell it. Trading posts eventually had crude pumps installed and found a company that would keep the tanks filled. Ben Whitehorse remembered that before this time, Cortez, Colorado, was where a lot of people obtained gasoline in small barrels that they carried in their cars as they traveled. "You could smell the gas and it was strong. I think gas lasted longer in those days; it seemed that just five gallons could take you for a long distance."[12] Around 1924 Jack Lameman, a Navajo who owned a lot of cattle and had money, bought a Ford in Farmington and drove it in low gear to Aneth, approximately one hundred miles away. The next day he started for the trading post but went only a short distance before the vehicle died. Next, he sought out Redshaw, who looked at the gas tank and found it empty. Lameman was chagrined. He swore that it could not be, because he had looked in it the day before and it was full. When he learned that a person had to put gas in on a regular basis, he vowed to go back to Farmington and return the vehicle, but Redshaw pointed out the problem of depreciation, so Lameman decided to "make the best of a very bad bargain."[13] He eventually became known to other Navajos by his auto and was called Mr. Red Car (Hastiin Bichidí Łichíí'ígíí).

Driving the Desert

The development and maintenance of roads has always been an issue in southeastern Utah—whether on or off the reservation. The government, through its employees like Shelton and Redshaw, urged that networks of transportation be developed for a number of reasons including governance (greater access to local leaders and control in law enforcement), economic development (not only for the traders but also for the fledgling oil wells starting to develop during the 1920s in the Shiprock area), education (moving students to and from school as well as encouraging the growth of other, smaller boarding schools), and construction jobs for local people. As these undertakings expanded, other needs developed. Old Mexican was on the tip of the spear when it came to a large-scale government approach in the Aneth area to improve wagon routes. Between 1904 and 1906 Agent Shelton employed many Navajo men to fix the road network emanating from the agency to distant Navajo communities. He paid them with practical items that furthered their own home industry.

> It was springtime. They announced again that they were going to continue the work on the road. They wanted a lot of men to work. "If any of you want a wagon, you have to work for forty-five days, and for a shovel, one day, and an ax, one day, and a saw, one day and a pitchfork, one day, and for a scraper, five days. If you want to work with a team to earn a scraper, two and a half days. If you want to work with a team to earn a wagon, you have to work twenty-two days and a half," they said. My older brother said he was going to work for a wagon.
>
> My wagon was no longer stout. It was getting old. It couldn't stand anymore hard work. I had put in a lot of expense having the wheels shrunk and for other repairs, and I was thinking about getting a wagon there, but it was kind of hard, and I was all alone. If I wanted others to help me, it would take lots of grub to feed them so I did not

Navajo workers earned tools as simple as an ax or hoe and as expensive as a wagon for their labor on the roads and irrigation ditches that serviced various communities. Many men saw this as an opportunity for gainful employment to provide goods otherwise difficult to obtain in a cash-strapped economy while also improving routes of travel and agricultural endeavors.

sign up. Slow had a wagon but he wanted another. He took over a bunch of men; they were driving a horse and a cow, and when they got to the place where they were going to work, they killed the horse and the cow to feed these men. In seven days, they had earned a wagon for him. Others were working for themselves, earning a shovel or an ax for a day's work. Slow earned his wagon and had already gone back, when my brother took his bunch over. I helped my brother and after we had earned the wagon we kept working for shovels, axes, and hoes. Some were working for saws and hammers. Several others earned wagons there. Before we got the road to the store, they let us off and told us to go ahead and work on our ditches.[14]

The adoption of cars led to a higher standard of roads, which had first been horse trails, then were upgraded to wagon tracks, and eventually were improved to a packed gravel road before Macadam was later applied. The fits and starts between these changes created some frustrating but interesting situations. Mary Jay's father saw a need and formed a local work crew who went to work to improve their route for commerce. At the time there was nothing but horse paths in most areas with only one wagon trail that came up from the place called Mesa Joins. Her father and some neighbors built a section of this wagon road out of huge granite rocks piled higher than a house. People were amazed at the strength of the men who built this road that went up against a ledge that helped to support it. Navajos used this wagon trail a lot, sometimes hauling large loads of firewood to sell to the trader. On the return trip the wagon was filled with large sacks of grain for their horses.[15]

Nakai Begay went through this transition period when there were only horses, later wagons, and finally cars. In his view, "When a person had a good wagon and a good horse, it almost equaled an auto. If there is no vehicle, a wagon with a horse can be used the same way."[16] But there was a problem mixing wagons and cars on dirt thoroughfares.

> The roads were sandy, and those little old narrow-wheeled wagons and buggies had wooden spokes with a metal rim that cut through the sand, making it loose and deep. I had a wagon that would cut that dirt and fill in the ruts, then push the sand to the side. Some of those old wagons were broad gauge and about six inches wider than the regular ones, so they pushed the sand around in the rut in a different way. This happened every time a car or wagon went through. The next car would come along, and if it got going a little too slow or was given too much gas, it would spin out and remain there until someone pulled it free. People had a heck of a time in that sand with a "V" on both sides of the rut.[17]

Inclement weather increased the challenge of motoring in less traveled regions, especially when dealing with livestock. An early fall snowstorm interfered with moving a herd of sheep to the Hatch Trading Post. The snow was too deep for the vehicle to move, and water coursed down a neighboring gully; still, a delivery had to be made. The stockmen herded their sheep down the road, trampling and packing the snow sufficiently to allow the vehicle to reach its destination—an early solution for a snowplow.[18]

This stretch of road between Aneth and Montezuma Creek is a section of the earliest road system joining these two communities. In the 1880s there was a measured system that originated in Bluff, with each mile marked with a cairn. The network of roads went along the river, then either up Montezuma Canyon or to Aneth and McElmo Canyon, and on to Cortez and Durango, Colorado. Later roads were built above the floodplain to avoid being washed out by the river.

Times have changed, but for those Navajos in the early days who pioneered the use of the car and truck, their descendants are grateful for the current ease of travel. Charlie Todacheenie, an elder who lived through those times, summarized this gratitude:

Around 1950 a lot more people started to get automobiles. Wagons were hardly used after this. When traveling in wagons, it took days to get from one place to the other. A one-way trip might take a day, but then you would have to spend the night wherever you were and the next day return home. Today, it might take 30 minutes to do the same trip. It required about three days to go to Cortez, whereas now, it can take one day to get there, do your business, and return. Travel is so very fast that we do not think much about going in an automobile, while horses and wagons are things of the past. After we learned to drive a car or truck, we grew to like them very much.[19]

CCC-ID

When the Great Depression hit the United States, the government instituted the Civilian Conservation Corps (CCC) with also an Indian
Division (CCC-ID) program in 1933 to serve on federally recognized reservations. The CCC-ID ran independently of the major CCC
program, allowing tribes to recruit their own members, to determine the
projects they would like to develop, and to receive technical assistance
not from the military like the CCC, but rather from the BIA. Instead of
employing unmarried young men ages eighteen to twenty-five, there were
no age restrictions for Native Americans, who could choose to remain at
home and travel to a worksite or could live in tent camps with other men
and families, and in some instances could bring their families with them.
They also had no curfew or rules for departing camp, were reimbursed
for shelter and travel if not provided, and could establish different sizes
and types of camps as determined by the tribe and project requirements.
The intent of both nationwide programs was to employ workers in rural
areas to improve roads and water facilities, conduct firefighting and
fencing projects, build structures, expand agricultural and range management, and generally upgrade a region's infrastructure. Not only did
this modernize certain conditions on the reservation from outhouses to
windmills, introduce workers to a more structured lifestyle, and familiar-
ize them with the latest construction equipment and techniques, but it
also provided a thirty-dollar monthly wage, which for Native Americans
could cover additional costs. Education played a major role, not only in
trade skills, but also in learning English, math, and other topics useful in
the dominant culture. This lifestyle unintentionally prepared participants
for World War II and the changes that occurred for those who enlisted
in the military or worked in the war industries. The program ended in
1942.

Many of the tasks on the Navajo Reservation, such as water projects
including wells, windmills, and dams; pest control; fencing operations;
and road construction, were fairly straightforward and common undertakings on tribal land in southeastern Utah. Yet there were also some
projects that were more unique, as Harvey Oliver attests. What follows
is his understanding of what he did and who benefited.

I have worked in that program, much of which went to assist the Utes, when we built their boundary fence. We worked in Towaoc [Ute Mountain Ute Reservation headquarters] at their "Blue House" school, building a fence near Cortez. That's when the white men said Ute Mountain belonged to the Navajos and not the Utes. Lee Jacket, our CCC supervisor, pulled a tag like those found on salt bags from an iron survey post. It stated this was Navajo land, that all of Ute Mountain was on the Navajo Reservation, and that it should not be called Ute Mountain but Navajo Mountain. He told me and Sam Antes this when he pulled the tag to show us. "This tag indicates there's another survey post on top of Bedrock and another on the mesa beyond that point and one down below it. This tag tells where all the survey boundary posts are located as well as the boundary that extends to Cortez and along the ridge to Cahone Mesa. This is where the boundary should have been. The white men are lying to you." Officials ordered white men to remove these posts and put them all the way back to the Ute Reservation boundary, thus diminishing Navajo lands by a long way, but still saying it was ours. This entire fencing project began at the Four Corners area, extending the fence to Ute Mountain, then to Towaoc, through the base of the ridge "Tsé Dah Sítaní" (Base of the Ridge), over the mesa and down to below "Taazléi" (Scattered Streams) to "Red Valley," then to "Tsé Doogai" (White Rock), and down to the ridge and the mesa's edge, to the San Juan River. All of the Navajo boundaries were moved in.

I helped put in the water tanks on top of Mesa Verde, another on the ledge of Ute Mountain, and one at its base at a place called Salt Water. Back then, the roads to Towaoc were not good, so the CCC workers improved it. That highway used to run along the fence, but now it is lower, since the white men built a new one recently. We built another road leading up to a ridge as you enter Cortez. This went up "Tsé Dah Sitáán (Rock Ridge)" and was only passable with horses, so we hauled all the material up there in saddle packs. Even the fence that runs along the ledge of Ute Mountain we built using horses, not trucks. I worked on our reservation, too. We built the irrigation canals up to the Ute Reservation fence as well as dams in Skunk Canyon, but they are gone now. There were others around the Ute boundary fence, one in Aneth, which is still intact, and three others on this side of the river and three on the other side. It didn't pay much, sometimes being paid with secondhand clothes.[20]

The 1950s through 1960s was also a time of road development. While the CCCs of the 1930s worked hard to mend and straighten some of the main arteries on and off the reservation, the roads of the 1940s remained dirt, subject to ruts and washouts. Navajo land was considered under the care of the federal government, road enhancements could be expensive, and no one had the time or money to update the infrastructure in distant southeastern Utah. Not much happened. However, after World War II, improvements in technology and materials, an increase in tourism, and a desire to do more for the Navajo people made it possible to support building a better road network. But it was the discovery of oil in the Aneth area in 1953 and the drilling of the first well in 1956 that put the pieces in place to start paving all-weather routes for heavy trucks, moving their loads to refineries and distribution points, and greatly increasing graveled dirt roads to reach drill sites. A spiderweb of access arteries now crisscrossed the barren deserts and rocky mesas on the land of the river Navajos.

Flying Metal

Flying over these lands were airplanes. Known to the Navajos as "the car that flies about" or "metal that flies about," this creature was initially just as strange as the auto, although it had little direct application to reservation life. It was thought of as the thing that moved through the heavens. The tail was said by some to be a person standing up, directing the rest of the plane. One woman believed that its noise came from dragging over rocks and mesas, while another was told that the shining specks in the sky were two supernatural beings returning to earth.[21] Ben Whitehorse recalled his first reaction:

> I was small. We were living on the hill at our winter camp at the time, when early in the morning I heard the strange sound of a motor, then glancing into the sky I saw it—my first airplane. It had two wings, one on top of the other [biplane]. It had a bunch of beams running between the wings and body. I could see the driver sitting inside. My

During the Great Depression of the 1930s, the federal government instituted the Civilian Conservation Corps–Indian Division (CCC-ID) to work on Indian reservations throughout the West. Managed under different rules than the Anglos' CCCs, it allowed Navajo men to bring their families, implemented fewer age and work restrictions, and involved projects closer to home. This flood control effort is one of a number of different undertakings including range management, predator control, forestry labor, road and bridge improvements, and water projects.

mother was so frightened when she saw it, she crawled under a rock ledge because she thought the plane would drop something down on top of us, knowing that white men do such things. It flew down to Bluff City, landing on a runway where they now have the Indian Days Pow Wow. After that, we would see one occasionally.[22]

Another person spoke of this same event as a time of great celebration. Word filtered through the Navajo community that on a certain day a plane was going to land in Bluff for the first time. A lot of people went to see this phenomenon and to help clear sagebrush for a place to taxi. The gathering became a social event, with roasted goat for the main course of the feast. At noon a reddish object appeared overhead. Everyone raced on horseback to the landing strip and spent a long time inspecting the strange contraption of the white man.[23]

World War I and II helped introduce more of this technology to the Navajos as an increasing number of planes appeared in the sky overhead. Ada Benally from Bluff remembered an incident during World War II.

> We heard about the war across the ocean and seemed to see more planes at that particular time. I was then twelve years old and knew more about what was going on. We were at war with Smelling His Mustache (Dágha'Yilchįįh), also known as Talkative German (Adágha' Yáłti'ii, also known as Talking Mustache—Adolph Hitler). My uncle went to fight in this war and told us about it. When we first heard the war was coming, we were encouraged to hide. The Navajos rode their horses to Mexican Water Trading Post to get more news about the situation because that was the only place there was a phone for communication. At that time, we called it "wire messages" and not a phone. We prepared for an attack. On the morning the war began, we brought in our donkeys and left the sheep by the water, then moved up a narrow canyon. We tied the donkeys at the base of the slope and carried our belongings up the ridge. If a bomb had been dropped on us that day, we could have been buried under the rubble of rocks. I don't know why we chose such a place for refuge, but we spent the entire day up there. Every now and then someone would go up on the hill to see if there was anything. We saw many planes flying low, which made the war seem real. In the evening, the people descended but continued to do this for two weeks. I believe other Navajos did likewise. Later we heard the war was over. It was our victory.[24]

The Influenza Epidemic of 1918

In addition to technology-driven changes like cars, roads, and airplanes, there were also things that expanded and changed the world of the Navajos such as new diseases and off-reservation employment. A few brief examples from the Navajo perspective will hint at the type and direction of change. Cataloguing the struggles to overcome health challenges such as tuberculosis that attacked the lungs, trachoma that caused blindness, and diabetes and cancer that affected different parts of the body, may be discussed another time. Glimpses of the influenza epidemic of 1918 will suffice for an example that was prominent in the minds of the elders interviewed here.

The Navajo response to influenza came in two forms—spiritual and physical. To them, the roots of the epidemic lay in religious beliefs, and it was on this level that the most successful prevention and treatment was found, since there was no serum to combat the airborne virus and many other Anglo measures proved fruitless. For the Navajos, there were two types of ceremonies to cure the patient's illness or to prevent people from becoming ill: the Blessingway and the Evilway, neither of which were specific to this new disease. The former is a ritual that encourages beauty, health, and harmony to surround a person, and was generally used as a prayer for well-being. The latter fends off evil, particularly associated with the spirits of the dead, and was used for those surrounded by death and burial. Both ceremonies share the ultimate outcome of protecting a person from harm and providing prayers acceptable to the holy people, who in turn give necessary help. However, there was no specific ritual to deal solely with influenza, a white man's disease that erupted during the very last stages of World War I and took a heavy toll on the Navajos. Medicine men remained busy, traveling about, performing ceremonies, and praying for the sick; how much of the disease was spread through these unwitting vectors and the close contact required in the ceremonies will never be known, but in the minds of the Navajos, these healers saved many lives and performed a valuable service. Prayers, not vaccines, held the cure.

Cyrus Begay was twelve or thirteen years old when the fatal epidemic arrived in the Aneth area.

> I remember my mother and older brother sick with the flu. The same with Hastiin Schlibby. He could barely raise himself to beckon us to come over to see him, during the times we cared for his sheep. My older brother and I never got the flu, so we remained busy, going from one camp to the next helping the sick. We brought in bundles of dry sagebrush to build a fire and made cornmeal mush for them to eat, before coming home to take care of our chores, then leaving in another direction to help someone else. There was so much work to do. Many people died with some families secretly carrying them off to bury. I believe the war must have been the origin of this epidemic, which caused our people so much suffering. Many of our elderly men and

women as well as children died from influenza. Those who survived managed to grow in numbers again. Red Mexican (Naakaii Łichíí'ii) was one of the medicine men in our area who treated the sick by performing the "charcoal sing" or "the good way" ceremony. Other medicine men also helped the people overcome the sickness. There were no hospitals except in Shiprock and no transportation other than horse and wagon. The river was narrow, so people used to use logs for a bridge. In some areas, they had two or three logs where the river became separate streams.[25]

Harvey Oliver remembered people "dying by the household" and, later, that white men came to burn the homes with the dead inside. He told of a cure where Navajos boiled herbs and "drank pine gum mixed with shortening oil or put it on their bodies. If that did not work, they rubbed on skunk fat, then prayed to the disease to leave them alone."[26]

David Lansing, as a seventeen-year-old living in Aneth, said:

The sickness took the lives of many Navajo people. This happened in the fall. Most of the people in our area were hit by the flu and laid up in bed for quite a while. There were no hospitals nearby. One old man and wife were not affected by the sickness. This man was a medicine man and he and his wife went from home-to-home praying for people. One day they came to our house because all of us were ill and brought something that looked like a piece of tree bark. He advised all of us to spit in it so we did. He told the same thing to all the other really sick people. I do not know what he did with this collected sputum, but about two days after the medicine man paid us his visit, we were all up and around again. The other people he had visited all got well, too. This seemed mysterious, but we were cured.[27]

The Northern Navajo Agency reported having 6,500 residents within its boundaries, but no specific number of deaths to report because there was so much isolation, hogans burned with bodies inside, and no one officially appointed to keep tally. If the Shiprock Boarding School, with a much more controlled, recorded, and cleaner environment, is any indication of the severity of the illness, of the 225 pupils, 200 became sick, 18 of whom died, giving a mortality rate of 9 percent.[28] By March 1919, the epidemic had run its course on the reservation, emphasizing the need for hospitals and greater medical care in the future.

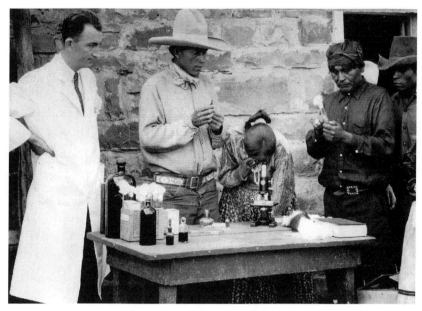

The influenza epidemic of 1918 was one of the worst outbreaks of sickness to impact the Navajo people, but it was not the only one. Traditional teachings did not cover this type of illness, and so even though ceremonies and medicinal plants were used, they often did not produce the desired effect. Not until the germ theory of disease became available could infectious diseases like tuberculosis, trachoma, and various poxes be effectively combatted through doctors like this working for the Indian Health Service.

Off-Reservation Employment

As the reservation became less insular, with less barter, greater cash flow, and an increased desire for material wealth associated with Anglo society, and as transportation networks and automobiles became more prevalent, Navajos looked beyond reservation boundaries to itinerant employment. Traders often identified and notified men seeking job opportunities, while Anglos living near the reservation also established their own pool of workers. Depending on the year, the worker's individual skills and reputation, the type of labor, and the availability of workers, Navajo men might travel a few miles or find employment hundreds of miles away from home and remain on the job for a month or a year. Work possibilities included harvesting crops of everything from hay to potatoes to apples, laying track for the railroad, doing pick-and-shovel digging and cleaning of irrigation ditches, and utilizing specialized individual skills. One job that Navajos often excelled in was taking care of livestock. Whether herding, branding, castrating, feeding, healing, or delivering newborns, Navajos generally had an excellent reputation among white livestock owners, who were anxious to employ those who had proven themselves capable. Sheep, goats, cattle, and horses benefited from traditional Navajo cures as well as patient, gentle ways of working with them. Over the years, hundreds of Navajo men found employment in this trade they were ideally suited for.

Charlie Blueyes provides an example of a typical, faithful, and conscientious shepherd whose reputation landed him successful employment. He originally traveled to Blanding to attend a five-day ceremony, spending the first night and the next day there before being asked to help with the ritual. He agreed and remained. During that time, he met a man who needed someone to look after his sheep. As the white man asked the people who were there, he eventually ran into Charlie.

Finally, I was asked, so I agreed to herd for him and was taken to Montezuma Creek. The white man who owned the sheep was called Yellow Teeth's Son (Biwoo' Łitsoi Biye'). I stayed in Devil's Canyon for two years, herding about sixty head. Sheepherding pay was very low so I only earned seventy-five dollars a month, but if I needed food, I could just butcher an animal. It was there for my use, as was the horse he provided. He had me move the livestock up onto Blue Mountain during the summer and herd the animals down to a lower elevation in the fall. This white man would visit me and bring food after asking what I wanted, then tell me when he was returning. The place I herded the livestock was beautiful and there were other shepherds nearby. Sometimes they would lose sheep, but I never did over the eight years I worked for this white man. I learned how to count them as they ran past me, with my employer counting the ewes and me counting the lambs. There was competition with other herders as to whose sheep were the fattest. If you had the best animals on paper, there was a bonus. I have helped many people around here when there were lots of sheep. The wool used to fill three sacks. This is where home is, and herding sheep was my life's work. You can also learn from cowboys by observing them. One of them would walk his horse until he saw what he came for, then he would race after the animal he wanted.

White people take care of sheep the way they should. I sometimes still herd sheep around here, which becomes my food and money. This is how you get visitors, too. You call grandfather and grandmother and they will come if you have sheep. I am not a learned person in terms of knowing all of the songs and stories, but I do know the sacred mountains because of being with the sheep.[29]

There were other men who moved well beyond the borders of southeastern Utah for employment. In many instances, an entirely new world opened up to them. John Knot Begay provides an example of such a man who worked well in the Anglo world and experienced many different things not common to reservation life.

It all began when I was an adolescent in the 1930s. I remember selling lambs to the traders in the fall when a wealthy white man [probably Charles Redd] from La Sal, Utah, bought all the lambs from the reservation. These animals were to be driven to the railroad station beyond the Naturita Mountains. Randolph Benally came to see me and requested that I help him move the sheep, starting from Bluff City the next day. He always asked me to help him with different things. We did not own any fancy sleeping bags. Instead, we used a sheepskin wrapped in blankets.

Our journey began the following morning, taking us through Blanding, Monticello, to the north past the Hole-in-the-Rock, then across the Colorado River. It required several days to reach our destination [Thompson, Utah]. When we arrived, we drove the lambs aboard the train, joining several other flocks that came in from different places. There were many, many herds. Some had already been shipped off, including cattle. In fact, we were the last to come in.

It was while we were there that the white man who bought the lambs was choosing his men to work for him. He selected me and Randolph along with others, some of whom were Mexicans. The white man told us to board the train for Kansas City, where we would herd these lambs for the winter. We got on the train with many other Navajo men. None of us had ever gone on a long trip like this before; it was all new to us. We went through many mountain tunnels on our way, which is a sacred thing to do for Navajos, so we sang a song each time we went through. The trip seemed to go on and on until finally we arrived at a strange place. The lambs who were shipped ahead of us were off the train, so we rested there for a couple of days, fed and took care of them, then reboarded the train and continued on our way.

We finally arrived in Kansas City, where we spent the winter herding the lambs, while some men went home to the reservation. Randolph left in the spring, but I stayed behind and was one of the few who did not return until after the job was over. Our boss paid for this trip, and I received a dollar an hour, which was high compared to the twenty-five to fifty cents per day on the reservation.

During our return trip, we stopped in Denver long enough to do some shopping. To make sure we were able to get around, we followed the one who spoke and understood English, probably looking like baby chicks following their mother. We went on a shopping spree, buying things like saddles and other practical items, then ate at the depot and were about to leave when a white man walked in. There was much talk about something interesting. Randolph always informed me as to what was happening, but he had already left, and the person I was with hardly said anything. I asked what they were talking about and found out that they had some job openings for railroad workers close to the city and were now hiring. The men discussed whether they should stay and work, but most of them wanted to head home. I wanted to stay but followed everyone's decision to leave, and so we did.

I then spent a year at home, when I again heard that a group of Anglos were recruiting railroad workers for a job in Las Vegas. Many Navajo men were leaving to take it. I joined them, bringing my readied bed roll. Some of these men took their mohair goat skins to sleep on, but we later learned that the train had beds made available for all of us. We also realized that the weather was quite warm there.

Upon our arrival, we discovered we had some furnished bunkers for our homes. After filling out some papers, time sheets, etc., and settling in, we ate dinner at the cafeteria, where there was plenty of food, took showers after work, and had everything we needed. We started working in separate groups. Everyone in my team carried a sledgehammer and drove nails into the railroad ties along the steel tracks. Some carried the ties and placed them, others came behind and hammered the nails to keep the rails in place, while a third group followed behind us and spread gravel.

Following World War II, after many Navajo men and women had left the reservation for either enlistment in the service or war industries work, off-reservation itinerant labor became a prominent way of life. John Knot Begay, like thousands of other Navajos, worked hard in various types of manual labor. In his case, railroad work paid well for its hard, physical demands.

There was a mixture of minority groups including Mexicans, Blacks, several different Indian tribes, and some whites, but no Orientals. I think the Navajos and Mexicans worked the hardest. We were able to communicate with each other just enough to ask for coffee. The Navajo men built a sweat hogan and took baths, which was good, because our job was tiring.

I worked digging with a shovel, hammering at big spikes, carrying steel rails, operating an automatic nailing machine, constructing and shaping rails to fit together, and surveying sections of route, all the time progressing in my job. I also spread gravel along the finished tracks with a rail cart machine, used a jack hammer and stapling machine, and worked with several other types of equipment that secured the ties firmly to the rails. I got pretty good at my job in all of these areas while learning the mechanical operation of the machines and how the railroad tracks are switched from one position to the next.

As for social activities with women, I have heard about women being brought in for the men, but I never saw this personally. There were men who lived for the weekends, then left for downtown after work, but I did not go often because I did not trust anyone. Once in a while I tagged along, but only if there were several of us. Some of the men took home small pieces of a hardened steel railroad track to hammer on when silversmithing, but I did not. I was always careful to not get myself in trouble, since I was brought up in a strict manner and lived by those standards. I mostly stayed home.[30]

Change has been a constant element of Navajo life. During the twentieth century, the Anglo world encroached upon the Navajo world—sometimes as a desirable thing, other times pushing the people from their known, traditional perspective. This chapter has looked at elements that were, with the exception of the influenza epidemic, fairly desirable—introduction of the car, road development, airplanes, CCC projects, and off-reservation employment. Some of these things were even courted for lifestyle improvement. On the other hand, accompanying each of these changes was a different worldview that encouraged adopting values of the dominant society. Although much of it was helpful, alleviating the drudgery and difficulty associated with life in a high desert environment, it also prompted the Navajos into a way of thinking, a brand of ownership, and subsequent actions that took on more and more of an appearance of what destroyed the Anasazi. The elders used these new things to warn against many of the pitfalls troubling even today's society. But it was livestock reduction, the topic of the next chapter, that irrevocably changed Navajo culture forever. It created circumstances that were anything but desired by the people.

CHAPTER ELEVEN

Livestock and Land

Conflict on the Range

Nothing on the Navajo Reservation accelerated change faster and more divergently than the period of livestock reduction, occurring primarily in the 1930s, but with fits and starts in the 1920s and vestiges in the 1940s. This is a topic that has been discussed extensively in terms of scale and impact, outcomes comparable in some aspects to the effects of the Long Walk period, another series of devastating events that changed the Navajo people sixty to seventy years previously.[1] In this book's companion piece, *Stories from the Land: A Navajo Reader about Monument Valley*, the emphasis of this shared experience is on the personal horror and traumatic disruption of daily life, while here, there is an examination of a more unified effort to stop the slaughter and resist law enforcement. The Navajos living along the San Juan River, although under greater control by the agency in Shiprock, were also more organized in their efforts to hold on to their livestock and maintain their present economy. Beyond the years of the Great Depression and into the mid-twentieth century, conflict remained between livestock owners and government officials over control and management of the ranges. The following personal accounts provide an inside picture of how perhaps more than half of the livestock on the entire reservation was obliterated, and why this gave birth to a volatile resistance that fostered chaos and deprivation. The second half of this chapter examines the relocation of Navajos in the Bluff area during the 1950s, when the Bureau of Land Management (BLM), local white cattlemen, and Navajo livestock owners clashed over land use and prior agreements. Again, chaos and deprivation ensued.

"Sheep Are Life"

To put this thirty years of conflict in perspective, it is good to return to fundamental beliefs concerning relationships with animals. Everything in the Navajo universe was a living entity with a spirit that communicated, a power that could either bless or harm, and a reason for existence as ordained by the holy people. When man interacted with each being in a positive way, paying homage and following guidelines of appropriate behavior, a harmonious relationship resulted and the world remained peaceful, in a state of hózhǫ́. Charlie Blueyes gave an explanation of how he viewed this relationship between man and animals by using the horse and sheep as examples. Much of what he said can be extended to other creatures.

> I believe that animals understand what is said to them. There was a man who had a horse that understood him, when he said to the stallion, "Bring in the horses in the morning." That morning, the stallion would herd the horses in. They have special powers. A long time ago, some medicine men knew how to use this power to draw horses to themselves. They knew the prayer of the horses, and when they said it, the horses would turn clockwise because they understood people. It is believed that a horse is a brother, so this is why you do not curse them. If you do that to a horse or sheep, you are cursing yourself. Just as if you curse your food, it will start to kill you by bringing illness that required the help of a medicine man. This is of your own doing. When you curse your children or your wife, you only curse your own heart. Who is going to fix that harmony because you are doing this to yourself. It is said if you curse another human, you are cursing yourself even though they might curse you first. When a person says this to you, all you have to do is make an offering to the river. All living things understand what is being said to them. If they cannot hear, what is their purpose for living?
>
> You are living, and it is through those things we are living. The plant is eaten by sheep, and we eat the sheep. We are living through

them. Sheep do not go by time and will not say, "It is time to feed us or give us water." As soon as they are free to go wherever they please, they start walking and eating. They want to feed, even on the coldest day. When it is time for lambing, a good shepherd will take care of that, too. This is how I made a living and it is hard work, but the pleasure is in eating. The horse is also an essential help by taking you any place you want to go as well as assisting with the cattle and sheep.[2]

John Joe Begay echoed Charlie's thoughts on the purely practical side of keeping livestock.

My maternal grandmother had lots of sheep. I was constantly told to herd them when I was young, so I did not have much opportunity to travel very far. If there were things going on, I was not allowed to attend. All I heard was "Herd the sheep. Herd the sheep," and was told, "Your grandparents will grow to old age. Your mother and father will too. When they are gone, this livestock will be your mother and father." This has proven true to this day because I have only the sheep to look to as I take care of my children with them.[3]

These sentiments were common expressions of a worldview held by many Navajo families.

Livestock to the Navajo was both literally and figuratively wealth on the hoof. One could no more have too many sheep or goats than an Anglo person could have too much money. A small family herd might have had a couple dozen sheep to provide wool and meat, but to maintain the flock meant balancing between slaughtering so many each year for food, obtaining enough wool for the weaving of blankets and other products, and having sufficient lambs to either sell or replace sheep lost or killed during the year. The small-herd owner could end up in a precarious position if any of these scales tipped in the wrong direction. On the other hand, there were plenty of large herd owners whose livestock numbered in the thousands and whose power and influence dominated the ranges. In some instances, these "ricos" might have had two or three camps, each with large herds of thousands of animals and plenty of "buffer" to survive winter kill, fluctuation in market prices, and livestock reduction. Take someone like Old Mexican, who might be considered "upper middle class" in the Navajo society of 1902. He had 2,500 sheep and goats, which was not particularly notable.[4] While every owner of sheep, goats, horses, and cattle was affected by the policies emanating from Washington, D.C., in determining how many animals could graze on a specific area of land, those with the most animals suffered the least. Prime rangeland, thick with grass and abundant in water, supported more animals than a sparse, scrubby desert section that could be quickly depleted of forage. Little consideration was given to an individual family's economy when compared to the amount of vegetation on the ground. The concern was soil erosion, not people's well-being. Grazing districts, as defined in the Taylor Grazing Act (1934), eventually regulated the number of animals allowed on a particular piece of range. But in order to get to that point, the size of the herds had to be greatly reduced.

Beginning Trauma

No other name during this period of trauma was more on the tip of the Navajos' tongue than that of John Collier, commissioner of the BIA between 1934 and 1945. Although they generally refer to him in connection with livestock reduction, he was also instrumental in providing many New Deal reforms through the Indian Reorganization Act. Self-determination, positive changes in tribal government, shifts in education and training, and the Indian Division of the Civilian Conservation Corps were just some of the programs he introduced on the reservation. That did not matter. Regardless of how helpful these other initiatives were in giving an unfettered voice to the People, he was still permanently enshrined in the tumult of livestock reduction. His name became synonymous with coercion and destruction. Many Navajo people mentally linked reduction and some of the CCC programs together as a type of payment for reducing the animals. For instance, John Knot Begay regarded the many sheep, who knew the songs and prayers that brought rain and abundant plant life to the land, as providing a time of plenty. This all ended when the government removed the animals.

> Our land was rich with vegetation back then; many different flowers, like sunflowers, grew thick. The evening clouds brought plenty of rain from every direction. You could hear the roaring thunder. Water puddles formed wherever there was a dent in the ground. Then came livestock reduction. The Navajos were first required to brand their

Livestock reduction of the 1930s was more than just a matter of reducing sheep, goats, cattle, and horses on the land. While Anglos also had to follow the rules outlined by the Taylor Grazing Act, it was far more traumatic for the Navajos. The sacred relationship they had with the sheep, who were thought to control rain and therefore were respected, put their slaughter in a more religious and social realm. It was not just the killing of the sheep, but also how it was done. The taking of this animal's life had to be performed in a specified, sacred way.

animals with a circle, not an "X," because it was not good. Later, the Soil Conservation Service told the people they had too many sheep and that they would deplete the land. The trails they left behind would turn into deep crevices, eroding the land when it rained and destroying the vegetation. This caused them to give up their animals. Along this same line of thinking, the [CCC] poisoned the prairie dogs and extinguished them, followed by the rabbits, then the grasshoppers. That's how it all took place. People's livestock were destroyed, then burned. Our women wept as they watched their sheep being slaughtered and dumped into a ditch to be burned and buried.[5]

Jane Silas, as an adult, remembered vividly how it all started.

First of all, reservoirs were built here and there [CCC projects], but before that took place, my husband came home saying that everyone was to get rid of their old sheep. By doing so, the government would provide jobs for us. We had a lot of sheep, so we separated all the old ones from our flock and drove them to the trading post. Upon our arrival, we saw hundreds of other animals in the corral. Shortly thereafter, my father went to the store and brought back news that our people were butchering the sheep free of charge, keeping all the fat mutton, but throwing all the lean ones away in a pile. Some butchered three sheep at a time and took the meat. My husband and I went to investigate and sure enough, it was true. We then butchered our three sheep. Our son, Dickie Silas, brought down the donkey, which we packed the meat on and took it home. I prepared it for drying as soon as we arrived. That is when livestock reduction began, as everyone continued to herd in their sheep. If we didn't obey, they said we would go to jail and they would confiscate all our livestock, including our horses. We did not herd them in, but instead sold them individually to other Navajos or white men.

A man named Hastiin Biálátsoh (Mr. Thumb), who lived in Montezuma Creek, owned a lot of sheep and refused to give them up. We heard rumors that government men were going to cut his throat. At this time, we were living by the river; my husband and I decided we had better move away because we feared they would come after us next, since we owned too many horses. We drove them up on the mesa, staying out of sight. While we were up there, we heard some Navajos were going to hold a ceremony regarding what was happening to our animals. A medicine man named Red Mustache (Dághaa' Łichíí'ii) was performing the sing. We went back to camp, then attended the ceremony, which is called Putting Down the Sacred Pebbles (Ntł'iz Ni'nil) for all of the livestock. When we came home, we were told that some police had moved into the area, so we left again to attend another sing, the same kind we had attended before in Montezuma Creek. This time, Mr. Thumb was singing. We were encouraged to take part in these types of ceremonies and not to run from anything. By then the police, which were a combination of white men and Navajos, had moved to the "stone building." We crossed the river, where my husband and father went to meet some people who had brought news that some of these law enforcement officers had blocked off the entrance to our trail. We decided to leave again and detour around on the west side to the mesa where the water tank is now in order to avoid contact. There our group stopped and waited. A man named Billy Beard (Billy Bidághaa) told me and the other people to remove our necklaces and bracelets and then wrap them up because the jewelry would cut us when we started fighting.

"Here come the police," someone said. We saw our present Navajo councilwoman named "Baal," a former councilman, and "Bilį́į́' Dijádí" (The One Whose Horse Runs Fast) among the government officials who came up to us. They themselves owned a lot of livestock, so I don't know why they came after us. We gathered at the tank, where we heard one of the policemen had shot himself by accident. Mr. Thumb, whose throat was to be cut, was with us, but he left on his horse, going down into the canyon, then up the river when he heard the police were coming. "The police are coming with their guns; do your best," we were told. We stayed to face them, not really caring what happened. Once they arrived, my uncle confronted our councilwoman, scolding, "Baal, I thought you taught us differently, to be good and all that, and here you are doing the opposite. You are doing the worst and have become a leader of chaos. What happened to your wise teachings? Have you gone crazy? Which mouth did you speak those good words from? It must have been from your ass!" The woman hung her head. My uncle continued, "We will now whip and beat you. I will knock that crazy head off your shoulders, Baal!" She broke down and cried, begging us not to harm her, saying, "This is it. Let's quit this conflict and have peace; it is alright, go ahead and keep your sheep, horses, and other livestock. Keep them and let us stop this conflict." Then we all scattered on our horses. After this, the police left us alone.

Today it seems we are headed in that same direction again. We are told that our horses will be gathered and locked up in the corral at the store. Our boys said it will not happen because if it did, they would beat them. Horses are important and useful to us. It is our form of transportation to difficult places where vehicles cannot go. We also use horses for special occasions, like squaw dances, in which a rider carries the "sacred stick." Why is it that people want to abuse our horses? They do not care for the horse's needs or feed and water them; the horses do this on their own. They have not done this people any harm and were formed in a sacred way along with everything else on this earth, including the water, heavens, and all the animals. There is no sense in abusing horses since they were created with sacred songs and ceremonies.[6]

Mary Jay, when recalling events that occurred sixty years previously, did not mince words about the feelings of horror that this government program fostered.

The goats' throats were slashed. People drove in their herds of animals from miles around, just like it was a sheep-dipping event. They waited with their herds around the big corral that used to be located near today's trading post in Aneth. People sold their goats for a dollar a head, which seemed like such a waste, especially for the ones that were good and fat. They were immediately slaughtered after being sold, with the blood running deep—such a horrible sight. I do not really know the reason behind this, but I was told that it was John Collier's idea and that his men were carrying out his plans. I never saw the man but heard a lot about him. All I know is that he wiped out our livestock, and to this day, we never received any compensation for it. My mother and family drove in fifty goats but were never paid for them. I often complained, doubting that we would ever be compensated. They might have failed to write it into a report, but why doesn't somebody do something about it?

I remember how I used to herd the sheep to the sheep-dipping site. Herds and herds of cattle roamed our land then, but they must have belonged to the white men, their livestock taking up all the space. Just across the river from Aneth, there was another trading post called "Toohgi (At the River)." The white men's cattle and horses covered the land across from here. Some Mexicans took care of an Anglo named Gray Ears' (Jaa Libá) livestock and sheared sheep for another named Wooden Legs (Jáád Tsin), who could ride a horse by standing up on top of the saddle. He also ran a small trading post there too. He forced the other trader out.[7]

Sally Lee in Aneth remembered government workers taking many of her goats, butchering them, and then having the remains sent off in wagons, while all she received were the hides. She was told later that all of her livestock would be taken away and that if she and the other Navajos did not cooperate, they would be handcuffed and sent to jail. This frightened the people. Sally recalled, "There were many police officers to go against us, so we gathered together to confront them. They drove our horses away during the night, but the Navajo people did not do anything. During this time, powerful medicine men conducted their ceremonies against this, so things calmed down, causing the offenders to back away from having to fight us."[8] Navajo Oshley also captured the frustration and disgust at seeing the People's livelihood disappearing under the butcher's knife with nothing to show for it.

The government bought old sheep for only two dollars a head, and for old goats, the price was very low. Trading posts such as the ones at Dennehotso, Kayenta, and Mexican Water bought many sheep and goats under this program. One time I was on the east side of the Dennehotso Trading Post, when one of our leaders came to the corral and said to kill all of the sheep that were in it. He had been told to say this and to tell the people that if anyone needed meat, that they could butcher the fat ones, but that we also had to dig a hole for all of the carcasses. I asked why we were doing this and suggested that at least we should do the butchering someplace else. There were people there just butchering away. I butchered one even though I did not like the idea. All of these living things were going to waste. From then on, even though I did not like it, I participated in the project and felt the anguish. The digging of holes began. The people threw the heads, the insides of the animals, and the feet into them. I did not like what I saw.

A lot of older men and women died from this because the livestock was their life, and it was being taken away. They killed my sheep, too; I can still feel the hurt.[9]

Two women, Mary Tsosie and Ella Sakizzie, supplied graphic accounts that speak to the senses and gave a firsthand feeling of what so many Navajos endured, in their mind, because of John Collier and the agent at Shiprock, E. Reeseman Fryer. Mary Tsosie remembered:

People drove their sheep and goats to Mexican Water, where they were killed. The people responsible for this act must have been at that place. The stench of death was too much. I went over just once. Sheep heads and feet were strewn all the way down the bed of the wash. Some people came to salvage the sheep heads that were rotting everywhere. Barren Woman (Asdzáán Doo Ashchíida) kept collecting and bringing home sheep heads and feet, while others took only the fat meat. We had lines and lines of cut-up meat at every household, but all the sheep guts were left behind, strewn everywhere. I heard that even the dogs didn't care to bother the remains anymore. "This was all a cruel and sorry scene," said the people, as they returned home from the rotting stench. That was the end of our herd of goats.[10]

Ella Sakizzie, who later went with a group of Navajos to Washington to protest their treatment, testified:

We took part in it, and the government men arrested my father and put him in jail. We had to reduce our sheep, goats, and horses, which were marked with paint, then driven away. A local Navajo named Joe and a white man called One-Who-Leads-His-Horse-Around [term for Soil Conservation employees called range riders who traveled about identifying excess livestock] forced us to get rid of about thirty goats, leaving us only forty, then told us ten more. The women herded the sheep to the Aneth Trading Post corral, where there were many people butchering the animals. We were asked to get rid of some, so we killed three, which we took home. All of the old and lean ones remained in the corral and were slaughtered. Their throats were cut, then they were thrown into a truck and hauled to the ditch near the store. The animals filled the gully to the top, had gasoline poured on them, and were burned. You could hear all the gurgling and popping sounds as the flames consumed the carcasses. When it happened back then, we had more vegetation, whereas now, we have none.[11]

Resistance

The Navajo people living along the river became increasingly resistant. Prominent leaders voiced complaints, some of which moved community members to coalesce into groups that started to exert pressure against outside influences that made demands on their livelihood. John Holiday, who lived in Monument Valley, was very much aware of this growing resistance in Montezuma and how the people wanted to be free from sacrificing their animals.

> John Nakai helped the Navajos to keep their livestock during this reduction period. From my home, I had to take the horses and sheep to the "reduction" office near Montezuma Creek, where the animals were marked with red paint for extermination. Everybody was mad at me, including John Nakai. They said, "For sure, all of your livestock will be killed." But instead, I was given a piece of white paper and told that it would keep officials away from my animals, even though I had more than the allowed number. The government did not take any away.
>
> John Nakai dealt with livestock reduction problems in the Montezuma Creek area. A group of stock-reduction policemen and representatives was sent out to the people at White Rock Point [Bluff area]. A man named Fat Yucca Fruit was a messenger who rode his horse back and forth between the Navajos and police, who were camped at Spring Water Coming Out. He told the police that the Navajos were given big guns from Salt Lake City to use against them. The policemen looked through their binoculars and said, "Sure enough. We see the big guns sticking up from behind the volcanic ridge." The Navajos had cut down some large tree trunks and laid them up against the top of the ridge so that the tip of the logs showed along the hill. Fat Yucca Fruit had lied to the police about the big guns, and so they turned around and went back.[12]

Ben Whitehorse explained that in Aneth, sheep were bringing twenty-five to fifty cents a head; after they were sold and killed, the Navajos believed the government would eventually take any other animals that remained.

> What was left of the herds, they wanted to wipe out, too. But the Navajos refused. This caused the BIA from Shiprock to send their police out to arrest our people. These policemen were dressed in uniforms with a five-pointed star badge on their shirt, carried a handgun, and rode in their BIA patrol vehicles. They arrested and jailed many of our people, but our men guarded their land and chased the policemen off. They told Navajos their amount of livestock was beyond the limit and against the law on what the grazing permit allowed and that having too many sheep would overgraze the land and ruin it. "If you don't obey, you will be taken to jail." Some went to jail for months, but were not mistreated and later released.[13]

To the Navajos, this was all Collier's fault. "He was the one who put the people into poverty. All that represented life went sour because of this. It came about by jealousy, cheating, scheming, and lying," John Joe Begay explained.[14] Tribal policemen, Soil Conservation officers, range riders, and local BIA officials who administered the program were also credited with anxiously abetting Collier.

As more animals disappeared, physical confrontation became much more of a reality. For instance, in Aneth, range rider Emmet D. Harrington, with his interpreter Benjamin Harvey, arrived at the hogan of White Man Hair on April 8, 1938. The owner, along with Jim Hammond, a Navajo man named Sakizzie, and seventeen other people, had gathered there for a protest meeting. Harrington told Harvey to give each Navajo a paper on which they could declare how many animals they owned. This was a poor time, a poor place for such an action. The men had already agreed that they would not accept these papers. Tall Man criticized Harvey as being a "school boy" who "lined up with the white people like Harrington, causing trouble for us." At this, Sakizzie jumped down off a nearby rock, approached the range rider, and told him, "Now I have given up my heart, my head, and my life, and I am going to take that paper away from you people. We can use sticks or stones or whatever weapon we might have to do this." As Sakizzie spoke, he

Barren desert lands were always a difficult place to tend grazing livestock. As flocks of sheep and herds of cattle expanded, something had to be done. In the 1920s there were a number of attempts to have Navajos self-regulate the amount of livestock they owned, but as time progressed, the urging turned into force, as livestock reduction became an unyielding government policy.

moved to the left side of Harrington's mount, while a man named Black Horse went to the right, and White Man Hair held the bridle. Sakizzie rummaged around through Harrington's pouches after the Anglo's interpreter warned him to let them do what they wanted. The Navajo took the hated papers in a sack, harangued the interpreter again that he was working against the Navajo people and that he had "never been taught by his mother and father." Sakizzie concluded by testifying, "I have given up myself to die. You can kill me now if you want to." Harrington and

Harvey left, feeling lucky that the angry group had not gone further. Later the police arrested the five major antagonists, who were released eight days later.[15]

Other government employees were not as fortunate. In Teec Nos Pos, some Navajos spotted a range rider and an official. They captured, tied, and beat the two men with their fists and a board, giving the range rider the severest punishment.[16] Later, in this same area, five Navajos visited the district supervisor at his home. They clubbed him, tied him and his interpreter up, put them in the back of his pickup truck, drove a few miles north, and stopped. Six policemen quickly pursued and exchanged shots with the kidnappers, but no one was injured. Although the antagonists released their two captives, the fugitives went into hiding, and the search resumed, culminating in seven arrests. The culprits spent three months in a Prescott, Arizona, jail.[17]

Gradually, toward the end of the 1930s, enough livestock had been removed from Navajo hands to comply with demands of the Taylor Grazing Act, but with it came a huge shift in economy and lifestyle. The same was true of the Anglo stockmen who had similar issues concerning their own livestock and grazing rights. Ever since the 1880s there had been active competition between Navajos and whites over access and use of rangelands, sometimes developing into violent confrontation. As both groups expanded in population and livestock, matters grew increasingly troubled, with each side arguing its justification. For the Navajos, there was every reason for them to file for homesteading and ownership on the public domain beyond the reservation; a recent (1905) addition of lands on the northern side of the San Juan River had given them legal title to what is now Montezuma Creek and the Aneth area, while the Shiprock agents were eager for them to develop economic independence. From the Anglo perspective, the Navajos had their own lands, which grew at first by presidential executive order and later by congressional legislation. Most had clearly defined boundaries like the San Juan River that separated rangelands and some of the contested area known as the Paiute Strip, which included part of Monument Valley, then serving as winter range for some of the Bluff cattlemen. At this time, it did not officially belong to the Navajos. The details to this conundrum are outlined elsewhere.[18] Since the orientation here is to examine the Navajo perspective of the conflict, an example will suffice.

Cyrus Begay offered the typical Navajo view of this general conflict:

Our living condition was alright, except the Navajos were restricted
to cross the river. The white men grazed their livestock on that side
and did not want our people to use that land. Hastiin Ashlibby was
a stubborn man. He refused to abide by what others said and took
his sheep over by Hatch in spite of all the squabbles. My two older
brothers, Pat and Tony, and Mr. White Hair's son, Jim Henry, used to
work there. The white men released their huge herds of cattle toward
our land, where seven families lived and shared the range. Everyone
else moved away, leaving hardly anyone here. Red Mexican lived at
Chííh Deez'á (Red Ochre Basin), unbothered by the white men. Our
people were accused of a lot of things. I was at school then, but I heard
many stories. My older brother told me all the news from back home
when he came on horseback to visit each month. The Navajos did not
exactly say what part of the land was theirs to use, but the white man
pretty well established their border lines by grazing their livestock in
those areas, choosing the best pasture lands on the points of each mesa.
This included the top of McCracken Mesa. They would leave their
large herds of sheep and cattle there, then accuse us of stealing their
livestock, even though this was untrue. The Navajos had their own
livestock, so why would they? These Anglos lied, and their accusations
became increasingly worse. Our people were labeled as savages, crazy,
and troublemakers, some being tried for it.[19]

There were, of course, incidents on both sides that fueled the dissension.

Land Lost, Land Gained

In order to understand the culmination of this conflict in the 1950s, it
is important to return to 1930 and see what seemed like a solution that
everyone agreed upon. In March, Navajos with their representatives and
Anglo stockmen with government officials met to resolve the damaged
relationships and solve the issues.[20] The two sides reached a verbal
agreement that divided the range between Montezuma and Recapture
Creeks so that the Anglos would be "assured that the Indians would not
use their winter range during the summer time and so that the Indians

might be assured that the white stockmen would not come on their range at any time during the year."[21] Both parties, keying on natural terrain features, understood the boundary line and agreed to abide by it. This gave the Indians approximately seventy-five thousand acres in the public domain and placed the Comb Ridge area under the control of white residents. By reaching this agreement, the cattlemen were also willing to concede control of the lands in the Paiute Strip to the Indians as an addition to the reservation.[22] However, the State of Utah and nonlocal business interests did not agree, and so for two more years, the question remained in limbo—not for lack of interest, since the cattlemen wanted a conclusive boundary and settlement. So did the government, who was worried about not only friction over range, but also the new allotments being made primarily by Navajos on public land north of the river. Finally on July 15, 1932, a decisive meeting in Blanding ended the issue. A wide array of luminaries with varied views graced the meeting. In attendance was Utah governor George H. Dern, who came opposed to the loss of state land but had an open mind; Charles J. Rhoads, commissioner of Indian Affairs from Washington, D.C.; J. M. Stewart, section chief of the Land Division, also from Washington; M. K. Sniffen from the Indian Rights Association in Philadelphia; Navajo and Ute superintendents Walker, McCray, and Peacore; C. E. Faris, superintendent of the Santa Fe Indian School; and Maxwell Yazzie, councilman from the Navajo Nation. Local representation coalesced into the "Council of Nine," comprising local livestock owners. Their point of discussion was "the [Don B.] Colton Bill that argued for addition of the Paiute Strip and 46,000 acres of land north of Aneth to be added to the Navajo Reservation."[23] The result was a finalized bill that moved to Congress in the form of House Bill 11735, passed on March 1, 1933.[24] Thus ended "the largest land deal ever made in the state, as it involves approximately 500,000 acres of land lying south of the San Juan River that run[s] to the Arizona line. Also in the deal is about 46,000 acres in the east corner of the state north of the present Indian reservation."[25]

The major points in the bill, besides designating the boundaries of the additions to the reservation including the Aneth Extension and Paiute Strip, had a significant impact on Navajos. The second of nine items specified that there would be no further allotments or Indian homesteads outside of the lands now a part of the Navajo Reservation.

Other items included existing Indian allotments north of the river being fenced, and Indians driving livestock across non-Indian land following standard rules established by white law.[26] Based on what would ensue, it is important to emphasize that this transaction was very desired by the Navajo Nation. Tribal chairman Deshna Clah Cheschillige wrote a strong letter of support in December before passage of the bill, offering to bring a delegation to Washington to ensure its passage. Communicating on behalf of the Navajo and Paiute people, he urged that Congress pass the bill to "protect" the Navajos and their stock.[27] By doing this, forty-three pending applications for allotment were then canceled, because the San Juan River was the northern limit of Navajo land.[28] A year later, the vice tightened again on range for Navajo herds when the government placed controls on land use through the Taylor Grazing Act.

Politically and intellectually, the Colton Bill seemed to be the solution, with clear boundaries and agreed-upon rules. The one thing it did not take into consideration was human nature. Historically, Navajos for centuries had sought good grassland for their animals. This urge did not stop with the passage of legislation. One by one, either Navajo families crossed the boundary lines to graze animals in areas set aside for white livestock owners, or families already there refused to move. No doubt there were infractions on both sides, leading to feelings rubbed raw on a daily basis. Mary Jelly testified as to how heated the confrontation had become, both before and after this legislation passed.

> Many livestock owners used "Spring under the Rock" on Little Cahone Mesa for domestic purposes. A white man called Jack Major directed an assault on Navajo families who lived in the Aneth Extension, particularly around Cahone Mesa. He grazed his cattle in the entire area and did not want Navajos bothering them, so he ordered his Mexican employees to frighten our families away from those places he used for his cattle by burning their hogans, corrals and shelters, and killing their horses. He received the name "He Who Kills Horses" (Łíí Neł Ts'edi') because he did such things as chase a herd of livestock to the foot of a mesa, butte, or ridge and shoot them. He also had his Mexican workers hang a dead coyote, a symbol of evil, from the ceiling of a cribbed-log hogan because he understood how this would bother them, and then after they abandoned the site, burned it.[29]

With the limited resources in a high desert environment, one can understand the animosity grown on both sides. Mary reported that while Major had his cattle, "Hastiin Sleepy who lived in this same area had over a thousand head of horses and 600 sheep, while Biłį́į́ Yishtłizhii had a total of 500 horses, while sixteen other men 'all used the same water-holes and grazed in this same area.' She had 370 sheep and 40 horses. A little after this, Commissioner Collier reduced our sheep and goat herd to 60 head and our horses to six head. During this time, we had trouble with the government and tribal representatives concerning livestock."[30]

Ella Sakizzie shared what it was like from her perspective in understanding both sides.

> Glenn and Jack Major used to kill our livestock if they wandered outside of the fence line. Some ranchers hired Navajo men to work for them. When the land was sold, white ranchers chased the Navajos away from Blanding, and so many of these Navajos moved to our area. Grazing permits had been passed out to their rightful owners, yet they were told to leave. It makes me think that these permits are worthless and do not mean anything. Back in 1978, I went to Washington with a group, and I asked, "Why were our people chased off their old land?" The people in the land claims office said that these permits were not from Washington, and that our tribal leaders from Fort Defiance and Window Rock were behind it all and responsible for ripping us off. Our tribal leaders were weak and uneducated in those days; therefore they were "fooled" into negotiating an agreement.[31]

This understanding, accompanied by the encroachment of Navajo families on land across the river, led to additional conflict over the same issue. From the local cattlemen's perspective, it was a matter of following the agreement passed in 1933; for the Navajos, many of whom were unaware of it, they were being forced off lands that they had used traditionally.

Navajo Relocation, 1950s

Anthropologist Beth E. King conducted interviews in the 1990s with many of these Navajo people who had been forced out of their homes and off of certain grazing areas and removed south of the San Juan River.

No person is identified with the government's livestock reduction program more than John Collier. As the commissioner of Indian Affairs (1933–1945) he instituted many programs to help Native Americans—all of which pointed toward self-determination. To a host of Indian tribes, he was their champion, but to the Navajos, he was the architect of and solely responsible for the traumatic program that decimated the herds and sent many people into abject poverty.

In an article entitled "The Utah Navajos Relocation in the 1950s," she captures their feelings and experience of what they considered unfair treatment.[32] Because of its oral history approach and the fact that it presents the culmination of a seventy-five-year conflict important to the river Navajos, I have decided to reprint it in its entirety with some edits. Appreciation and recognition is expressed for Beth's good work. I have retained the use of her informants' initials for anonymity.

This is the story of one of the last big relocations of Navajos in Utah's San Juan County told by people who were pushed south of the San Juan River through force and threat in the early 1950s. These people lost their homes, their livestock, and the land their ancestors had inhabited for centuries. In the oral histories that follow, Navajos who directly experienced the relocation describe the series of events that uprooted them and devastated their families for years afterward.

The Navajo families living in the canyon tributaries north of the San Juan River inhabited the country from the Valley of the Gods, through Comb and Butler Washes and east to McCracken Mesa. Many of them had lived there for generations. From their parents and grandparents, they had inherited rights to use certain areas for grazing and farming. Although their rights were recognized only within the Navajo community, for 70 years these families had shared their grazing areas north of the river with the local white stockmen in relative peace. A series of events starting in the winter of 1950 abruptly ended that peace. During that time, terrible drought devastated the range throughout the county. Navajo families, who usually grazed south of the river, moved north across the San Juan searching for forage for their animals. Several northern stockmen watched in frustration as Navajo livestock consumed their limited winter forage. In the spring, when grazing conditions improved, most of the newly-arrived Navajos returned south of the river. Navajo families who had regularly used the areas north of the San Juan remained. They would bear the blame for the influx of Navajos into areas which the northern white stockmen considered their range. They feared that the Navajos had come to stay and that the Indians wanted to extend the reservation boundaries north of the river past Bluff and Aneth. White livestock owners reacted first by seeking legal solutions to this problem through the U.S. Bureau of Land Management (BLM) and the Utah courts. In 1952 the Utah Supreme Court ruled in favor of the white stockmen and declared that the Navajos were trespassing. Armed with a favorable court verdict and a fear that the Indians were trying to permanently claim lands north of the river, the local cowboys, BLM employees, and others decided it was time to permanently remove them.

Ever since Mormon pioneers had settled Bluff in 1880, they had used the northern tributaries of the San Juan River for travel and grazing livestock. Migrating Navajo families with their animals co-existed with the settlers for the first fifty years. While relations were generally friendly, this period was also marked by repeated conflicts over grazing areas and livestock. As the white population of San Juan County moved from the southern town of Bluff to Blanding and

Monticello, they also changed their economic base from irrigated farming to one increasingly dependent on livestock and the rangelands within the county. Many of the stockmen had witnessed the loss of large sections of the county to the Navajos as the reservation boundaries expanded north of the San Juan River in the 1933 Paiute Strip and Aneth Extensions. Each extension of the reservation required a re-division of the remaining federal grazing lands. However, the white stockmen were not powerless in their struggle to confine the boundaries of the Navajo Reservation. They had the ear of their state legislatures and the U.S. Congress as well as ready access to the courts.

Local Navajos in 1950 still led a primarily migratory life with their sheep and horses, concentrating their family migration to summer and winter grazing areas. Among themselves, they recognized customary use areas inherited from their parents and grandparents, living in small groups, usually as extended families. Most did not speak or read English and were also experiencing a time of change. Many families had sons and brothers who had traveled extensively as soldiers in World War II or as employees at military plants. Most families had at least one member, usually male, working for wages in some far-off place like Colorado, New Mexico, or California. The young children in the area were more consistently enrolled in schools and several families had automobiles.

Navajos living north of the river watched the influx of Navajos from south of the river during the drought of 1950. They noted that most of these families returned to the south when grazing conditions improved, while those on the north side believed their ancestors had always lived in that area. Stories passed down through generations tell of the first encounters with white settlers in the region, while local stories also described ancestors who escaped captivity at Fort Sumner by living in the isolated canyons north of the San Juan River, all of which connected the people to their land. Families north of the San Juan had no home or customary use area south of the river, giving them no place to "return" to.

Local Navajos were willing to share their experiences in the stories that follow. First, they describe their former homes and life before the relocation, including their relations with white stockmen, followed by the terrifying events of removal, most of which occurred in 1952–53, and the hardships of building a new life.

"We used to live about 3–4 miles north of the San Juan River in Butler Wash. I was mainly brought up in this area. There were others who also lived in this area, as well as near the footbridge upriver from Bluff. In the old home, everything you needed was close by, it was a nice place to live, and people kept to themselves. For many years the river was a provider, giving plants to our livestock, but it was also very unpredictable. That is why we stayed in the northern gulches. We survived many difficult times along Comb Ridge. In my grandmother's time, the family lived along Butler Wash and encountered the Spanish in that area, my great-grandfather being taken hostage by them. During hard times, they almost lived like the Anasazi. When you were at the top of Comb Ridge, you could see the whole area around you so that scouts on the top of the ridge could warn people if anyone was coming." —K. M.

"My first memory of this area is traveling through right by Butler Wash on the way to our winter home. I was turning six, about 61 years ago. We traveled through here on the way up north to our winter home which was down in the canyon. We had another home directly across from the mouth of Chinle Wash on the San Juan River, among the cottonwood trees. Another home, a summer place, was east of Comb Wash on the north side of the river where we had a big garden patch. We moved around in this area where families knew each other. There were many place names. One was called "Wagon Trail" or "Pass Where a Wagon Could Travel." At the mouth of Fish Creek there is a hogan made out of stone. My brother Carl built that. There were also a couple of tents around the hogan. It was a beautiful place but hard to get fresh water." —A. N.

The Navajo families believed that their relations with the people of Bluff and the cowboys who they encountered near their homes were good. They had known these individuals and their families for generations. Many of the local cowboys and traders spoke Navajo and people felt that good relations could have continued.

"We lived there for many years and many of our loved ones are buried there. We lived well with the people in Bluff, with some of the whites speaking our language as we did business with them, while others did not want anything to do with us. The ranchers were very helpful, held onto wandering livestock, and fed them while they were under their care. We used to help one another that way." —K. M.

"The cowboys knew of our home, would come and visit, giving a feeling of co-existence, until it suddenly became bad. Usually, the cowboys would be in the area, working with their animals and even hire some of our young boys for day labor to gather the cattle. We had worked around each other for many years." —A. N.

Not all white stockmen felt this way, insisting on greater use of grazing lands. Ranchers and BLM employees got ready to take action. They posted notices on sagebrush and dead trees, warning the Navajos that their livestock would be impounded, even though they knew that most Navajos did not speak or read English. It is not known why the cowboys didn't send their bilingual speakers around to explain the notices and their intentions to remove the Navajo north of the river.

Later, Navajos reported that the relocation took several forms. In some areas, their livestock was rounded up and loaded into trucks, adults arrested or physically restrained with handcuffs, property confiscated, and homes set on fire. In other areas, the stockmen drove large herds of cattle through the homes and camp areas of the Navajo. Groups of men with guns and whips forced some of the Indians across the river with their livestock. When other families heard rumors of the relocation, they hid many of their material possessions in the crevices of cliffs. Some people packed their children off to the safety of St. Christopher's Mission east of Bluff. Despite the relocation efforts, many Navajo families had no choice but to continue grazing their livestock near their old homesites since there was no place to go.

"For many months before the people were forced off the land, the ranchers had been coming by every once in a while, riding horses among the people and talking to them. Then one day, suddenly, a bunch of these men told the people to move immediately with no extension. It was really cold when they were forced across the river just below Desecration Panel. I later met my father, who told me his family was pushed across the river. Some people were escorted while others just left. Many did not have time to pack and so later sneaked back for their things. Father was very worried about possessions left behind and felt a great loss. Some of the women were very disturbed, although no one protested before being forced off the land. If people had been aware of what was going on, there would have been more resistance." —K. M.

"At that time, most people didn't speak English. We heard that the cowboys were driving big herds of cattle with lots of bulls through people's camps. Houses were burnt, people lost everything, and only had time to grab their children. My father was thrown in jail for living in that area, probably for trespassing. My family had established another home by the mission in case they were forced to leave and kept most of our belongings in that place." —J. M.

"My family lived in Comb and Butler Wash. My aunt used to herd livestock in the Valley of the Gods until the BLM took our family's livestock and burned our homes and shade houses. Some people were tied up and whipped. Many of the adults in my family and I had spent a month on Blue Mountain collecting sumac berries until a man from our area told us that there was chaos back home as people were forced off the land. When we returned to Bluff, I caught up with the last group of people crossing the river. We took our herds to the Sand Island area where we crossed, even though it was very cold. When the people were forced off the land, many of them took up living at Saint Christopher's Mission." —M. S.

"All of a sudden, things got bad. People were losing animals and we didn't have any money to buy them back, so were told it was better to move them south of the river. We—my mother, a five-year-old boy, and myself—started from Fish Creek at sundown, with the child strapped on a horse. It did not seem to bother him since he slept through the entire night. We were the only ones to herd the animals; some of them drowned when we crossed the river. We had heard we were being pursued by people with horses loaded on stock trucks and recognized some of the men who pursued us. Two people on horseback caught up with us at the river, which was running very high. I was in my late teens and remember being on my toes and the water coming up to my mouth. We lost many of our animals. I moved the horses across first as the cowboys harassed my mother, so I went back to help her. They were whipping our animals to get them to move across the river." —A. N.

The families forced south of the river were in poor shape. Many had only the clothes on their backs and had lost their garden produce and food storage for the winter. The lucky ones had family south of the river, but others had no one as well as no grazing privileges. Everyone faced the immediate problems of getting through the winter and building a new home.

"Some people tried to salvage their hogans and shade houses, by disassembling them and floating the logs across. The south side of the river became our second home. People would have resisted and protected their areas, but it happened so quickly, just in one day. One time my husband and I went back to the old homes. Everything was still standing—the hogans, shade houses, and sheep corrals—but it all looked sad. Everyone was hoping they could move back and live there again, but that never happened." —K. M.

"The house was left as if someone just walked out of it. I never saw it again. The kids took what they could carry and left. Most of my belongings are still there. When I came across the river, there was no place to go. I met some clan relations at the sand dune near the swinging bridge who said, 'We will take you to a place where there is a home for you,' which ended up being Shiprock. I left my herd at the sand dune, so I lost most of it. It was like being a forgotten individual. I didn't know who I was, where I was going to sleep next, where food for me and my children would come from; it was like a dream. I started roaming around with people in the Shiprock area. I had a small boy so concentrated on him and left everything behind. After a while people started to get themselves back together again on the south side of the river. I worked as a migrant laborer in Shiprock and Alamosa, picking potatoes. By that time, the people were getting back together again and my family started to ask questions about me while my mother sent a vehicle to bring me back. I was really surprised when I returned to find everyone living near the cliffs east of White Rock, trying to start over again. My mother passed away before I got home. It was very hard to start over during the early fall when it was getting cold. I only had a sack of potatoes and a bag of corn which everyone ate during the winter, then in the spring, my father passed away. I felt so discouraged. Everyone kept the expulsion a secret. It was like a curse. No one wanted to talk about it. At that time, all of my concerns and concentration were focused on surviving—how to live through the winter, how to get along, pick potatoes, and work, work, work." —M. S.

"We were afraid when we returned. We had left the camp when the vines were out on our garden and were fearful when we returned. The watermelons by then were very large, but I could not take them with me, so I ate what I could. We just abandoned the garden with all of its produce; what a waste. Everything we could remove, except for my grandmother's old Dutch oven, was taken during several trips. We headed to a place called 'Peaches' along Chinle Wash, where we had an orchard. There were hogans there when we arrived, so we fixed them up and built a new one. Our Navajo neighbors tried to take the hogan apart; it was like being pushed on both sides." —A. N.

People scattered and sought life and a future where they could. In the short term, they concentrated on surviving the winter, finding a new home, and rebuilding their herds. In the long term, people slowly worked through the trauma of relocation. To this day, many do not want to discuss these events, while others still wonder why relocation was necessary and why it had to be done in such a terrible way. A group of Navajos, only a small portion of the relocatees, brought legal proceedings against the BLM and received $100,000 for their lost livestock. They caravanned to Salt Lake City and camped in the field behind their lawyer's home. In court, the BLM agents and their volunteers repeatedly professed ignorance about the livestock they had rounded up. As reported in the *San Juan Record* of November, 1953, a BLM ranger aide testified that "he did not know who the horses belonged to. However, he did say that he knew the cornfields in many of the areas from which the horses were gathered belonged to the Indians." The BLM's lack of knowledge about livestock ownership angered the judge. He reportedly said, "It's nonsense, pure nonsense, and I don't want to hear any more about it." The judge also stated the BLM agents had violated state statutes and BLM regulations. He ordered further investigation into the entire matter in addition to the monetary award.[33]

Today the omnipresent herds of sheep and goats of yesteryear are gone. Navajo people still strongly identify with their livestock, but more as a symbol of their heritage as opposed to an all-encompassing family livelihood. Livestock reduction and subsequent constriction of the ranges, the dictates of the Taylor Grazing Act, the enforcement of the AUM (Animal Unit Months) that measure the carrying capacity of the land subject to the type of livestock grazing in a certain area, and a growing population making different demands on the land ensured that Navajo herds would diminish. Now, there are only memories of the past, when "sheep were life."

CHAPTER TWELVE

Legacy for the Future

Concerns and Hope

A ll of the elders who have shared their thoughts and experiences within these pages have walked the Old Age Road and reached the Old Age Home, a spirit dwelling of peace. Their most important legacy for the living is their family and friends left behind and the teachings shared for all. They witnessed dramatic change, shifts in their world that were almost incomprehensible. Consider the humble start of their life around the turn of the twentieth century as seen through the eyes of Old Mexican: "Three days after Christmas, as we were moving toward Blue Mountain, my wife gave birth to a baby girl in camp, just before midnight. We set up a post, tied a woman's belt around it, and placed a knot near the end of the belt to which she held, facing the post, while I held her about the waist from behind. My mother acted as midwife. It didn't take very long. The afterbirth we hid in a tree. If there are no trees, you bury it. I came after them and took them to Blue Mountain."[1] Now compare that to the modern clinics in Montezuma Creek, Oljato, and Navajo Mountain operated by the Utah Navajo Health System (UNHS), who offer dental, emergency medical (EMS), pharmacy, and other services as well as patient transport to hospitals in Blanding, Monticello, and Shiprock. This, as well as the growth of electricity, water, telecommunications, road networks, stores, motels, and educational facilities ranging from preschool through college that are now available in the nascent communities of yesteryear, is a story that needs to be told another time. Here, we close with the concerns of the elders as they saw them in the early 1990s filtered through their historical perspective. Many were unhappy with what they were experiencing as they watched their land, traditional beliefs, and grandchildren become an amalgam of the closing twentieth century's dominant culture.

Polluting the Sacred

There is no doubt that for the two largest Navajo population centers along the San Juan River in Utah—Aneth and Montezuma Creek— the biggest issue was oil. People were well aware of its presence long before Humble Oil and Shell Oil opened negotiations to lease part of the 230,000 acres of oil-rich land in 1953. By 1956 Texaco was hard at work pumping some of the first petroleum out of what became known as the Aneth Oil Field. That year alone, long before it reached its peak, the field yielded $34.5 million in oil royalties to the tribe.[2] Large sums of money went into tribal coffers over the years, but the Navajo residents in southeastern Utah received a much smaller amount that was not a per capita payment but was dispersed across the entire Utah portion of the reservation through services and community development. The elders, living in the area of the oil field, felt they were sacrificing all that had sustained them and their traditional culture in the past. This is their story.

Many Navajo people living in Montezuma Creek had little idea what was going to happen when the oil companies started to work in their area. The people in the T'áábíích'įįdii (Aneth) Chapter had certainly held discussions with oil company officials and tribal representatives prior to the work beginning, but what was said in those gatherings and what took place on the ground were two different things. Jerry Begay remembered some of the confusion that arose in those early days:

> The papers explained what was going to happen. During this time, we did not have a chapter house, and so we just met in front of the Hatch Trading Post. We were told that the land was set aside for lease for ninety-nine years and that this information should be relayed back to the people. It was probably already agreed upon. They wanted to know what the response was to the paper bill. A man named Hataałii

(Medicine Man) carried these papers around. He did not really tell us about it but just let the papers that contained all the information lie around. He then told the committee that the people were not talking about it and so the lease was alright. The workers moved in and started to drill and pump oil.[3]

John Norton captured the feelings of surprise and concern when the oil field began to be exploited:

The land is messed up when it was once very livable. It had vegetation that the horses and sheep lived on and water coming out of the ground that we drank. We did not even know that the land had been given out without our knowledge by our leaders and that we had oil under our feet. The oil field workers came, and it just happened. For ninety-nine years they will drill for oil and continue to pump until the land is dry. They just went to work on it, when all of a sudden, it was like that. The Anglos drove all over the place, put up ribbons to outline what they were going to do, started drilling and looking for oil, and then put in their pumps. One of the first ones was just over there, but then they spread through the whole area. No one bothered these workers, but we soon learned this was not a good thing and wondered why we were not told of their coming. Now they are going back over where they have drilled and putting in more pumps, which has ruined our water. When they drill, they let whatever is coming out drain into the washes without fixing a place for this liquid to go. The horses and sheep drink the water and oil, which kills them. This wastewater then goes into our drinking water. The whole place is ruined and the air stinks. People from the outside ask us how we can live like this. We cannot do anything about it; there are no alternatives. Whatever they were drilling with came back out in the underground water, our vegetation is very sparse, grass does not grow, and rain just bypasses us. The soil is dried out and there is nothing now.[4]

John Knot Begay, comparing the past to the present, echoed similar thoughts:

In my early years, I remember how beautiful our land used to be. Green vegetation grew in abundance and prairie dogs lived in its midst. These animals would stand on their hind legs and chatter as the tall grass waved in the breeze. It was a beautiful sight. Then came the oil wells. Bulldozers tore up the land, removing all of the vegetation and its roots. Our water was pure so that we could get a drink of cool, unpolluted water anywhere without getting sick. It did not cause heart problems, bone disease, headaches, or cramps like it does today. All of these health problems began when the oil wells were put in, polluting and ruining what we had. We used to have many medicine plants such as "Iináají Ch'il" (Lifeway plant), used for treating an injured bone during a ceremony. Where we once had medicine plants, we now have nothing but alkali and barren, polluted soil.

The water is unclean. If a sheep, horse, or cow drinks from these springs, they get sick. It is a pitiful sight to see them suffer. Even our underground water supply is polluted by chemicals in drainages and runoffs that kill the vegetation's roots. Our people experience heart attacks, high blood pressure, and diabetes, some people dying in their sleep. The air smells horrible, the stench covering our land like a cloud, especially when the wind drifts in our direction. We have some oil tanks sitting in the middle of my livestock grazing area and they smell terrible. The ground around them is dry and dead with its thick vegetation gone. The sagebrush has uprooted itself. This is how it has affected our environment.

The white men are rich, own many companies so that they can stuff their pockets with our land's mineral money and haul it back to their "unbroken land" to enjoy. What about us? Our water supply? I'm not about to go to Cortez or to the mountains to fetch some clean drinking water. It's too far. We have pleaded with these white men to set up clean water wells for us, but they have done nothing and will not listen. Furthermore, they claim that "this land does not belong to you, but to the BIA," and that we have no rights to it but are only borrowing it for a short time. Why do they lie to us? They send our children, some of whom are females, overseas to a foreign country to risk their lives defending other people's land for them? Why do they say this land is not ours?[5]

Every elder interviewed in the Aneth Oil Field area had similar comments, enough to fill the remainder of this chapter. A potpourri of their thoughts will be sufficient to understand the general feelings associated with this burdensome situation. Florence Norton agreed: "It not only destroyed what is on top, but underneath the ground too. The white men might look at us and think that we are very rich to have all these oil pumps surrounding us, but that's not the case. I live here without electricity and now my water is polluted and our land excavated everywhere, even in some of our sacred places. They have made too many roads all over and destroyed us. We have to haul our water great distances now, where we used to have it close to our homes. That is how we live today."[6] Isabelle Lee felt the whole process unsightly: "We didn't have all these oil pumps, but today you see our land dotted with red, greasy spots, leaving no space to build another house. The oil smells bad, especially in hot weather. People probably think I'm being paid for these oil pumps, but they are wrong."[7] Jane Silas reported: "One night, awhile back, a pump broke and the oil drained into one of our reservoirs and cornfield. My husband went down to our garden that morning to find it half full of black water. The corn was a few inches tall, but was now destroyed. Our field used to produce corn that was higher than a horse's back, but not anymore. Even our melons used to be huge, but now they are small."[8] Jerry Begay was very aware of the chemicals put into the ground to help move the oil to the surface. "In the wash below us, there used to be a hot spring used by people and livestock for drinking. The oil field workers drilled right on top of it, so now it is harmful to us because of something called CO_2 [carbon dioxide] in the water, which dissolves the hard rock and causes the oil to flow. This information came from an Anglo who does not work around here. This is not right that the chemical seeps through all the water. There were two springs that were analyzed, and neither one could be used by humans or animals."[9] Finally, Margaret Tso Weston commented on the social casualties caused by these disruptive influences: "We can see chemical waste seeping from the ground on the other side of this hill and it smells bad. They warned us that it is hazardous to our health because of the dangerous chemicals. That isn't all. People used to live in harmony without a lot of arguments, but the oil fields have totally destroyed their relationships. It separated the people; now they don't look at one another. It ruined everything."[10]

Through some Navajo eyes, the physical situation was so bad that the land and its animals were rebelling against the environmental degradation. The holy people had been ignored, the sacredness of the land was disrupted, and so it was reasonable to view a drought and sickness—in this case the hantavirus spread by infected mouse droppings—as two of the consequences. Cyrus Begay, for instance, complained of living in a

One of the biggest complaints of Navajo elders living in the Aneth–Montezuma Creek area between the 1960s and 1990s was the pollution and abhorrent living conditions caused by the oil extraction industry. Fouled air, contaminated water, noise, reckless driving, loss of sacred gathering sites for plants, and general disregard for residents created a volatile situation.

physically dangerous world abetted and manipulated by tribal political figures. After remembering what the land was like in the early days, he suggested that the earth, like the Navajos, were suffering. Excerpts from his lengthy statement follow.

> Our earth, our land is wearing down. I often think and wonder why it looks that way. When I was younger, the land was beautiful in every way. . . . These oil wells are very hazardous to our health and are too close to our homes. When the pollution blows our way, it fills our dwellings at night. . . . The oil field workers are dangerous to be around. They ignore the speed limit and drive at 60–70 miles per hour. I was almost hit in front of the store, when a pickup truck that I saw from a long way off approached me going 70 miles per hour, screeching and swerving past me. The tire marks are still visible in this 40 mile-per-hour speed zone. They drive like that everywhere, every day, and do not care about other people's safety. The oil wells have destroyed everything: the sagebrush, grass, stock feed, and water. It has stopped

raining, where it used to rain a lot. We haven't had a good rain in ten years, and when it does rain, it is only a little bit. It is our land that's producing oil, but the money it makes is all going to Window Rock, where Peter McDonald [Navajo Nation president] has stashed the royalties. Oil pollutants are thick like smoke or gas and smell terribly. It irritates our eyes, ears, and throat, and gives us headaches. Sometimes you wake up with all of these problems. Once in a great while, the wind will blow in a different direction and it feels better.[11]

Jerry Begay also felt that the land was rebelling against existing conditions. "The gas is escaping from somewhere so it smells when a person is driving through. There are chemicals in the gas that are harmful and will knock you out if you inhale too much. They have really ruined Mother Earth. Because of this mist of gas that hangs over us, the good rain clouds do not come here anymore. There would be a good rainstorm heading our way, but then would detour around us."[12] Fernandez Begay, building on the same concept of a dangerous world, attacked the polluted state of the Aneth–Montezuma Creek area, then commented on the various types of sickness, concluding with the hantavirus:

Perhaps because of all of the pollution of the land, these viruses and fevers are here now like they have not been before. In the past there was not all of the smoke and noise from trucks or from machines running at the El Paso [petroleum processing] plant. Things are being taken out of the ground like natural gas as well as smoke from burning fumes. Until these things occurred, these illnesses were not here. When you got a shot for such illness, you would get better. Right now, there are many kinds of sickness from oil drilling, and these illnesses came from them. What I think is that all of this pollution must have affected the mouse, and it is now said that these mice are what is bothering us. Maybe that is what is happening; it is from the mice. In the past, they would be around your home, but it was not said that they were going to kill you. Back then, there was only one kind of smoke, no butane, and no gas that you pump out. A wood fire was the only thing that boiled your coffee, and that was all. After butane became available, so did the sickness, which comes and sticks to you. It is like that.[13]

The Aneth Oil Field Takeover

All of these widespread complaints about the oil field led to an active resistance and eventual takeover in 1978 of the Texaco plant servicing the field. Occupation of the property lasted for approximately two and a half weeks until citizen demands had been met. Reminiscent of the backlash during the livestock reduction era, when community members took action against the BIA agents, range riders, and those sympathetic to the government's plan to rid the Navajos of half of their livestock and move land use to the restrictions of the Taylor Grazing Act, the Navajos of the Aneth–Montezuma Creek area set out to impact the power structure. Local people, tribal bureaucrats, American Indian Movement members, oil field representatives, federal agents, BIA supervisors, county and state government officials, and a host of tribal and nontribal activists all joined in to support—either pro or con—the negotiations. It was a complex process with many strident voices insisting their position was the correct one. The politics became heated, a warmth that spread in newspapers across the nation.

Perhaps the best way to understand what happened from a more personal, oral history perspective is to listen to the account of Ella Sakizzie, one of the organizers and protesters. She was uniquely suited due to her involvement, yet typically representative of what local people saw and felt.

> We didn't know what was going on when suddenly one day, a small drilling vehicle came around checking out our land. We were all wondering what these big trucks were doing. Some said they were drilling for oil, some said for uranium. We did not know. Our councilman and chapter representatives never informed us. Why didn't they tell about this transaction? They should have warned us about what was taking place and what the oil companies would guarantee our community, if there was an agreement. They could have offered us, in exchange, some funds to improve our situation by paying for electricity, good water wells, and other things, but they did not. Instead, they silently pushed their way onto our lands without any explanation. My father-in-law and Red Mexican used to own a lot of cattle and sheep that roamed in the area of the oil field, but that is all gone now. This was before the land was depleted. When you compare yesteryear

with today, it's more dangerous to eat a sheep now than back then because of these "injected" oil wells. All the chemicals and explosives used when drilling have contaminated our vegetation so that it does not grow anymore. Whenever there is an oil spill, it destroys every bush and plant in its path. It killed several of our cows, the veterinarian said, because it had eaten too much tumbleweed. But they have eaten tumbleweeds for years and were never hurt. There was an oil spill up on the hill, and this drained down into the waterholes below. I saw the cattle down there, and the next day, I found one sick cow, while the rest had gone elsewhere. He finally died, so those people dug a hole and buried it on the spot. The vet sided with the oil company, because he had met with them before he came to see us. These spills killed horses and sheep, too, the chemicals probably eating their insides. One of my goats got sick, so I took it to Cortez to the vet. When they pumped its stomach, it contained traces of oil and cost me forty dollars for the procedure.

Later, in 1957, more Anglos came in with their rigs and machinery. Before too long, we saw tall smokestacks popping up here and there, and more drilling. At first it did not bother us, until we noticed that there were more Anglos moving onto our land. These white men became very careless and ignorant and started running over our dogs, goats, and other animals with their vehicles. In fact, they killed several of my goats that way. It happened at the airport by the Texaco Company site. Someone failed to slow down and stop, so they plowed through my herd of goats with the animals rolling out from under the truck like balls. Later, while my son-in-law was herding sheep with his horse, an oil driller employee shot at him with a rifle. The horse reared and took off with my son-in-law hanging on. When he arrived home and told us about the incident, several of us went to investigate where it took place. Sure enough, we found some empty bullet shells and a cartridge box. I took those with me to use as evidence. While we were still looking, another oil worker came up to us, so I told him about the incident. He replied he was not responsible for handling such cases, that he was from Texas and only here to check on his workers. He did not listen to me or say anything. I then went to the main office and told them, "Ever since this oil company came here, you have not listened to or noticed us and mistreated our people. Why are you like that? Exactly who gave your company the rights to our land? You have absolutely no respect for the Navajos and it is getting worse. You could care less if you killed one of us, but just carry on as you please. You have already killed my goats by driving over them, and another died when he trapped his head in the small fence around the oil pump. I stopped a worker from clearing the ground for a new 'location' near my trailer. Then another worker came by and I protested to him when he showed up for work, saying, 'No! You cannot do this! Why are you clearing off my only grazing spot for my sheep? This greasewood pasture is where I take them every morning, but now look at what you have done! You have completely stripped my land. Turn that bulldozer off right this instant! I mean it! I am not kidding you!' He shut off the bulldozer and left in his truck. He probably came back here to see you, his boss. What are you trying to do to us? And now, with this most recent shooting incident against my son-in-law, I definitely will not let you get away with that!"

All of this disruption caused us to form the "Coalition" group. Our community was tired of this disrespectful treatment, so many men and women joined us from this area. We held our meetings at night, and heard similar stories of "sheep killing" in other places, but it was the shooting incident with my son-in-law that made me furious. We decided to invade the company's territory. I think Texaco was the biggest company, so we set out to block every access road that went to their main offices. We barricaded the roads with huge rocks, moved in, and prevented anyone from entering. We wanted to know who gave this company permission and authority to carry out their operation. Who was responsible for "giving us up" to be the victims of disrespect? We did not know who had made these agreements. Any transactions and agreements should have been settled in a more open and agreeable manner, but the Anglos had no respect for us whatsoever. There were fistfights with some white workers, too.

It was 1978 when we moved in to occupy the Texaco facilities, hauling wood and water in our trucks. We blocked the main entrance, where the horses usually entered, then secured all other roads with huge boulders. We asked the boys to help us do this and they did. "Let's see what happens now; let it happen. Let it be heard all over the world if it has to. We'll see what happens to us. We don't care if we get thrown in jail; it's okay!" The men stayed to block the roads, while us women went home to bring back some food. We spent the rest of the night at home, while the men stayed behind with their blockade and night fire. The next morning, the men stopped the company employers and employees at the point of entry, where they confiscated any weapons or sharp objects and stashed them in the pickup trucks parked in two locations so that if one was filled, we could use the second one.

Officials from Washington had been called in to meet with us. They were of different races and representation, Blacks and Justice Department officials, I can't remember all who came, but we were all given a list of their names. For eighteen days we protested, although the newspapers said it was seventeen. We camped at the site and slept on the ground, raided their office buildings and overturned everything, rampaged through their files and desks unconcerned about important and untouchable documents, put the keys to their trucks hanging out in the open, and left everything in disarray. We wanted them to see how it felt; let them experience the affliction they had been causing our people so that we could watch and see how they reacted.

Not until then did they tell us how this all came about. Many years ago, shortly after our people returned from "the Long Walk," our nation's council delegates, whoever they were, held a meeting concerning land use. The BIA did the translating for this meeting. They negotiated with the oil company and the department in charge of drilling minerals and resources in Washington. None of our people knew about this, only the BIA spoke for the Navajo Tribe. They were not Navajo! So they are the ones who jeopardized our lives and left us to suffer the consequences. They gave the company the right to invade our land; this is what we now realized.

Then we said, "Although the BIA pretended to be the spokesman for the Navajos, we now realize and understand what has taken place. Because of our current turmoil, we refuse to let you continue any further!" We made these kinds of speeches loud and clear—into the microphones, all day long, throughout the ordeal. I shared my thoughts, too.

We made several proposals to the company: that it should agree to install our electrical power lines, make water wells for us, dig graves with their equipment for our dead, provide scholarships for young Navajos, reimburse us for livestock killed by oil field activity, assist in building dams, and other things that I cannot remember offhand. "Only if and after you agree to these terms, help us when we ask, and

For two and a half weeks, Navajos living in the oil-producing area in southeastern Utah rebelled and took over the offices of the Texaco refinery plant. Residents blocked roads, controlled administrative areas, gave daily speeches, and made public demands of those they saw as trespassers of their homeland. Tribal leaders; members of the American Indian Movement (AIM); federal, state, and county officials; and well-meaning sympathizers joined the fray. Not until some of the demands were met did things settle down.

abide by our jurisdiction will you be able to continue your work. If not, then we won't leave," we said. They told us to leave, but we stubbornly refused, until they finally agreed. We wrote down all these demands, but our councilman, Robert Billie, made the biggest mistake. He was "bought" by the company and intentionally disposed of our written proposals, causing us to totally despise him up to this day. The same thing happened with [name deleted], who was also "bought" by the company. We wanted to meet and negotiate this case at our chapter house, but the officials met in Denver instead. I still confront Robert Billie about this.

A new company runs it now, and the one we negotiated with has moved out. This new one knows nothing about our past negotiations. Sometimes they get out of hand, but we always hold a meeting to voice our complaints. We will take the oil field again if it becomes necessary.

We proposed that our local people get employment there and should any company employee become disrespectful, he would not be allowed to work there. If his employer does not want to let him go because he is a good worker, then he should be transferred elsewhere, off the reservation, even if he is native. We value "life" and demand respect within its guidelines. These were some of the agreements we wrote and spoke about at the meeting. A huge crowd showed up for the negotiations. The Civil Rights Commission kept in touch with us for approximately three years. They wanted to stay informed about how we were being treated. After three years, we let them know we were fine. Sometimes representatives would come by to personally check on us and ask questions. The company paid for the power lines, but only for those who lived within the leased sites. Some people had their water wells fixed too, but several did not, including me.[14]

Bars, Booze, and Bickering

While Ella Sakizzie may have been mistaken in some of her information, there is no missing the intensity of her feelings and her perception of what the underlying problems were. She was concerned about current events, but like so many Navajo elders, she was also worried about the future of the young people and the community. There were other things that were viewed as threats and challenges when moving toward the twenty-first century. For instance, there has been a long-standing concern about alcohol and Native Americans, the Navajos being no exception. Certainly, the oil field with its roustabouts exacerbated the problem on a "dry" reservation that had bars and package stores on its periphery but no tolerance for sales on Navajo land. Regardless of where it was purchased, alcohol consumption was a reality that stared Navajos in the face, and was a cause of broken homes and death on the roads. John Knot Begay expressed the problem of mixing oil field workers, young Navajos, and alcohol.

> The oil field workers introduced harmful substances like wine, whiskey, and beer to our people and into our land. It has destroyed our young men and women, killing them on our highways, then setting up more laws and blaming us for what the white man did in the first place.

Nobody admits or cares to notice that we are suffering, nor do they want to put an end to it, but when we stand up to defend our rights, the judge decides to put us in jail. This whole system holds us as prisoners so we cannot speak for ourselves. I cannot stand to live here in this polluted land as our poor children suffer from health problems. Some are already deformed at the time of birth because their mother drank polluted water during pregnancy. Look around; our young people have gone astray because they have followed in the wrong footsteps leading in a different direction. It was not our fault.[15]

Given the preceding discussion about the oil field, it should not be surprising to hear that Ella Sakizzie threw her hat into the ring concerning alcohol distribution in Montezuma Creek. Before this area became annexed to the reservation in 1905, there were some sections that had been homesteaded for trading posts and designated as school sections of land that were under the control of the state. On one of these pieces, close to the mouth of Montezuma Wash, stood a building that became a bar and sold alcohol, which followed state and county regulations but not those of the Navajo Nation. Ella saw the damage it was doing to people in the community and took action.

I got involved, or rather started another revolt, against the bar. We raided it and threw out their beer before they called the police. When they arrived, we climbed on top of their patrol cars. One policeman wanted desperately to use the bathroom, but we refused to let him, saying, "You sit still, because you've asked for it. You favor the side of bloody violence and suffering. Is that why you came here, to stop us from ending all of this chaos? You are a policeman because you don't want violence and are responsible for people's safety."

"So why can't this bar decrease its selling of beer and shorten its business hours? It could close at sundown instead of midnight or later to avoid violence and criminal behavior. This is what we don't like," I told Fern, the bar owner. She was furious and asked someone to throw me out or shoot me, but her son, Preston, told her not to talk like that because the cops were outside. I went outside and told everyone to stay on top of the patrol vehicles. At that instant, a couple of men, who belonged to a different tribe, came to us to say something, but the cops arrested one, then left to take him to the Monticello jail. That made me angry again. "The boy you have arrested just so happens to be a visitor to our community from a distant place. Why did you do this? We demand that you release him from jail or else we won't let you go either." The cop kept asking to use the restroom and that he was ready to wet his pants, but we told him to stay put. Finally, the other one made a phone call, and before too long, the young man was brought back and released. We let the cops go, too.

This business has brought nothing but trouble and suffering to our community. There is no reason why it should stay open until midnight or later; it should close around six or seven in the evening to avoid bloody fighting or killing. Several people have either been killed or committed suicide. We don't like it. Even though they have a license to be open and say it is their means of income, can't they find something else worthwhile to sell or live on? Why sit and sell something putrid, then claim they are earning a living, while people fight around you and crying babies stumble among the crawling drunkards. This was our reason for revolting and seeing this situation as definitely inappropriate. We did it because we did not like it one bit and witnessed intoxicated students ruining the school. Whenever it has an activity like a dance or ball game, the students always wreck it by showing up drunk, and then we hear how they vandalized others' cars. Our people once lived in harmony, so we never heard about children drinking or fighting. They used to chase horses or we would learn that they went rabbit hunting on their horses or held foot and horse races; not anything like "They were drunk and crawling around." Those were our activities in those days. But today, that's all we hear. It's no good. Our children don't listen to us because of alcohol. That's why we don't want that bar; I despise it.[16]

Future Generations—Where To?

The issue of school and education reaches far beyond that of youths drinking alcohol. Indeed, it goes to the very heart of the elders seeing the next few generations losing much of what was held dear in the past. Language loss, ignorance of the ceremonies, disrespect for elders, adopting values from the dominant culture, and laziness are concerns that shake the traditional culture core. The strict, no-nonsense approach of yesteryear, spawned by the Long Walk era, a work-or-starve situation in the early reservation years, conflict over the introduction of white values running contrary to tradition, the influenza epidemic, livestock reduction, a national depression, two world wars, and an ever-changing economy inured the elders to tribulation, encouraging them to stoically accept what life dished out. Perhaps that is one reason why their voices heard throughout this chapter often sound a pessimistic warning cry. Formal education, one of these concerns, has played an important role, both good and bad, in the ongoing process of cultural change.

Whitehorse High School, founded in 1978, has a staff of Navajo and Anglo teachers who provide a curriculum that is sympathetic to Navajo history and culture. Indeed, the reason for this school's existence derived from a lawsuit against San Juan County that brought education into two communities—Montezuma Creek and Monument Valley—to stop the long bus rides to Blanding and introduce culturally sensitive materials to Navajo high school students. Even so, there are still concerns. Margaret Tso Weston felt that those charged with raising children are also failing to promote traditional teachings and language.

> The parents are trying to pass on their teachings, but their children are not interested. The young people recognize their language, but fail to speak it. Only a few parents and children still follow the old ways and know their language. Some speak half and half, but most of them end up using English. Many of our young people are being too careless by doing forbidden things, which are dangerous for them. Television has been a bad influence on our young children. They watch too much violence that is not good for them. Some will be led astray by it. Before we had television, our children listened and obeyed us. All they do now is stare at the screen for their pastime. It keeps them from doing what they need to do. This is how we live now.[17]

Isabelle Lee agreed.

> Today we live without all of these teachings. We used to be asked to "fetch the horse," "take the sheep out," herding them in a cloud of dust in the early morning light, before it got hot. But we don't do these things anymore. We depend on the automobile for everything we do; nobody wants to set their foot on the ground. We used to walk

everywhere back then. We would card wool and weave during the night. They don't do this anymore; they say "the wool stinks" and they don't know how to card or spin it or how to use the weaving sticks. All they do is "paper and pencil," "paint their lips," then off they go, not giving a second thought about the undone chores around the home.[18]

Cyrus Begay was concerned with what was happening to his grandchildren, not just in school but also at home.

One grandson is graduating soon. His assignment was to write a paper and give a report in Navajo. He came to me for help, but I had to teach him how to speak our language. His mother was there, and I told her, "See what you've done to him?" His father, my son, was there also, so I pointed out how they had created their son's language problem. I told my son, "If you would address your child as 'son, do this,' and not use his English name, which he does not respond to, he would obey. If parents taught their children the Navajo culture until they left home, these young people would be more than willing to explore and research their own culture and respect themselves and others. He would have the urge to learn the sacred sandpaintings and songs and a desire to become a medicine man for all occasions." My grandson was in trouble because he did not know how to speak his native language. He had to learn by repeating the words I wrote down for him, but when we visited him later, he was good at it.[19]

Ella Sakizzie, once again trying to return order to what she considered chaos, did not like the statement in the school ordinances that said a child was on his or her own at age eighteen. "It's not good. I don't like it. Children believe this, and once they turn eighteen, they leave, while you're still cooking and feeding them. They tell you that they are no longer under you and that 'Whatever I'm doing is none of your business, because I'm eighteen years old now.' Then they go to the bar and drink, steal, or do something like that. It's no wonder our people are labeled as being obnoxious."[20] Jerry Begay agreed and hearkened back to the old days. "The young people are moving along. They do not know what is being said when spoken to in Navajo, so they do not grasp the meaning of their language. They will ask about a word when I speak, but only a few understand the meaning—those taught in their homes. When I was their age, I was told things. I did not go to school, but only herded sheep. At the age of eighteen, I was no longer home, but herded sheep for the Anglos. This was my foundation for life. This was why I did not go to school."[21]

One can see from these comments that although the schools are not teaching the Navajo language in a way that creates fluency and that the curriculum still emphasizes Anglo education, there is much more to the problem of culture loss in the family. Traditional teachings are not emphasized in the home either. John Norton, longtime resident of Montezuma Creek, who lives within a couple of miles of Whitehorse High School, has children and grandchildren educated there. He remarked:

> The school itself is probably good. If the teaching is straightforward, then the learning situation is good. There are many other activities like sports and dances that also take place. Then there are TV, movies, and the things the young people listen to. When these things are involved, it is not good. They are looking at these things, and that is why they don't listen. They are seated in front of the TV, which has unpleasant things on it. Anglos are in this TV and sometimes the movies are too embarrassing. The children are watching it, and it goes into their mind so that they think in crazy ways. There are other things like the smoke that makes a person crazy [marijuana] or other harmful drugs. If there was nothing like them, it would have been better. All of their activities are held at night, so they come in late. They are found walking beside the road because their ride left earlier. If they did not have these activities, but only school, it would be good. Now there seems to be gossip, violence, and many other things that are going on.[22]

Concern, unrest, and friction extends much further than just alcohol, education, and modern Anglo influences. Much of the cohesion that used to be generated by traditional culture through shared involvement in ceremonies, neighborly assistance in harvesting crops, joint activities during sheep shearing and lambing times, leisurely interaction at the trading posts, horse racing, involvement at the Shiprock Fair, and general community events has now been replaced with competitive values, marked concerns over ownership, emphasis on the nuclear instead of the extended family, dependence on technology including television and social media, and employment that takes both parents out of the home.

Perhaps the greatest concern of all the elders who have spoken in this book is that younger generations are losing their way, losing their distinctive Navajo heritage, and losing the determination to maintain that culture. For many, the days of sitting around a fire in a hogan on a winter night have been replaced with technology, social media, and an incessant bombardment of images and practices from the dominant culture. In this twenty-first-century world, the choice has become crucial.

In one sense, the world has become smaller and more sterile in terms of interpersonal relationships, even though in the words of Cyrus Begay:

> Our population is overwhelming and our world is getting old. I am a grandfather of four generations with about one hundred or more grandchildren from my seven daughters and five sons. Others of my age have just as many children, and many of them live here. We are overpopulated and crowded. There is no more room as people begin claiming areas of land. My wife lost the right to her grandfather's land up at Red Ochre Basin. People are mad at each other because of the land. For example, here on our property there is a dispute going on. Mr. Canyon (Hastiin Tsé Yiini) used to live here, and Red Mexican lived on the other side, where their children live now. Red Mexican's grandchildren claim part of our land, get furious when our sheep wander that way, and beat my wife when this happens. We do not know what to do about it, especially if it gets worse. It seems impossible to resolve, for it is not like it used to be.
>
> People are everywhere and seem unstable as we become more overcrowded. They complain to us about this land, and sooner or later, they will tell us to get out and chase us off. It is impossible to live like this. Our plans and what we say might sound great, but physically we aren't getting along like we should. In our chapter meetings, we discuss land and livestock, but people are always cussing at one another. We don't accomplish anything because they argue over who owns what land. I think that the problem lies within the chapter officials themselves. The grazing committee chairperson will often claim others' lands, creating trouble against his own people. These representatives resent it when I mention this at the meetings. I say the same thing to the delegates from Shiprock. I tell them how they take over and approve property for others that is not theirs. I say they are to blame. Our livestock are barely thriving. These oil wells are the main cause in our area, but for those people who live away from the pollution, they have better livestock and their sheep are fatter and healthier. I observe these things wherever I go. In fact, I saw some sheep down by the road in Aneth the other day and they looked good, but there is nothing up here near the oil fields. It is ugly. We would appreciate it if our tribe and government officials reconsidered our people's special needs.[23]

Cyrus raises an important issue. As the Navajo population grows exponentially and distant employment can now be handled through telecommunications, there is increasing pressure on the land base for those who wish to live on the reservation. In the past, land could often belong to the family that got there first and put it to use. Take for instance Old Mexican's experience noted previously, when he just came in, selected a piece of land that was not under use, and began farming. There certainly were disputes over grazing areas as wandering herds entered what another owner considered his territory, but through discussion, community influence, or suggestions of witchcraft, the arguments were pushed under the blanket. In today's society, litigation and conflict remain on the surface. Legal papers, government and tribal regulation, fence lines, and lawyers argue for ownership rights that were first established when there was no such concern or process for resolution. Imagine defending through today's court system what Isabelle Lee described as an early claim to land by Asdzáán Blanding when she and her grandmother, Bimásání, accompanied by a white lady, climbed on top of a hill overlooking Montezuma Creek.

> Here Grandma Bimásání outlined the boundaries of our future Clauschee Clan's existence—"from that juniper covered hill to White Point (Łigai Desaaha) on down the gray ridge to Stair Formation Rock (Nahaz'áí) and across to Fallen House (Kin Náázhoozh) and to that mesa where the land markers are still." She spoke to us, saying, "This is how big our land will be. This land is not mine alone, because it will also belong to the Clauschee Clan. They will multiply here, so I declare this much land for them." In fact, that prediction has been fulfilled and we now live here. She also said, "No one shall move onto our land," but many have done just that, and now they are telling us to move out.[24]

Land covered with housing and construction to support the oil industry has replaced the open range of the past. What seemed so available for livestock has turned into cramped quarters for individuals or types of development unsupportive of raising animals or planting corn. Jane Silas recalled her dad's warning:

> My father used to say, "There is some kind of oil, way down under this ground." I didn't know what he was talking about, but sure enough, it has become a reality. Today we see "galloping" oil pumps overtaking the

land where our horses once galloped. Livestock, sheep, cattle, horses, covered our land as far as the eye could see. We used to own a portion of this livestock, but now we have only a few animals. That's how it is. I don't know what our future holds. Everything that was foretold is taking place as predicted, like the housing that would someday be here and there. My father was right. Houses have been built. We are told to "move in, move in." When you do move in, you have to pay the bills. If you can't afford it, you are forced to leave and make room for rich people.[25]

Mary Jay briefly summarized her concerns:

Our sheep corrals were made from chopped juniper branches and we never had to buy hay, there was plenty of vegetation for the animals to graze on. It's not like that anymore, we have to buy hay these days. The same with firewood. It scares me each time I think about it. I question, "What is happening to our society and environment? What will happen?" It wasn't like this before. We have many land disputes today. We were taught by our folks that the land, "Mother Earth," should not be fought over. It is a place where "life is lived and buried," so it was forbidden to fight, speak, or bother Mother Earth. That is why I leave it alone. I live in this small space, but my children are constantly told to move. It bothers me sometimes. I feel they have the right to live here because they were all born right here.[26]

There were, of course, some real benefits with modern conveniences that made life easier. Labor-saving devices powered by electricity brought in lighting, heating, washing machines, cooking appliances, and other amenities that used to require hours and hours of work to accomplish when done by hand. John Knot Begay was happy with his situation.

I think the installation of electricity in our homes was a great idea, but I worry whether we will be able to afford it in the next several years. As it is now, our people are getting some assistance through the federal government from the oil wells to pay for these services. If it stops, what will happen to us? As you know, the white men know how to budget their money, usually saving to make ends meet. But not us. People are paying for and living in ready-made housing with all of its conveniences, none of which were built by the individuals themselves.

What will happen if all the funds run out or when the oil wells are gone? Progress is good, though.

I have electricity in my home. I am able to pay for these expenses through my social security benefits, which I earned by working at odd jobs all my life. I have labored on railroads and herded sheep for several Anglo ranchers in my younger years. I have also labored as a construction worker on highways, buildings, and schools. We are living on these earned benefits and hope to continue to do so for a long time. The new generation, however, is not working; they only look forward to getting another check from general or public assistance programs. They don't bother with hauling wood and water anymore. They don't know how to use the sacred corn grinding stones or plant a cornfield that can produce food, or harvest and store it for the winter. They ignore such things. That is what causes me to wonder what will happen to them if they are turned out in the open with no assistance.[27]

Jane Silas recognized that it was because of the questionable oil pumps that she received electric power. "Last winter we received electricity in our homes. Long ago we were warned that electricity was dangerous and that you could be electrocuted if it was in your home or if you went near an electric power line. We never had electric power lines around here until the oil pumps came into being because the pumps run by electricity."[28]

The last word goes to Isabelle Lee, who put the entire past and contemporary Navajo lifestyle of those living along the river in perspective. Her concerns and interpretation of what she had encountered during her lifetime fit into the mythological pattern understood by many of her people. The dissolution of the world and a change to a new order is exemplified by the Anasazi, whose experience serves to use the past as prologue. Isabelle's statement, cited previously in chapter 10, bears repeating:

It seems like the end will come soon because everybody's going the white man's way. Once our people leave our culture and traditions, we will no longer have an identity. No one partakes of the sacred corn pollen anymore. That's how the Anasazi destroyed themselves. They got carried away with their inventions, just like we are doing today. Our technology is overpowering the human race. The Anasazi "outdid" themselves, and that is where we are now, close to destruction. When it happens again, the world will end. We are drying out our earth by digging up the land and pumping up its water and oil, so it will soon collapse. I think the end is near. Our elders used to tell us, "When the end comes, it will take place in the wink of an eye," because this is how the Holy Creator said it would be. The holy ones exist in the fog that often covers our land. Some warning signs for the end are if a horse bears twins, if planted corn seed fails to grow, or if a baby is born with teeth and white hair—these signs mean the end is here. We will perish like the Anasazi did, dying with their babies in their arms. Likewise, the end will come in sudden death for us too.[29]

Life along the San Juan River has never been an easy, carefree experience for the Navajo. Conflict with Ute and Anglo neighbors, years of drought or floods, and pressured change in cultural beliefs are only part of the history that has encouraged these people to become resilient and practical. Perhaps one reason that the elders speak so highly of the past is that the present seems difficult. Most older people, regardless of their culture, think of the "good ole days" but recall them through selective memory, while contemporary issues stare one in the eyes. The elders have had an opportunity to share their thoughts and concerns with those who have the future lying before them. The old one's voices are preserved, as they wished, to serve as a guide for the young people who will experience the issues that lie ahead. They have shared their legacy with the hope for a brighter future.

NOTES

Introduction

1. Robert S. McPherson and Perry J. Robinson, *Traditional Navajo Teachings: A Trilogy* [hereafter *TNT*], vol. 3, *The Earth Surface People* (Boulder: University Press of Colorado, 2020), 108.

2. Walter Dyk, *A Navaho Autobiography* (New York: Viking Fund Publication in Anthropology, 1947).

3. David M. Brugge, "Navajo Use and Occupation of Lands North of the San Juan River in Present-Day Utah to 1935," unpublished manuscript, in possession of author. Used with permission.

4. Margaret K. Brady, *"Some Kind of Power": Navajo Children's Skinwalker Narratives* (Salt Lake City: University of Utah Press, 1984); Terry Tempest Williams, *Pieces of White Shell: A Journey to Navajoland* (New York: Charles Scribner's Sons, 1984); J. Lee Correll, *Bai-a-lil-le: Medicine Man or Witch?*, Biographical Series no. 3 (Window Rock, AZ: Navajo Historical Publications, 1970).

5. See James M. Aton and Robert S. McPherson, *River Flowing from the Sunrise: An Environmental History of the Lower San Juan* (Logan: Utah State University Press, 2000); and Robert S. McPherson, *Comb Ridge and Its People: The Ethnohistory of a Rock* (Logan: Utah State University, 2009). Both books examine not only the topographical features of these two places but also detailed histories of people and events associated with them.

6. Robert S. McPherson, *A History of San Juan County: In the Palm of Time* (Salt Lake City: Utah State Historical Society, 1995), was written for the Utah Centennial. Half of this book concerns Native Americans—Navajos, Utes, and Paiutes—and their interaction among themselves and

with the Anglos who settled in the area. It provides a good overview of some of the topics covered in this book.

7. Robert S. McPherson, *The Northern Navajo Frontier, 1860–1900: Expansion through Adversity* (Logan: Utah State University, 2001).

8. Robert S. McPherson, *Stories from the Land: A Navajo Reader about Monument Valley* (Boulder: University Press of Colorado, 2021).

9. McPherson, *Northern Navajo Frontier*, is particularly helpful here with its first four chapters discussing the interaction with the Utes, Paiutes, and Mormons; the Long Walk period; and the role of Henry L. Mitchell, a real firebrand who settled in Aneth. Two chapters in Robert S. McPherson, *Fighting in Canyon Country: Native American Conflict, 500 AD to the 1920s* (independently published, 2016; 2021), discuss Navajo and Ute forms of warfare and the Long Walk period. In Robert S. McPherson, *Both Sides of the Bullpen: Navajo Trade and Posts* (Norman: University of Oklahoma Press, 2017), there is a chapter about the earliest posts—both Mormon (Bluff and Montezuma Creek) and non-Mormon (Aneth). Robert S. McPherson, "Howard R. Antes and the Navajo Faith Mission: Evangelist of Southeastern Utah," *Utah Historical Quarterly* 65, no. 1 (Winter 1997), is about a little-known boarding school established close to Aneth, the name given to this area by Antes.

10. See Robert S. McPherson and Perry J. Robinson, *TNT*, vol. 2, *The Natural World*, for a general understanding of what the land—from the heavens to geologic formations to water to creatures—represents in the Navajo world. Robert S. McPherson, *Sacred Land, Sacred View: Navajo Perceptions of the Four Corners Region* (Provo, UT: Brigham Young University Press, 1992), devotes seven short chapters to an overview of how the Diné think about their environment, while McPherson, *Comb Ridge and Its People*, has a lengthy chapter dealing with the land formation called Comb Ridge and its environs.

11. For a general history of the role that the San Juan River played in the lives of Navajos and settlers alike, see Aton and McPherson, *River Flowing from the Sunrise*. In Robert S. McPherson, *Traders, Agents, and Weavers: Developing the Northern Navajo Region* (Norman: University of Oklahoma Press, 2020), there are two chapters devoted to trying to harness the river to provide irrigation water in the Shiprock area as well as detailed information about the flood of 1911. Robert S. McPherson, *Navajo Land, Navajo Culture: The Utah Experience in the Twentieth Century* (Norman: University of Oklahoma Press, 2003), has a chapter

on the government farmers of Aneth, their role in teaching twentieth century agricultural techniques, and their success and failures. Herbert Redshaw was a particularly notable contributor.

12. In Robert S. McPherson, *Dinéjí Na'nitin: Navajo Traditional Teachings and History* (Boulder: University Press of Colorado, 2012), there are two chapters—one on divination and another on witchcraft— that give detailed explanations about the power of these two forces. A good overview of Navajo religion, ceremonial behavior, and thought, as well as additional information on the Bearway ceremony can be found in McPherson and Robinson, *TNT*, vol. 1, *Sacred Narratives and Ceremonies*.

13. For information about the life stages outlined in traditional culture, see McPherson and Robinson, *TNT*, vol. 3, *The Earth Surface People*, which covers activities from prebirth to the death and burial of an individual. In addition to Old Mexican's autobiography previously mentioned, Robert S. McPherson, ed., *The Journey of Navajo Oshley: An Autobiography and Life History* (Logan: Utah State University, 2000), is the story of a man who spent a good part of his life in Bluff and experienced many of the things discussed in this chapter.

14. See McPherson, *Northern Navajo Frontier*, in which there is one chapter on earliest posts. McPherson, *Navajo Land, Navajo Culture*, has two chapters, one describing trade as a cultural undertaking, the other looking at the issue of slaughtering the deer herds for hides to trade. McPherson, *Both Sides of the Bullpen*, entire book. See Will Evans, Susan E. Woods, and Robert S. McPherson, *Along Navajo Trails: Recollections of a Trader* (Logan: Utah State University Press, 2005), for the experience of a trader living in Shiprock who was heavily involved with many Navajos living along the river. To understand the government's view emanating from Shiprock and the problems from a marketing perspective, see McPherson, *Traders, Agents, and Weavers*, which has three pertinent chapters.

15. McPherson, *Traders, Agents, and Weavers*, has a detailed chapter on the Shiprock Boarding School—how it was staffed, how it functioned, how it expanded, and how it was involved in the community. In addition to the Navajo Faith Mission previously mentioned, there was also an Episcopalian school run by Father H. Baxter Liebler outside of Bluff. The Navajo perspective concerning him and his success is found in a chapter in McPherson, *Dinéjí Na'nitin*. A medicine man named Ba'álílee reacted against the presence of the Shiprock school, Agent

William T. Shelton, and government policies in general. He rebelled in 1907 and was arrested at his home near Aneth by the U.S. cavalry under the direction of Shelton. His story is found in McPherson, *Fighting in Canyon Country*.

16. For an in-depth explanation of how the Anasazi experience served as a template for contemporary change in Navajo culture, see *Viewing the Ancestors: Perceptions of the Anaasází, Mokwič, and Hisatsinom* (Norman: University of Oklahoma Press, 2014), and eight short chapters in McPherson, *Sacred Land, Sacred View*. McPherson, *Navajo Land, Navajo Culture*, provides further explanation of how the car and airplane were first introduced on the reservation, while McPherson, *Traders, Agents, and Weavers*, outlines general improvements in roads and infrastructure, and McPherson, *Dinéjí Na'nitin*, explains the impact of the influenza epidemic of 1918.

17. McPherson, *Northern Navajo Frontier*, has two chapters that look at the conflicts over livestock management in San Juan prior to 1900, while McPherson, *Navajo Land, Navajo Culture*, offers one chapter in which Navajos compare the events of livestock reduction to that of the Long Walk, when hunger and fear stalked the people. McPherson, *Traders, Agents, and Weavers*, follows the thinking about this program as it emanated from the government in Shiprock; McPherson, *Both Sides of the Bullpen*, tracks its effects on the trading posts of San Juan.

18. For background information about what Navajos faced previously in this area concerning alcohol and white relations, see one chapter in McPherson, *Northern Navajo Frontier*; a chapter in McPherson, *Traders, Agents, and Weavers*, looks at the initial drilling for oil in the Shiprock area, while another chapter in McPherson, *Navajo Land, Navajo Culture*, examines the Aneth takeover of 1978 and the widespread repercussions of that action.

19. Cyrus Begay, interview with author, May 14, 1991.

Chapter 1

1. For the earliest Spanish documentary evidence of interaction with the Navajos see J. Lee Correll, *Through White Men's Eyes: A Contribution to Navajo History*, vol. 1 (Window Rock, AZ: Navajo Heritage Center, 1979). For documentary evidence of Navajos living north of the San Juan River, see David M. Brugge's unpublished manuscript, "Navajo Use

and Occupation of Lands North of the San Juan River in Present-Day Utah to 1935," in possession of author.

2. Richard Van Valkenburgh, "Synopsis of Statements Regarding Navajo Residence North of the San Juan River," series of interviews ending in 1953, Berard Haile Papers, Box 9 Miscellaneous, Special Collections, University of Arizona, Tucson [hereafter cited as Van Valkenburgh]; Doris Duke Oral History Project, Special Collections, Marriott Library, University of Utah, Salt Lake City [hereafter cited as Duke].

3. Scotty Jones, interview, January 27, 1961, Duke no. 229; Hastiin Nez Begay, interview, January 18, 1961, Duke no. 706; Mary Jelly, interview, January 21, 1961, Duke no. 722; Jimmy Holiday, interview, Van Valkenburgh; Netty Hezpah, interview, Van Valkenburgh.

4. Mary Jelly, interview, January 21, 1961, Duke no. 722.

5. George Littlesalt in Broderick H. Johnson, ed., *Navajo Stories of the Long Walk Period* (Tsaile, AZ: Navajo Community College Press, 1973), 159–60.

6. Hashk'áán Dííl, interview, Van Valkenburgh.

7. Old Lady Bitsili or Old Lady Sweetwater, June 11, 1958, Land Claims Statement no. 13, Duke.

8. White Sheep, interview, Van Valkenburgh; Blind Weaver, interview, Van Valkenburgh; John Hart, interview, January 19, 1965, Duke no. 709.

9. White Sheep, interview, Van Valkenburgh.

10. White Horse, interview, Van Valkenburgh.

11. Blind Weaver, interview; Jimmy Holiday, interview; Hashk'áán Dííl, interview, all Van Valkenburgh.

12. For a more complete history of Weeminuche Ute and Navajo interaction, see Robert S. McPherson, *As If the Land Owned Us: An Ethnohistory of the White Mesa Utes* (Salt Lake City: University of Utah Press, 2011).

13. Charles Kelly, "Chief Hoskaninni," *Utah Historical Quarterly* 21, no. 3 (Summer 1953): 220.

14. Brugge, "Navajo Use and Occupation," 1–2.

15. White Sheep, interview, Van Valkenburgh.

16. Tsekizzie [Tsék'izí], interview, Van Valkenburgh.

17. Eddie Nakai, interview, January 21, 1961, Duke no. 723.

18. Eddie Nakai, interview, January 21, 1961, Duke no. 723.

19. Lucille Hammond, interview with author, October 18, 1985.

20. See L. R. Bailey, *The Long Walk: A History of the Navajo Wars, 1846–68* (Pasadena, CA: Westernlore Publications, 1978); Peter Iverson, *Diné: A History of the Navajos* (Albuquerque: University of New Mexico Press, 2002); Broderick H. Johnson, ed., *Navajo Stories of the Long Walk Period* (Tsaile, AZ: Navajo Community College Press, 1973); and Gerald Thompson, *The Army and the Navajo: The Bosque Redondo Reservation Experiment, 1863–1868* (Tucson: University of Arizona Press, 1982).

21. Tom Jones (aka Tomas), interview, Van Valkenburgh.

22. Martha Nez, interview with author, August 2, 1988.

23. Louise Big Mouth, January 22, 1961, Duke no. 726.

24. Sally Draper Bailey, interview, January 29, 1961, Duke no. 740.

25. George Littlesalt in Johnson, *Navajo Stories of the Long Walk Period*, 159–60.

26. Ada Black, interview with author, December 15, 1991.

27. Old Man Bob, testimony, January 27, 1961, Duke no. 734.

28. Old Ruins (Kit'siili [Kints'iilnii]), testimony, January 18, 1961, Duke no. 704.

29. Mexican Woman, January 23, 1961, Duke no. 731.

30. Eddie Nakai, interview, January 21, 1961, Duke no. 723.

31. Eddie Nakai, interview, January 21, 1961, Duke no. 723.

32. Garrick Bailey and Roberta Glenn Bailey, *A History of the Navajos: The Reservation Years* (Santa Fe, NM: School of American Research Press, 1986), 19; James L. Collins, "New Mexico Superintendency," August 30, 1857, *Report of the Commissioner of Indian Affairs* (Washington, D.C.: Government Printing Office, 1857), 273. Collins estimated 12,000 members of the Navajo Tribe. Others suggested as many as 20,000, but this seems too high, although no one will ever know. For an interesting discussion of tabulating how many did not go to Fort Sumner, see Marilyn R. Wagner, "Navajo Settlement Patterns, 1846–1870: A Geographical History" (master's thesis, University of Utah, December 1978), 122–66.

33. Mary Bitsili or Old Lady Sweetwater, testimony, January 19, 1961, Duke no. 710.

34. For a discussion of friendly relations with the local Utes and Paiutes living in the Bears Ears area, see Billy Holiday, testimony, July 21, 1961, Duke no. 668; George Martin Sr., interview, March 22, 1961, Duke no. 913; Cecil Parrish, interview, January 6, 1961, Duke

no. 667; Paul Goodman, testimony, January 6, 1961, Duke no. 689; Pat Shortfinger, interview, January 11, 1961, Duke no. 694; Anderson Cantsee (Ute), interview, January 28, 1961, Duke no. 739.

35. White Sheep, March 15, 1953, and January 6, 1961, Duke nos. 687A and 687B.

36. Paul Goodman, testimony, January 6, 1961, Duke no. 689.

37. Mexican Woman, interview, January 23, 1961, Duke no. 731; Hastiin Claw, interview, January 7, 1961, Duke no. 672; Hastiin Nez Begay, interview, January 18, 1961, Duke no. 706; Hetty Nepah, interview, January 7, 1961, Duke no. 671; Tom Stash, interview, July 17, 1968, Duke no. 386; Hastiin Toh Tłizhini Bitsi, interview, January 28, 1961, Duke, unnumbered.

38. John Hart/John Rockwell, interview, January 19, 1961, Duke no. 709.

39. Eddie Nakai, interview, January 21, 1961, Duke no. 723.

40. Warrior Woman, interview, January 18, 1961, Duke no. 703.

41. Desbaa' [Deezbaa'], interview, January 18, 1961, Duke no. 703.

42. Desbaa' [Deezbaa'], interview, January 18, 1961, Duke no. 703; Sally Draper Bailey, interview, January 29, 1961, Duke no. 740. Sally did not tell the person's name but described him as "my mother's mother's father . . . who was born near the Bears Ears."

43. Paul Jones, interview, January 19, 1961, Duke no. 712.

44. Major Albert Pfeiffer to A. K. Graves, December 10, 1866, Record Group 75, Letters Received by Office of Indian Affairs, New Mexico Superintendency, 1866, National Archives, Washington, D.C.

45. Tsekizzie [Tsék'izí], interview, Van Valkenburgh.

46. See Robert S. McPherson, *The Northern Navajo Frontier, 1860–1900: Expansion through Adversity* (Albuquerque: University of New Mexico, 1988).

47. See Ronald F. McDonald, *Fort Montezuma, 1879–1884: An Account of the First Mormon Settlers in San Juan County, Utah* (self-published, 2015).

48. Tódich'íínii, interview, Van Valkenburgh.

49. White Sheep, interview, Van Valkenburgh.

50. Hashk'áán Dííl, interview, Van Valkenburgh.

51. Hashk'áán Dííl, interview, Van Valkenburgh.

52. Maimi Howard, interview with author, July 19, 1988.

Chapter 2

1. There are many excellent versions of the creation story and beginnings of Navajo culture, including the emergence and the events surrounding Changing Woman, Monster Slayer, and Born for Water. Here I have included, in alphabetical order, some of the most readily available examples. See Stanley A. Fishler, *In the Beginning: A Navaho Creation Myth*, Anthropological Paper no. 13 (Salt Lake City: University of Utah, 1953); Pliny Earle Goddard, "Navajo Texts," in *Anthropological Papers of the American Museum of Natural History*, vol. 34, part 1 (New York: American Museum of Natural History, 1933), 127–79; Berard Haile, *The Upward Moving and Emergence Way: The Gishin Biye' Version*, ed. Karl Luckert (Lincoln: University of Nebraska Press, 1981); Jerrold E. Levy, *In the Beginning: The Navajo Genesis* (Berkeley: University of California Press, 1998); Washington Matthews, *Navaho Legends* (Salt Lake City: University of Utah Press, 1897, 1994); Franc Johnson Newcomb, *Navaho Folk Tales* (Albuquerque: University of New Mexico Press, 1967, 1990); Aileen O'Bryan, *Navaho Indian Myths* (New York: Dover Publications, 1956, 1993); Mary C. Wheelwright, *Navajo Creation Myth: The Story of the Emergence by Hasteen Klah* (Santa Fe: Museum of Navajo Ceremonial Art, 1942); Leland C. Wyman, *Blessingway: With Three Versions of the Myth Recorded and Translated from the Navajo by Father Berard Haile, O.F.M.* (Tucson: University of Arizona Press, 1970); and Paul G. Zolbrod, *Diné Bahane': The Navajo Creation Story* (Albuquerque: University of New Mexico Press, 1984).

2. The complexity of these teachings, the nature of the language used to present them, and the contextual fabric of a wide variety of ceremonies and chants makes it impossible to deal in depth with that material here. For more information on these concerns, see Robert S. McPherson and Perry J. Robinson, *Traditional Navajo Teachings: A Trilogy*, vols. 1, 2, and 3 (Boulder: University of Colorado Press, 2020).

3. Mary Blueyes, interview with author, July 25, 1988.

4. Robert W. Young and William Morgan, *Navajo Historical Selections* (Lawrence, KS: Bureau of Indian Affairs, 1954), 15.

5. Charlie Blueyes, interview with author, June 7, 1988.

6. Florence Begay, interview with author and Nelson Begay, April 19, 1988.

7. Florence Begay, interview with author and Nelson Begay, April 19, 1988.

8. Jane Byalily Silas, interview with author, February 27, 1991.

9. Florence Begay, interview with author and Nelson Begay, April 19, 1988.

10. Florence Begay, interview with author and Nelson Begay, April 19, 1988.

11. Matthews, *Navaho Legends*, 211; Charlie Blueyes, interview with author, June 7, 1988; Florence Begay, interview with author and Nelson Begay, April 19, 1988; Ada Black, interview with author, October 11, 1991; Fred Yazzie, interview with author, November 5, 1987; Joe Manygoats, interview with author, April 8, 1992; Editha L. Watson, essay presented March 17, 1968, p. 22, Duke no. 796.

12. Florence Begay, interview with author and Nelson Begay, April 19, 1988.

13. McPherson and Robinson, *TNT*, vol. 1, *Sacred Narratives and Ceremonies*, 199–200.

14. See McPherson and Robinson, *TNT*, vol. 1, *Sacred Narratives and Ceremonies*, 73–83.

15. Barre Toelken and Tacheeni Scott, "Poetic Retranslation and the 'Pretty Language' of Yellowman," in *Traditional American Indian Literature: Texts and Interpretation*, ed. Karl Kroeber (Lincoln: University of Nebraska Press, 1981), 90.

16. Florence Begay, interview with author and Nelson Begay, April 19, 1988.

17. Charlie Blueyes, interview with author, June 7, 1988.

18. Tallis Holiday, interview with author, November 3, 1987; see also Charlie Blueyes, interview with author, June 7, 1988.

19. Florence Begay, interview with author and Nelson Begay, April 19, 1988.

20. Charlie Blueyes, interview with author, June 7, 1988.

21. Sally Manygoats, interview with author, April 8, 1992.

22. For discussion of the concept of sacred versus profane space, how it is delimited and handled, see Mircea Eliade, *The Sacred and the Profane: The Nature of Religion* (New York: Harcourt, Brace, and World, 1959).

23. For a more in-depth explanation of Navajo beliefs of this region, and in particular Comb Ridge and the Bears Ears, see Robert S. McPherson, *Comb Ridge and Its People: The Ethnohistory of a Rock* (Logan: Utah State University Press, 2009).

24. Ada Black, interview with author, October 11, 1991.

25. Ada Black, interview with author, October 11, 1991. Other

people who have mentioned that Comb Ridge is a boundary include Charlie Blueyes, Stanley Holiday, John Holiday, and Florence Begay.

26. Stanley Holiday, interview with author, June 14, 2000.

27. Mary Blueyes, interview with author, July 25, 1988. For one of the most complete versions of this story, see Berard Haile, *The Upward Moving and Emergence Way: The Gishin Biye' Version*, ed. Karl Luckert (Lincoln: University of Nebraska Press, 1981).

28. McPherson and Robinson, *TNT*, vol. 2, *The Natural World*, 33.

29. Florence Begay, interview with author and Nelson Begay, April 19, 1988.

30. Martha Nez, interview with author, August 2, 1988.

31. Martha Nez, interview with author, August 2, 1988.

32. Maimi Howard, interview with author, July 19, 1988.

33. Harvey Oliver, interview with author, May 14, 1991.

34. Florence Begay, interview with author and Nelson Begay, April 19, 1988.

Chapter 3

1. Washington Matthews, *Navaho Legends* (Salt Lake City: University of Utah Press, 1897, 1994), 160–94.

2. Matthews, *Navaho Legends*, 166.

3. Matthews, *Navaho Legends*, 168.

4. Franc Johnson Newcomb, *Navajo Folk Tales* (Albuquerque: University of New Mexico Press, 1967), 63–64.

5. Matthews, *Navaho Legends*, 73–74, 77, 212; Gladys Reichard, *Navaho Religion: A Study of Symbolism* (Princeton: Princeton University Press, 1963), 490; Franciscan Fathers, *An Ethnologic Dictionary of the Navajo Language* (Saint Michaels, AZ: Saint Michaels Press, 1910), 156–57, 507.

6. Matthews, *Navaho Legends*, 170.

7. Aileen O'Bryan, *Navajo Indian Myths* (New York: Dover Publications, 1993), 109.

8. Gerald Hausman, *The Gift of the Gila Monster* (New York: Simon and Schuster, 1993), 101–70.

9. Matthews, *Navaho Legends*, 183–84.

10. Mary Blueyes, interview with author, July 25, 1988.

11. Harvey Oliver, interview with author, May 14, 1991.

12. Mary Blueyes, interview with author, July 25, 1988.

13. Jim Dandy, interview with author, October 24, 2007.

14. Jim Dandy, interview with author, October 24, 2007.

15. Florence Begay, interview with author, January 30, 1991.

16. Isabelle Lee, interview with author, February 13, 1991.

17. Ada Benally, interview with author, February 6, 1991.

18. Walter Dyk, *A Navaho Autobiography* (New York: Viking Fund Publications, 1947), 70.

19. Don Maguire, "The Third Arizona Expedition," Don Maguire Papers, Utah State Historical Society, Salt Lake City, Utah, 93–99.

20. Isabelle Lee, interview with author, February 13, 1991.

21. Florence Begay, interview with author, January 30, 1991.

22. Ben Whitehorse, interview with author, January 30, 1991.

23. Cyrus Begay, interview with author, May 14, 1991.

24. Sally Lee, interview with author, February 13, 1991.

25. Sally Lee, interview with author, February 13, 1991.

26. Jane Byalily Silas, interview with author, February 27, 1991.

27. Ada Benally, interview with author, February 6, 1991.

28. W. W. Hill, *The Agricultural and Hunting Methods of the Navaho Indians* (New Haven: Yale University Press, 1938), 25.

29. Hill, *Agricultural and Hunting Methods of the Navaho Indians*, 26–27, 30.

30. Isabelle Lee, interview with author, February 13, 1991.

31. Dyk, *Navaho Autobiography*, 24.

32. Dyk, *Navaho Autobiography*, 36–37, 39.

33. Dyk, *Navaho Autobiography*, 57–58.

34. See Robert S. McPherson, *Navajo Land, Navajo Culture: The Utah Experience in the Twentieth Century* (Norman: University of Oklahoma Press, 2001), 44–64.

35. William T. Shelton to R. Cook and Sophus Jensen, July 10, 1911; Shelton to H. B. Noel, August 1, 1911, Letters Received—New Mexico; R. Clayton Brough, Dale L. Jones, and Dale J. Stevens, *Utah's Comprehensive Weather Almanac* (Salt Lake City: Publisher's Press, 1987), 290; Harold and Fay Muhlestein, *Monticello Journal: A History of Monticello until 1937* (Monticello, UT: self-published, 1988), 105, 108.

36. Dyk, *Navaho Autobiography*, 155.

37. Dyk, *Navaho Autobiography*, 156–57.

38. Martha Nez, interview with author, August 2, 1988.

39. Mary Jay, interview with author, January 27, 1991.

40. "Pushed Back the Floods," *Mancos Times-Tribune*, October 20, 1911, p. 1.

41. Ray Hunt, interview with author, January 21, 1991; Robert Howell, interview with author, May 14, 1991; Kay Howell, interview with author, May 14, 1991; Helen Redshaw, interview with author, May 16, 1991.

42. Ray Hunt, interview with author, January 21, 1991; Margaret Tso Weston, interview with author, February 13, 1991.

43. Ray Hunt, interview with author, January 21, 1991; Jane Byalily Silas, interview with author, February 27, 1991.

44. C. L. Christensen, "Tells of Strange Navajo Ceremonies," *The Times-Independent*, February 9, 1922, p. 3.

45. Christensen, "Tells of Strange Navajo Ceremonies."

46. Ben Whitehorse, interview with author, January 30, 1991; Jane Byalily Silas, interview with author, February 27, 1991; Margaret Tso Weston, interview with author, February 13, 1991; Mary Jay, interview with author, February 27, 1991; Ella Sakizzie, interview with author, May 14, 1991; Cyrus Begay, interview with author, May 14, 1991.

47. John Meadows, interview with author, May 30, 1991.

48. For further information about this event, see Robert S. McPherson, *Traders, Agents, and Weavers: Developing the Northern Navajo Region* (Norman: University of Oklahoma Press, 2020), 183–84.

49. John Knot Begay, interview with author, May 7, 1991.

50. Margaret Tso Weston, interview with author, February 13, 1991.

Chapter 4

1. Good sources to study for the use of plants as food and medicine are found in the following works (arranged alphabetically by author): Flora L. Bailey, "Navaho Foods and Cooking Methods," in *American Anthropologist* 42, no. 2 (Spring 1940): 270–90; Sam and Janet Bingham, *Navajo Farming* (Chinle, AZ: Rock Point Community School, 1979); Charlotte J. Frisbie, *Food Sovereignty the Navajo Way: Cooking with Tall Woman* (Albuquerque: University of New Mexico Press, 2018); Charlotte J. Frisbie, ed., with Rose Mitchell, *Tall Woman: The Life Story of Rose Mitchell, A Navajo Woman, c. 1874–1977* (Albuquerque: University of New Mexico Press, 2001); W. W. Hill, *Agricultural and Hunting*

Methods of the Navaho Indians (New Haven, CT: Yale University Press, 1938); Vernon O. Mayes and Barbara Bayless Lacy, *Nanise': A Navajo Herbal: One Hundred Plants from the Navajo Reservation* (Chandler, AZ: Five Star, 1994); Leland C. Wyman and Stuart K. Harris, *Navajo Indian Medical Ethnobotany* (Albuquerque: University of New Mexico Press, 1941); Leland C. Wyman and Stuart K. Harris, *The Ethnobotany of the Kayenta Navajo*, Publications in Biology 5 (Albuquerque: University of New Mexico Press, 1951).

2. Martha Nez, interview with author, August 2, 1988.

3. Mary Blueyes, interview with author, July 25, 1988.

4. Robert S. McPherson and Perry J. Robinson, *TNT*, vol. 2, *The Natural World* (Boulder: University Press of Colorado, 2020), 118–19.

5. Mary Blueyes, interview with author, July 25, 1988.

6. Gladys Yellowman, interview with author, August 2, 1988.

7. Mary Jay, interview with author, February 27, 1991.

8. Charlotte J. Frisbie and Tall Woman, *Food Sovereignty the Navajo Way: Cooking with Tall Woman* (Albuquerque: University of New Mexico Press, 2018).

9. Jane Byalily Silas, interview with author, February 27, 1991.

10. Fernandez Begay, interview with author, February 2, 1994.

11. John Knot Begay, interview with author, May 7, 1991.

12. Gladys Yellowman, interview with author, August 2, 1988.

13. Stewart Hatch, interview with author, May 30, 1991.

14. Charlie Blueyes, interview with author, June 7, 1988, and August 28, 1988.

15. Mary Blueyes, interview with author, July 25, 1988.

16. Mary Blueyes, interview with author, July 25, 1988.

17. Mary Blueyes, interview with author, July 25, 1988; Gladys Yellowman, interview with author, August 2, 1988.

18. Margaret Tso Weston, interview with author, February 13, 1991.

19. Gladys Yellowman, interview with author, August 2, 1988.

20. Charlie Blueyes, interview with author, June 7, 1988.

21. Mary Blueyes, interview with author, July 25, 1988.

22. Gladys Yellowman, interview with author, August 2, 1988.

23. Gladys Yellowman, interview with author, August 2, 1988.

24. Mary Blueyes, interview with author, July 25, 1988.

25. Mary Blueyes, interview with author, July 25, 1988.

26. Mary Blueyes, interview with author, July 25, 1988.

27. Ada Benally, interview with author, February 6, 1991.
28. Gladys Yellowman, interview with author, August 2, 1988.
29. Gladys Yellowman, interview with author, August 2, 1988.
30. Mary Blueyes, interview with author, July 25, 1988.
31. Gladys Yellowman, interview with author, August 2, 1988.
32. For two excellent studies of the introduction of peyote on the reservation, the growth of the Native American Church, and its religious practices, see David F. Aberle, *The Peyote Religion among the Navaho* (Chicago: University of Chicago Press, 1982); and David F. Aberle and Omer C. Stewart, *Navaho and Ute Peyotism—A Chronological and Distributional Study* (Boulder: University of Colorado Press, 1957).
33. John Joe Begay, interview with author, September 18, 1990.
34. Isabelle Lee, interview with author, February 13, 1991.

Chapter 5

1. The David Kindle interviews were a series of fourteen taped discussions ranging in length from short (2–3 transcribed pages) to long (15 pages). Most were conducted between 1973 and 1977, with half of them being recorded in 1975. Done at Kindle's and Robert W. Putsch III's convenience as schedules permitted, they were recorded at different locations, times, and seasons. Because the tapes were not archivally catalogued, there is not a useful way to distinguish between them. Considering that and the fact that the material is organized topically in this book, there did not seem to be any benefit in endnoting every shift in a discussion or topic. Also included is material recorded in an interview with Robert Putsch conducted in August 2017 where he provided important contextual information to me and archaeologist Kevin Conte.
2. The use of divination in Navajo society is extensive. There are three major forms—listening (íists'ą́ą́); star (sǫ'ni'į), with its subsidiaries of sun and moon gazing and their affiliate, crystal gazing (dést'į́); and hand trembling (ndishniih)—all of which have their own procedures. For a more complete explanation of how each works, see Robert S. McPherson, "Wind, Hand, and Stars, Reading the Past, Finding the Future through Divination," in *Dinéjí Na'nitin: Navajo Traditional Teachings and History* (Boulder: University of Colorado Press): 13–43.
3. DNA (Diné be'iiná Náhiiłna be Agha'diit'ahii) is the Navajo people's legal service, a nonprofit organization with locations in Crown Point, Shiprock, and Farmington, New Mexico.

Chapter 6

1. As noted in the previous chapter, I wish to recognize the tremendous efforts of Robert W. Putsch III for recording this material, having it translated, and making it available for this project and for Kevin Conte in organizing and writing a first draft of what follows. These two individuals have worked long and hard; their efforts are greatly appreciated.

2. Martha Nez, interview with author, August 2, 1988.

3. Mary Blueyes, interview with author, July 25, 1988.

4. W. W. Hill, *The Agricultural and Hunting Methods of the Navaho Indians* (New Haven: Yale University Press, 1938), 132.

5. To best understand the role of bears and the complex teachings within the story shared by David Kindle, I enlisted the assistance of medicine man Perry Robinson, who was familiar with the narrative and could add detail that Kindle had omitted. See McPherson and Robinson, *TNT*, vol. 1, *Sacred Narratives and Ceremonies*, 172–92.

6. Leland C. Wyman, *The Windways of the Navaho* (Colorado Springs, CO: Taylor Museum, Colorado Springs Fine Art Center, 1962).

7. Robert W. Putsch recorded much of the material about the Windway ceremony with David Kindle on January 7, 1974.

8. There is some confusion here. There are four types of Navajo ceremonies: (1) Blessingway (Hózhǫ́ǫ́jík'ehgo); (2) Holyway (Diyink'ehgo), which includes the Windway; (3) Lifeway (Iináájík'ehgo); and (4) Evilway (Hóchxǫ'íjí). Kindle's discussion puts three of the four together and jumps back and forth between them. The majority of this paragraph is his commenting on a Lifeway ceremony.

9. Prostitutionway is a chant used to restore one's well-being altered by the effects of frenzy witchcraft. This ceremony employs the use of datura, a plant that has both hallucinogenic and poisonous properties. Frenzy witchcraft was a negative practice employed in bewitching a woman to come under the influence of a man through "love magic," or when trading and gambling in order to induce bad judgment in an opponent. The Prostitutionway ceremony was a five-night cure to free a victim from these negative influences. Clyde Kluckhohn, whose definitive study was entitled *Navajo Witchcraft* (Boston: Beacon Press, 1944, 1970), believed that this form of witchcraft was no longer practiced by the 1940s when he conducted his research.

Chapter 7

1. For a detailed explanation of the life stages of a Navajo woman or man from birth to death, see McPherson and Robinson, *TNT*, vol. 3, *The Earth Surface People*.

2. Ben Whitehorse, interview with author, January 30, 1991.

3. Martha Nez, interview with author, August 2, 1988.

4. Mary Blueyes, interview with author, May 6, 1992.

5. Ella Sakizzie, interview with author, May 14, 1991.

6. John Knot Begay, interview with author, May 7, 1991.

7. Jerry Begay, interview with author, January 16, 1991.

8. Florence Begay, interview with author and Nelson Begay, April 19, 1988.

9. Jerry Begay, interview with author, January 16, 1991.

10. Mary Jim, interview with author, June 7, 1988.

11. Martha Nez, interview with author, August 2, 1988.

12. Florence Begay, interview with author and Nelson Begay, April 19, 1988.

13. Mary Jay, interview with author, February 27, 1991.

14. Mary Jay, interview with author, February 27, 1991.

15. Mary Jay, interview with author, February 27, 1991.

16. Florence Begay, interview with author and Nelson Begay, April 19, 1988.

17. Florence Begay, interview with author and Nelson Begay, April 19, 1988.

18. Mary Jay, interview with author, February 27, 1991.

19. Florence Begay, interview with author and Nelson Begay, April 19, 1988.

20. Jerry Begay, interview with author, January 16, 1991.

21. Mary Blueyes, interview with author, May 6, 1992.

22. The standard work on this topic from an anthropological perspective is by Clyde Kluckhohn, *Navaho Witchcraft* (Boston, MA: Beacon Press, 1944). Margaret K. Brady, *"Some Kind of Power": Navajo Children's Skinwalker Narratives* (Salt Lake City: University of Utah Press, 1984), is of particular interest here because the children interviewed in this study were from the Montezuma Creek and Aneth area. Robert S. McPherson, "Sacred Evil: The Dark Side of Life along the San Juan River," in *Dinéjí Na'nitin: Navajo Traditional Teachings and History* (Boulder: University Press of Colorado, 2012), 72–99, provides a wide-ranging context and

analysis of practices that examines the topic through Navajo testimony.

23. Walter Dyk, *A Navaho Autobiography* (New York: Viking Fund Publications, 1947), 138.

24. Harvey Oliver, interview with author, May 14, 1991.

25. Charlie Blueyes, interview with author, February 28, 1988.

26. Mary Blueyes, interview with author, May 6, 1992.

27. Mary Blueyes, interview with author, May 6, 1992.

28. Martha Nez, interview with author, August 2, 1988.

29. Margaret Tso Weston, interview with author, February 13, 1991.

30. Harvey Oliver, interview with author, May 14, 1991.

31. See McPherson and Robinson, *TNT*, vol. 3, *The Earth Surface People*, 168–88, for a more complete discussion of the Navajo view of death.

32. Florence Begay, interview with author and Nelson Begay, April 19, 1988.

Chapter 8

1. For the early years along the San Juan River, see Robert S. McPherson, *The Northern Navajo Frontier, 1860–1900: Expansion through Adversity* (Albuquerque: University of New Mexico Press, 1988). Robert S. McPherson, *Both Sides of the Bullpen: Navajo Trade and Posts* (Norman: University of Oklahoma Press, 2017), examines the trading post phenomenon as a cultural scene of exchange as well as individual posts in southeastern Utah and southwestern Colorado. Robert S. McPherson, *Traders, Agents, and Weavers: Developing the Northern Navajo Region* (Norman: University of Oklahoma Press, 2020), centers on the Two Grey Hills Post and others in the Shiprock area, the evolution of weaving in that region, and developing government policy that affected the livestock industry, wool sales, and the Shiprock Agency. Susan E. Woods and Robert S. McPherson, *Along Navajo Trails: Recollections of a Trader* (Logan: Utah State University, 2005), tells the life story of Will Evans, a Shiprock trader for over forty years, who not only encouraged innovative weaving and the study of Navajo ceremonial design, but also recorded the history of the area and Navajo personalities.

2. Frank H. Hyde, "Testimony, October 1930, p. 1208; Ernest B. Hyde, "Testimony," October 1930, pp. 700–707, Colorado River Bed Case microfilm, Utah State Historical Society, Salt Lake City.

3. Mary Jay, interview with author, January 27, 1991.

4. Martha Nez, interview with author, August 2, 1988.

5. Maimi Howard, interview with author, July 19, 1988.

6. Sally Lee, interview with author, February 13, 1991.

7. Ray Hunt, interview with author, January 21, 1991; John Meadows, interview with author, May 30, 1991.

8. John Meadows, interview with author, May 30, 1991; Cyrus Begay, interview with author, May 14, 1991; Ray Hunt, interview with author, January 21, 1991.

9. John Meadows, interview with author, May 30, 1991.

10. Mary Blueyes, interview with author, May 6, 1992.

11. Walter Dyk, *A Navaho Autobiography* (New York: Viking Fund Publications, 1947), 37.

12. Jerry Begay, interview with author, January 16, 1991.

13. Martha Nez, interview with author, August 2, 1988.

14. Maimi Howard, interview with author, July 19, 1988.

15. Martha Nez, interview with author, August 2, 1988.

16. John Knot Begay, interview with author, May 7, 1991.

17. Ada Benally, interview with author, February 6, 1991.

18. See Robert S. McPherson, "Navajo and Ute Deer Hunting: Consecration or Desecration," in *Navajo Land, Navajo Culture, The Utah Experience in the Twentieth Century* (Norman: University of Oklahoma Press, 2001), 21–43.

19. Dyk, *Navaho Autobiography*, 40.

20. Robert S. McPherson, *A History of San Juan County: In the Palm of Time* (Salt Lake City: Utah State Historical Commission, 1995), 20.

21. Jane Byalily Silas, interview with author, February 27, 1991; John Knot Begay, interview with author, May 7, 1991.

22. Mary Jay, interview with author, January 27, 1991.

23. Jane Byalily Silas, interview with author, February 27, 1991.

24. John Meadows, interview with author, May 30, 1991.

25. Stewart Hatch, interview with author, May 7, 2010.

26. Harvey Oliver, interview with author, May 14, 1991; Cyrus Begay, interview with author, May 14, 1991.

27. Stewart Hatch, interview with author, May 7, 2010.

28. Mary Blueyes, interview with author, May 6, 1992; Mary Jim, interview with author, June 7, 1988; John Joe Begay, interview with author, September 18, 1990.

29. Stewart Hatch, interview with author, May 7, 2010.

30. Stewart Hatch, interview with author, May 7, 2010.
31. Stewart Hatch, interview with author, May 7, 2010.
32. Ira Hatch, interview with author, May 30, 1991.
33. Stewart Hatch, interview with author, May 7, 2010.
34. Ira Hatch, interview with author, May 30, 1991.
35. Stewart Hatch, interview with author, May 7, 2010.
36. Stewart Hatch, interview with author, May 7, 2010.
37. Stewart Hatch, interview with author, May 7, 2010.
38. Stewart Hatch, interview with author, May 7, 2010.

Chapter 9

1. "The Shiprock Agency," *Farmington Enterprise*, September 21, 1906, p. 3.
2. William T. Shelton to Commissioner of Indian Affairs (CIA), July 23, 1907, Record Group 75, Letters Received—New Mexico.
3. John L. Conway, "San Juan School," *Farmington Enterprise*, April 15, 1908, p. 3.
4. Shelton to CIA, January 21, 1909, Letters Received—New Mexico.
5. Walter Dyk, *A Navaho Autobiography* (New York: Viking Fund Publications, 1947), 86.
6. Dyk, *Navaho Autobiography*, 125.
7. Margaret Tso Weston, interview with author, February 13, 1991; Ada Benally, interview with author, February 6, 1991.
8. John Joe Begay, interview with author, September 18, 1990.
9. Mary Jay, interview with author, February 27, 1991.
10. Martha Nez, interview with author, August 2, 1988.
11. Ella Sakizzie, interview with author, May 14, 1991.
12. Florence Begay, interview with author, January 30, 1991.
13. John Norton, interview with author, January 16, 1991.
14. John Norton, interview with author, January 16, 1991.
15. John Norton, interview with author, January 16, 1991.
16. Ben Whitehorse, interview with author, January 30, 1991; Jane Byalily Silas, interview with author, January 27, 1991; Margaret Tso Weston, interview with author, February 13, 1991; Mary Jay, interview with author, February 27, 1991; Ella Sakizzie, interview with author, May 14, 1991; Cyrus Begay, interview with author, May 14, 1991.

17. Florence Begay, interview with author, January 30, 1991.

18. Margaret Tso Weston, interview with author, February 13, 1991.

19. John Norton, interview with author, January 16, 1991.

20. Cyrus Begay, interview with author, May 14, 1991.

21. Cyrus Begay, interview with author, May 14, 1991.

22. Cyrus Begay, interview with author, May 14, 1991.

23. Cyrus Begay, interview with author, May 14, 1991.

24. Ira Hatch, interview with author, May 30, 1991.

25. Ira Hatch, interview with author, May 30, 1991.

26. Maimi Howard, interview with author, July 19, 1988.

27. Maimi Howard, interview with author, July 19, 1988.

28. John Knot Begay, interview with author, May 7, 1991.

29. Sally Lee, interview with author, February 13, 1991.

30. Ella Sakizzie, interview with author, May 14, 1991.

31. John Knot Begay, interview with author, May 7, 1991.

32. Harvey Oliver, interview with author, May 14, 1991.

Chapter 10

1. See Robert S. McPherson, *Viewing the Ancestors: Perceptions of the Anaasází, Mokwič, and Hisatsinom* (Norman: University of Oklahoma Press, 2014).

2. Harvey Oliver, interview with author, March 6, 1991.

3. Buck Navajo, interview with author, December 16, 1991.

4. Fred Yazzie, interview with author, November 5, 1987.

5. Isabelle Lee, interview with author, February 13, 1991.

6. John Knot Begay, interview with author, May 7, 1991.

7. Jane Byalily Silas, interview with author, February 27, 1991.

8. Mary Jay, interview with author, February 27, 1991.

9. Ben Whitehorse, interview with author, January 30, 1991.

10. Cyrus Begay, interview with author, May 14, 1991.

11. John Meadows, interview with author, May 30, 1991.

12. Ben Whitehorse, interview with author, January 30, 1991.

13. Albert H. Kneale, Indian Agent (Caldwell, ID: Caxton Printers, 1950), 368–69.

14. Walter Dyk, *A Navaho Autobiography* (New York: Viking Fund Publications, 1947), 97–98.

15. Mary Jay, interview with author, February 27, 1991.

16. Nakai Begay, interview with Bette Benally, February 24, 1991, used with permission.

17. John Meadows, interview with author, May 30, 1991.

18. Nakai Begay, interview with Bette Benally, February 24, 1991, used with permission.

19. Charlie Todacheenie, interview with Bette Benally, February 20, 1991, used with permission.

20. Harvey Oliver, interview with author, March 6, 1991.

21. John Norton, interview with author, January 16, 1991; Nakai Begay, interview with Bette Benally, February 24, 1991, used with permission; Mary Blueyes, interview with Bette Blueyes, March 10, 1991; Hilda Nakai, interview with Bette Benally, March 3, 1991, used with permission.

22. Ben Whitehorse, interview with author, January 30, 1991.

23. John Knot Begay, interview with author, May 7, 1991.

24. Ada Benally, interview with author, February 6, 1991.

25. Cyrus Begay, interview with author, May 14, 1991.

26. Harvey Oliver, interview with author, March 6, 1991.

27. David Lansing, in *Stories of Traditional Navajo Life and Culture*, edited by Broderick H. Johnson (Tsaile, AZ: Navajo Community College Press, 1977), 108.

28. Garrick Bailey and Roberta Glenn Bailey, *A History of the Navajos: The Reservation Years* (Santa Fe, NM: School of American Research Press, 1986), 119; Albert B. Reagan, "The Influenza and the Navajo," *Proceedings of the Indiana Academy of Science* 29 (Fort Wayne, IN: Fort Wayne Printing Company, 1921), 245.

29. Charlie Blueyes, interview with author, August 28, 1988.

30. John Knot Begay, interview with author, May 7, 1991.

Chapter 11

1. For more information on Navajo livestock reduction, see Kenneth R. Philp, *John Collier's Crusade for Indian Reform, 1920–1954* (Tucson: University of Arizona Press, 1977); Richard White, *The Roots of Dependency: Subsistence Environment and Social Change among the Choctaw, Pawnees, and Navajos* (Lincoln: University of Nebraska Press, 1983); Ruth Roessel and Broderick Johnson, eds. *Navajo Livestock Reduction: A National Disgrace* (Tsaile, AZ: Navajo Community Press,

1974); L. Schuyler Fonaroff, "Conservation and Stock Reduction on the Navajo Tribal Range," *Geographical Review* 53, no. 2 (April 1962): 200–23; Fern Charley and Dean Sundberg, *The Navajo Stock Reduction Interviews of Fern Charley and Dean Sundberg* (Fullerton: California State University–Fullerton Oral History Program, 1984); and Robert S. McPherson, "History Repeats Itself, Navajo Livestock Reduction in Southeastern Utah, 1933–1946," in *Navajo Land, Navajo Culture: The Utah Experience in the Twentieth Century* (Norman: University of Oklahoma Press, 2001), 102–20.

2. Charlie Blueyes, interview with author, August 28, 1988.

3. John Joe Begay, interview with author, September 18, 1990.

4. Walter Dyk, *A Navaho Autobiography* (New York: Viking Fund Publications, 1947), 68.

5. John Knot Begay, interview with author, May 7, 1991.

6. Jane Byalily Silas, interview with author, February 27, 1991.

7. Mary Jay, interview with author, February 27, 1991.

8. Sally Lee, interview with author, February 13, 1991.

9. Robert S. McPherson, ed., *The Journey of Navajo Oshley: An Autobiography and Life History* (Logan: Utah State University Press, 2000), 132.

10. Mary Tsosie, interview with author, January 30, 1991.

11. Ella Sakizzie, interview with author, May 14, 1991.

12. John Holiday, in McPherson, *Journey of Navajo Oshley*, 133.

13. Ben Whitehorse, interview with author, January 30, 1991.

14. John Joe Begay, interview with author, September 18, 1990.

15. H. E. Holman (Navajo Service) to U.S. Attorney (Utah) with accompanying statements, June 11, 1938, Record Group 75, Navajo Service Personnel File, Denver Records Center, Denver, Colorado.

16. Tacheadeny Tso Begay, in Roessel and Johnson, *Navajo Livestock Reduction*, 111.

17. Capiton Benally interview, in Roessel and Johnson, *Navajo Livestock Reduction*, 33–37.

18. See Robert S. McPherson, *The Northern Navajo Frontier, 1860–1900: Expansion through Adversity* (Albuquerque: University of New Mexico Press, 1988), 51–62.

19. Cyrus Begay, interview with author, May 14, 1991.

20. For a more detailed discussion of this and other proceedings culminating in the Don B. Colton Bill signed in 1933, see Robert S. McPherson, *Comb Ridge and Its People: The Ethnohistory of a Rock* (Logan: Utah State University Press, 2009), 174–79.

21. B. P. Six to Commissioner of Indian Affairs, March 20, 1930, J. Lee Correll Collection [hereafter cited as JLC Collection], Navajo Archives, Window Rock, Arizona.

22. C. L. Walker to Commissioner of Indian Affairs, March 21, 1930, JLC Collection.

23. J. M. Stewart to Assistant Commissioner of Indian Affairs, July 19, 1932, JLC Collection; "'Piute Strip' Controversy Settled at Last," *San Juan Record*, July 21, 1932, pp. 1, 5.

24. U.S. Congress, House, "Permanently Set Aside Lands in Utah . . . Navajo Indian Reservation," Report No. 1883, 72d Cong., 2d Sess., January 19, 1933, pp. 1–4; U.S. Congress, Senate, "Addition to Navajo Indian Reservation in Utah," Report No. 1199, 72d Cong., 2d Sess., February 10, 1933, pp. 1–4.

25. "'Piute Strip' Controversy," 1.

26. "Memorandum of Agreement Made Between Council of Nine Representing the Citizens of Blanding, Utah, and the Commissioner of Indian Affairs, Regarding the Piute Strip," July 15, 1932, JLC Collection.

27. Deshna Clah Cheschillige to Charles J. Rhoads, December 11, 1932, JLC Collection.

28. "The Official Addition of Indian Land," *San Juan Record*, May 25, 1933, p. 4.

29 Mary Jelly, interview with Aubrey Williams, January 21, 1961, Duke no. 722.

30. Mary Jelly, interview with Aubrey Williams, January 21, 1961, Duke no. 722.

31. Ella Sakizzie, interview with author, May 14, 1991.

32. Beth E. King, "The Utah Navajos Relocation in the 1950s," *Bluff Legacy Project: Life Along the San Juan River*, July 1996, pp. 1–4.

33. King, "Utah Navajos Relocation in the 1950s," 1–4.

Chapter 12

1. Walter Dyk, *A Navaho Autobiography* (New York: Viking Fund Publications, 1947), 25.

2. For a detailed discussion of the development, economic impact, depletion of oil, social chaos, and political infighting surrounding the Aneth Oil Field, see Robert S. McPherson and David A. Wolff, "Poverty, Politics, and Petroleum: The Utah Navajo and the Aneth Oilfield," *American Indian Quarterly* 21, no. 3 (Summer 1997): 451–70. Here, the focus is upon what Navajo elders felt about what was happening.

3. Jerry Begay, interview with author, January 16, 1991.

4. John Norton, interview with author, January 16, 1991.

5. John Knot Begay, interview with author, May 7, 1991.

6. Florence Norton, interview with author, March 6, 1991.

7. Isabelle Lee, interview with author, February 13, 1991.

8. Jane Byalily Silas, interview with author, February 27, 1991.

9. Jerry Begay, interview with author, January 16, 1991.

10. Margaret Tso Weston, interview with author, February 13, 1991.

11. Cyrus Begay, interview with author, May 14, 1991.

12. Jerry Begay, interview with author, January 16, 1991.

13. Fernandez Begay, interview with author, February 2, 1994.

14. Ella Sakizzie, interview with author, May 14, 1991.

15. John Knot Begay, interview with author, May 7, 1991.

16. Ella Sakizzie, interview with author, May 14, 1991.

17. Margaret Tso Weston, interview with author, February 13, 1991.

18. Isabelle Lee, interview with author, February 13, 1991.

19. Cyrus Begay, interview with author, May 14, 1991.

20. Ella Sakizzie, interview with author, May 14, 1991.

21. Jerry Begay, interview with author, January 16, 1991.

22. John Norton, interview with author, January 16, 1991.

23. Cyrus Begay, interview with author, May 14, 1991.

24. Isabelle Lee, interview with author, February 13, 1991.

25. Jane Byalily Silas, interview with author, February 27, 1991.

26. Mary Jay, interview with author, February 27, 1991.

27. John Knot Begay, interview with author, May 7, 1991.

28. Jane Byalily Silas, interview with author, February 27, 1991.

29. Isabelle Lee, interview with author, February 13, 1991.

INDEX

Italicized page numbers correspond to images.